The Complete Illustrated Guide to

Everything Sold
in Hardware Stores

Completely Updated Edition

The Complete Illustrated Guide to

Everything Sold in Hardware Stores

Completely Updated Edition

by Steve Ettlinger

Illustrations by
Robert Strimban

Conceived and Edited by
Ettlinger Editorial Projects

Macmillan•USA

MACMILLAN
A Simon & Schuster Macmillan Company
1633 Broadway
New York, NY 10019-6785

Macmillan Publishing books may be purchased for business or sales promotional use. For information please write: Special Markets Department, Macmillan Publishing USA, 1633 Broadway, New York, NY 10019.

Library of Congress Cataloging-in-Publication Data

Ettlinger, Steve.
        The complete illustrated guide to everything sold in hardware stores / by Steve Ettlinger ; illustrations by Robert Strimban ; conceived and edited by Ettlinger Editorial Projects.—Rev. ed.
                p. cm.
        Includes index.
        ISBN 0-02-862575-7
        1. Hardware—United States—Catalogs.   2. Hardware—Terminology.
I. Title.
        TS405.E77   1998
        683'.029'6—dc21   98-42142
                                                 CIP

Printed in the United States of America

10 9 8 7 6 5 4 3 2 1

Book design by Barbara Kordesh

This book is dedicated to anyone who has ever walked into a hardware store, home center, or lumberyard and asked for a whatchamacallit or thingamajig.

Contents

PART III: General Hardware

PART IV: General Materials

PART V: Paints, Stains, Finishes, Wall Coverings, and Related Products and Tools

PART VI: Wood and Wood Products

PART VII: Wall, Floor, and Ceiling Materials and Tools; Doors and Windows

PART VIII: Plumbing Hardware, Materials, and Tools

PART IX: Electrical Products and Tools

PART X: Masonry Materials, Products, and Tools

PART XI: Safety Equipment

Preface

Why This Book

Whether you are a homeowner, an apartment dweller, or renovator, you no doubt have often entered a hardware store, lumberyard, or home center full of fear prior to making a small purchase. This uneasiness generally stems from two facts: first, people rarely know the actual, correct name of even the most everyday item and are reduced to visual descriptions that often leave a lot to be desired—and often leave the customer with an unusable and unreturnable purchase. Second, store clerks may often be unavailable, unknowledgeable, or downright rushed (or is it just that we feel guilty with all those folks in line behind us?).

Probably the most frustrating thing is that after you ask a clerk for an item, whether a succinct request for a paintbrush or pliers, or the more typical "whatchamacallit that fits over the thing that you turn to make the doohickey work" (accompanied, no doubt, by broad, dramatic, descriptive hand gestures), the clerk will come back at you, nine times out of ten, with a barrage of questions: "Well, what are you using it for?" "What size do you want?" "You want top-of-the-line or cheap?" "Silicone or acrylic?" "Galvanized or plain?" If you haven't thought these questions through, this can be pretty demoralizing, embarrassing, and intimidating. I know. That's just the kind of experience that gave birth to this book.

The Complete Illustrated Guide to Everything Sold in Hardware Stores should serve to end your intimidation, help you avoid wrong purchases, and enable even you, too, to walk fearlessly into a hardware store or lumberyard and get exactly what you need. I will expose the choices available to you so that you can be prepared for those rapid-fire questions.

How This Book Got Inspired

A cat's paw did it. No doubt about it—a cat's paw inspired this book. A few years ago, while I was helping a friend renovate her apartment, I asked a passing carpenter for advice about my next task—removing an old floor. The carpenter said casually, "Get yourself a cat's paw, and you'll have those floor-boards ripped up in an hour!" So, armed for once with specific professional guidance, I strode boldly into the local hardware store and asked self-confidently for a cat's paw, even though I had never seen or heard of one before. "Cat's paw? Cat's paw?" The clerk reacted sarcastically. "Wha' d'ya think this is, a butcher shop?" Rolling his eyes, he completely demolished my assertive frame of mind. I mentioned almost apologetically that I wanted to rip up some old floorboards. After much gesticulating, the clerk said, "Ohhhh, what *you* want is a pry bar!" Relieved, he proceeded to sell me one. It turned out he was quite wrong.

About a week later I finally finished ripping up the floor, cursing the new tool all along and wondering why the carpenter had suggested it. Well, if you check Chapter 3, you'll understand what went wrong—the cat's paw and the pry bar are distinctly different tools, though they are members of the same family. I checked all the indexes of the heavy-duty complete how-to books and found them listed nowhere. And I thought, "someone ought to write a book that just lists all the items mentioned elsewhere—I don't want to keep looking past all those articles on how to install a garage door or a deck every time I want to check out some small item that is mentioned somewhere!"

And thus was this book born. I hope it answers your questions too.

Notes on the Revised Edition

What's changed in ten years? While the inventory of hardware stores and home centers has not changed dramatically, it certainly has increased. More importantly, the stores themselves have expanded. The prevalence and success of immense home centers is the norm, while they were more just a new trend back when I started research. With their extensive inventory (and increasing crowds of do-it-yourself folks), a revision and updating of this book was called for, and here it is.

A lot of the traditional tools are now made with better materials and ergonomic designs; there is also a general increase in the availability of top-quality, longer-lasting versions. Of course, the cheap stuff is still with us. Innovation is healthy: More gadgets are being introduced each month, it seems, most in the painting tools and fastener departments. Advances in electronics have led to a wide array of fully electronic measuring devices; advances in engineered wood have led to new products there, too. It seems that many improvements are found among paints, finishes, and materials like caulk and insulation, partly in response to environmental concerns.

One thing that hasn't changed is the need for a book that describes all the items and lists all the names people have for them—something no other book in this field does, despite the publication of several excellent, how-to books in the intervening years. Most of the how-to books' indexes don't even list the tools and gizmos that you need to buy. And contractors and sales clerks are still telling us to get some gizmo or some adapter by vague description, or use, or nickname, so the descriptions, including items merely referred to, have been made more detailed to help you make that purchase with a minimum of confusion.

A final note about the motivation for a revised edition: Over the years, I've heard again and again how much people really liked having this book. Some (even from outside my immediate family!) claim it's their favorite, though I doubt they mean to include all books in that praise. I've been told of at least one spouse who was kept up late at night while her husband read it voraciously in bed. With that kind of response, I felt that I owed my readers a thorough revision. Happy hardware hunting!

—Steve Ettlinger

New York City, 1998

Acknowledgments

Generous research assistance for the first edition of this book was provided by the editors of *The Old House Journal*, Brooklyn, New York, especially Patricia Poore and Gordon Bock.

This book began with a simple idea that I discussed over time with a variety of people ranging from friends and relatives to mere acquaintances. Their enthusiastic responses sustained my efforts and without them it is unlikely that this book would have happened. To those people who gave me such early encouragement I will be ever grateful. In particular, though, there are some people whose responses provided as much emotional as professional support at a time when the project was just a gleam in my eye. I will never forget Clem Labine's and Patricia Poore's quick response to my initial phone call. The original enthusiasm and help of designer Leslie Smolan of Carbone, Smolan Associates will be appreciated forevermore. My parents' continuous contributions of thoughts, critiques, and suggestions for both the manuscript and concept were truly wonderful and essential.

The following people and companies proved invaluable and patient in their generous assistance and technical expertise when reviewing sections of the manuscript, allowing me to explore their stores, and, in all cases, answering endless lists of questions: J. C. Valentine of J & G Plumbing and Heating Supplies, Brooklyn; Dan and the staff of Dan's Hardware, Brooklyn; Matthew Pintchik, Tom Mariano, John Heemer, Larry Reingold, Leon Cummings, Rudy Gentik, Floyd Stanislaw, and Allen Cohen of Nathan Pintchik, Inc., New York; James P. Balis and Dennis J. Vanette of APS Locksmith and Hardware, Brooklyn; Marvin Pereira and Lorenzo Otero of City Lighting, New York; Milton and Adam Greebler and the staff of Gurrell Hardware, New York; Byron Hathorn of SITA Construction Company, Ely, Vermont; Clem Labine (now of Historic Trends, Brooklyn); Jean McGrane, industrial hygienist, New York; Paul "Hocky" Hochberg, Chicago; Paul Murphy, Chicago; Gary Chinn of Garrett Wade Tools Catalog, New York; Chris Wadsworth of Peter Gisolfi Associates, Architects, Hastings; Gregory Warock, master mason, Asheville, North Carolina; and Martin Daly and Harlow Haagensen of the New York District Council of Carpenters Labor Technical College, New York.

I am also very grateful for the friendly expertise of the many manufacturers who responded to my numerous requests for technical information and catalogs.

I would especially like to extend my heartfelt thanks to: Al Barrett, The Stanley Works; Jack Murray; Stanley Zuba; Hugh and Mary Devaney of Centerport Hardware; and Henry Wetzel. John Trench, the incomparably articulate owner of A&B Hardware, Huntington, New York, contributed much important information and spent many long hours on the book for which I am extremely grateful.

Many friends and colleagues provided valuable editorial and administrative assistance, including Laura Anderson and Karen Richardson; Debnee Steele; Paul Wheeler of Wheeler Pictures (including a generous loan of a Macintosh); Sharon Rappaport; Johnny Truman; and Gusto Graphics, which provided graphic and editorial consulting services.

And special thanks to—

Robert Strimban, whose encouragement, generosity, enthusiasm, and upbeat attitude added to the pleasure of working with his beautiful illustrations.

The friendly, helpful staff editors of Macmillan who have been a delight to work with, and especially my first editor, David Wolff, who has always been a true, patient colleague, and who has always understood what I wanted.

Rick Smolan, whose early enthusiasm and suggestions were fundamental to the birth of this book, and who has shown that the book business can be a great entrepreneurial one.

The carpenter who suggested long ago that I buy a cat's paw, and especially to the obnoxious, anonymous hardware-store clerk who sold me a pry bar instead of the cat's paw I requested, neither of us aware of the difference. His attitude and error actually inspired this book—I understand he is no longer employed in this field.

The many hardware-store clerks around the country of whom I inquired about cat's paws, without ever buying one—I was just testing the need for the book. My apologies and sincere thanks.

And certainly I could never have done anything like this without the support of my wife, Gusty Lange. Projects like this take too many hours away from the pure pleasure of being together, and I will always be thankful for her sacrifices, understanding, suggestions, and shared pride. What more could you want?

For the Revised Edition

I am grateful for publisher Natalie Chapman's longtime enthusiasm and editor Betsy Thorpe's guidance on the revised edition. A note of thanks goes to Ed Lanctot, legendary co-founder of True Value Hardware, for his enthusiasm for my book.

A special acknowledgment goes to Dylan and Chelsea Ettlinger for their extraordinary patience during numerous mysterious trips to hardware stores and home centers. The most patient and helpful staff at those stores earned my respect and gratitude, especially at Home Depot, Norwalk, Connecticut; M. D. Joyce, Deer Isle, Maine; Lumberland, New York City; and (again!) Pintchik's Ace Hardware, also here in New York City. You're great. Thank you!

—Steve Ettlinger

Introduction

How This Book Is Organized

This book is organized in a way similar to a large hardware store or home center. However, it is not a perfectly clean breakdown. For example, though there is a section on hand tools, specialized tools for particular products or projects, such as masonry tools, are found in their own section.

I have put what I think are the more common items in the front of each section, and groups of items follow this in a logical sequence wherever possible. Also, do make use of the index, as it includes every item alphabetically.

The item names are the result of months of research with manufacturers and catalogs, and though these names reflect the most accurate and common terms you'll find on a store's label, in many cases it may not be the name with which you are most familiar, the name you hear on the job site, for example. That's where the "Also Known As" element comes into play. This section comes from the original inspiration for this book, when someone told me to get a cat's paw, which is not the most common name for the tool I needed, a nail claw.

We all call these tools by the names we've learned informally—from where we grew up, in the Navy, on the farm, from some old boss who picked up hardware nomenclature from who knows where. It has been fun collecting all the various aliases that might be out there (tongue-and-groove pliers are the tool with the most aliases: 19) and I continue to try to collect them (please send me any you come across). Some are dead wrong and may come from authoritative sources (even a popular TV show host), others are rare and folkloric, but someone somewhere calls the thing by that name, and so it finds its way into print.

"Use" and "Use Tips" are meant to be succinct, with just enough information to help you identify the item and avoid common problems.

There is also a conscious avoidance of extensive "how-to" advice. The tips we give are meant to echo the friendly advice a good clerk would give you as you leave a store; they are definitely not the comprehensive and detailed instructions required for many projects. I would never have been able to do justice to them in a book of this size.

This is, after all, a buying guide, so the individual "Buying Tips" with each item are essential, as are the more general ones in the various "About" sections. And please also keep in mind the following generalities:

- So many items are available in different sizes, models, and materials that you should always try to take in an old item in order to purchase proper replacement parts or materials.

- Most small hardware items sold "carded" in see-through plastic packages are much more expensive than the same item sold in bulk. Always ask if something is available in boxes of 100, or by the pound, or merely loose.

- While the technical terms concerning metals and finishes of tools and devices may be complicated, you can often determine quality merely by hefting the item and comparing weight and finish quality to other brands. (See Appendix A for information on metal finishes.)

- Most stores group their merchandise in a manner similar to our book. However, there are many overlapping uses as well as interior-design considerations that may make it difficult for you to find something. Be sure to ask—even small stores may have over 15,000 items in stock!

What This Book Does Not Include

Though a good hardware store, lumberyard, or home center carries tens and even hundreds of thousands of items in stock, I have included only those that the average homeowner/handyperson will find necessary for typical repairs, do-it-yourself projects, renovation, and restoration.

You will not find heavy construction materials, or professional tools, or esoteric cabinetmaking tools, or hobby materials. I drew the line at including automotive, boating, electronics, gardening items, home security items, and housewares.

Yet these items may all be sold in many hardware stores. Nonetheless, for practical reasons, which I trust you understand, I had to stick to my decision: this is about traditional do-it-yourself hardware, products, and materials, and not meant to include anything more.

How to Use This Book

It's very simple. When you are preparing for your next foray into the hardware world, check out the relevant sections in this book. Wherever it is noted that a particular item "comes in various sizes" (or types, or styles, or colors, or grades) you should be alerted that you have some thinking and shopping to do. These are questions that must be answered prior to a purchase.

In other words, there is no such thing as "just a door lock" or "just a paintbrush" and so on. When you ask for these items the clerk will ask you questions back, and invariably they are questions you can anticipate. This book tells you in advance what you have to figure out before you leave home. The key word is "usage." You have to think about what you are going to use your purchase for before you go to the store.

A Personal Note to Readers

I hope you find this book helpful and would like to hear of your comments and experiences. I am also always in search of more alternative names—"also known as" aliases—for any item. Please write to me c/o Macmillan General Reference, 1633 Broadway, New York, NY 10019.

Common Hand Tools

About Common Hand Tools

This section includes the more common tools used in do-it-yourself projects, particularly those used with wood, plastic, and metal. Although many of these tools have more specialized applications, those tools that are more often used with specific types of work are not listed here but are found at the ends of their respective sections, such as tools for **painting and finishing** (Part V), **hanging drywall** (Part VII), **plumbing** (Part VIII), **electrical work** (Part IX), and **masonry work** (Part X). Many innovative, ergonomic designs have been introduced recently, making shopping for even the simplest tool exciting.

Hammers

About Hammers

A hammer is usually the first tool for most of us and indeed was one of mankind's first tools.

Safety glasses or goggles are recommended, as a hammer can send a chip flying like a shot into your eye. Never strike another hammer or other striking tool—both could chip or be damaged so that they chip later. Never use a hammer with a loose head. Never use the side, or "cheek," of the head to strike anything—it is likely to crack.

Search for the most comfortable handle you can find—many new materials and ergonomic designs are now available.

Claw Hammer

Also Known As: Curved claw hammer, nail hammer, carpenter's hammer

Description: The most common, standard hammer. Metal head, with a striking surface (the face) and opposite it a notched, curved claw for pulling nails out of wood. Usual head weight is 16 ounces; sometimes lighter or heavier. *Rip hammers*, also called *straight claw, ripping claw* or *flooring hammers*,

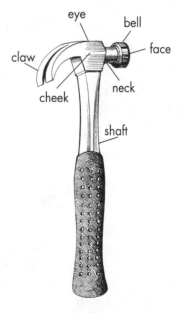

Claw Hammer

have a straighter claw. *Casing hammers* (8 ounces) are for cabinetwork. Hammer handles can be of wood, steel, or fiberglass.

Use: Driving and pulling nails. Rip hammers are useful for demolition. Also, their straight claw can be jammed into a roof deck if you start to slide off.

Use Tips: The 16-ounce size is best for most carpentry, but the 20-ounce size is highly recommended for construction work when driving long nails into soft wood—the weight of the head gives the hammer greater momentum. Some models have magnets or slots that hold nails for starting.

Buying Tips: Quality hammers have heads with slightly beveled, or "chamfered," edges to avoid chipping, and slightly curved, or "crowned," faces, which are well polished. Research with friends and experts the choice of handle material.

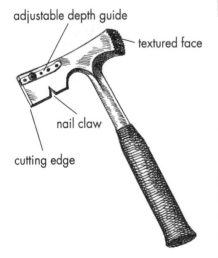

adjustable depth guide

textured face

nail claw

cutting edge

Shingler's Hatchet

Shingler's Hatchet

Also Known As: Roofing hatchet, shingling hatchet

Description: Hammer-sized hatchet with notch in lower edge and thumbscrew and small, sliding, replaceable metal blade along top edge; "heel" of blade has a milled pattern and is square. A *shingler's hammer* is a similar tool but without the sharp hatchet edge, while the small *roofing knife* has only the edge.

Use: Ripping up and replacing old shingles in a small repair or re-roofing job. The sliding metal blade with holes in it can be set to keep the blade from going too far under old shingles; it is used for cutting asphalt or fiberglass shingles, while the hatchet blade is for splitting shakes. The hammerhead is for driving roofing nails. The notch is for prying out nails from the roof decking.

> $ **Buying Tips:** A specialized tool that helps a big job go faster. For a larger job, get the larger **roofing shovel (Part IV, Chapter 33).**

Drywall Hammer

Also Known As: Drywall hatchet

Description: Smallish hammer with a notched blade instead of a claw. Hammerhead is scored.

Use: Driving drywall nails when hanging drywall and removing old drywall and nails. The notch in the blade is for removing exposed nailheads.

> $ **Buying Tip:** Screws are the preferred method for hanging drywall.

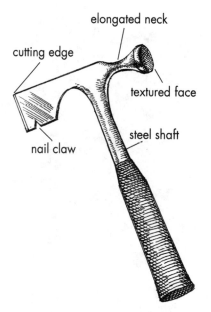

elongated neck

cutting edge

textured face

nail claw

steel shaft

Drywall Hammer

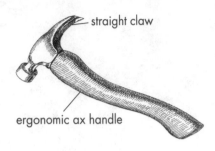

straight claw

ergonomic ax handle

Framing Hammer

Framing Hammer

Also Known As: California Special, California Framer's hammer, Framer's hammer

Description: Extra-long (up to 17") and heavy (21 to 30 ounces) hammer with straight claw, available with either a smooth or patterned (milled, checkerboard) face. Handle is usually straight but some models are available with an "ax-handle" curve to them. Developed by framers in California during the post-war housing boom. Quite similar to the lighter, smaller **rip hammer (above)** but sturdier.

Use: Rough carpentry, such as framing in a house with 2 × 4's, where accuracy is less important than power and speed. The extra length and weight give the carpenter more leverage, reducing the number of blows needed to drive a nail home. Straight claw is more useful for prying than for nail removal.

> **$ Buying Tips:** Checkerboard-patterned faces reduce the chance of glancing blows and flying nails. Top-quality models reduce vibration and arm fatigue. Look for unique features such as square heads and side-pull claws.

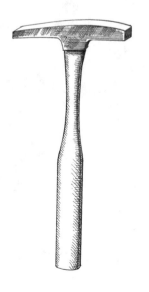

Tack Hammer

Description: Light, narrow, square head, with one face split and magnetized. Similar, but lighter and with a rounded head, is an *upholsterer's hammer*.

Use: For driving tacks or small nails. The magnetized face holds tacks that are too small to be held by hand.

Tack Hammer

Use Tip: Likely to be damaged if used on heavy nails.

Brad Driver

Also Known As: Brad pusher

Description: Round handle on short, spring-loaded, two-piece metal shaft. Brads are loaded into the open end of the shaft.

Use: Drives brads (small finishing nails) without a hammer.

spring-loaded barrel

Brad Driver

Ball Peen Hammer

Also Known As: Ball pein hammer, machinist's hammer

Description: A flat striking surface on one face, like a standard hammer, and a rounded striking surface on the other. A similar model, a *Warrington pattern* or *cross-pein hammer*, has a horizontal wedge-shaped face instead of the rounded face. A *straight-pein hammer* has a vertical wedge.

Use: Driving metal punches, working on sheet metal or rivets. Warrington model has a wedge face that can be used for starting small brads without hitting your fingers. The ball-shaped end is used for forming metal.

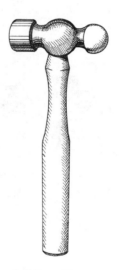

Ball Peen Hammer

Mallet

Also Known As: Soft-face hammer

Description: Large cylindrical or square wooden, rubber, plastic, or rawhide head with a wooden handle. A *carver's mallet* has a vertical cylindrical wooden head; a *carpentry mallet* has a big, squarish wooden head; a *deadblow hammer* is rubber filled with shot to eliminate rebound.

Use: For striking wood-handled wood-carving chisels; for bending metal; for tapping wood into place in cabinetmaking (a metal hammer face would mark the wood).

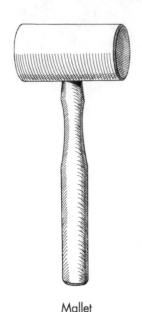

Mallet

Sledgehammer

Description: Oblong, faceted, extra-heavy head secured to a wooden handle. Available in a range of weights and lengths, the longest ones being two-handed tools. Common small one has a 3-pound head. *Double-face* means both faces are the same; a *single-face sledgehammer,* or *maul,* has one flat striking face and one wedge-shaped face for splitting wood. It is also called a *log splitter.*

Types:

Drilling, hand drilling, or *stone cutter's, hammer:* For striking masonry chisels, such as a **star drill (Part X, Chapter 75)**.

Engineer's hammer: Very small sledge (or metal mallet).

Blacksmith's hammer: One face wedge-shaped ("New England pattern").

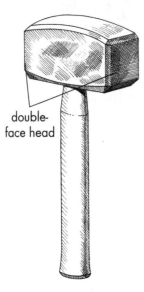

double-
face head

Sledgehammer

Note: Some manufacturers consider same as engineer's.

Use: Heavy work, such as driving chisels into brick or stone, driving heavy spikes or stakes, or breaking up concrete.

Wedge

Description: Heavy forged steel wedge about 7 to 9 inches long weighing 3 to 5 pounds, with a straight V-shape that has a cutting edge on one end and a wide striking surface on the other.

Use: Splitting logs for firewood. Must be struck with a sledge-hammer. Can only work *with* the grain—not a cutting tool.

$ Buying Tips: Quality steel is worth the expense. The striking end on cheaper wedges will "mushroom" out with use and the blade dulls quickly.

Hammer Wedge

Description: Tiny steel wedge with slight steps. Sold in various widths and thicknesses.

Use: Driven into the head ends of wooden hammer, ax, hatchet, and mallet handles to expand the wood and better hold the head in place.

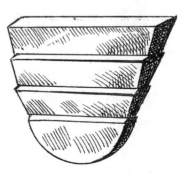

Hammer Wedge

Struck Tools: Nailsets, Punches, and Chisels

Nailset

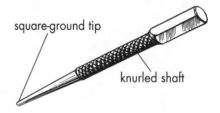

square-ground tip

knurled shaft

Nailset

Also Known As: Countersink

Description: Small shaft of metal, a few inches long, with one end round or square and one tapered to a point. Tapered point is usually blunt, but on some models is concave, or cupped, to hold nailheads. Nailsets come with various-sized tips—$1/32$" to $5/32$" at $1/32$" increments. This tool is often confused with a **center punch (below)**.

Use: Countersinking nails, i.e., driving nailheads beneath the surface of wood.

 Use Tip: Use the nailset sized to the nailhead being driven to avoid enlarging the hole.

 Buying Tip: Get a set of three: $1/32$", $2/32$", and $3/32$".

Punches

Description: Short, cylindrical steel shape like a **nailset (above)** with square head and knurled (or hexagonal) area for gripping. Tapers to a point. *Self-centering* models have telescoping sleeve.

Types:

> *Center punch* (point has short bevel, also known as a *nail punch*)
>
> *Drift punch* (long taper to a flat tip)
>
> *Pin punch* (straight shaft to a flat tip)
>
> *Prick punch* (point has long bevel)

Use: For marking and starting holes in metal or wood (*prick* and *center punches*), for aligning bolt or rivet holes (*drift* or *center punches*), or for driving out bushings (*pin punch*) or rivets after their heads have been removed (*center punch*). A *prick punch* makes a first, light mark that can be enlarged by a center punch.

 Use Tips: Punches should always be hit with a ball peen or light sledgehammer with a head slightly larger than the end of the punch. Safety glasses are recommended. Self-centering models are helpful when making holes in hinges and the like.

Buying Tip: The center punch can take care of most punch jobs.

About Chisels

Chisels are classified according to the kind of material they cut—wood, metal, and brick or **stone (masonry tools, Part X, Chapter 75).** Very few are interchangeable. Wear safety goggles when striking these tools.

Cold Chisel

Also Known As: Flat chisel, rivet buster

Description: Thick, short, hexagonal steel bar about 6 to 10 inches long, with a flat, tapered point.

Other Types:

Diamond point chisel (sharp square end, for sharp corners and V-shaped grooves)

Round nose chisel (for curved grooves)

Cape chisel (arrowhead-shape tip, for shearing off rivet heads and mashing bolt threads to keep nuts in place)

Use: Strike with a ball peen hammer or small sledge to cut and chip such "cold" metals as brass, copper, aluminum, and unhardened steel. Also good for removing bolts and rivets.

> **Use Tips:** Do not use for cutting masonry, which is a common mistake with cold chisels. There are specialized chisels for **masonry (Part X, Chapter 75)**. Always wear safety glasses to protect your eyes from flying chips. Deformed tips can be reground.

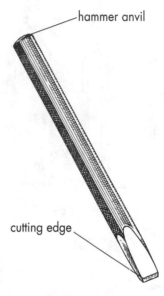

hammer anvil

cutting edge

Cold Chisel

plastic hand guard

Cold Chisel with Hand Guard

Wood Chisels

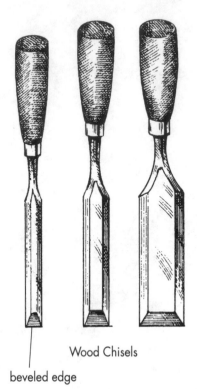

Wood Chisels

beveled edge

Description: Long, narrow steel blades in a variety of shapes, ranging from 2¹/₂" to almost a foot long and ¹/₈" to 2" wide, with a wooden or plastic handle. Only the beveled, front cutting edge is sharp. If the sides are beveled, then it is a *bench*, or *bevel-edged*, chisel, which is the most common style.

Types:

Butt chisel (short blade)

Firmer chisel (medium duty, square-sided)

Framing chisel (long and up to 2" wide, for deep furrows)

Flooring chisel, or *Electrician's chisel* (3" wide, 10" long, all steel)

Mortise chisel, or *mortising chisel* (narrow, thick, and strong)

Paring chisel, or *cabinet chisel* (light duty, for trimming)

Use: Making cuts in wood by chipping small pieces away at each hit.

Use Tips: Protect and keep sharp. Hit with a mallet rather than a hammer, except for the all-steel models. Wood-handled chisels should be hit only with a wooden mallet.

Buying Tips: Some top-quality chisels are works of art, and there is great competition among woodworking tool suppliers in this area. Bevel-edged chisels are common for the home workshop. Get a set.

Bars and Claws

About Pry and Wrecking Bars

While the following lineup of demolishers will help you take a house to the ground, they also do other jobs. Some tools allow you to remove nails and boards with minimal damage to treasured wood or plaster. Since some old trim may be irreplaceable, it is desirable to have, as usual, the right tool for the job. Happily, most bars are not expensive. The choice is easy. And lots of specialized bars are available (but not included here).

Safety note: When standing on anything other than flat, firm floors, don't put all your weight into pulling on a wrecking bar. When the piece you are wrecking pulls free, all your pulling energy is released, and you can go right down unless you are braced and ready.

Wrecking Bar

Also Known As: Crowbar, ripping bar, pig's foot, gooseneck bar, pinch bar

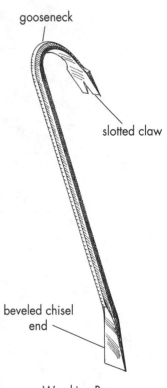

gooseneck

slotted claw

beveled chisel end

Wrecking Bar

Description: High-carbon steel bar, from 1' to several feet in length, with ends designed for prying and nail-pulling. Typically, one end is bent back in a hook and has a forked, nail-grabbing tip. The opposite end has a solid chisel shape and is slightly angled. Cloven appearance of nail puller is the source of the nickname *"pig's foot."* T-headed *wrecking bars* (or *rocker bars*) are common alternatives, too.

> **Note:** To some the *crowbar* or *iron bar* refers to a wrecking bar without a curved end. A bar with a curved end is known as a *gooseneck bar*. However, common usage is as presented above.

Use: Heavy prying and wrecking, particularly where some damage is acceptable. Also popular for lifting heavy objects, such as flagstones or crates, the distance necessary to place wedges and other items under them.

> **Use Tip:** The longer the model, the more leverage you'll have (and the more weight to maneuver).

> **Buying Tip:** A 24" or 30" model is handy for most jobs.

Pry Bar

Also Known As: Wonder Bar™, Super Bar (brand name), Utility Bar (brand name), Action Bar (brand name), pinch bar, molding chisel, shipscraper (small models), flat bar

Description: Flat, thin steel bar, a foot or so long, with beveled notches in both chisel-type ends, one slightly curved and one bent at 90 degrees. Some smaller, lighter models, less than 10" long, are called *pry bar scrapers.*

Use: For prying paneling, molding, crates, and the like where a thin, flat tool is needed and you are trying to avoid damage. Also for removing nails and spikes whose heads are exposed, either by using the notches in the ends or the teardrop-shaped hole (the "eye") in the middle.

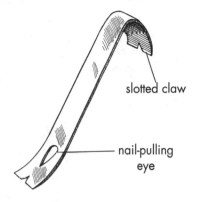

slotted claw

nail-pulling eye

Pry Bar

Use Tips: Not for extremely heavy prying. The flat shape is less strong than the hexagonal shape of **wrecking bars (above)**.

Buying Tips: Useful to have around, in both light and heavy weights (short and long, 6" and 14").

Ripping Chisel

Also Known As: Ripping bar, rip chisel, angle bar, flat bar, double-end ripping bar

Description: Hexagonal or I-beam steel rod, usually 18" long, with a wide chisel end, a beveled notch, and a teardrop-

Offset Ripping Chisel

shaped nail slot for removing nails. Also made in an *offset* version, with a short, beveled, and notched end bent at a 90-degree angle opposite the wider chisel end.

Use: Basically a heavy-duty model of the **pry bar (above)**, for removal of items with small gaps between them. Made to be driven with a large hammer and used like any chisel.

 Use Tips: Particularly useful when removing floorboards. Don't overload.

 Buying Tip: Many variations exist. Get the one you need.

Cat's Paw Nail Claw

Nail Claw

Also Known As: Cat's paw, nail puller, nail puller bar, cat's paw puller, tack claw (smaller models)

Description: Hand-sized, hexagonal or round steel bar with a small, nail-grabbing slotted tip at one or both ends. Typically each tip is cup- or spoon-shaped, and at 90 degrees to the shaft. Some models are L-shaped. Usually around 1' long.

Use: Pulling out sunken nails. Driven below nailheads with a hammer so that nails can be pulled all the way out with the claw of a **hammer (Chapter 1)**, **pry bar, ripping bar,** or **wrecking bar (above)**.

Double-End Cat's Paw

 Use Tip: Try to avoid driving the claw too deeply into the wood.

$ Buying Tips: Sometimes available in a combination model with a chisel end, or with a small claw for tacks and small nails.

Tack Puller

Description: Short metal shaft with flared, slightly curved, notched end and cylindrical handle, no more than 6" long.

Use: Prying out tacks.

Tack Puller

Lumber Wrench

Also Known As: Tweaker® (brand name), board bender (brand name), warped lumber straightening tool

Description: Foot-long, heavy, octagonal steel bar with uneven U-shaped end, the points of which are tapered to resemble hammer claws. The inside of the U is squared off. Some models have an angled handle with a hinge.

Tweaker®

Use: Multiple uses, but its distinctive shape is primarily for tweaking 2 × 4 studs and deck joists or any other 2"-**dimensional lumber (see Chapter 48)** into place with a gentle twist. The hinged model also squeezes deck floorboards tight. Also suited for wedging a door or other panel to move it slightly, and for removing nails, as well as miscellaneous demolition jobs.

$ Buying Tips: If you are building a deck, or working with slightly warped studs or rafters, this is the tool for you.

Screwdrivers

About Screwdrivers

There are a number of screwdrivers of potential use to the handyperson, but two kinds predominate: the *slotted* and the *Phillips.* Both types are available with square or round shanks. A *square shank screwdriver* can be gripped with a wrench for added turning power; some brands have a round shank with a hex bolster (a small section just under the handle) for the same purpose. The slot must conform to the type of **screw (Part III, Chapter 21).**

Slotted Screwdriver

Also Known As: Standard screwdriver, straight-slot screwdriver, machinist's screwdriver, mechanic's screwdriver

Description: Narrow steel shank with flat tip, or blade, and a plastic or wooden handle. *Machinist's screwdrivers* have blades with a slight shoulder and taper. *Cabinet, electrician's,* or *thin-blade* screwdrivers are similar, but the blade tip is narrower and there is no shoulder (straight sides); for finish or electrical work. Cabinet models have a wide blade under the handle.

Use: Driving and removing standard, slotted screws.

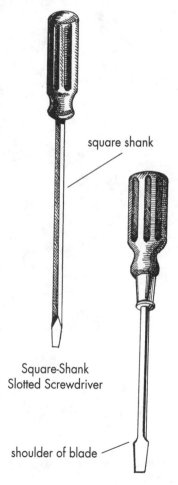

square shank

Square-Shank
Slotted Screwdriver

shoulder of blade

Machinist's (Standard)
Slotted Screwdriver

narrow
blade tip

Electrician's Slotted Screwdriver

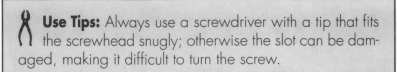

Use Tips: Always use a screwdriver with a tip that fits the screwhead snugly; otherwise the slot can be damaged, making it difficult to turn the screw.

Buying Tips: Cheap, low-quality screwdrivers are worthless. Get screwdrivers with the bigger, softer handles.

Phillips Head Screwdriver

Also Known As: Cross head screwdriver, star screwdriver, Phillips-type screwdriver

Description: Long, narrow steel shank with pointed, crisscross end and a plastic or wooden handle. Comes in a range of five sizes: 0 (smallest) to 4 (largest). Industrial variations are the *Reed & Prince,* and *Pozidriv* screwdrivers.

Use: Driving and removing Phillips head screws.

Use Tip: Always use a properly sized screwdriver. Using the wrong size can ruin the screw slot.

Buying Tips: Buy at least a #1 and a #2 so you can use the right size each time. The smallest sizes are good for electronic devices. Get good quality only.

Phillips Head Screwdriver

Torx® Screwdriver

Description: One of several new styles of screw slots found in manufactured items, Torx® screwheads are designed with an internal, faceted hole. Sizes are denoted by numbers, such as T8, T15, T40, etc. Somewhat similar to Phillips or Hex Head, Torx® screws are most often used on automobiles (in headlights and the dashboard) and computer cases.

Use: Driving Torx® screws only.

Torx® Screwdriver

 Buying Tip: You must match the Torx® screw size to the driver.

Stubby Screwdriver

Description: Standard or Phillips blade but only about 1¹/₄" long.

Use: Good in tight spots where a regular-size screwdriver won't fit.

 Buying Tip: Handle should be large enough to grip comfortably.

Stubby Screwdriver

High-Torque Spiral Ratchet
Screwdriver

High-Torque Spiral Ratchet Screwdriver

Also Known As: Ratchet screwdriver, wrist ratchet screwdriver, mechanical screwdriver

Description: Has a ball or a T-handle instead of a regular handle and a ratchet mechanism enabling you to turn the tool without regripping the handle. Has more turning power, or torque, than an ordinary screwdriver. Most models have interchangeable blades, for both slotted and Phillips screws.

Use: For easier driving and removing of screws.

 Use Tip: Good in tight spots where gripping and regripping the handle is difficult.

Return Spiral Ratchet Screwdriver

Also Known As: Ratchet screwdriver, auto-return screwdriver, Yankee® screwdriver, in-and-out screwdriver, mechanical screwdriver

Description: Crosshatched shank, with short, interchangeable, ratchet-operated blade and large handle. Turned by pushing down on the handle. Some models can store different type blades in the handle.

Use: Driving and removing screws quickly. Can also drill small holes in soft materials.

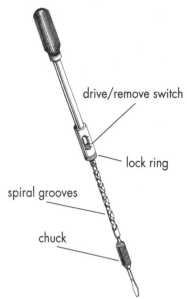

drive/remove switch

lock ring

spiral grooves

chuck

Return Spiral Ratchet Screwdriver

Use Tips: Particularly good when there are a number of the same-size screws to drive. The ratchet mechanism makes repetitive work easier and faster. Hard to control at first. An old and venerable design.

Offset Screwdriver

Also Known As: Cranked screwdriver

Description: 4" or 5" long, S-shaped shank with either standard slot head blades or Phillips head blades on each end, perpendicular to the shank; some combination models have both. Also sold in pairs with one of each kind. Available in an *offset ratchet* version made plain **(see ill.)** and with a large handle. For the hardest to reach spots, there is a *flexible screwdriver*, a rare accessory that has a spring-like shank.

Use: Primarily for turning screws in tight places, its added leverage is also helpful in turning difficult screws.

Offset Screwdriver

Offset Ratchet
Screwdriver

 Use Tip: Don't forget to hold the screwdriver tip firmly on the screw.

 Buying Tips: A plain slotted version is easier to use than the combination model. Because the blades are at right angles to one another, you can alternate ends as you turn the screw. This can be a big advantage in a tight space. If you need this often, get an **offset screwdriver head (Part II, Chapter 16)** for a cordless drill-driver.

Screw-Holding Screwdriver

Screw-Holding Screwdriver

Also Known As: Screw-gripper screwdriver

Description: Similar to a standard screwdriver, but with a split blade that holds screws on the tip of the blade. A variation is a *spring-clip*, which has two springs, or arms, and fits on the end of the blade.

Use: Starting screws in places where they are difficult to hold.

 Use Tip: Screwdriver size must match size of screw being driven.

Saws and Accessories

About Saws

Saws come with various-sized teeth and specific numbers of teeth per inch (tpi) simultaneously designated by "points," such as an "8-point" or "8-tpi" blade. The higher the number, the finer and slower the cutting. All saws should be kept sharp through careful use and, if possible, professional sharpening. They should be of fine-tempered steel. A little lubricating spray helps keep things moving more easily, too.

Crosscut and Rip Saws

Description: Wood or plastic handle secured to a wide, slightly tapered, steel blade with jagged teeth along one edge. Lengths run from 20" to 28"; 26" is most popular.

Use: *Crosscut saws* are used to saw boards across the grain. *Rip saws* have teeth designed to saw along, or with, the grain going the length of the board.

> **Use Tips:** The crosscut saw is *the* basic handsaw for most projects. Use a rip saw at a slightly steeper angle than a crosscut saw—60 degrees as opposed to 45 degrees.

Crosscut Saw

> **$ Buying Tips:** Taper-ground blades (thinner along the top), which reduce binding, are recommended, as is purchasing brand names. *Skewback saws*, which have slightly curved topsides, are lighter and better balanced. The 8-point size is best for general crosscut work on most home projects; 10-point is for finer work and for plywood and paneling. Rip saws are in the 5- to 6-point range, and are not needed if you have power saws Also, a crosscut handsaw can suffice for the occasional rip job.

About Specialized Handsaws

Saws come in a wide variety of specialized models, but the most useful ones are listed here. Only serious cabinetmakers will need more models. There are also a number of particularly useful Japanese saws; typically, such saws are made of harder steel and cut very well but, unlike American-made saws, cut on the "pull" rather than the "push" stroke, giving you more control for a smoother, more accurate cut.

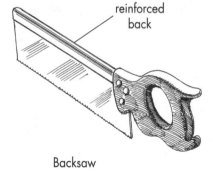

reinforced back

Backsaw

Backsaw

Also Known As: Miter-box saw, miter saw

Description: Rectangular, fine-toothed saw with a stiff reinforcement piece along the top or back. Smaller versions of the backsaw, the smallest having handles in line with the blade, are for very fine joint work and include *the dovetail saw, cabinet saw, blitz saw, gent's* or *gentleman's saw, slotting saw, razorback saw,* and *tenon saw*. The reinforced back gives greater control for fine cutting. Generally smaller than a regular saw—12" to 16"; 18" to 30" models are for use in **miter boxes (below)**.

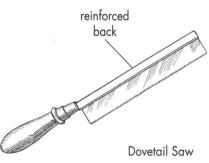

reinforced back

Dovetail Saw

Use: For making very accurate cuts, such as for molding. Also for use in a **miter box (below)**.

Miter Box

Also Known As: mitre box

Description: Wood or plastic box with matching slots on both sides cut at 45-degree and 90-degree angles. Also available in metal with guides for the saw rather than slots.

Use: To cut wood at precise angles.

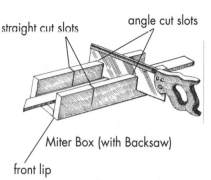

straight cut slots   angle cut slots

Miter Box (with Backsaw)

front lip

> **$ Buying Tips:** Indicators of a quality metal miter box are roller bearings in the saw guide and grips, which allow the stock to be held so both hands can be used. Some miter boxes have magnetic mounts, which make it easier to cut more accurately.

Compass Saw

Also Known As: Keyhole saw, nesting saw

Description: 12" to 14" long, thin, tapered blade. Similar to a **drywall or wallboard saw (Part VII, Chapter 50)** but finer-toothed. Smaller versions are called *keyhole saws* and have fine teeth, which can often cut metal as well as wood. Also very useful are still smaller models with metal, open construction, *pistol grip* or *turret-head* handles, which can hold the smaller blades at various angles. All of these saws are often sold with several different-sized blades, and are therefore sometimes called *nesting saws* or *nest of saws*. When the handle is in line with the small blade, it may be called a *jab saw*, or *pad saw*, as well as a *keyhole saw*.

Use: Cutting holes and curves.

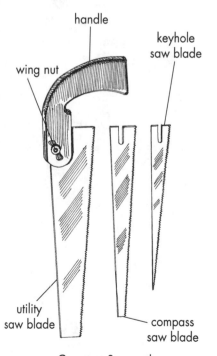

handle

keyhole saw blade

wing nut

utility saw blade

compass saw blade

Compass Saw and Interchangeable Blades

Use Tips: You must drill a hole to start a cut. Some of the smaller blades may cut on the "pull" stroke.

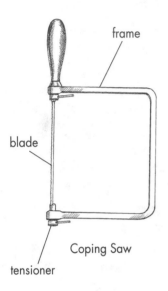

frame

blade

Coping Saw

tensioner

Coping Saw

Description: Extremely thin blade, usually around 6½" long, held by a C-shaped metal frame. Deeper-throated models are known as *fret saws, scroll saws,* and *deep-throat coping saws.*

Use: Extremely fine cutting of all decorative patterns and curves.

 Use Tips: Keep blade highly tensioned. Adjust angles and direction of teeth for the work at hand.

 Buying Tip: Many specialized blades exist for cutting plastic, metal, and wood.

Japanese Saws

Also Known As: Pullsaw

Types:

Ryoba saw

Dozuki saw

Azebiki saw

Keyhole saw

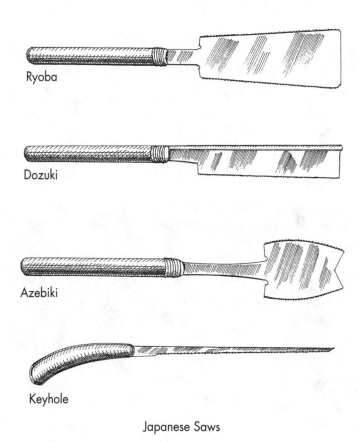

Ryoba

Dozuki

Azebiki

Keyhole

Japanese Saws

Description:

Ryoba: Thin-bladed *combination saw* with fine teeth on both sides—crosscut teeth on one and ripsaw teeth on the other.

Dozuki: Thin, fine-toothed saw with very sharp teeth and stiffening weight rib (usually of brass) along backside. Cuts very fast.

Azebiki: Short, thin, slightly curved blade with fine teeth on both sides. Similar to small **flooring saw (below)**.

Keyhole: Very narrow, pointed blade with large teeth.

Use:

> *Ryoba:* Traditional carpenter's general-use saw; also flush cuts.

> *Dozuki:* For fine cabinetry work and joint cutting, such as for dovetails.

> *Azebiki:* Starts cuts in middle of panels; also for flush cutting in awkward places.

> *Keyhole:* Like its American counterpart, for cutting holes with very small radii; "pull" stroke method allows for a finer blade.

Use Tips: As mentioned, Japanese saws cut on the "pull" stroke rather than the "push" stroke. This certainly aids accurate cutting, makes it easier and faster, and prevents blade buckling. It also allows the use of thin blades. Warning: They are easily damaged.

Buying Tips: An absolutely superior design. The *ryoba* as a combination model is an excellent gift item for anyone of any skill level. A definite purchase for all tool boxes.

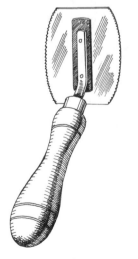

Veneer Saw

Veneer Saw

Description: Small handle secured to small, slightly rounded blade with large-toothed edges.

Use: Cutting veneer (extremely thin pieces of wood) and any small cuts flush with a surface.

Flooring Saw

Description: Short, 8-point crosscut saw with a curved bottom cutting edge and a short cutting edge on the topside of the front end.

Use: Cutting floorboards and baseboards where you need to keep the blade away from neighboring surfaces.

Buck Saw

Also Known As: Bow saw

Description: Extremely large-toothed blade secured between two ends of a metal bow, or handle. Not to be confused with a *frame saw,* popular with cabinetmakers, which is a rarefied traditional saw made of two parallel wooden pieces joined at one end by a blade and at the other by a tension cord or wire, with a bar of wood in the middle.

Use: Rough cutting of logs for firewood or pruning.

 Buying Tip: Get a long one, about 36".

Flexible Saw

Also Known As: Pocket saw

Description: Flexible wire coated with sharp tungsten-carbide particles. Has a ring on each end instead of a solid handle.

Use: Limited rough cutting. Made to be portable, used by hikers.

Hacksaw

Description: An adjustable or fixed-frame saw that holds a narrow, fine-toothed blade 8" to 16" long. Number of teeth per inch varies from 14 to 32 tpi, and they may be of various designs such as *wavy* or *raker*. The frame is bought separately from the blades, which are easily (and often) replaced. Some models are extra-strong and have many convenient features such as blade storage and special shapes, called *high-tension* hacksaw frames. Others have just a small handle in line with the blade for use in close quarters, called *mini*, *jab*, *handy*, *close-cutting*, or *utility hacksaw*, depending on the manufacturer. Blade may be mounted at a 90-degree angle for flush cutting.

Use: Cutting metal or plastic.

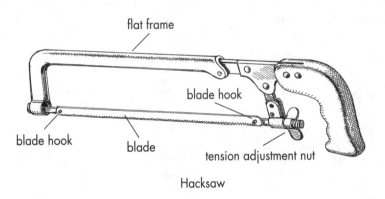

flat frame

blade hook

blade hook   blade

tension adjustment nut

Hacksaw

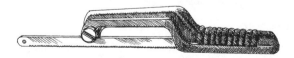

Mini-Hacksaw

Use Tips: The thinner the material to be cut, the finer the blade should be. Use an 18-tpi (teeth per inch) blade on soft metals; a 24-tpi blade on medium metals; and a 32-tpi blade on hard metals. Always use higher-tpi blades on thinner material. Blade should have three teeth on the work piece.

Buying Tips: Keep a supply of different-toothed blades on hand. Specialized blades are available for cutting glass or tile. Both the *rod saw*, a wire or rod covered with bits of tungsten carbide, and the *grit saw*, with a normal-shaped blade also covered with abrasive material, can cut almost anything. A 10" simple model is sufficient for most DIY jobs. Standard, high-carbon steel blades are usually fine, but a few more expensive, tougher bi-metal blades are good to have on hand.

Saw Set

Description: Pliers-like tool with thumbscrew and small vise for holding a saw blade. Some models have a small magnifying glass built in.

Use: Setting (bending back) teeth on all kinds of hand saws, from 4 to 12 tpi, and on some fine-toothed circular saw blades. The goal is to prevent the saw from binding in the kerf (cut) after getting banged up or worn out.

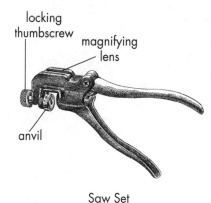

locking thumbscrew

magnifying lens

anvil

Saw Set

Buying Tip: Not your usual weekend handyman necessity, but a good way to save money and extend the life of a tool.

Knives and Cutting Tools

Utility Knife

Also Known As: Trimming knife, carpet knife, Sheetrock knife, drywall knife, mat knife

Description: Two common models: either a hollow metal handle with a large angular blade that is held in place by screwing the two sides of the handle together or else a push-pull type. Some *breakaway utility knives* have sectioned narrow "breakaway" blades; each section can be broken off with pliers when it dulls. Then the new blade section is slid forward. One model even stores blades in a rotating barrel inside the handle.

Use: Cutting wallcovering, drywall, tape, string, roofing, and most any soft material. *Hook blades* allow cutting without damaging material underneath.

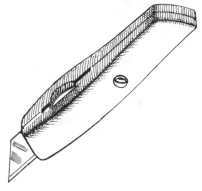

Utility Knife

Use Tips: Be sure to use sharp blades only; dull blades are inefficient and unsafe. You can reverse the large angular blades and use the opposite end before replacing them. Store with blade retracted for safety's sake. Keep away from children. Hide it in your tool box.

Buying Tips: One of the handiest tools to have around. Look for the newer ergonomic models (some even have holsters—wow!).

Razor Knife

Razor Knife

Description: Wooden- or plastic-handled grip that holds single-edged razor blades.

Use: Cutting wallcoverings, paper, etc. Slices and trims with precision.

 **Use Tip:** Change blades as often as every cut, depending on material.

Precision Knife

Also Known As: X-ACTO®, hobby knife

Description: Pencil-sized metal knife that holds a variety of triangular and curved blades in a chuck. The blades are made from surgical steel and are especially sharp. Some models can store blades in their hollow handle. Larger, heavy-duty models are available.

Use: Precision cutting of paper and other lightweight materials, usually on a flat surface. A regular staple of the graphic design business.

Precision Knife

Use Tips: Use a metal rather than a plastic straight-edge to guide your cutting, as the knife will cut into plastic. Wrap worn blades in tape before discarding to protect anyone who might handle the waste basket.

Linoleum Knife

Also Known As: Vinyl knife, flooring knife, hook-bill knife

Description: Short, hooked, wide blade with short, thick handle.

Use: Cutting resilient flooring, such as linoleum or vinyl sheets.

Use Tips: Keep blade sharp. A small file works as well as an **oilstone (below)**.

Linoleum Knife

Oilstone

Also Known As: Whetstone, benchstone, sharpening stone, Arkansas stone, waterstone, carborundum, craftsman's stone, hone stone

Description: Polished stone, either silicon carbide or aluminum oxide. Comes in various sizes. The standard oilstone is $1/2$" to 2" wide by $6^1/2$" to 8" long and 1" thick. It is kept in a holder and the blade is ground on it. If the stone is shaped, small, and can be ground against the blade, it is known as a *slipstone*. A *combination stone* has a different roughness on each side. *Japanese waterstones* are now becoming popular with craftspeople.

Oilstone

Use: Sharpening ("honing") tool and knife edges.

> **Use Tips:** Clean the stone with a stiff brush and kerosene if it becomes clogged with metal shavings. Treat with honing oil.

> **Buying Tips:** Oilstones come in a range of coarseness, or grit: fine, medium, and coarse. Medium is best for most uses.

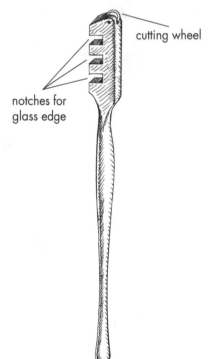

cutting wheel

notches for glass edge

Glass Cutter

Glass Cutter

Description: Pencil-like metal tool with one notched end with a small cutting wheel on the tip. Roller may or may not be carbide.

Use: To cut glass by scoring and then breaking glass along the line. Models are made for cutting plastic, too.

> **Use Tips:** Warmed glass cuts more easily than cold glass. Never go over the same score twice.

> **Buying Tip:** Table model also available for cutting circles.

Plastic Cutter

Description: Short metal blade and flat handle

Use: For cutting and scoring acrylic plastic sheets.

Tin Snips

Types:

Aviation snips

Duckbill snips

Hawk's bill snips

Offset snips

Straight snips

Universal snips

Aviation Tin Snips

Also Known As: Metal shears, tinner's snips.

Straight: Standard, flat blade (duckbill pattern, with pointed tips)

Aviation: Compound action, compound leverage

Description: Large, heavy, scissor-like tool with different-shaped noses. *Aviation snips* are smaller, with spring hinges and smaller noses. *Offset snips* have jaws that are at a slight angle to the handle.

Use: Cutting thin metal, as follows:

Aviation: For cutting both straight and curved lines, but spring action gives you better leverage. Available in left- and right-cutting models.

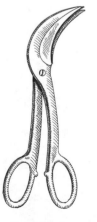

Hawk's Bill
Snips

Straight Tin Snips

Hawk's bill: For cutting tight circles without distortion.

Straight and duckbill: For cutting straight lines.

Universal: For cutting both straight and curved lines.

 Use Tips: Wear gloves when cutting metal. Cut edges are very sharp.

$ **Buying Tips:** For really thin materials, smaller, lighter models called *shears* are available. Offset and aviation snips are slightly easier to use than the large, heavy, *straight* snips.

Bolt Cutter

Bolt Cutter

Also Known As: Rod and bolt cutter, cutter

Description 14" or 24" long blade-and-anvil type shears. Handles work with two sets of hinges and a compound cutting action for extra leverage. Even larger models are made, some over 3' long.

Use: Cutting chain, bolts, rods, small padlocks, or other thick wire.

 Use Tips: The 24" model cuts up to $^3/_8$" diameter bolts; the 14" model only up to $^1/_4$" diameter. Keep lightly oiled to prevent rust, as this is not a tool one uses often.

Ax (or Axe)

Description Heavy steel, slightly curved wedge with a cutting edge, about 4" to 8" long, attached to a handle, usually of hickory, which ranges in length from 20" to 36"; 36" is most common. Some handles are now made of fiberglass. Handle is curved to increase leverage.

Types:

Single-bit ax has only one sharp edge, for cutting; the other is slender but blunt, for driving large stakes and the like. (A *maul* has a wedge-shaped head with a large, blunt heel.)

Double-bit ax has two sharp cutting edges and a straight handle.

Shapes of the ax head vary slightly and carry many different names, some of which are regional, such as *Western* and *Michigan* single edge. Names also vary with the specialized use, such as *fireman's* and *forester's*. Smaller versions of axes are known as **hatchets (below)**.

Use: Chopping trees and branches, splitting logs for firewood.

Double-Bit Ax

Use Tips: Double-bit axes are very dangerous for beginners. Safety glasses to protect eyes from flying chips are recommended when using any ax. Don't use the blunt end of a single-bit ax for striking anything hard, like stone or a steel post—use a *sledgehammer* instead. An ax no heavier than $2\frac{1}{4}$ pounds is recommended for the average user; heavier heads are harder to control and therefore slightly risky to use. A *maul* and *wedge* are best for splitting logs.

Half-Hatchet

Hatchet

Also Known As: Hunter's belt ax

Description: Hammer-sized single-bit ax. Half-hatchet model has a hammerhead where the heel normally is.

Use: Demolition, splitting of small logs into kindling, making stakes.

Adze

Also Known As: Adz

Description: A heavy steel head with a cutting edge perpendicular to the handle, resembling an ax head turned sideways. Often sold as a head only, and you must supply the handle. A general-purpose adze has a 3-pound head, while a finishing adze is a little slimmer and lighter. Finishing adzes may come with slightly curved or straight blades, depending on their intended use.

Use: Shaping and smoothing logs and timbers into beams, notching logs for log cabins, or for wood sculpture. Cuts can be made only with the grain, not across it.

 Buying Tip: Rarely found in stock, but easily ordered from major manufacturers.

Adze

Pliers

About Pliers

Pliers are some of the most common and useful tools around the house. Some can be up to 20" long, with the jaw opening getting progressively wider as the handles get longer. The variety is necessary—a good toolbox should have a number of types. Many pliers have the capacity to cut wire, with, in most cases, just a small notch on the outside edge or a cutting edge inside, near the hinge. Special-task models abound.

All pliers are scissor-like, usually made of drop-forged steel, with handles on one side of a joint and jaws on the other. Some pliers handles are plastic-covered for improved grip and identification, but this plastic is not protection from electrical shock. Insulated pliers are marked as such, but are very rare.

Slip-Joint Pliers

Also Known As: Pliers

Description: Slightly curved, toothed jaws, and a hinge that can be "slipped" to make the jaw opening wide or narrow. The classic, standard pliers. Some models with a large, round

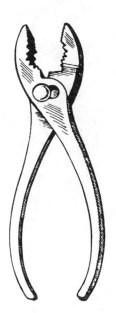

Slip-Joint Pliers

opening in the jaws are called *gas pliers.* Sometimes a type of **tongue-and-groove pliers (below)**, which have a similar slip-joint, are called by the same name.

Use: Gripping small objects.

> **Use Tips:** Not always the best tool for gripping—the specialized pliers described below are better for many jobs. It may slip.

> **Buying Tips:** One of the most common tools to have around, but one that is easily out-performed by more up-to-date models.

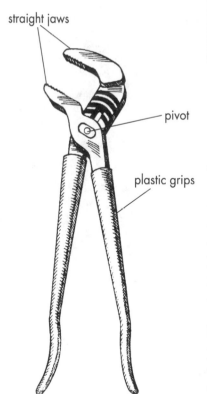

straight jaws

pivot

plastic grips

Tongue-and-Groove Pliers

Tongue-and-Groove Pliers

Also Known As: Channellocks® (brand name and most commonly used name), Channel-type pliers (referring to brand name), arced pliers, curved jaw pliers, jointed pliers, mechanic's pliers, pump pliers, water-pump pliers, pump-house pliers, pipe-wrench pliers, slip-groove pliers, groove-joint pliers, rib-joint pliers, multiple-joint pliers, channel-joint pliers, C-joint pliers, utility pliers, adjustable pliers—and, incorrectly but often, just plain "pliers."

Description: Pliers-like tool with long jaws and a movable pivot that allows jaws to be set at a variety of widths. Choice of models is large; jaw widths range in size from about 1" to over 5". $1\frac{1}{2}$" is average. Jaws may be either flat or curved. Some manufacturers make two models: *tongue-and-groove,* which has a number of slots or channels for positioning the jaws, and *water pump, box joint* or *slip-joint,* which has a long slot with scalloped edges for different jaw positions.

Use: For gripping items too large for standard pliers; their jaws remain parallel, making them more secure than slip-joint pliers. Plumbers use them for small repairs all the time. Curved jaw models are frequently used to hold pipes. Thinness allows access to tight spots.

Use Tips: Long handles allow for great leverage and gripping power, which can cause you to dent or mar soft metals like brass and copper. Those with solid rivets at the pivot hold better than those with nuts and bolts.

Buying Tips: Larger sizes are harder to handle; 7" and 10" are best to have around. Very versatile—useful also in cars and on boats.

Robo Grip® Pliers

Also Known As: Self-adjusting pliers

Description: Pliers-like tool with an adjustable pivot and handles connected by a moving bar for compound action. Jaws are curved, with deep teeth. Handles and jaws stay roughly parallel as they are moved.

Robo Grip® Pliers

Use: Where extra-strong gripping is required, this design provides needed leverage.

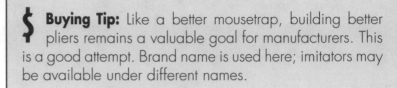

wire-cutting jaws

box joint

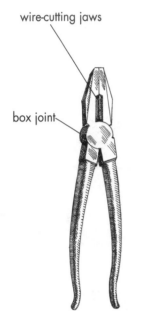

Lineman's Side-Cutting Pliers

Lineman's Side-Cutting Pliers

Also Known As: Lineman's pliers, linesman pliers, electrician's pliers, engineer's pliers (uninsulated handles), telecommunications pliers, wiring pliers, side-cutting pliers

Description: Similar to **diagonal side-cutting pliers (below)**, but of heavier construction and insulated handles with square jaws for gripping and cutting. Those with rounded jaws are known as *New England style*. Combination or universal models have a middle section in the jaws that has a more concave set of gripping teeth, and these may be called *gas* pliers. The pivot is a "solid joint" or "box joint."

Use: For heavy-duty cutting and handling wire with more control than **slip-joint pliers (above)**.

 Use Tips: As mentioned before, plastic handles are for comfort only—not for protection against shock.

§ Buying Tips: Heavy-duty models are very good to have. The combination model, which is quite versatile, is the standard design of pliers in Europe. *Solid-joint* or *box-joint* design is superior.

Locking Pliers

Also Known As: Vise-Grips®, combination plier-wrench, plier wrench.

> **Note:** These are more often called by the brand name Vise-Grips®.

Description: Curved or straight, short jaws and what appears to be one double handle. Jaws may be opened and set as needed by turning a knurled screw in the back of one handle. The jaws are then clamped together by squeezing the handles. Available in a smaller, long-nose version, too, as well as **clamp versions (Chapter 9)**, and flat, smooth jaws for holding sheet metal, etc.

Use: Works like a clamp—they can provide up to a ton of pressure—and can be turned with two hands to free frozen nuts—or used with no hands, just to hold something in place.

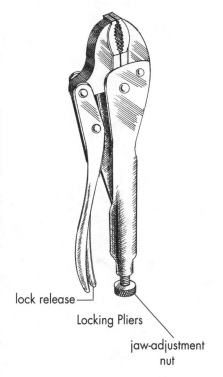

lock release ——

Locking Pliers

jaw-adjustment nut

Long-Nose Pliers

Also Known As: Needle-nose pliers, thin-nose pliers

Description: Short, curved handles with long, thin, tapered jaws. Most have a wire-cutting area by the hinge. Those with the longer, more slender noses are more often called *needle-nose pliers*. Many specialized, hooked designs are available.

Use: For reaching into tight spots and/or to hold and bend wire, such as for the small radii necessary in electrical connections or for delicate work.

Long-Nose Pliers

Diagonal Side-Cutting Pliers

Diagonal Side-Cutting Pliers

Also Known As: Wire cutters, diagonal cutting pliers

Description: Small pliers with curved handles and short, pointed nose with cutting jaws (no teeth) at a diagonal to the handles.

Use: General cutting of wire and thin metal items like cotter pins.

Use Tips: Cutting a "live" wire can cause a dangerous short. Don't do it. And again, plastic-coated handles are not necessarily insulated. If you need to cut something thicker than wire, such as a bolt, a lock hasp, chain or cable, use a **bolt cutter (Chapter 6)**, which are huge versions of wire cutters.

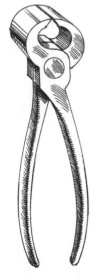

End-Cutting Nippers

End-Cutting Nippers Pliers

Also Known As: Nippers, end nippers, end cutters, carpenter's pincers, nail outener, end nipper plier, nail puller/cutter

Description: Beveled, wide jaws that meet at a right angle to the handles.

Use: For cutting off or pulling nails whose heads are close to the surface.

Use Tips: If you are pulling a nail, don't grip so tight as to cut its head off. These pliers have great leverage.

Fence Pliers

Also Known As: Prong and hammerhead pliers, fenceman's pliers or tool, fencing pliers, fence tool

Description: Pliers-like tool around 10" long with a head that consists of jaws, a hooked part, and a flat, hammer-like end. Combination wrench, pliers, hammer, and stapler puller/driver.

Use: Made for the erection of wire fencing, but good for all wire work. The flat section is used to hammer staples into fence posts, the hook part to pull staples out, and the jaws to pull wire. Generally handy around the house too.

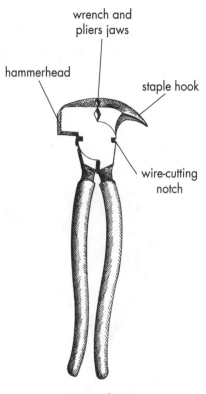

wrench and pliers jaws

hammerhead

staple hook

wire-cutting notch

Fence Pliers

Wrenches

About Wrenches

Within the variety of wrenches available there are generally two kinds: those for general use and those for plumbing. The **plumbing**, or **pipe wrenches**, as they are known, are detailed in **Part VIII, Chapter 63**. Basically, the wrenches described below are for turning any type of hex or square nut or bolt or object with flat surfaces, while most pipe wrenches can grip round surfaces with their teeth. All wrenches are available in either fractional (inches) or metric (millimeters) sizes, and only their openings are noted.

The quality you pay for at purchase time will be evident over the years: heavy, good-quality wrenches do not wear out. Cheap ones do, and can slip when in use, damaging the nut you are trying to loosen.

The rare term *spanner* is sometimes used for wrench terminology. It is in general use in England to denote a variety of wrenches, and it may have been used almost as often here prior to World War II. However, our research shows that usage here limits it to plumbing wrenches for large, special nuts.

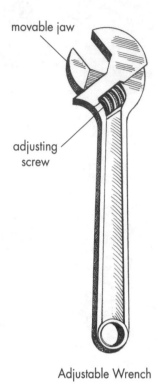

movable jaw

adjusting
screw

Adjustable Wrench

Adjustable Wrench

Also Known As: Crescent® wrench, adjustable open-end wrench, knuckle-buster

Description: Long, narrow, polished steel handle with parallel jaws that open or close by adjusting a screw gear. Typically 4" to 16" in length; the size of the jaw opening is proportionate to the length of the tool.

Use: For tightening or loosening nuts and bolts, spark plugs, and small pipe fittings, and larger, chrome-plated pipe fittings that would be marred by the teeth of a pipe wrench. Considered by some to be the modern replacement of the **monkey wrench (Part I, Chapter 8)**.

Use Tips: Not intended for really heavy turning pressure—it may slip. Turn toward the movable jaw. Jiggle as you tighten it for best fit.

Buying Tips: Of all the wrenches you buy, this one should be of the highest quality as it tends to be used quite often around the home and lower-quality wrenches do not grip as well. Helpful to have both a small (6") and a large (10" or 12") model. Check out new versions that may replace this standard such as a *self-adjusting wrench*, which may even have a ratcheting feature.

About Open-End, Box, and Combination Wrenches

These three similar wrench types are available in sets of various sizes. Their openings are fixed, as opposed to the adjustable opening of the wrench described above. All are sold in sets. Ingenious new universal, adjustable, designs may render the fixed style obsolete.

Open-End Wrench

Also Known As: Double-end open-end wrench

Description: Narrow steel handle with ends that have open, fixed jaws. 4- to 16" length; the openings getting larger as the tool gets longer. Like **box wrenches (below)** wrench sizes are described by the size of the nut that each end can fit, such as $3/8" \times 7/16"$. Usually ends are of different sizes.

Use: For tightening or loosening nuts and bolts, especially those accessible only from the side.

Open-End Wrench

 Use Tip: Generally can be used in tighter quarters than an adjustable wrench.

Buying Tips: A completely flat version with several different-sized jaws on each end is made for bicycles, but is not very usable around the house.

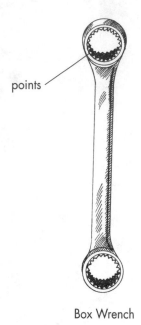

points

Box Wrench

Box Wrench

Also Known As: Ring wrench, double-end box wrench, offset box wrench, box-end wrench

Description: Long, narrow, polished, plated steel handle with two ring-shaped ends with six or twelve interior facets called *points* or *teeth*. Typically 4" to 16" long; the size of the rings is proportionate to the length of the tool. The rings are usually different sizes ($^3/_8$" and $^7/_{16}$", for example) and may be slightly offset from the handle, so this is sometimes called an *offset wrench*. Also available in a ratchet form, called a *ratcheting box wrench*. Sizes are denoted by the size of the nut that each end can fit, not the wrench length.

Use: For tightening or loosening nuts and bolts when the wrench can be slipped over the end of the work.

 Use Tip: Generally can be used in tighter quarters than an adjustable wrench and with more leverage.

 Buying Tip: 12-point rings are faster and more versatile.

Combination Wrench

Also Known As: Combination open-end box wrench

Description: Literally a combination of the open-end and box wrenches described above. A narrow steel handle with one ring end with six or twelve points (as described above) and one open end with fixed jaws. Typically 4" to 16" long; the openings are larger if the tool is longer. The two ends are usually for the same size nuts, and that is the size denomination for the wrench, i.e., a $^5/_{16}$" wrench is for removing or installing $^5/_{16}$" nuts. Also available as a *ratcheting combination wrench*.

Use: For tightening or loosening nuts and bolts.

 Use Tip: Generally can be used in tighter quarters than an adjustable wrench.

 Buying Tips: Most common type of fixed-end wrench. The ratcheting version is very handy.

Combination Wrench

Adjustable Box End Wrench

Also Known As: Pocket socket wrench

Description: 8", 10", or 12" long steel bar with slightly angled head containing small sliding, notched jaws. Jaws are tightened in place with a thumbscrew or lever, depending on the make. Other designs use an eccentric oval head.

Use: Gripping and turning nuts and bolts of all sizes, metric or standard. Eliminates need for a set of different-sized wrenches or sockets.

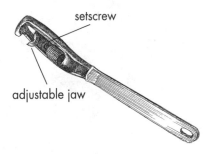

setscrew

adjustable jaw

Adjustable Box End Wrench

 Use Tip: Angled handle allows you to work without endangering your knuckles.

> **\$ Buying Tips:** Much cheaper than buying set after set of **sockets (below)** or standard **open-end** or **box wrenches (above)** and less likely to slip than an **adjustable wrench (above)**. Despite the appeal of its efficiency, some people prefer the solidity of size-by-size wrenches.

Bone Wrench

Description: Shaped like a small toy dog bone, usually made of cast aluminum. The two spherical ends have various-sized hex openings. Sort of a spherical version of the **box wrench (above)**.

Use: Light-duty nut tightening and loosening around the house, boat, or on a bicycle.

Nut Driver

Nut Driver

Also Known As: Hex nut driver

Description: Round steel shaft and handle, like a screwdriver, but with a small hex opening in the end (which fits over nuts) instead of a screwdriver tip. Available in a variety of fractional and metric sizes from $3/16$" to $1/2$", denoting size of nut to be driven, but $5/16$" is most common. An *adjustable nut driver* uses a **socket (below)** that tightens down to size.

Use: Driving and removing hex nuts or bolts. Works like a screwdriver.

Use Tips: Commonly used in plumbing for turning gears on *hose clamps* ($5/16$"). Very helpful in confined spaces, such as in automotive work, where a wrench would be difficult to "swing."

Socket Wrench

Also Known As: Ratchet wrench

Description: Long steel handle (the "drive") with a round head containing a reversable ratchet mechanism with a square point sticking out. The point snaps into short, cylindrical sockets. The size of this drive point is the size of the wrench, i.e., $3/8$" or $1/2$". Each socket has an interior opening with either six or twelve points, or in the case of the single-socket, *universal socket,* a spring-loaded pin system that fits a wide range of nuts and bolts. Sold in sets of drives and sockets. A socket wrench set may also include an *extension,* which fits between the socket and the handle to allow better access to certain jobs; and an *adapter,* which allows a combination of socket sizes.

Also made with a hinged handle *(universal joint, flex joint,* or *flexible head ratchet socket wrench)* for tight spaces. Ratchet mechanisms with more, smaller teeth *(fine tooth ratchet socket wrench)* allow for working in tight spaces with a smaller ratcheting arc. At least one model ratchets with a squeeze-action handle. Available in a cordless electric version.

Use: Driving and removing nuts and bolts that are accessible from their ends and in work where a lot of turning power is needed. The ratchet mechanism allows it to work well in limited space.

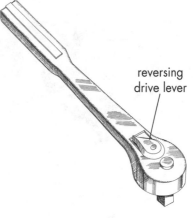

reversing drive lever

Socket Wrench

12-point socket

Sockets

Crow's-Foot Wrench

Crow's-Foot Wrench

Also Known As: Gimmick wrench, crowfoot wrench

Description: An abbreviated (just the head), open-end wrench with a square hole into which a socket wrench or extension can be inserted for driving.

Use: Tightening and loosening nuts accessible only from the side and in places difficult to reach.

Open-Back Socket Wrench

Open-Back Socket Wrench

Description: Steel rod with open ends that fit over long bolts. Ends contain hex-shaped openings that fit over nuts and bolts of various sizes. Sold in standard and metric sets. Also available in ratchet version, with a hole in the center of the head for bolts to pass through.

Use: Installing nuts on long, threaded rod or bolts. Eliminates the need for deep sockets designed for special uses, such as spark plug removal.

Buying Tip: Considered a specialty item, but extremely helpful if needed. Similar effect can be had just by using the old-fashioned **open-end** or **box wrench (above)**.

Finger Wrench

Description: Probably the world's smallest wrench, this small stainless-steel sleeve just barely fits over any size fingertip (it is adjustable). A small notch in the end holds nuts or bolts.

Use: Holding a small nut (up to $7/16$") or bolt in an awkward spot so that the matching nut or bolt can be tightened.

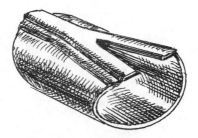

Finger Wrench

Buying Tip: An inexpensive (and lightweight) gadget worth its weight in gold.

Allen Wrench

Also Known As: Hex-key wrench, setscrew wrench, hexagon key, L-wrench, hex-L

Description: L-shaped, short hexagonal metal bar, ranging in diameter from $1/20$" to $3/8$". Also available in a set (see illustration) in a screwdriver form and in a T-handle (or T-head) form as well. Some have a rounded "ball" tip for ease of use.

Use: For turning screws or bolts with a hexagonal opening. Typically found in setscrews on machinery.

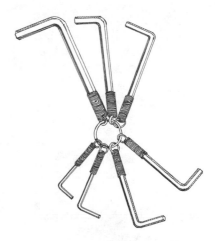

Hex-Key Set

Nut Splitter

Description: Small, hardened steel, P-shaped device with hex-head knob on the tail and small jaws in the P part that have a sharp cutting blade.

Use: Splits open nuts that are "frozen" onto a bolt or whose hex edges have become rounded, rendering a wrench useless.

Clamps and Vises

About Clamps

Clamps (and their mirror image, *spreaders*) are used for holding items in place on a workbench while they are being glued or otherwise assembled. They come in a variety of types. Clamps should not be tightened so much that they damage the surface of the clamped item; often it is wise to insert a piece of scrap wood or cloth in between the clamp and the item. It is always good to have a number of types and sizes in your workshop.

C-Clamp

Description: A piece of cast iron in the shape of the letter C with an adjustable screw on one leg, which actually makes it look more like the letter G. Comes in a variety of sizes ranging from 1" to 12" deep, measured by the gap, known as the throat, between back, or vertical, part of the C and the clamping part, at the opening. The opening between clamping faces can be as large as 8".

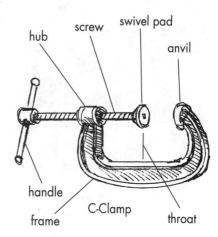

Types:

Deep-throat c-clamp (deepest gap)

Square-throat c-clamp

Heavy-duty c-clamp (rounder shape)

Use: For a wide variety of clamping jobs. Most common kind of clamp.

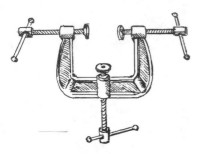

3-Way Edging Clamp

3-Way Edging Clamp

Description: C-clamp with an additional screw in the center of the throat. A plain-edge clamp is a **bar clamp (below)** with two spindles on the side for pieces too big for a C-clamp.

Use: Applies right-angle pressure to the edge or side of work. Ideal for holding trim in place while glue sets.

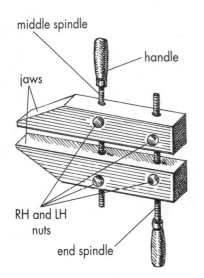

middle spindle

handle

jaws

RH and LH
nuts

end spindle

Hand Screw Clamp

Hand Screw Clamp

Also Known As: Jorgenson®, screw clamp

Description: A pair of hardwood (usually maple) jaws connected by two large screw spindles.

Use: General clamping of woodwork, especially where protection of the work is important. Can be adjusted to clamp at various angles.

Hold-Down Clamp

Description: Clamp that attaches to workbench surface and has a vertical screw.

Use: Holding work against the workbench.

Pipe Clamp

Also Known As: Furniture clamp, cabinet clamp, Pony® clamp

Description: Clamping devices that slide on pipe and are locked into place where desired. Can be as long as any length of pipe. Generally made for $1/2$" and $3/4$" pipe.

Use: For clamping very large, flat objects.

 Use Tip: For smooth operation, use black iron pipe, not galvanized.

Buying Tips: Tend to be cheaper than **bar clamps (below)**. Look for reversible models that can be converted into spreaders.

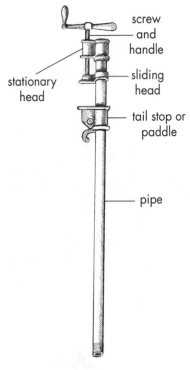

Pipe Clamp

Bar Clamp

Also Known As: Furniture clamp, cabinet clamp, joiner's clamp

Description: Similar to the **pipe clamp (above)** but has flat bars 6" to 4' long instead of pipes. Some models, called *quick-action one-handed clamps,* have a wedge-type trigger mechanism for locking one head in place.

Use: For clamping large objects.

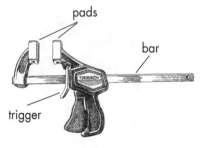

One-Handed Bar Clamp

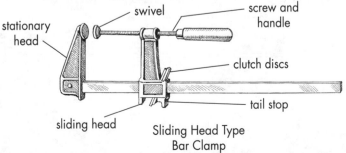

Sliding Head Type
Bar Clamp

Buying Tips: Trigger-grip models are great for one-handed use. Always buy in pairs.

Pinch Dog

Pinch Dog

Also Known As: Joint clamp, joiner's dog

Description: Small, U-shaped metal piece with two sharp, pointed legs.

Use: Holds boards together edge-to-edge while glue sets. The pinch dog is driven into the ends of abutting boards and naturally pinches them together.

 Use Tip: Edges of boards must be truly flat.

Vise-Grip® Clamp

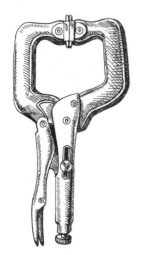

Vise-Grip® Clamp

Also Known As: Locking pliers clamp

Description: Oversized jaws that function and look like a C-clamp with a handle—actually a pair of Vise-Grip® pliers. Various sizes and shapes available.

Use: Clamping irregularly shaped items. Squeezing the Vise-Grip quickly locks the clamp onto the item.

Spring Clamp

Also Known As: Jiffy clamp

Description: Two flat metal pieces linked by a hinge and a spring, much like a large clothespin. Comes in a variety of sizes.

Use: For quick use with thin materials when not much force is required.

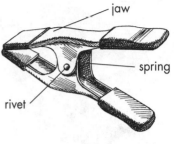

Spring Clamp

Web Clamp

Also Known As: Band clamp, tourniquet clamp, strap clamp

Description: Belt a few feet long made of hard nylon or cloth material that is locked into place with a buckle-like device. Some consider a 1" wide, light-duty clamp a *band clamp* and a 2" wide, heavy duty model a *web clamp*.

Use: For applying even pressure to an irregular shape, such as a chair, or around a large object, such as a box.

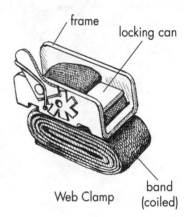

Web Clamp

Corner Clamp

Also Known As: Splicing clamp (same, but with ability to move small vises alongside one another to hold two pieces in a line), miter clamp, or miter box vise (same, but with adapter that holds a guide for sawing)

Description: Flat base with small vises that are at a 90-degree angle.

Use: For gluing picture frames, screen frames, and trim.

Vise

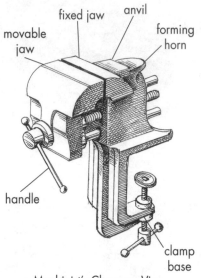

movable jaw · fixed jaw · anvil · forming horn · handle · clamp base

Machinist's Clamp-on Vise

Description: Two flat jaws drawn together and opened by a gear device. If the jaws are made of steel, known as a *machinist's vise;* if made of or faced with wood, known as a *woodworker's vise,* which is generally screwed to and flush with the edge of the bench. If bolted to the top of a workbench, known as a *bench vise.* May have a swivel base or just clamp to the bench.

Use: Holding pieces steady during a job.

Use Tips: Vises designed to hold pipe are also available. Lining the jaws of a machinist's vise with wood allows it to hold wood workpieces without damaging them.

Buying Tips: Models with a half-thread screw handle are easier to work. Most machinist's vises have a swivel base, allowing rotation of the jaws.

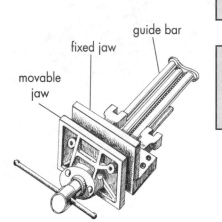

movable jaw · fixed jaw · guide bar

Woodworker's Vise

Measuring and Layout Tools

About Measuring and Layout Tools

Electronics have changed this category more than any other in recent years, now that there are electronic measuring devices of all kinds. Some are merely enhanced versions of the classics, such as a tape measure with digital readout. Others are really quite evolved, such as laser levels. Most are big improvements, but at a cost. In fact, the bulk of the state-of-the-art, high-tech measuring devices are designed, both price-wise and function-wise, for the professional. However, that still leaves a few models of interest to the DIY worker, and they are certainly a big help.

Tape Rule

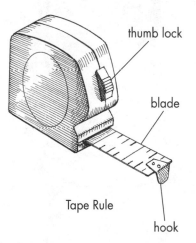

Tape Rule

Also Known As: Measuring tape, tape measure, rule, tape, push-pull tape, flex or flexible tape or rule, power return rule, pocket tape (if very small), steel tape, blade tape

Description: Slightly concave steel tape coiled inside a case, from 3' to 33' long and from $\frac{1}{4}$" to 1" wide. Retracts automatically after use. Another type has flat tape that can be up to 100' long and may be known as a *reel tape* or *engineer's tape*. A small hook is riveted loosely on the end for hooking over the edge of the object being measured (the looseness

Reel Tape

compensates for the thickness of the hook). Some tapes have clips on the back for hanging onto a belt or holster. Available with electronic, digital readout, as well as with a small recording/playback device for dictating measurements.

Use: Measuring objects.

Use Tips: If you are working with someone else, make sure you both use the same brand rule, as the actual dimensions may vary somewhat from brand to brand. Note that the case can be part of the measurement if you want; it is marked and is usually 2". Be careful not to touch the edge of the tape as it is returning to the case—you could get a nasty cut.

Buying Tips: Signs of quality are epoxy or Mylar coating on the tape, solid cases, and reliable return mechanisms. Domestic brands are generally better than imported. A wider, $3/4$" tape is easier to handle at long distances and may more easily be extended beyond your reach, say to a ceiling, which is a convenience that makes up for the bulkier size. Buy a small one to carry in your pocket if need be.

Electronic Distance Measuring Tool

Also Known As: Electronic measuring tool, rangefinder

Description: Palm-sized, calculator-like tool with an ultrasonic transmitter/receiver on one end and an LCD display, plus an acoustical signal on some models. Contains a microprocessor and several command buttons. Available in a variety of

Electronic Distance Measuring Tool

models, which vary in range capacity (such as 1'6" to 60') as well as computing ability and accuracy. A separate target extends the range exponentially.

Use: Measuring linear dimensions and computing them into volume measurements for estimating wallpaper, flooring, or paint work. Works from one spot; no need to move furniture or walk to different spots in the room being measured.

> **Buying Tips:** An excellent time-saver that can convert a two-person job into a solo job. Some of the extra functions in the better models are well worth the price, such as automatic shutoff, ability to display distances in a variety of units, and memory.

Bench Rule

Also Known As: Ruler, steel ruler

Description: Plain, flat steel bar from 6" to 36" long with various measuring markings, usually down to $1/16$" or $1/32$" and metric increments down to millimeter increments.

Use: Measuring pieces around the workshop.

Folding Rule

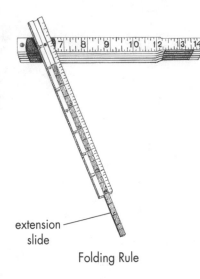

extension
slide

Folding Rule

Also Known As: Zigzag rule, carpenter's rule, folding wood rule

Description: A number of 6" to 8" segments hinged together. Made of hardwood, steel, or aluminum. Segments lock to form a long rule when folded out. A model with a small extension in the end segment for small measurements, called an *extension rule,* is also available.

Use: Measuring distances when it would be difficult to extend a tape rule.

 Use Tip: Take care of rule so that the markings remain clear and the hinges tight.

 Buying Tip: Quality rules have easily read markings, highlighted common measurements, and protective coatings.

Try Square

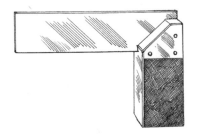

Tri/Miter Square

Also Known As: Tri-square, rosewood square, engineer's square

Description: L-shaped tool with a thick wooden section that has a flat metal blade projecting at a right angle from it. Sizes range from 6" to 12". A similar tool, called a *miter square,* has its handle at 45 degrees and is used only for measuring and marking 45-degree miter cuts. A try/miter square has a 45-degree edge at its corner.

Other Types: *Engineer's,* or *machinist's,* try squares, which are made completely of steel.

Use: Checking, or "trying," workpieces to see if they are square. Good also for making 90- and 45-degree marks.

Combination Square

Also Known As: Machinist's square, 45-degree miter square

Description: Straight steel rule, usually 12" long, to which is attached a head section containing a small level (short tube with a bubble inside). The head can be slipped along the rule and then locked in place at any point. A center head is available.

Use: As its name denotes, it can be used for a variety of functions: a level, a steel rule, a try square, and for measuring or marking miter cuts.

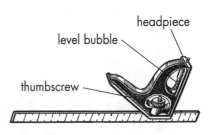

Combination Square

 Buying Tip: A versatile but sometimes expensive combination tool good to have in your workshop.

Framing Square

Also Known As: Square, rafter square, steel square, carpenter's square, flat square, carpenter's framing square, roofing square, builder's square

Description: L-shaped piece of flat steel or aluminum with one long section, the *blade,* and one shorter section, the *tongue.* Typically 24" by 16". Both sections have measure-

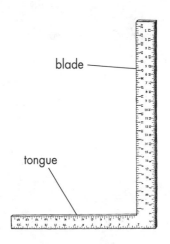

Framing Square

ment marks, including common carpentry measures such as the standard distance between studs (sargent tables); hence the names above.

Use: Mostly for laying out, for squaring up large patterns, and for testing the squareness and flatness of large surfaces. Use **stair guides (below)** for marking repetitive measurements.

> **Buying Tip:** The best-quality square has engraved, not stamped, markings.

thumbscrews

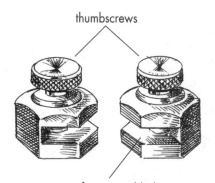

gap for square blade

Rafter and Stair Gauges

Rafter and Stair Gauges

Also Known As: Stair gauges, stair gage fixture attachments, stair gage fixtures, square gauge, square gauge set, angle gauge

Description: Small ($3/4$"–2" wide) hexagonal or sometimes tear-drop-shaped cast iron, zinc, or steel clamp with a thumb-screw and a large slot that fits over a **framing square (above)**. Brass clamp screw available on better models. Always sold in pairs.

Use: When attached to a framing square forms a handy gauge for laying out stair stringers, hip, valley, and other rafter cuts, or any other repetitive measurement.

> **Buying Tip:** Worth its reasonable price for even a small job.

Speed Square

Also Known As: Pocket square, quick square, deck and rafter square, rafter square, rafter triangle square, rafter angle square, rafter layout square, angle square

Description: Small (6" × 10") plastic or light metal triangle with one wide, thick edge and various angle measurements marked on its surface and edges.

Use: Laying out a variety of cuts in ways similar to other, more specialized squares such as the **try square** and the **framing square (above)**. Its wide edge can be used as a *power saw guide,* and it also functions as a *protractor.*

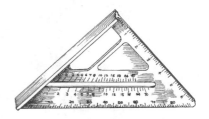

Speed Square

Bevel Gauge

Also Known As: Bevel, T-bevel, combination bevel, sliding T-bevel, sliding bevel, adjustable T-angle, angle bevel, bevel square, adjustable try square

Description: Flat metal blade about half a foot long with a wooden or plastic handle. The handle slides along the blade and can be locked into position at any angle.

Use: Marking a wide range of angles—more than other measuring tools—by copying them for transfer to another piece.

tongue or blade

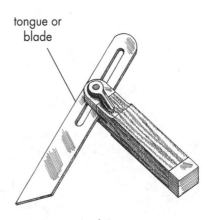

Bevel Gauge

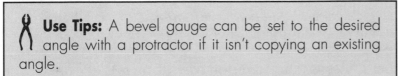

Use Tips: A bevel gauge can be set to the desired angle with a protractor if it isn't copying an existing angle.

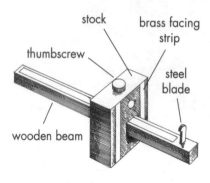

stock
brass facing strip
thumbscrew
steel blade
wooden beam

Marking/Cutting Gauge

Marking Gauge

Also Known As: Cutting gauge

Description: A long wooden, metal, or plastic bar, up to 9" long, with a marking pin on one end and a round section that slides along it and is locked where wanted with a thumbscrew. A *mortise gauge* has two marking pins; a *cutting gauge* has a small blade in place of the pin.

Use: Scoring lines parallel to the edge of a board. The round section is pulled along the board edge and the pin in the end of the long piece marks the face of the board.

 Use Tip: Before scribing, double-check desired dimensions with a ruler.

window vials

Carpenter's Level

Carpenter's Level

Also Known As: Level, spirit level, bubble level, magnesium level, aluminum level

Description: Wood or wood and metal (magnesium or aluminum) piece usually around 3" by 24" to 48" long containing from three to six small glass tubes ("vials") with bubbles in them. A *mason's level* is similar, but 48" or longer. Some levels have adjustable and replaceable bubble tubes. Some have magnets. A *bubble stick* or *bubble level* is a lightweight plastic ruler with one or two bubble tubes.

Use: Checking the level, or *true* (flatness), of surfaces or pipes. The glass vials are positioned for measuring the level of surfaces at horizontal, vertical, and 45-degree angles. A bubble stick is for installing wallpaper.

> **Use Tips:** Make sure bottom of level and surface are clean before placing the level to ensure accurate readings. Test occasionally for accuracy by reversing it in one spot.

> **Buying Tips:** Look for a light one. Before buying a level, check it out on a surface that has been established as perfectly level. Sight along edge to check for warping. A special clamp that holds the level onto a stud is a big help.

Torpedo Level

Also Known As: Canoe level, marine level

Description: Typically 1" × 9" lightweight bar containing three glass vials with bubbles in them. Some have magnets to hold them against pipes.

Use: Handy where a longer **carpenter's level (above)** won't fit, as in many electrical and plumbing jobs. Small enough, and shaped to fit in your pants pocket.

Torpedo Level

Electronic Level

Description: Plastic, electronic version of a **carpenter's level (above)** or **torpedo level (above)** with either a video or digital LED display as well as an audio signal to indicate level or off-level instead of the traditional bubble (some models include a traditional bubble as well). May have a pipe groove

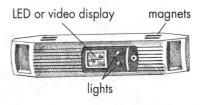

LED or video display   magnets

lights

Electronic Level

for stability on uneven surfaces, magnets for attaching to pipes and studs, or other accessories. Better models have memory and instant recalibration. Models intended for professionals (in other words, very expensive models) incorporate a laser beam as well, or angle measures (protractor arms) with digital readouts.

Use: Finding level or plumb (vertical) as well as (depending on the model's abilities) slope, pitch, or grade stored in memory. Visual and audio displays allow for ease of use in dark areas

> **$ Buying Tip:** Easier to use and more precise than traditional levels.

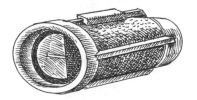

Sight Level

Sight Level

Description: Small viewing tube with bubble level and crosswire.

Use: Simple leveling work, such as lining up the tops of fence or deck posts, or for grading jobs.

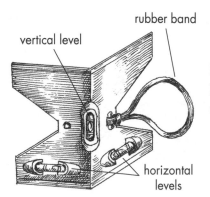

rubber band

vertical level

horizontal levels

Post Level

Post Level

Description: Small, plastic L-shaped item with a large rubber band on one side and three bubble vials (two horizontal and one vertical).

Use: Hands-free, one-person installation of posts that are plumb.

Line Level

Description: Short length of tubing containing a glass vial with a bubble, with hooks on each end for hanging from a line.

Use: Hung from a taut *mason's line* prior to laying bricks; also used when installing a ceiling or constructing a floor.

Line Level

 Use Tips: Make sure line is really taut before using level.

Water Level

Also Known As: Flexible Tube Level

Description: Clear tubing containing colored liquid and bubble, 25' to 200' long. Also available in an electronic version that beeps when one end is level with the other.

Use: Establishing level over long distances, such as when making suspended-ceiling lines, in landscaping, or around corners.

> **$ Buying Tips:** Some hardware stores will make up flexible tube levels to any length you wish. Or you can try making your own with a ¹/₄" plastic tube filled with water. Hold up the two ends in a U shape and the water will be at the same level at both ends. Add some food coloring for easier viewing.

Surface Level

Also Known As: Bull's-eye level, circular level

Description: Small liquid-filled circular plastic piece with a bubble in the middle.

Use: Determining the levelness of a surface over a range of 360 degrees, such as for record turntables or washing machines.

Contour Gauge

> **Use Tips:** May give misleading reading if surface is uneven; because of its small size, it can "read" only the levelness of the actual point it is touching, not the entire surface.

Plumb Bob

Plumb Bob

Also Known As: Plumb line

Description: A pointed, tapered weight a few inches long that is suspended from a cord. The bob commonly weighs from 6 to 24 ounces.

Use: Determines true verticality, or *trueness*, when hung by a cord.

> ✂ **Use Tips:** Because a plumb bob is a precision instrument, it should be handled carefully. Dangle into a bucket of water for use on windy days.

> $ **Buying Tip:** Some plumb bobs' tips are replaceable.

Contour Gauge

Description: Hand-sized bunch of parallel, thin metal or plastic rods held together by a metal bar. See illustration on previous page.

Use: Making a template for transferring shapes to various materials, such as when cutting floor tiles or carpeting to fit snug against an odd-shaped piece of molding in a doorway. The rods are adjustable and are moved by pushing them all against a contoured piece. The result is an exact, traceable contour of that piece.

Calipers

Description: Precision metal instrument about 10" long consisting of two legs and a spring-type hinge with a small handle on the end about half a foot long. *Inside calipers* have straight legs slightly turned out at the ends; *outside calipers* have tips pointing in. Another version, *vernier calipers,* consists of a steel bar with a measuring scale on it and a sliding head.

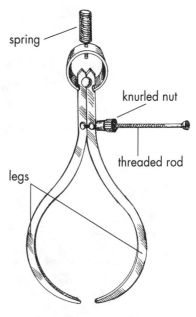

Outside Calipers

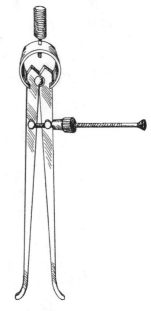

Inside Calipers

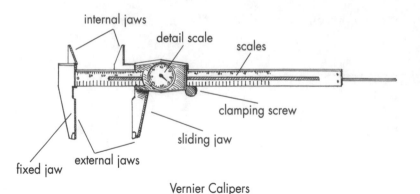

internal jaws
detail scale
scales
clamping screw
sliding jaw
fixed jaw
external jaws

Vernier Calipers

Dial calipers are like vernier calipers, but the measurement is read on a dial rather than on the bar itself. Extremely precise.

Use: For measuring the inside or outside of round objects, for transferring dimensions, or for precision measuring.

wing

Compass

Compass

Also Known As: Wing dividers

Description: Two pointed metal legs, hinged at the top, with a metal band that locks the legs in a desired position. One leg may or may not have a small pencil attached to it for marking; if not, this is more often known as a *pair of dividers*.

Use: Scribing circles or transferring measurements from one item to another.

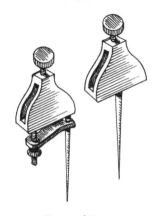

Trammel Points

Trammel Points

Also Known As: Trammel heads, trammels

Description: Pencil-like metal points with adjustable clamps (or setscrews) for securing on a suitable beam or bar.

Use: Duplicates measurements or marks large arcs when a compass or divider is too small for the job.

Use Tip: A pencil can often be substituted for one of the points.

Carpenter's Pencil

Description: Wide, flat pencil containing soft lead. A similar item, *lumber crayon,* is a 6" long hexagonal crayon.

Use: Like any pencil, for marking measurements and cut lines, etc. Its advantage is that, being flat, it won't roll away. Its design makes it easily sharpened with a penknife.

Chalk Line Reel

Also Known As: Chalk line, chalk box, snapline

Description: Coiled string in a metal or plastic housing containing powdered chalk. Line may be 50' or 100' long. Chalk is available in various colors.

Use: Marking long, straight lines on large, flat surfaces, such as floors, ceilings, and walls.

Chalk Line Reel

 Use Tips: Can be used as a **plumb bob (above)** by simply hanging it by its own string. Chalk for refilling is sold in plastic bottles; replacement string is also available. Rewind after each use to re-chalk string.

> **$ Buying Tip:** Much easier to use than the old-fashioned system of a half sphere of chalk, which was rubbed onto the string each time it was used.

lights

Electronic Stud Sensor

Stud Finder

Also Known As: Stud and joist locator, stud sensor

Description: A small magnetic or electronic device that comes in many types of designs. Small magnets, or metal detectors, indicate nails in studs; some use sonar to sense density, shown in LED's or audio tones.

Use: Indicating locations of studs behind finished walls or under floors for hanging cabinets, shelves, or light fixtures (studs are the vertical pieces of wood holding your wall up).

> **$ Buying Tips:** The more expensive electronic models can search through thicker walls, flooring material, and even concrete. They are also more accurate.

Drills and Braces

Hand Drill

Also Known As: Eggbeater drill

Description: Straight tool with a crank handle and gear on the side very similar to an eggbeater. Drives bits up to $1/4$" in diameter. The handle is usually hollow and used to store assorted bits.

Use: Basic, simple drill for making holes up to $1/4$" in diameter.

 Use Tip: Can use most standard drill bits and accessories intended for power drills.

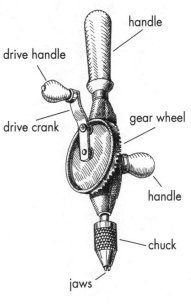

Hand Drill

About Drill Bits for Hand Drills and Braces

Most drill bits and accessories can be used both in hand and power drills. Because of the popularity of power drills today, we have placed all information about interchangeable drill bits in the **power tools section (Part II, Chapter 16)**. Those bits that can be used only by a hand drill or brace are described below in this chapter.

Push Drill

Also Known As: Yankee push drill

Description: Ratchet screwdriver-like tool whose end rotates a bit when the handle is pushed down. Uses special drill bit, sort of a small gouge, called a *drill point*.

Use: Drilling small holes in soft material.

Gimlet

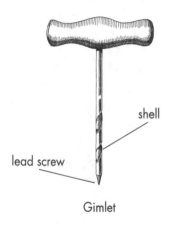

shell

lead screw

Gimlet

Also Known As: Screw starter

Description: Short steel shank with a sharp, fluted tip and a wooden T handle.

Use: For starting screw holes in wood up to around $^3/_8$".

> **Use Tips:** Be sure gimlet is pushed in straight because the screw will follow the hole. Don't use a hammer—the gimlet would then be hard to remove.

Awl

Awl

Also Known As: Scratch awl

Description: Ice pick–like tool with wooden handle and pointed rod about 3" long.

Use: For starting holes for drill bits, screws, and nails, and for making "score" marks.

Brace

Also Known As: Hand brace, carpenter's brace, bit brace, brace and bit

Description: A type of large hand drill made of a crank handle with a knob on one end and a knurled nose that holds large drill bits with specially designed square or hex ends, called **auger bits (below)**.

Use: To bore large holes in wood.

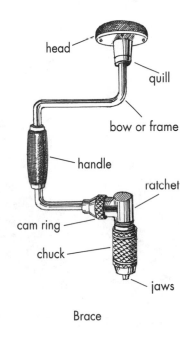

Brace

 Use Tips: Traditional way to use brace is to press against the knob with your body. Some braces have ratchet mechanisms that allow the brace to be turned in very tight quarters.

Buying Tips: Not available much anymore, having been replaced by power drills.

Auger Bit

Description: General name for bits used in a **hand brace (above)**. Large spiral bit that averages 10" long but available as long as 30". Tail end of shank is a tapered square or hex. Common designs include the *Jennings,* or *Russell Jennings* (high-quality, double twist), and solid center (most common design—single twist). Special versions are made for end grain, creosoted timbers, wood containing nails, and so on.

Some Special Types:

> *Ship auger:* Deep boring, often used with power drills.
>
> *Ship head car:* Deep boring in soft wood.
>
> *Dowel bit:* Short, 5" long, for precision work.
>
> *Door lock bit:* Wide, for installing cylinder locks or piping.

Use: For drilling large holes in wood with a **brace (Part I, Chapter 11)** and with a ³/₈" or larger power drill if shaft end is round or otherwise adapted for power drills. *Power* auger bits are designed specifically for use with power drills and will have the properly designed shaft (round end) as well as other features that make them more suitable for high-speed use.

Use Tips: To avoid splintering where the bit leaves the piece, drill just until the small screw point emerges, then turn the piece over and drill back in the opposite direction. Solid center bits are less susceptible to bending.

Files, Rasps, and Abrasives

About Files and Rasps

Many people confuse rasps and files. The distinction is essentially one of use: rasps (technically a "cut" of file) are used on wood, whereas files are used on both wood and metal. They also differ in that rasp teeth, which are rougher, are individually shaped teeth, while file teeth, which are finer, are actually a series of lines or grooves cut into a metal bar.

When you buy or use a file, there are four basic distinctions that need to be made, depending on the work you want it to do:

1. **Length.** Length is measured from the tip, or *point,* to the *heel,* the shoulder where the file narrows to the *tang,* the narrow part that fits into and is secured to a handle **(see ill.).** The coarseness of a file or rasp is also affected by its length: longer files and rasps have bigger teeth than shorter ones, and are therefore coarser.

2. **Shape.** The biggest distinction among the various types of rasps and files is their shape, as detailed below. However, some basic shapes are **(see ill.):**

   Flat (mill, flat, and *hand,* in order of thickness)

   Pillar (thick and flat)

   Half-round

Wood Rasp with Handle

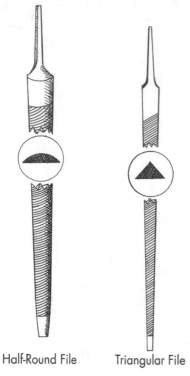

Half-Round File   Triangular File

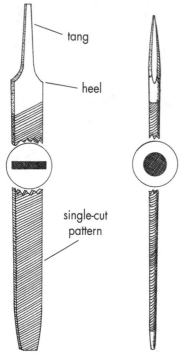

tang

heel

single-cut
pattern

Flat File   Rattail File

Round (also known as *rattail*)

Square

Taper (also known as *three-square* or *triangular*)

3. **Cut, or coarseness.** There are three common grades:

Bastard-cut (coarsest; for rough work)

Second-cut, or *double-cut* (medium rough; for quick work)

Smooth-cut, or *single-cut* (smoothest; for finish work)

Two more extreme cuts are sometimes found—coarse and dead smooth. It is good to have a range of coarseness in the files of your workshop.

Rasps themselves are often rated with a slightly different set of names: *wood* (coarsest, for quick removal work), *cabinet* (finer), *bastard* and *cabinet rasp second cut* (finest).

Swiss pattern or *European patternmaker's* files range in seven cuts from 00 to 6.

4. **Kind or pattern of teeth.**

In one of the more confusing traditions in the world of tools, the terms for tooth pattern and coarseness are identical: cut. Good luck!

Single-cut (parallel rows of teeth)

Double-cut (two sets of parallel rows of teeth in a crisscross pattern)

Curved-cut (slightly curved rows, used primarily in autobody work)

Rasp-cut (short, triangular, separate teeth—just called a rasp)

> **General Use Tips:** Files should be cleaned with either a wire brush, or a specialized **file brush** or **card (below)**. They should be stored carefully—not piled in a box with other tools—so as not to chip teeth. Clamp whatever you are working on in a vise or clamp for better control.

Files

Description: Long, narrow metal bar of various shapes with shallow grooves or teeth. **(See About Files and Rasps section, above.)** Most are slightly tapered; they are known as *blunt* if they are not.

> **Note:** Usually the teeth are not cut on the edges of files, and the edges are then known as *safe* or *uncut*. When they are cut they may have a different coarseness than the face, and also may differ from side to side, being safe on one side only. Some "handy" or "utility" models have different cuts on each working side of the file, which is very convenient.

Common Types, Description and Uses:

Cabinet file (half-round, blunt tip)

Cantsaw, also known as *cant file, lightening file* (diamond shape, for certain saw-blade sharpening or other small work)

Equaling file (blunt, rectangular, for rapid stock removal)

Flat file (rectangular, for general work on metal)

Half-round file (one side flat, one side curved, pointed tip, for general use on curved surfaces)

Hand file (thick, flat)

Knife file (wedge shape, for sharpening crosscut saws, etc.)

Mill file (thin, flat, single cut, good general-purpose metal or tool sharpening)

Needle file (very small and slender, for finishing work; also known as *die sinkers*)

Pillar file (rectangular, thick)

Rattail file, or *tapered round* (slender, round, for enlarging holes and various detail work)

Round file (slender, round, usually tapered, also known as *rattail,* for enlarging holes and various detail work)

Square file (slender, square shape for corners and slots)

Taper saw file (triangularly tapered, very fine and slender, for sharpening saw teeth and other fine work)

Warding file (smaller, for fine metal work, such as keys)

rasp-cut pattern

double-cut pattern

Four-in-Hand Rasp

Four-in-Hand Rasp/File

Also Known As: Shoe rasp, combination shoe rasp, horse rasp

Description: Steel bar with one flat face and one convex face, with vertical sides. Half of each face is file cut and half rasp cut.

Use: Variety of typical shop filing tasks.

Surface-Forming Tool

Surface-Forming Tool

Also Known As: Surform® tool, surface-forming rasp, surfoam

Description: Basically an open-weave zinc alloy metal that looks like a cheese grater. Shapes include plane-like, rasp-like, and hand scraper–like forms.

Use: Very fast removal of wood, plastic, rough drywall edges, hardboard, soft metals, plastic fillers and patchers, etc. Popular in auto-body repair work.

 Use Tips: Comes with replaceable blades.

 Buying Tips: Versatile and easy to use, especially in smaller, curved version. Good to have around.

Riffler Rasps and Files

Also Known As: Rifflers, bent rifflers

Description: Small, fast-cutting rasps or fine-cutting files. Only the tips have teeth; the center portions are very thin. Most tips are curved. Available in various shapes such as flat, triangular, round, and half-round. Sometimes rifflers are referred to by their country of origin, as in *German* or *Italian* rifflers.

Use: For finishing details in wood or metal.

Rifflers

File Card

Also Known As: File brush, file cleaner

Description: Small, wide brush with fine wire teeth.

Use: Clearing metal scrapings from file teeth.

> **Use Tips:** Use a file card frequently to keep files working efficiently. When filing nonferrous metals, use chalk on teeth to help prevent clogging teeth.

Wire Brush

Block Handle Wire Brush

Also Known As: Painter's wire brush

Types:

> *Block wire brush* (rectangle filled with bristles, like a scrub brush)
>
> *Curved handle wire brush* (curves slightly up)
>
> *Shoe handle wire brush* (finished, arc-shaped handle)
>
> *Straight handle wire brush*

Shoe Handle Wire Brush

Description: A wooden handle with several rows of stiff wire bristles embedded in it. Some models have a scraping blade at the tip for scraping before brushing.

Use: Cleaning material from rough surfaces, such as files, or old, flaking paint from metal or concrete.

> **Use Tips:** Keep dry—bristles will rust easily, making a mess of the next job.

§ **Buying Tips:** A concave handle that curves away from the bristles may be more comfortable to hold than a straight one, and will protect your knuckles.

Sandpaper

Also Known As: Abrasive paper, coated abrasive, garnet paper, production paper

Description: Sandpaper is made in various degrees of coarseness, with different abrasive materials adhered to various backings. Some (the very finest grades) can be used dry or wet—that is, moistened with water or oil. This keeps the dust down—very important indoors.

Sandpaper comes described both by number—either of two kinds—and verbally. The higher the number, with either system, the finer the paper. The range commonly available includes:

Very fine (8/0 to 6/0, or 280 to 220 grit)

Fine (5/0 to 4/0, or 180 to 150 grit)

Medium (3/0 to 1/0, or 120 to 80 grit)

Coarse (1/2 to 1 1/2 or 60 to 40 grit)

Extreme ranges include 12/0 or 600 on the fine end to $4^{1}/_{2}$ or 12 on the coarse end. Grit numbers refer to the size of the abrasive grains themselves; the numbers are higher for finer grades because there are more pieces of grit per square inch.

This classification is only relative and varies somewhat from manufacturer to manufacturer and material to material. Remember that the grit, or mesh, is your most accurate guide from brand to brand.

Sandpaper also comes with *closed* and *open* coat, meaning the grit is farther apart or closer together. If closed coat, the grit covers 100 percent of the surface, while it covers only 60 to 70 percent of open coat. Open coat tends to clog up less with sawdust, which is a big advantage on *belt sanders,* and lasts longer, but closed coat will cut faster.

Three common kinds of paper are *flint* (least durable and least expensive), *emery* (called *emery cloth* or *paper*), and *aluminum oxide* (most common). Flint is cream or tan, emery black, and aluminum oxide a reddish color. It is the most commonly used abrasive. The backing weight is designated by letters A–E, thin to thick. C or D is best. X-rated sand paper is a medium-weight cloth used for heavy-duty and power sanding.

The material is normally available in small sheets, but can also be purchased with peel-and-stick or Velcro backing for easy adhering to power sanders. Abrasive cord or tape *rubber contoured sanding grips,* and *flexible sanding sponges* are also available, though not widely, for detail sanding work of contoured surfaces.

Sanding Block

Use Tips: For even hand sanding, secure the sandpaper to a *sanding block* or a long, narrow *sanding stick.* You can make this with a block of wood or buy a rubber one of various shapes. Many common materials, some types of paint, plaster, and treated wood, yield a toxic sawdust. Use wet sandpaper and/or a respirator in such situations.

Steel Wool

Description: Steel thread of various finenesses loosely woven into hand-sized pads; also sold in bulk packages. *Bronze wool* is also available and is simply steel wool made of bronze. Now *synthetic steel wool* (also known as *abrasive nylon pads* or *sanding pads*) is widely available. Pads are made from synthetic fibers and abrasive particles in various thicknesses that resemble dishwashing scouring pads.

Use: Steel wool is used for a variety of purposes, including a final wiping of wood and other surfaces prior to finishing, taking the gloss off a surface prior to painting or finishing, removing hardened substances such as dried paint, and applying final finishing materials such as wax.

Steel wool comes in six or seven grades ranging from 0000, which is super-fine, through 000 (extra-fine), 00 (very fine), 0 (medium fine), No. 1 (medium), No. 2 (medium coarse) and No. 3 (coarse).

Use Tips: Bronze, stainless steel, and synthetic pads are better for use with water-based finishes as loose strands will not rust.

$ Buying Tips: For removal jobs, synthetic steel wool is the way to go. It won't shed, splinter, or rust. It can be rinsed and reused a few times, and it is generally longer-lasting, safer, and cleaner to use.

Planes and Scrapers

About Planes

Planes are one of the oldest designs of hand tools still in use. They are all used to shave wood from boards, and to do this their blades should be kept very sharp. There is quite a variety of planes, and we have omitted some that are really just for advanced cabinetry. The art of plane-making is a fine one, and they can be very expensive. And no matter how well they are made, you must fine-tune them—adjust the blade angle and so on—for best results.

> **Note:** See also **paint- and finish-removal tools, Part V, Chapter 45,** for more specialized scrapers.

Bench Planes

Also Known As: *Jointer*, foreplane, gage plane

Types:

Jack plane

Jointer (or *joiner*) *plane*

Smooth, or *smoothing plane* (most common)

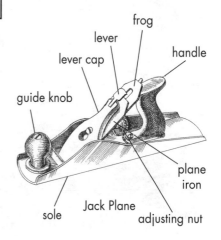

Jack Plane

Description: Metal or wooden device generally 9" to 22" long and several inches wide, with two handles—a knob in front and a grip in the back for pushing. Planes contain blades that protrude at an angle from the smooth wooden or steel bottom by a small, usually adjustable, amount. The *smooth plane* is smallest (9"–10"); *jack planes* are medium-sized (around 14"); and the *jointer* is the longest model (around 22" long).

Use: Smoothing, trimming, shaping, beveling wood along the grain.

> *Jack:* Heavier, high capacity for rough work, medium size, popular model.
>
> *Jointer:* Heaviest, for trimming long board edges prior to joining, or door edges.
>
> *Smooth:* Lightweight, wide, good for most home workshop tasks.

 Use Tips: Cut with the grain, using both hands, and at a slight angle across the board.

Buying Tip: The better-quality planes are more adjustable.

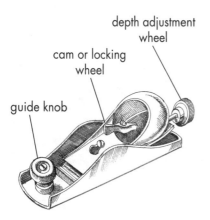

depth adjustment wheel

cam or locking wheel

guide knob

Block Plane

Block Plane

Description: Small plane, adjustable in many ways, with blade at 12–20 degrees, not 45–50 degrees as with most other planes.

Use: Shaping end grain and finishing cuts.

> **Use Tips:** For fine finishing, a plane with a very narrow mouth is desirable; a wider mouth removes wood faster. Keep a scrap piece of wood against the end of a board when planing end grain to keep from splintering off the edge. Plane in from the edges toward the middle. Common, handy model.

Rabbet Plane

Description: Similar to others, but blade projects from side as well as bottom.

Use: Cuts a rabbet, a recess, or step, in the edge of a board.

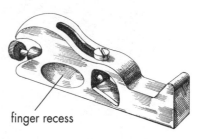

finger recess

Rabbet Plane

Bullnose Plane

Description: Extremely small, compact, usually metal block with small handle and blade right near the front of the plane.

Use: Very detailed work inside corners.

Router Plane

Description: Unlike other planes, a flat metal plate with a small blade in the center.

Use: Makes recesses, called *dadoes,* and grooves in a board.

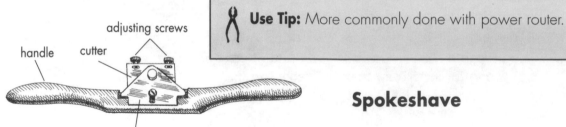

> **Use Tip:** More commonly done with power router.

handle   cutter   adjusting screws

cap iron

Spokeshave

Spokeshave

Description: Winged, two-handed handle with a small blade in the middle. There are many specialized variations for different types of work and wood.

Use: Fine scraping and planing of curved wood such as spokes.

Cabinet Scraper

Also Known As: Scraper plate

Description: Either a small **spokeshave (above)**, or sometimes just a flat piece of metal, rectangular or curved, with a cutting burr on one edge.

Use: Very fine shaving, as in removing glue.

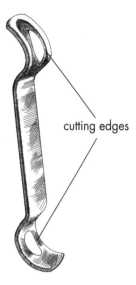

cutting edges

Cornering Tool

Cornering Tool

Also Known As: Chamfering tool, edge-rounding tool

Description: Looks something like a beer-can opener with holes that have cutting edges in each curved end. There are different sizes on each end, two tools to a set.

Use: Beveling corners of boards. Cuts a specific radius and no more.

Fastening Tools

Glue Gun

Description: Smaller models look like a regular gun, with a long handle and a triangular trigger. Cigarette-like *glue sticks* (*hot melt* glue) are melted inside the gun and the glue extruded either by pushing the stick in with your thumb or, on some models, merely by squeezing the trigger; it generally dries within a minute.

Use: For any large wood or household gluing jobs using hot melt glue. It can also be used with caulk sticks, and various specialized glue sticks for different materials.

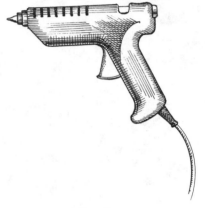

Glue Gun

Glue Injector

Description: Syringe-like tool with a long probe-like applicator that can be filled with a variety of glues. Epoxy glue injectors have two cylinders.

Use: Applying glue in furniture joints and other narrow places.

Glue Injector

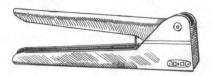

Rivet Tool

Rivet Tool

Also Known As: Rivet gun, Pop® Rivetool, riveter

Description: Consists of two pliers-like handles with a nose that accepts special nail-like **rivets (Part III, Chapter 23)** that form a sandwich bond when squeezed.

Use: Good for repairing anything made of thin metal, canvas, or leather, items ranging from toys to briefcases to gutters, especially when only one side of the material can be reached.

 Use Tips: Rivets come in various diameters (typically from $1/8$" to $3/16$") and "grip ranges"—determined by the thickness of the two pieces to be fastened together (typically from $1/16$" to $5/8$"). Selection of the proper rivet is easily made by following directions on the rivet-gun package. Rivets may be aluminum or steel; steel rivets are stronger.

$ Buying Tip: Some rivet guns have interchangeable noses and can set rivets of three different diameters.

Staple Gun

Also Known As: Staple gun tacker, hand stapler

Description: Essentially a stapler with a grip and lever handle for shooting staples that are rectangular in shape. Comes in a variety of sizes and with varying degrees of power. Also made in an electric, power model. The *hammer tacker* is a heavier-duty model that is swung to hit against the surface, not squeezed.

Use: Securing a wide variety of thin materials to wood by shooting staples with great force: insulation, stair treads, carpet, ceiling tile, plastic sheet, poultry netting, etc. Much faster than nails and more secure.

 Use Tips: Standard staple guns can accept staples from $1/4$" to $9/16$" long. Choice of staple length is based on the material being secured, but the width and type of staple that you can use are limited to your particular brand and model, and these must be specified when purchasing staples.

Buying Tip: The *hammer tacker* is a real time-saver for large projects.

Soldering Gun

Description: Similar to a **soldering iron (below)**, but shaped like a gun. Has a finer tip.

Use: Melts solder for making electrical connections.

Soldering Gun

Soldering Iron

Also Known As: Soldering tip

Description: Resembles a fat pencil with a copper rod or broad blade at the tip and an insulated handle that has a wire cord and plug attached to the tail end. Tip heats to 15 to 240 watts.

Use: Melts solder for making electrical connections.

> ⚡ **Use Tip:** As soldering irons are available in a variety of sizes and types, be sure to use the proper one for your job.

Power Hammer (gun type)

Power Hammer

Also Known As: Low-velocity powder-actuated fastening tool

Description: Gun-barrel device in either a trigger or hammer-activated version, operated with bullet-like *power loads* (that look like .22 cal. bullets) and fasteners (hardened steel nails) sold separately, often called *powder-driven* or *power fasteners*. A back-up disc helps control the depth of the fastener.

Use: Fastening items such as door frames or studs to concrete or other masonry.

> ⚡ **Use Tips:** These fasteners are actually shot out of the hammer, so make sure that the receiving wall is thick enough to "take" the hit; should the fastener continue through and exit a wall, it could injure someone. Make sure that fasteners are solid in the masonry, and that they have not shattered the wall instead.

Miscellaneous Tools and Equipment

Drop Light

Also Known As: Trouble light, safety light, work light

Description: Incandescent bulb housed in protective cage, secured to a long electrical cord and plug.

Use: Provide light for working wherever needed.

Use Tips: Hang carefully where it won't be snagged or bumped as you move around the worksite. Keep a few spare bulbs on hand, though. You might want to try using **construction grade bulbs (Part IX, Chapter 67)**.

Buying Tip: Could be replaced in some situations by a battery operated, portable mini-fluorescent lamp that is commonly sold for auto or camping use.

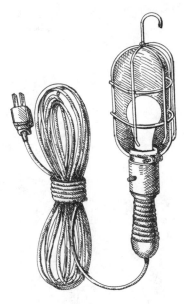

Drop Light

Grip Light

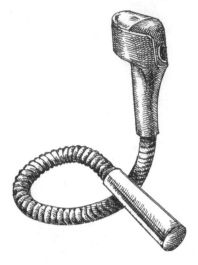

Grip Light

Description: Cordless flashlight with long, flexible snake-like neck that twists and holds position on horizontal surface or snakes around pipes. Light bulb is generally more intense than regular flashlight bulb. Some models have heads that pivot for more control.

Use: Providing hands-free light at worksite.

 Use Tip: Try wrapping it gently around your neck and shoulders for light that moves with you.

 Buying Tip: A terrific improvement over older models of portable lighting equipment.

Halogen Work Light

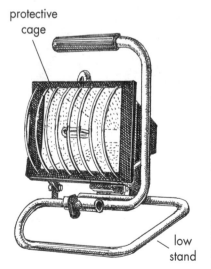

protective cage

low stand

250-Watt Halogen Light

Description: Aluminum housing and caged reflector holding a halogen bulb. Available in a variety of forms, including clamp, low stand, and tripod for heights up to 8'. Bulbs offered in 250 and 500 watt versions.

Use: Lighting up an entire jobsite such as a room under construction with no other light source.

Use Tips: These lights get dangerously HOT! They can easily cause a fire if they come into contact with combustible material. Exercise extreme caution around them! Stay clear of them, and make sure that nothing flammable is directly above them.

> **$ Buying Tips:** Extra-bright, pure white light is a pleasure
> to have, especially if you are used to making do with
> **clamp-on lamps (Part IX, Chapter 67)** with their small in-
> candescent bulbs and small reflectors. Especially good for
> large painting jobs where reflections help you keep track
> of wet edges and drips.

House Jacks

Also Known As: Jack post, single post shore

Description: Two heavy steel pipes, one inside the other, in
various lengths up to about 8', with flat metal plates on either end. A large screw extends the post a short distance for
raising. A similar-looking item is the *lally column,* which has
no jacking ability and may be filled with concrete once in
place.

Use: For temporarily raising a sagging floor joist. Can be
boxed off and left permanently in place, though this is not
recommended (a lally column is used for a permanent installation). Shorter, heavier versions are used to jack up an
entire house for moving or major repairs.

> **Use Tips:** Jack up floor joists, or any house framing
> member, very, very slowly—like less than an inch a
> day. Make sure the bottom part of the jack is well sup-
> ported on thick concrete or wood. A hydraulic house jack,
> a large-scale version of a standard jack, may be useful for
> heavier loads.

House Jack

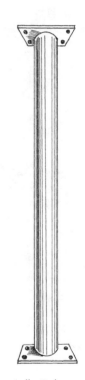

Lally Column

Jay Roller

Description: Small wooden roller and handle

Use: Pressing down freshly glued veneers and laminates to help bond them.

Siding Removal Trool

Siding Removal Tool

Description: Hand-sized metal tool with slightly angled, 1" wide blade that has a hooked tip.

Use: Grabbing underside lip of vinyl siding to unlock it for easy removal and replacement. Eliminates cutting and scoring.

Ladder

Also Known As: Rung ladder

Description: Made of aluminum, fiberglass, or wood. Consists of two parallel rails flanking round or rectangular steps. *Extension ladders* are made of two similar sections that fit together and are linked by a line or mechanical device and locked into place with hinged hooks called *dogs*. Extension section can be pulled out to almost double the height of the ladder. *Folding* or *articulating* combination ladders are more expensive but can act as scaffolds and stepladders as well.

Use: For climbing heights.

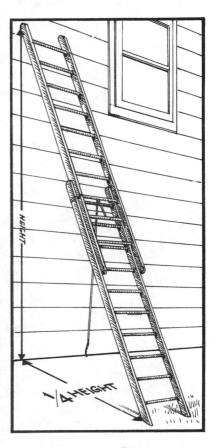

Extension Ladder

> **Use Tips:** For safety, (1) extreme care should be exercised in securing the base so it doesn't slip, such as by using a ladder with rubber grips, by tying the bottom rung to a stake between it and the wall, or by having an assistant hold it; (2) the ladder base should be one-fourth of the height of the ladder away from the wall (an arm's length at shoulder height is usually correct); (3) move the ladder often rather than lean too far to one side when working; (4) look up before raising an aluminum ladder to avoid hitting electrical wires; (5) and never place a ladder in front of an unlocked door or on muddy ground. (6) Try using *ladder stabilizers*, or *guards*, C-shaped aluminum arms about twice as wide as the ladder, for better stability when leaning a ladder against a wall. Triangular metal brackets called *ladder jacks* can be attached to a heavy-duty **(Type 1A—see below)** ladder to make scaffolding. Tie off rope, check your dogs to see that they are locked.

$ Buying Tips: Aluminum ladders are lightweight and easier for one person to handle than wood, but they can be hazardous if there are electrical wires nearby. Flat "D"-shaped aluminum rungs are more comfortable and safer to stand on than the round ones found on wooden ladders. Look also for resilient rubber *ladder mitts end caps,* and rubber or metal swiveling *ladder shoes.* Ladders are rated for safety and construction four ways: *type 3:* household; *type 2:* commercial; *type 1:* industrial; and *type 1A:* extra-heavy-duty industrial. The commercial type, type 2, is highly recommended. The ratings indicate load limits ranging from 200 pounds (type 3) to 300 pounds (type 1A).

Stepladder

Description: Consists of what appears to be two separate ladders connected by a hinge at the top. Actually only one side has rungs. Available in wood, aluminum, and fiberglass and in various heights.

Use: Self-supporting ladder that can be used without leaning against a wall. Ideal for interior painting and repairs up to heights of 10 feet.

Use Tips: Never stand on the top two rungs—it is unsafe, due to the increased leverage of your weight. Never leave a hammer or other tool on the top when you come down, as it is very likely that you will forget it's there when you move the ladder and then it will fall and cause real damage.

Buying Tips: Fiberglass is tops in quality and price. Get as large a one as possible so you will not be tempted to stand on the very top. New versions that act as scaffolding platforms as well (*articulating ladders*) are very useful and worth considering, although they are much more expensive.

Mechanical Fingers

Also Known As: Pick-up tool

Description: Long, narrow, flexible tube containing flexible springs that extend outside the tube by pressing on the handle.

Use: Retrieving small tools, jewelry, or other small items that have dropped into places you cannot reach with your hands.

Mechanical Fingers

Use Tip: A small magnet on the end of a string can provide the same function for metal objects.

Magnetizer/Demagnetizer

Description: Two part, magnetic cube with a large hole in its middle.

Magnetizer/Demagnetizer

Use: Magnetizing and demagnetizing screwdrivers, drill bits, wrenches, and other tools. Passing tools through the hole magnetizes items; passing tools repeatedly over the outside edge demagnetizes tools.

> **$ Buying Tip:** Magnetized screwdrivers and wrenches are much easier to use because they hold screws and bolts automatically.

Nail Apron

Also Known As: Nail bag, carpenter's apron

Description: Canvas or leather pouch or pouches that attach around your waist.

Use: Holds large amounts of nails and screws handy.

Propane Torch

Description: Self-contained gas torch. Canister of pressurized propane gas with a screw-on burner and valve assembly. Uses propane but also higher-temperature fuels such as Mapp® and butane gas.

Use: Supplies clean flame that can be used for a variety of purposes, including removing resilient tile (heating the tile softens and loosens the adhesive), softening putty, removing paint, soldering pipe.

Use Tips: Both wide and narrow burner tips are available, and one may be more suitable for a particular job than another. Take precautions when working with flame; this is very intense heat and always risky.

Buying Tips: In addition to the standard propane torch, there are mini-propane torches, self-igniting ones, and those that can be linked by hose to a large canister of gas.

Spark Lighter

Description: Looking somewhat like a 6" long safety pin, this spring-wire tool has a replaceable flint on the end of one arm and a bowl-shaped striking surface on the other. When the spring arms are squeezed together, the flint sparks as it is dragged across the striking surface.

Use: Lighting propane and other pressurized gas torches. The tip of the torch is placed in the striking bowl and then turned on while the spark is created.

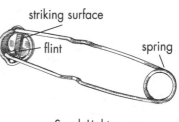

Spark Lighter

Buying Tips: This is the best way to light torches. Get one when you get a torch. Inexpensive.

Rubber Knee Pads

Rubber Knee Pads

Description: Flat rubber cups with straps

Use: Protects knees when installing floors or roofs.

Sawhorses

Also Known As: Horses

Description: Crosspiece supported by two pairs of legs set at angles. Typically made of two-by-fours.

Use: Temporary support for a worktable or shop work.

> **$ Buying Tips:** Sawhorses are typically homemade. Also, specially made hinged metal joints are available for making collapsible sawhorses from two-by-fours. Nonhinged metal or plastic *sawhorse brackets* are available as well. Both are big conveniences.

Toolbox

Description: Metal or plastic box with compartments for tools and hardware. Most have a piano-hinged top and a removable tray. Some small, open plastic models are designed only for use on a per-job basis—you load it only with the tools needed for a particular job.

Use: Carrying tools and miscellaneous hardware and materials to a work site (a *tool chest* is usually larger, with drawers, and designed for stationary use on a workbench or has built-in casters).

> **Use Tip:** Though they may seem convenient, larger toolboxes present a formidable problem when fully loaded with a complete set of tools—they are dangerously heavy and may be impossible to lift. Better to have a few smaller, specialized ones. The plastic boxes will not scratch floors or counters at the worksite.

5-Gal Bucket Pocket Tool Carrier

Description: Polyester sheet loaded with pockets that sit inside and out of an empty 5-gallon plastic bucket, such as that used for joint compound or paint.

Use: Definitely the modern, portable tool chest. Much better than dumping all your tools into an empty bucket. Plastic bottom is easy on floors, too.

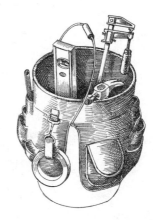

5-Gal Bucket Pocket Tool Carrier

> **Buying Tips:** Good gift item. Look for other bucket-related accessories, such as plastic compartment trays and seats that fit over the top, or removable screwtop lids that create an airtight, waterproof container.

Shop Vacuum

Also Known As: Shop vac, wet/dry vac

Description: Large canister or drum, some as large as several feet high, with a vacuum motor on top and $2^1/_2$" diameter vacuum hose. Most are wet/dry models. Six to 16 gallon capacity, with 2 to 6 hp motors. Smaller versions are designed to attach directly to portable electric tools with 1" or $1^1/_4$" adapters.

Use: Sucking up all kinds of workshop and worksite debris, such as sawdust, wood, glass, nails, gravel, water, paint chips, and the like. Also excellent for cleaning cars and gutters. Convertible to blower.

 Buying Tips: Invaluable time saver for any major interior project. Great gift item.

Portable Workbench

Also Known As: Workmate® (often used generically)

Description: Small, collapsible metal framework workbench with many convenient attachments and design elements, such as built-in clamp mechanisms (the two halves of the work surface slide open and shut).

Use: Home workshop and renovation projects—holding boards for sawing, clamping, and much more.

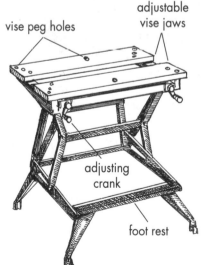

vise peg holes
adjustable vise jaws
adjusting crank
foot rest

Workmate® Portable Workbench

Power Tools

About Portable Power Tools

The real news in portable power tools is that not only are almost all of them now available in cordless form—you charge a battery for a few hours and off you go—but that many are now available in more powerful versions than ever before. This is a terrific convenience both for repairs at home and for major construction sites (just eliminating the mess of power cords is a major change). But in no way do cordless tools replace plug-in tools for steady use or for tasks where size and strength really matter. The smaller models, especially, are substantially weaker than their corded siblings.

When buying either kind of power tool, buy good quality and characteristics. With cordless tools, look for a short recharge time ("charge rate") and substantial voltage (upwards of 12 volts where power is important). Also compare cycle life, the number of charge/discharge cycles a battery can be expected to handle before failure—500 to as many as 3,000. With corded tools, check the amperages, not the horsepower, for determining the relative power—the more power, the better. The trade-off in both cases, besides price, is usually weight and size. Ball or roller bearings are better than sleeve bearings. Double-insulated tools are safer. Cheaper tools often are difficult to open for repair, if they can be opened at all.

In general, a good rule of thumb is to purchase a model somewhere in the middle range between heavy-duty professional and the lightweight, least expensive. "Light-duty industrial" is often best. You won't get every feature possible, but you'll get what is most often needed in a model that will last.

And remember, most power tools are available for rent.

Portable Power Drills, Tools, and Accessories

Power Drill

Also Known As: Portable electric drill, hole-shooter, drill-driver

Description: Gun-shaped tool with a chuck (nosepiece) that comes in one of the three common sizes: $1/4$", $3/8$", or $1/2$"; the size of the drill is denoted by the largest-size drill-bit shaft that can fit into the chuck. The better ones come with variable speed triggers and reversing switches (may be indicated by "VS" or "VSR"). Rpm's run 130 to 400 at low speed, and for corded models up to 2000 or so at high. A *close-quarters* drill has a head at 55 degrees to the handle.

Use: Drilling holes of various sizes. Also, with proper **accessories (below)**, a drill can be used to grind, sand, polish, and do other jobs. And with a **screwdriver bit (below)**, a VSR drill can be used as a very convenient power screwdriver. Can be mounted on a workbench on a special stand to work, use the half-inch drill, as the larger chuck means a more powerful motor; for major masonry drilling jobs, use a special model drill, the *hammer-drill*. This vibrates as it drills, and requires special *percussion* bits, also called *impact bits* (use the even larger *rotary hammer* for pure concrete and cement).

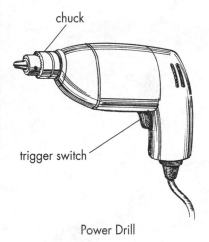

chuck

trigger switch

Power Drill

Use Tips: Get a proper, heavy-duty extension cord with two or three female receptacles. This will allow you to use two or three power tools on the same job without having to unplug and plug as you switch tools.

Buying Tips: Get a good one. The $^3/_8$" size is best for the do-it-yourselfer. Variable speed and reversibility are good features. If the plug is the two-prong type, the drill should be marked as "double-insulated" for protection from shocks. Cordless models of more than 12 volts are too heavy for most of us. Get the most amp-hours you can afford. A 9.6 volt cordless model is o.k. only for the casual DIY user.

Cordless Screwdriver

In-Line Cordless screwdriver

Also Known As: Compact cordless screwdriver

Description: Lightweight, straight cylinder of lower power and speed (under 200 rpm max) than the **power drill (above)**.

Use: Driving screws in light-duty household or repetitive small woodworking projects.

Buying Tips: Though less expensive than the *drill-driver*, for only a little more money you can purchase a much more versatile and useful tool—the **power drill (above)**. On the other hand, the screwdriver is a lot lighter and smaller, and may be easier to handle for the DIY'er.

Chuck Key

Also Known As: Key

Description: Small, L- or T-shaped steel piece with one conical, fluted end. Literally a small gear. Comes in various sizes and types that vary by manufacturer as well as universal models. Also made in a ratchet version.

Chuck Key

Use: Opens and closes the chuck on *electric drills* and *drill presses*. (The chuck—technically a *Jacob's chuck*—is the part of the drill that holds the bits.)

 Use Tips: Always good to have a spare. Check for the proper fit if replacing your key. Always tighten the bit securely, using all three holes.

Keyless Chuck

Description: Knurled knob about 2" in diameter and length.

Use: Allows hand-tightening of chuck to hold bits in cordless and corded drills and drivers, depending on model.

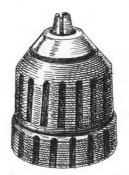

Keyless Chuck

$ Buying Tip: Much easier to use than a *key;* a real advantage if the bulkiness doesn't bother you.

Drill Guide

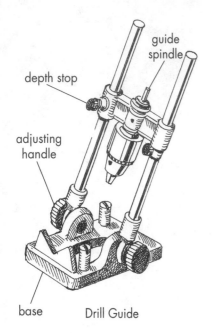

Description: Consists of a bracket to hold a portable drill, two steel rods, and a round plate. Might be confused with a *hinge bit,* another type of drill guide. (A hinge bit—a hollow, beveled jacket housing a drill bit—merely centers a drill bit in the hole of a hinge plate.) A larger version is a *drill press stand,* which converts a portable drill into a **stationary drill press (Chapter 19)** for use on a workbench.

Use: Enables you to drill perfectly perpendicular or angled holes with a portable drill. Particularly helpful for mounting items on door edges.

Drill Guide

Drill Level

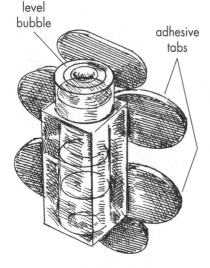

Description: Small *bubble level* (either horizontal, vertical, or surface **(bull's eye—see Chapter 10)** that attaches to a drill with self-adhesive rubber mounts. Different models are designed for different types of drills, and may fit either the front, top, or rear of a drill.

Use: Judging when a drill is exactly vertical or level; also useful for portable machinery that must be leveled.

Drill Level

 Use Tip: Useless if the piece being drilled is not also level or plumb.

Buying Tip: Some newer models of portable drills have built-in levels.

Dowel Jig

Also Known As: Dowel jointing jig, doweling jig

Description: Rectangular metal block with various-sized holes and brackets for holding it in place.

Use: Allows accurate placement of holes for dowels in furniture and cabinetry.

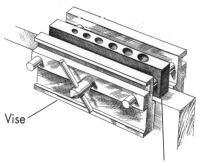

Vise

Dowel Jig

Flexible Shaft

Also Known As: Flexible drive

Description: A cable housed in a flexible cover material with a shank that fits into a drill on one end and a chuck that holds bits on the other. Various lengths up to 4'.

Use: Allows drilling in hard-to-reach places. Shaft can be snaked around various obstructions.

Flexible Shaft

Offset Screwdriver Head

Also Known As: Bevel gear offset screwdriver

Description: Though there are many different versions of this useful item available, the one shown here is smallest. $5^1/_2$" long, lightweight cylinder with a small chuck for screwdriver tips at 90 degrees to its axis. A small flange protrudes from one side and a hex shank extends out the back end. Magnetized. Also sold with a large, solid, standard screwdriver handle for hand use as a plain **offset screwdriver (Part I, Chapter 4)**. Sold with a set of various screwdriver tips.

hex shaft goes into drill chuck

Offset Screwdriver Head

Use: Converting a cordless or hand screwdriver to an *angle drive screwdriver* or just for more control, when you need to support the drill bit with your hand.

Right Angle Drive

Also Known As: Angle Drive

Description: Small gearbox that fits into the chuck of a power drill and has its own chuck at a 90-degree angle.

Use: Enables you to drill holes at right angles.

 Buying Tip: Less expensive than buying a whole *right-angle drill*.

Power Drill Accessories

Description: Small devices with shanks that fit like bits into power drill chuck just like regular hole-drilling bits, but for wood or metal shaping or finishing instead of drilling. Some are best used when the drill is mounted on a workbench in a horizontal or vertical drill stand, which turns a portable drill into a stationary tool.

Types:

Drill saw, or *router drill, saw bit:* A drill bit with cutting edges on its sides, made for either metal or wood.

Drum sander: Short, small cylinder wrapped in sand-paper.

Drill stand: Base and clamp for benchtop use.

Flap wheel, or *contour, sander:* Wheel with flaps of abrasive cloth, for rough contour sanding.

Grinder: Abrasive wheel.

Paint sprayer: Powers a small compressor.

Rotary file: Very small bit with file teeth in various shapes, such as cylindrical, cylindrical with round end, tapered round, conical, and ball.

Rotary rasp: Same as above, but with rasp teeth; some models have a knob on one end which you hold in your hand for control.

Flap Wheel
Drill Accessory

Grinder Drill
Accessory

Rotary Rasp Drill Accessory

Note: Rotary files and rasps are also known as *burrs.*

Sanding disk, or *wheel:* Rubber backing disk about 5" in diameter that supports all kinds of sandpaper.

Screwdriver and nut-driver (or *nut-setter*) *bits:* Short blades (1" to 3½") that turn a drill into a power screwdriver or nut driver. Magnetized tips are easiest to use. Available in straight-slot or Phillips head. Excellent for installing drywall or decks.

Socket wrench set: A power version of the standard socket wrench.

Water pump: Connects to garden hose; self-priming, up to 250 gallons per hour.

Wire brush, or *wheel:* Flat wire brush of various sizes. A wire cup brush has wires going parallel to the drill shaft.

Screwdriver Bit

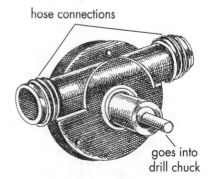

hose connections

goes into
drill chuck

Drill-Powered Pump

> **$ Buying Tip:** If you do a lot of very small-sized jobs requiring these attachments, you may want to purchase a precision, high-speed tool instead, called a **rotary tool (below)**. Get top-quality, hardened steel screwdriver bits with ribbed tips.

Screw Starter

Screw Starter

Also Known As: Bit finder and driver, screw starter/driver, bit holder, bit extender, drill bit holder

Description: Any one of a number of designs that consist of a short steel cylinder with a hex shank on one end (to fit into a power drill) and an open end that holds driver bits for screws up to a certain size (labeled by model). A *sliding sleeve* (plus, usually, magnetism) holds the screws in place; this is clear on some models so you can see the screw as it is driven in. A *manual screw starter* looks more like a hefty ballpoint pen (it even has a clip for pocket storage) and holds screws with springs and/or magnetism.

Use: Driving long screws or driving screws in hard-to-reach places, with more accuracy and less wobble. The nonpowered version is used only for starting or retrieving loose screws, not for driving.

> **$ Buying Tips:** Very handy item. Get the magnetized version, or magnetize yours. Look for one which can double as a quick-change bit for converting your drill into a driver and back again rapidly.

Quick Change Adapter

Also Known As: Quick change chuck

Description: Spring-loaded collar a little over 1" in diameter that slides back over a bit-holding hole; a hex shank sticks out one end and fits into the chuck of a $3/8$" or $1/2$" drill.

Use: Converts a power drill into a quick-change power screwdriver. Makes changing bits almost instant, as there is no need to tighten the chuck.

Quick Change Adaptor

 Buying Tip: Ideal if you have to change bits often.

Note: Works only with $1/4$" hex shank bits with a power groove, but hex adapters for round bits are available.

Screw Gun

Also Known As: Drywall screwdriver, drywall driver, drywall screw gun, power screwdriver

Description: Similar to power drill, above, but lighter, and with a clutch mechanism that disengages when the screw has reached its proper depth. Tips used should be magnetized for holding screws. Runs at a much higher rpm than a drill—around 4,000 rpm.

Use: Driving screws and removing screws, especially drywall and other self-tapping screws.

Screw Gun

> **$ Buying Tip:** Worth its price if you are hanging drywall in any quantity. Lighter than a drill with a screwdriver tip, and the clutch mechanism prevents driving screws beyond the paper surface of drywall or stripping the hole when driving into wood.

Drywall Adapter Bit

Drywall Adaptor Bit

Also Known As: Drywall screw adapter bit, depth driver, drywall bit

Description: Small, conical **Phillips #2 drill bit (above)** inside a larger cone, with a shaft that fits into $1/4$" and $3/8$" power drill chucks.

Use: Converting a power drill into a power screwdriver, expressly for driving drywall screws into **drywall (Chapter 50)** without piercing the surface paper, but with just enough of a dimple to make hiding the screwhead with **joint compound (Chapter 50)** more easy.

> **Use Tip:** Practice setting the depth and getting used to the speed on pieces of scrap.

> **$ Buying Tip:** Much cheaper but less effective than a **screwgun (above)**.

About Drill Bits for Both Power and Hand Drills

Many different bits and accessories may be used in drills. All drill bits are made of steel, have a pointed cutting edge or end, and are for drilling holes in wood and metal, unless otherwise noted. Many specialized types are made but not listed here. Oddly, the terms *drill* and *bit* are both commonly used to describe what we call *drill bits* (the actual hole-making instrument); we reserve the term *drill* for the tool that holds the bit. Buy many to save time on the job.

Twist Drill Bit

Twist Drill Bit

Also Known As: Drill bit (most common), twist drill, drill, drill point, screwdriver bit, bit

Description: Short steel rod ranging in diameter from $1/16$" to $1/2$" in increments of $1/64$", about half of its length spiral and half smooth. Typical bits range from about $1\frac{1}{2}$" to 4" long. Drill bit sets are available in $1/4$", $3/8$", and $1/2$" diameters; a $1/4$" drill takes bits up to $1/4$" in diameter; a $3/8$" drill takes them up to $3/8$", and so on. *Oversize,* also called *step-down* or *reduced-shank* twist drill bits, have narrower shanks at the chuck end than at the bit end, and therefore allow a $1/4$" bit to drill a $1/2$" hole, for example. Be careful to avoid overloading (drawing too many amps).

Specialized Types:

Brad point bits: Tip has a tiny screw-type lead point in front of the normal cutting teeth. For making $1/8$" to 1" holes in hardwoods with great precision and for preventing splintering (you can tell when the bit has reached the far side by the lead point protruding). For use in wood only.

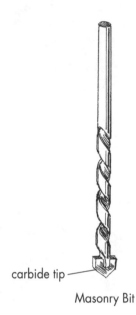

carbide tip —

Masonry Bit

Taper point bits (also known as *tapered shank drill bits*): Tapered to match profile of wood screws.

Masonry bits: Recognizable by the flat wedge in the drill-bit tip. Carbide-tipped for drilling into masonry, tile, and marble.

Cobalt bits: For drilling stainless steel and other hard metals.

Installer bits: (also known as *Bell Hanger bits*): Long (up to 18"), hardened steel, large bore for creating holes for wire and small pipe installation. May be able to drill through nails.

Use: The most frequently used small hole–boring instrument. Suitable for either power- or hand-operated drills. Though most work in wood or metal, some are for wood only. Check the label.

Use Tips: Be sure to replace dull bits. Smaller ones break easily, too, so it is not a bad idea to have extras on hand. To choose the right-sized bit, hold it in your line of sight next to the screw being used. Bit should be the diameter of the center shaft of the screw. Charts matching the exact bit size for screws can be found in hardware stores.

Buying Tip: High-speed steel (HSS) bits are recommended over carbon steel bits—they tend to last longer and are more efficient and versatile. Chrome vanadium steel bits can be used only in wood and plastic.

Countersink Bit

Description: Short, pointed, mushroom-shaped bit. Also made with a knob handle in a hand-operated version.

Countersink attachments are available that work simultaneously with the bit making the original hole. Bits with this feature are known as *pilot bits*. Another version is the *counterbore*, which makes a straight-walled hole, leaving room for a wooden plug. Combination drill bit/countersink/counterbore units do it all at once.

Use: To make beveled, recessed holes for screwheads, enabling them to be driven until the top of the screwhead is flush with or slightly below the surface of the piece into which they are screwed. Actually drills an angle around the hole itself.

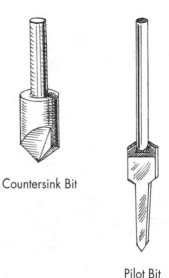

Countersink Bit

Pilot Bit

 Buying Tip: Adjustable combination models offer many advantages.

Spade Bit

Also Known As: Power wood-boring bit, flat boring bit

Description: Usually a 6" long bit consisting of a rod with a flat, paddle-like end with a triangular point. Width of paddle is diameter of hole, ranging up to about 2". A similar item, a *corner drill* or *3D-Bit,* has cutting edges on the sides too.

Spade Bit

Extension Bit

Use: For drilling large holes with power drills. May have a small hole in the blade for pulling wire through holes. Typical uses include holes for installing door locks and electrical wiring. A *corner drill* can cut curved holes and half-holes (grooves) and due to having cutting edges on its sides and rear, can be used for milling in all directions.

Extension Bit

Description: Similar to a regular drill bit, but extra-long, usually 6" to 12".

Use: Reaching places a regular bit would not fit, such as between studs.

> **$ Buying Tip:** Not to be confused with a *drill bit extension*, or *extension shaft*, a plain shaft with a collar and two setscrews, which can extend the length of any drill bit.

Step Drill Bit

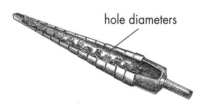

hole diameters

Step Drill Bit

Description: Conical metal drill bit with 6 to 13 steps and a gouge out of about a third of the whole bit. Dimensions are marked inside the gouge. Made of high-grade, high-speed, heat-treated molybdenum steel. Available in both $1/4$" and $3/8$" shank sizes and several different shapes, ranging from more squat to more elongated. Each shape cuts different sizes and quantities of holes, in different increments.

Use: Making perfectly round holes of various sizes in thin materials such as most metals.

Glass And Tile Drill Bit

Glass and Tile Drill Bit

Description: Plain steel diameter shaft with spear-like carbide tip. Shaft sizes available from $1/8"$ to $1/2"$. Different bits are suitable for different recommended drilling speeds, measured in rpm's, from 250 (the largest bit) to 1000 rpm's (the smallest bit).

Use: Smooth, accurate drilling in ceramic tile, mirrors, marble, and so on, usually for installation of fasteners or accessories.

Hole Saw

Also Known As: Saw-blade cutter

Description: Cup-shaped metal blade with a bit, called a *mandrel,* in the center and saw teeth on the bottom. Attaches to chuck on electric drill or drill press. Comes in small-range diameters up to 2 $1/2"$, all of which fit onto the same mandrel. Sold in kits for installing door locks.

Use: Cuts large holes in wood, drywall, and metal.

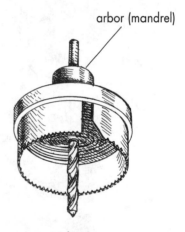

arbor (mandrel)

Hole Saw

> **Buying Tip:** Best quality are *bimetal blades,* that is, teeth are made of high-speed steel and welded onto a regular steel body.

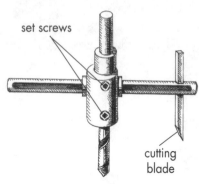

set screws

cutting
blade

Circle and Wheel Cutter

Circle and Wheel Cutter

Also Known As: Fly cutter

Description: Large drill bit with attached horizontal arm that has a cutting blade at the end.

Use: Cutting circles up to 7" in diameter, and, if adjusted to cut twice, wheel shapes.

 **Use Tip:** Primarily for use on a **drill press (Chapter 19)**.

Drill Stop Collar

Also Known As: Nail setters, stop collars, drill stop

Description: Circular steel piece that attaches to drill bits at any point and is held in place by a set screw.

Use: Limits the depth a bit can go so that you don't drill farther through the work than you want.

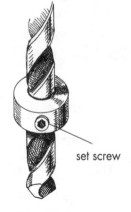

set screw

Drill Stop Collar

 Use Tip: The stop itself will mar a surface if you continue bearing down once it touches, so be careful on delicate surfaces.

Plug Cutter

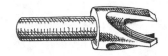
Plug Cutter

Description: Hollow bit with saw teeth. Various sizes up to $3/4$".

Use: Cuts plugs of wood for insertion into the tops of screw holes (to conceal the screws) or for dowel joints.

Forstner Bit

Description: Rimmed bit with small, pointed center guide. Available from $3/8$" to over 2".

Use: Drilling large-diameter, clean, shallow, flat-bottomed holes without great danger of the bit wandering, i.e., following the wood-grain pattern. Can replace any large bit where accuracy and cleanliness are desired. Best used in **drill presses (Chapter 19).**

> ✂ **Use Tips:** The precision of Forstner bits makes them particularly useful for drilling into veneer. To start the bit, tap it into the material first.

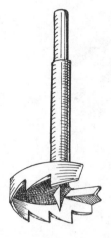
Forstner Bit

Expansive Bit

Also Known As: Expanding bit, adjustable bit

Description: Long bit with adjustable cutting bit on the end.

Expansive Bit

Use: Cutting large holes in wood. Diameter may be adjusted to avoid having to purchase different bits for different-sized holes. Different shaft designed for use in a **brace (Part I, Chapter 11)** or **power drill (above)**. Normally for use in a **drill press** too **(Chapter 19)** as opposed to a *portable drill*.

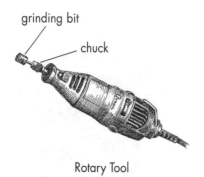

grinding bit

chuck

Rotary Tool

Rotary Tool

Also Known As: Dremel (brand name), hobby/craft tool

Description: Hand-sized, cylindrical, high-speed (up to 30,000 rpm) motor with many drill-bit like attachments available. Commonly has a $1/8$" collet for bits. Usually sold in kits, some with as many as 72 accessories or bits for grinding, drilling, sanding, and so on.

Use: Grinding, sharpening, drilling, polishing, sanding, and generally shaping small areas of all kinds of materials.

 Use Tips: Handy for furniture making and sculpture as the odd repair. Due to its high speed, the rotary tool can be used to drill small holes in hard materials.

Buying Tip: More useful to hobbyists than home repair nuts, but a great gift item for either.

Portable Power Saws

Circular Saw

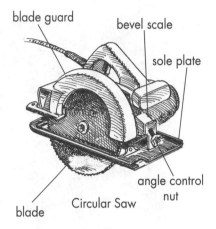

blade guard   bevel scale

sole plate

angle control nut

Circular Saw

blade

Also Known As: Power saw, cuttoff saw, Skilsaw® electric hand-saw, contractor's saw; sometimes confused with **table saw (below).**

Description: Handle on a housing in which a high-speed circular blade is mounted. Blades vary in diameter, but $6^1/_2$", $7^1/_4$", and $8^1/_4$" are most popular. Cordless models are smaller, starting at $3^3/_8$" **(see below for more details on blades).** Size of saw indicates the largest size of blade it can use. Can be adjusted to cut on an angle. Side-drive is most common, and worm (rear)-drive more common for heavy-duty models; this denotes the position of the motor relative to the blade. Various motor sizes and rpm capacities are available.

Use: To make straight cuts (either crosscut or rip) in a wide variety of materials such as plywood, lumber, particleboard, plastic, and so on. Probably the one power tool most often used by carpenters. Good for materials that are difficult to cut by hand. Cordless version can cut wood only up to about 1" thick.

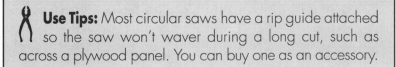

Use Tips: Most circular saws have a rip guide attached so the saw won't waver during a long cut, such as across a plywood panel. You can buy one as an accessory.

Note: The circular saw is proven the most dangerous portable power tool. Always use it with two hands on the saw, and make sure the guard snaps back into place before putting it down. Some models have a brake that stops the blade from spinning as soon as the trigger is released.

$ Buying Tips: A quality circular saw has a chute that directs sanding dust away from the cutting line. It also has higher amperage and rpm ratings. Look for one with at least 10 amps of power and ball or roller bearings. Cordless models are good for trim or clapboards.

Circular Saw Blade with Large
Carbide-Tipped Teeth

Circular (and Radial and Table) Saw Blades

Description: Blades for circular saws, **radial arm saws, compound miter saws,** and **table saws (Chapter 19)** are available in types and styles that can make jobs easier. The diameter and the arbor, or center hole, of the blade must be the right size for your model. Most blades have a "knockout" center piece that enables the blade to fit saws that take either round or diamond arbors. Some now have open slots for heat and noise reduction as well as to minimize resin build-up. Only some types are listed here.

Types:

Abrasive blade, masonry blade, or *abrasive cutoff wheel:* Different materials, such as metal, masonry, ceramic tile, concrete block, and the like can be cut by a circular saw as long as you match the blade to the material (carbide-tipped blades should not be used on such materials). Abrasive cutoff wheels should be used only if the saw has an aluminum or magnesium guard.

Carbide, or *carbide-tipped blade:* Expensive but last as much as ten times longer than ordinary blades. Use them if you do a great deal of cutting. Available in many styles.

Chisel-tooth combination blade: Excellent for exterior plywood, massive softwood-cutting projects where speed is most important, tempered plastic or hardboard laminates, and for other materials or contruction jobs that normally cause blades to dull rapidly and where a rough-edged cut is not a great concern. Common general-purpose blade.

Combination, combo, general-purpose, or *all-purpose blade:* The most commonly used blade, adapted for ripping, crosscutting, mitering hard- or softwood, plywood, composition board, and veneer. Generally has groups of medium-sized teeth separated by spaces every four teeth or so. Makes for a slightly rougher cut than you would get with specialized blades but smoother than a chisel-tooth blade. Usually included with saw when purchased.

Crosscut flooring, nail-cutting, or *remodeling blade:* Smooth cutting blade particularly good for hardwoods; stays sharp even when cutting old, nail-embedded lumber.

Crosscut and rip blades: Just like their handsaw counterparts, except that the crosscut has smaller teeth. Crosscut blades are sometimes called *cutoff blades,* as they cut boards off across the grain. Rip blades are sometimes called *framing blades,* designed for fast, rough cutting.

Flat ground blade: These have teeth angled a bit to each side, or "set" in such a way that the blade makes a wide cut and does not bind. Especially useful for plywood, fiberboard, and other hard materials.

Hollow ground blade: Also called *planer* or *taper ground,* this style of blade is sort of the opposite of flat ground. They are manufactured to be slightly concave so that when the cut is made the blade can go through the material smoothly, without binding. There is no "set" to their teeth, which means they are aligned. Look for this style in combination blades, as it makes for more precise, clean cutting, although it is more expensive. Little sanding is needed afterward.

Metal cutting blade: Available for cutting either ferrous or nonferrous metals.

Plywood and veneer blade: These have extremely small teeth and resist the abrasion of plywood glue and prevent splintering. The finest version of this blade is called a *thin-rim blade,* which cuts splinter-free.

Circular Saw Blade for Plywood

Use Tips: Many types can be resharpened. The center hole (the arbor) varies in size from brand to brand (usually $5/8$" but also $1/2$"), so it must be specified or the blade must come with an insert that fits. Wear safety goggles, especially when cutting wood that chips or has nails. Store blades carefully, and clean them after use if they have gum and pitch on the teeth.

> **$ Buying Tips:** Combination blades suffice for general use. In general, the more teeth per inch, the smoother the cut will be—and the slower. Make sure you get the proper-sized center hole to fit your machine. Carbide-tipped blades are worth the extra expense.

Ripping Guide

Description: Circular saw accessory. An adjustable metal rail that attaches to the saw.

Use: Helps guide the saw during very long cuts, such as of 8' long plywood sheets.

Saber Saw

Also Known As: Portable jigsaw, jigsaw, sabre saw, bayonet saw

Description: Has a short, thin blade that moves up and down, cutting on the upstroke. Barrel grip or overhand grip.

Use: For making intricate cuts in a variety of thin materials, but may be used for crosscutting and ripping. Heavy-duty saws can cut through hardwood up to 1" thick and softwood up to $1^1/_2$" thick. It can also be equipped with a wide variety of specialized blades to cut through a variety of other materials, including metal and glass. Starting from a drilled hole, it can cut from inside a larger piece. Accessories include a rasp blade.

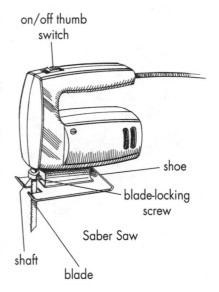

on/off thumb switch

shoe

blade-locking screw

Saber Saw

shaft

blade

Use Tips: If you are making straight cuts, you are better off with a circular saw as the saber saw does not have the high-speed stroking necessary to keep the blade straight. Toss blades the minute you suspect they are dull.

$ Buying Tips: Check for the following features:

- *Stroke.* Good machines have long ones, up to 1". May be adjustable. Some are orbital and some vertical—orbital is best for wood.

- *Adjustable cutting angle.* Blade can be oriented to cut at a 90-degree angle, for corners, or at angles for bevels.

- *Strokes per minute.* Quality machines have a stroke speed of around 3,000 strokes a minute. Look for variable speed settings.

- *Blade attachment.* Quick-blade change features make things go a lot easier.

Reciprocating Saw

Also Known As: Bayonet saw, Sawzall®, Cut Saw®, Supersaw

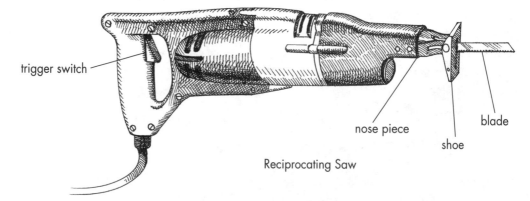

Reciprocating Saw

Description: Tubular housing with straight blade projecting from end. A cordless version is similar but smaller, and may be called a *multipurpose saw* or *utility saw*.

Use: A good saw to use in tight quarters and the only one for rough cutting in major renovation work, such as when cutting into existing framing members and through pipes and walls. Variety of blades available that simultaneously cut through nails and wood and the like.

Cordless Multipurpose Saw

> **Use Tips:** A large variety of specialized blades are available, developed for different materials (drywall, wood, metal) and types of cuts. The cordless model is handy for pruning.

Chain Saw

Description: Gasoline- or electric-powered motor with a long, wide blade around which a toothed chain revolves.

Use: Rough timber cutting, primarily for firewood or pruning.

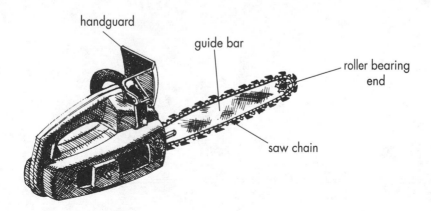

Chain Saw

Portable Power Sanders, Scrapers, Routers, Joiners, and Planes

Finishing Sander

Also Known As: Pad sander

Types:

>*Orbital* or *random orbit sander*
>
>*Oscillating sander*

Also Known As:

>*Orbital:* Speed finish sander (if high-speed type)
>
>*Oscillating:* Straight-line sander

Description: The finishing sander has a handle and a base pad of felt or other soft material to which pieces of sandpaper are secured. *Oscillating/orbital sanders* combined two models in one tool. The dimension of the pad is the *size* of the sander; sometimes the model name notes the size of a standard sheet of paper that it takes, such as $1/3$ sheet. The finest finishing is done with small *palm grip–type* orbital sanders called *palm sanders.*

The oscillating sander moves the pad in a straight line, back and forth, while the orbital moves the pad in a circular motion. The motion, in either case, is usually not more than $1/4$" and is extremely rapid. The more rapidly it oscillates, the finer the sanding action.

Use: For fine finishing—not for quick, heavy removal of wood.

 Use Tips: Use only aluminum oxide or silicon carbide paper; inexpensive flint paper will tear apart quickly. Paper cut to the correct size is sold in packages. Remember that an orbital sander will inevitably go across the grain and thus is not good for some sanding operations.

Buying Tip: Look for flush sanding in quality models, which allows you to sand right up to corners.

sanding pad

Detail Sander

Detail Sander

Also Known As: Corner sander, triangle sander

Description: Long, narrow, cylindrical tool (some would say "svelte") with small, offset, triangular flat head to which sanding pads are attached by hook and loop system or adhesive. Models available that vibrate (oscillate) up to 12,000 SPM (strokes per minute); 7,600 is average (orbital models may be rated in orbits per minute, or OPM). Accessories available include scraping blades and polishing or buffing pads; a *profile sander* includes small profile pads with rounded or cupped shapes; one brand even adds a saw blade. Some models are designed to vibrate only in a back-and-forth motion (*in-line sanders*).

Use: Sanding in small areas, such as corners and edges, where attention to detail is paramount and where discs and square pads of larger sanders can't reach. The sanding head on this tool is out in front of the handle, so you can get into spaces that other sanders can't. In-line sanders can be used specifically for sanding curves of millwork, with the help of narrow rubber profiles.

 Use Tips: Holding one of these for a long time may set your bones to vibrating. Don't overdo it.

 Buying Tips: Extremely welcome development in the world of sanders. Great gift item.

Belt Sander

Description: This sander has fore and aft grips to guide it, with a rapidly revolving (usually 1,300 feet per second) abrasive belt that rides on rollers beneath the housing and ranges, depending on the model, from 2½" to 4" wide and 16" to 21" long. Some models have bags for collecting sanding dust. Many come with a special stand for benchtop work, upside down. At least one company has introduced a compact belt sander to bridge the gap between the **detail sander (above)** and the belt sander. Made with a sharp point in place of the front roller, it takes 1½" wide belts and can sand close in to corners.

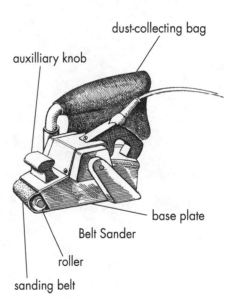

dust-collecting bag

auxilliary knob

base plate

Belt Sander

roller

sanding belt

Use: For the fast removal of finish or wood. You might think of a belt sander, with a coarse belt, as the first sander you'd use to remove a layer of wood or paint; with a fine belt it can also do the finish sanding (the belt going with the grain) better than **orbital sanders (above)**.

> **Use Tips:** Take care when using a belt sander. It removes material so rapidly that it's easy to gouge a surface without realizing it.

> **Buying Tips:** The heavier the model, the better. An occasional problem is the belt tracking off the pulleys. Most models have an adjustment feature that prevents this. *Open-coat sandpaper* is best, as it is less likely to clog. Get the biggest and heaviest model you can heft; sturdiness counts here. 3" × 21" models are good bets.

Disk (or Disc) Sander/Polisher/Grinder

Also Known As: Rotary sander

Description: Comes in two configurations. In the *vertical* type the disk, which revolves rapidly, operates in a plane perpendicular to the motor; in the more common *angle grinder*, or *angle-head grinder*, type the disk is parallel to the motor.

Use: Sanding, polishing, or grinding metal or wood, depending on the disk used. Disks for use on wood, plastic, and concrete are also available. Really for heavy-duty use; a disk sanding attachment on a power hand drill will take care of most homeowners' tasks.

 Use Tip: The extreme speed and heavy weight of this tool make it easy to gouge something by mistake.

Buying Tips: Especially suited for long-use periods and high pressure. Otherwise a **portable hand drill with a sanding disk accesory (Chapter 16)** will do. A good tool to rent.

Router

Description: Canister-shaped tool with two handles and a bit that revolves at high speed underneath the center of the tool. (A shaper performs similar functions but is a stationary tool.) Sold in two versions: *fixed-base router (see illus.)* and *plunge-type router.* A smaller, handle-less model is called a *cut-out tool* or *rotary cutter.*

Use: There are a few dozen bits available for use with a router that allow fast and accurate cutting of wood and plastic edges into molding shapes, making grooves (dadoes and rabbets) and mortising for door hinges. A special, smaller model, a *laminate trimmer,* is made for trimming plastic laminate, such as for countertops. A *plunge router* can start a cut in the middle of a solid surface. Cut-out tools are used for cutting electrical and plumbing openings.

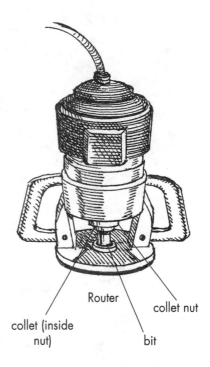

Router

collet nut

collet (inside nut)

bit

> **Use Tips:** Think of the router wherever you want to achieve a very smooth-cut surface along an edge; its high-speed operation ensures this. Because the router bit is exposed, make sure to exercise extreme caution. New bits may chip at first. Don't put bits snug against bottom of collet.

> **Buying Tips:** Ask for a tool that has both accurate depth adjustment of the bit and ball-bearing construction. Routers come with motors of various horsepower and higher rpm's are better. For the do-it-yourselfer a $7/8$- to $1/2$-horsepower motor is adequate, but home renovators need at least a $1 1/4$ horsepower model; also look for $1/4$" to $1/2$" collet capacity (or better, one with both). Check to see whether replacing bits is convenient or awkward. Bits come three ways: carbide-tipped, pure carbide, and heat-treated. Carbide is more costly than heat-treated but lasts longer. Plunge routers are more handy. *Cut-out tools* are a big help in new construction jobs. *Door hinge* and *strike and latch templates* are worthwhile accessories for big jobs.

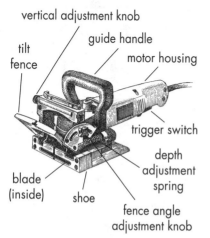

vertical adjustment knob

guide handle

tilt fence

motor housing

trigger switch

depth adjustment spring

blade (inside)

shoe

fence angle adjustment knob

Biscuit Joiner

Biscuit Joiner

Also Known As: Plate Joiner

Description: Cylindrical motor about a foot long, housed above a square base, with a handle on top and a vertical front (the "fence") with one sliding piece and thumbscrews for guidance for depth and angle of cuts. Contains a small cutting blade, usually about 3" to 4" in diameter, in the square base.

Use: Cutting half-circle slots in sides of pieces to be joined with glue and wooden or plastic inserts, called **biscuits (below)**.

> **$ Buying Tip:** Excellent and simple way to assure strong joints between pieces of wood, though not as strong as tenons or dowels—just much easier to make.

Joiner Biscuits

Also Known As: Plate joiner biscuits, splines, wood biscuits, plate, biscuit

Description: Thin oval ($^3/_4$" to 1" × $1^7/_8$" to $2^3/_8$") of wood (often compressed beechwood) or plastic. Sold in bags of 50 to 1000, by dimensions and thickness (#00 to #20 gauge).

Use: Joining two pieces of wood by placing wooden biscuits into slots cut by a **biscuit joiner (above)** with glue (some plastic biscuits are self-locking and eliminate the need for clamping).

Joiner Biscuits

> **$ Buying Tip:** Purchase the specialized glue and applicator that are offered along with biscuits for ease of use.

Power Scraper/Carver

Description: Hand-sized, cylindrical, vibrating motor with offset head that holds a variety of blade-like tools (scrapers, gouges, chisels, and knives) for scraping and carving.

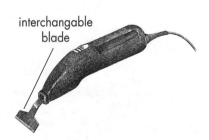

interchangable blade

Power Scraper/Carver

Use: Quick, uniform scraping or carving for quick removal of (depending on the choice of interchangeable metal blades) adhesive, caulk, glazing compound (from windows), foam carpet backing, wood filler, paint splatters, putty, stucco, mortar overflow or splatters, and of course, wood stock.

 Buying Tip: Good gift item.

Portable Plane

Types:

Block plane

Jack plane

Description: Just like hand planes, portable planes come in small and large versions. Rotating cutter blades protrude slightly from a smooth bottom; a high-speed motor and handle grip are on top.

Use: For smoothing surfaces and edges of wood and for some rabbeting (grooves on edges).

 Use Tip: Block planes, being smaller, are handier.

Engraver

Description: Hand-sized plastic tool with pencil grip and a small metal point that vibrates at high speed.

Use: Engraving identification on tool housings or other equipment.

Stationary Power Tools

About Stationary Power Tools

The ultimate power tool for the do-it-yourselfer is the stationary or benchtop one: Unlike portable tools, which you take to the work, you take the work to the stationary power tool.

Radial Arm Saw

Also known As: Cutoff saw

Description: A cutting table with an arm over it that houses a circular saw. The saw can be set to various angles, and turned 90 degrees for ripping. To operate, grasp the handle and pull the blade forward for cutoff operations. Move the work through the blade for ripping cuts.

Uses: Can be set to crosscut, rip, and do a variety of other jobs—shaping, dadoing, sanding, jigsawing—with the proper accessories, such as *molding heads,* **dado heads (below),** and *panel cutters.* Can also be set for compound and bevel cuts.

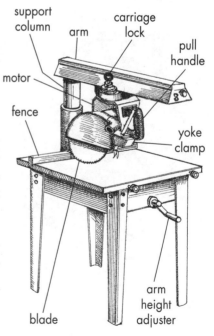

Radial Arm Saw

> ✂ **Use Tips:** Does many different things than a **table saw (below)**. Ripping especially can be very dangerous—be sure to feed the work to the blade from the correct side.

> ⚡ **Buying Tips:** Many people consider the radial arm saw the most useful stationary power tool of all, and it should be the first major purchase for your shop. The models that take smaller-sized blades are better for a first purchase. **Compound miter saws (below)** are a close competitor for that No. 1 purchase.

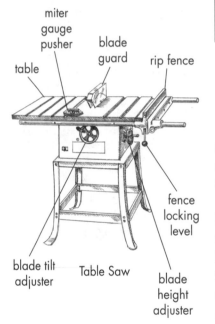

Table Saw

Table Saw

Also known As: Bench saw, contractor's saw, arbor saw, circular saw (not to be confused with the **portable circular saw, Chapter 17)**, variety saw

Description: Consists of a table with a slot from which the circular saw blade protrudes. The blade can be raised or lowered as needed for depth of cut, and either the blade or the table, depending on the model, can be tilted for angled cuts (tilting blades are much more common). To operate the saw, wood is fed into the revolving saw blade (unlike the **radial arm saw, (above)** where the saw is run across the stock). The motor and works of the machine are located under the table.

Use: Very good for ripping large pieces of wood, but how large depends on table size. Special blades such as *molding heads* or *panel cutters* can be used to cut special grooves and contours, like a router or a more advanced tool, a **shaper (Chapter 18).** Grooves are also cut by **dado heads (below).**

Use Tips: If you have to cut very narrow lengths of stock, protect your fingers by using a push stick to feed the stock into the blade. Floor stands with rollers are available for supporting extremely long workpieces.

Compound Miter Saw

Also Known As: Chopsaw, chop saw, chop box

Description: Benchtop-mounted, circular saw with blade and motor mounted on a hinged yoke-style arm that raises up and lowers for cutting at various angles. Not necessarily attached to the workbench, this saw can be used at the worksite. Small models start at about $1^1/_2$ hp, take eight $^1/_4$" blades, and can cut up to a limited degree of angle. Larger models are offered at 2 to $3^1/_2$ hp with greater amperage and can cut at a wider range of angles with 10" and even 12" saw blades. All saws are sold labeled by their various stock capacities, such as crosscutting up to $5^1/_2$" $\times$ $2^1/_{16}$" thick, and the like.

Use: Accurate and fast miscellaneous angled (miter and bevel) or cutoff (straight crosscut) cuts in trim stock.

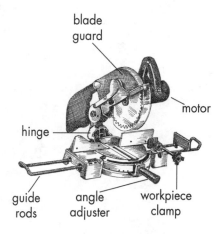

Compound Miter Saw

Use Tip: Use as often as possible for accurate cutting.

Buying Tips: One of the most successful developments in power tools in recent years. Extremely helpful tool for finish carpentry of all kinds.

Note: Not all miter saws are *compound miter saws* (angles off vertical *and* horizontal).

About Power Saw Blades

Radial arm, miter, and table saws use the same types of blades as circular saws, as mentioned above in **Chapter 17**, except that these stationary tools, due to their higher speeds, tend to use blades with larger diameters and greater thicknesses (and generally cost more). Be sure to check your old blade and tool model before purchasing replacement blades.

Dado Head Blades

Dado Head Blades

Also known As: Dado set, dado assembly

Description: Composed of two kinds of blades: small, thicker-than-usual *circular saw blades,* and *chippers,* which are cutters mounted, or flanked, by the blades when in use. Generally 6" to 8" in diameter. An alternative is a single-blade type, called an *adjustable dado*.

Use: To cut grooves or slots, called *dadoes,* across boards.

Use Tips: For most purposes the 6" size will be fine. To vary the dado size, use fewer and/or wider chipper blades or make multiple cuts. If you have it resharpened, be sure to sharpen the entire set so the sizes remain constant.

Band Saw

Description: Large tool with a saw blade in the shape of a loop or circle that rotates continually in one direction through a table guide that holds the workpiece. The table on many models can be tilted 45 degrees.

Use: For cutting intricate curves in wood, particularly in thick wood (6" or more). With the proper blades, a band saw can cut a variety of other materials, including steel, plastic, and aluminum.

 Use Tip: Sanding attachments can be substituted for blades for sanding intricate shapes.

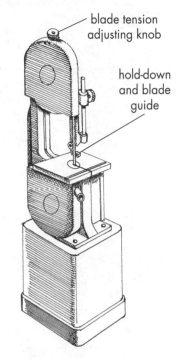

Band Saw

Scrollsaw

Also known As: Jigsaw, bench jigsaw

Description: Small blade in the middle of a steel worktable, supported by a long arm anchored in the rear. Blades are extremely narrow and of two types: the *jeweler's blade,* which is held at both ends, and the *saber blade,* which is a bit heavier and held only from below. Blade moves vertically in a reciprocating motion.

Use: For cutting curves and sharp corners in patterns and for cutting from within a starter hole inside a workpiece. Table tilts for miter and bevel cuts.

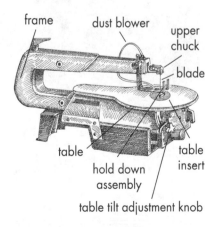

Scrollsaw

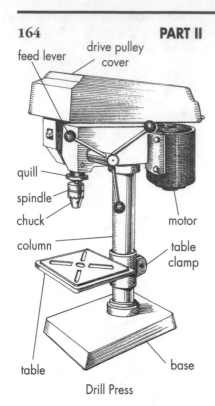

feed lever
drive pulley
cover

quill

spindle

chuck

column

table

motor

table
clamp

base

Drill Press

Drill Press

Description: Has a heavy base and a vertical arm that holds drill bits and can be raised or lowered with a crank or lever. The table or base can be adjusted to various angles. A variation on the regular drill press is the *radial* type, which can be rotated completely around the arm.

Use: A handy machine, though mainly for precision or production drilling. With accessories a drill press can shape, mill, groove, or rout. For metal as well as wood.

 Buying Tip: Recommended as the second stationary power tool in your shop, after the **radial arm saw (above)**.

Bench Grinder

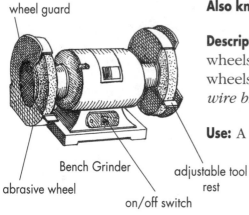

wheel guard

abrasive wheel

Bench Grinder

on/off switch

adjustable tool
rest

Also known As: Grinder

Description: Usually has a motor flanked by two grinding wheels. The tool itself is mounted on a workbench. Various wheels include *abrasive grinders, lamb's-wool buffers,* and *wire brushes.*

Use: A variety of polishing, grinding, and sharpening jobs.

Jointer

Also known As: Jointer-planer

Description: Table with a housing from which cutterheads protrude. Stock is pushed against housing into cutters that revolve at up to 4,500 rpm.

Use: A variety of jobs similar to a hand plane: to smooth, groove, taper, or bevel wood edges and surfaces. Particularly helpful prior to gluing precision joints. One of the basic cabinetmaking tools.

 Use Tip: For safety, use a stick to push stock into cutters.

 Buying Tip: One sign of a quality jointer is three or four cutters; lower-quality machines have only two.

Lathe

Description: Two heads ("stocks")—one movable, the other stationary—mounted on a metal bed, with wood inserted between them or attached to one. As the head spins so does the wood. A chisel, supported by a tool rest, is held against the wood.

Use: All kinds of wood shaping, from making bowls to adding a filigree to a piece of molding.

Lathe Gouges

Also known As: Gouges, turning tools

Description: Long, narrow, variously shaped high-speed steel blade set into a wooden handle, similar to a chisel. May be *flat* or *fluted*.

Basic Types:

> *Plain gouge:* For roughing shapes, cove cutting.
>
> *Roughing out gouge:* Trims square to round.
>
> *Spindle gouge:* For hollows and beads.
>
> *Skew and square end gouge:* General planing action.
>
> *Parting gouge:* Sizing and beading.
>
> *Scraping gouge:* Flat, for bowls and faceplates.

Use: Shaping wood on a **lathe (above)**.

 Buying Tip: Use only the highest-quality turning tools.

General Hardware

Nails

About Nails

There are two categories of nails: those ordinarily used for assembling wood members, be it fine work or rough construction, and specialized nails—those having a variety of single purposes. Actually, there are hundreds of different types when you include various esoteric coatings, ends, materials, and heads. We deal only with the more commonly found ones here. Most of the regular wood nails may be referred to as wire nails.

For wood, though you can get nails smaller and larger, nails are generally available in 1" to 6" sizes; as the nail gets longer it gets larger and thicker in diameter. After 6" in length, nails are often called spikes, and can range up to 18" long.

Basic wood nails are sized according to length, expressed by the letter d (verbalized as "penny"). Originally this was an early English symbol for a pound of weight—from the ancient Roman coin, the denarius—and related to the weight of 1000 nails in pounds. Sizes run from 2d (2-penny or 1") to 60d (6-penny or 6")—6d nails are 2" long, 10d nails are 3" long, etc. This is shown on the following table.

About Determining Nail Length and Quantity With the D System

As mentioned in the above About section, nails are commonly sold by length, which is denoted by the symbol d and a number. Here is how it works:

2d—1"	8d—2^1/$_2$"	30d—4^1/$_2$"
3d—1^1/$_4$"	9d—2^3/$_4$"	40d—5"
4d—1^1/$_2$"	10d—3"	50d—5^1/$_2$"
5d—1^3/$_4$"	12d—3^1/$_2$"	60d—6"
6d—2"	16d—3^1/$_2$"	70d—7"
7d—2^1/$_4$"	20d—4"	80d—8"

Approximate quantities of common nails per pound by size are, for example: 845 2d nails, 165 6d nails, 65 10d nails, or 30 20d nails. Check with your dealer for specifics regarding whatever nail you are purchasing.

Another antique term is still used too—*penny,* again probably referring to the number of nails you could get for this amount in England. Thus a 10d nail is sometimes called a *10-penny nail,* and a box of 3" long, common-type nails would be labeled *10 common.* Don't worry—these days you can order nails just by their length in inches if you want.

Finishing nails are sized by length in inches and diameters in gauge, with higher numbers denoting thinner nails.

Nails are generally not as strong as screws; however, the holding power (and driving ease) of nails is increased by coating them with resin. These are called *cement-coated ("c.c.") nails, resin-coated nails, coated sinkers* or *sinkers,* or *coolers.* Other coatings, such as zinc, are for rust resistance. Holding power is even more greatly increased by various deformations, or threading, of the shaft, such as *barbs, chemical etching, annular rings, spiral threads* or *flutes,* and by *clinching,* or *bending,* the tips. These nails, though, are very difficult if not impossible to remove without damaging the wood, while screws are easily removed. In general, if strength is your requirement, use screws.

Plain common nails with no coating are called *bright.*

> **Note:** Because of the increased holding power of coated or deformed nails, they are a little bit shorter than the same d-size common nail.

Nails come in boxes, brown paper bags, and carded; the latter is the most expensive way to buy them. If you are going to use a lot of nails, buy 25- or 30-pound kegs at a reduced price. Your dealer can show you a chart to help you figure out the quantity of a particular nail per pound.

Common Nail

Description: Fairly thick with a large, round, flat head

Use: General construction work such as framing and a wide variety of other purposes. Comes in many different sizes. Its large, flat head acts like a washer.

> **Use Tips:** When driving common nails with a hammer try to snap your wrist rather than hitting the nail with arm power. If you are using cement-coated nails, do not stop hammering until the nail is driven all the way in. If you stop, the cement, which is actually a friction-sensitive glue, will set, and when you start again the nail might bend.

Common Nail

Box Nail

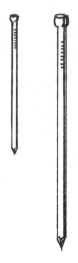

Finishing Nail

Box Nail

Description: Looks like the common nail but is thinner and a little shorter than the common nail d-length indicates. Smooth sides. Made of specially hardened wire.

Use: A variation on the common nail. It is used for the same purposes but its thinner diameter (lighter gauge) and slightly blunted tip make it good where there is a danger of the nail splitting thin wood. Does not hold as well as common nails.

Finishing Nail

Also Known As: Brad

Description: Thin, with a very small, cupped head. Comes in both very small and fairly long sizes and may be sized according to wire gauge (diameter) with a number from 12 down to 20 as well as by the d system.

Use: For wherever you don't want nailheads to show, such as when making cabinets, fine paneling, and the like. A very commonly used nail, it is also thinner than the common nail, but the real difference is the head: because it's small and cupped, it can be easily countersunk, that is, driven beneath the wood surface with a **hammer** and **nailset (Part I, Chapters 1 and 2)** and then the depression above the head filled with wood putty and sanded for a near-invisible finish.

Casing Nail

Description: Looks like a **finishing nail (above)**, but is thicker and has a flat rather than a cupped head.

Use: This is a close cousin of the finishing nail and gets its name from its main use: securing **case molding (Part VI, Chapter 49)** and other rough trim. It is thicker and harder than a finishing nail, so you can use fewer of them.

Casing Nail

Ringed, Threaded, or Barbed Nails

Types:

Annular ring (or ring shank, or ring drive, or underlayment) *nail*

Drywall nail

Roofing nail

Spiral (or spiral flooring, or spiral shank, or spiral screw, or spiral drive, drive screw, or underlayment) *nail*

Description: Nails with shanks that have been shaped to have the greatest holding power possible, such as

Annular ring: Shank has many sharp ridges. Various uses include underlayment, shingles, siding, paneling.

Drywall: Has a partially barbed or ringed shank and may be resin-coated; has a large head. A *plasterboard* or *lath nail* is another version of this, with a larger head and smaller barbs.

Roofing: Large head and a barbed shank, usually galvanized. Metal roofing model available with a lead or plastic washer under head. *Cap nail* has extremely large head—up to 1" (metal or plastic).

Spiral: Small head with a spiral shank.

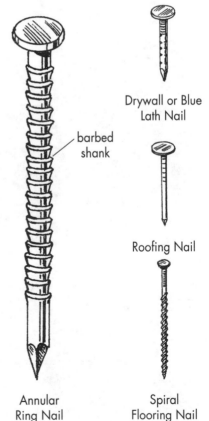

Drywall or Blue Lath Nail

barbed shank

Roofing Nail

Annular Ring Nail

Spiral Flooring Nail

barbed shank

Cap Nail

Use:

Annular ring: For generally increased holding power, such as in paneling or delicate floor repair work.

Drywall: Securing **drywall (Part VII, Chapter 50)** to framing.

Roofing: Securing asphalt shingles and roofing paper.

Spiral: Usually used to install or repair wood flooring but can also be used in rough carpentry.

 Use Tips: *Drywall:* Hit it just hard enough so that the nailhead dimples the surface paper but goes no deeper. Screws should generally be used with drywall.

Roofing: Comes in various sizes up to $1^1/_4$". Carefully size the nail to the thickness of the roofing being fastened. Available in rust-resistant materials, such as aluminum or stainless steel. Strike as few times as possible to avoid scratching off the rust-resistant coating.

Buying Tips: Galvanized roofing nails are the least expensive. Get double-hot-dipped galvanized nails.

Cut Flooring Nail

Description: Flat, tapered shank and head. Looks like old-fashioned, hand-forged nails.

Use: For nailing into sides of floorboards without splintering and for decorative purposes in restoration.

Use Tips: As it is very difficult to nail sideways at a precise angle, we recommend the use of a *nailing machine*. This can usually be rented from your hardware store or flooring supplier.

Duplex Head Nail

Also Known As: Duplex nail, sprig nail, double-head scaffold nail, staging nail

Description: Regular common nail with a flat ring about $1/4$" below the head.

Use: For temporary work, such as scaffolding. You drive it in up to the first head like a normal nail but can easily remove it by pulling on the second head.

Panel Nail

Description: Decorative brads available in a variety of colors. The best come with **annular rings** for better holding power **(see above)**.

Use: Securing wood paneling to wall when nails are to be inconspicuous.

Duplex Head Nail

Common
Tack

Ornamental
Tacks

Tack

Types:

Common tack

Ornamental or *ornamental tack*

Description:

Common tack: Short, flat- or round-sided nail, some with extra-sharp "cut" end.

Ornamental: Has a tack-like shaft, or shank, and a large, fancy head, often mushroom-shaped.

Use:

Common tack: Mainly used for securing carpeting.

Ornamental: For securing upholstery.

> **Use Tips:** Available with a blued finish or in copper and aluminum. The latter are impervious to weather and are good for boating applications but also for securing webbing on outdoor furniture. Starting tacks without a small-headed hammer, such as a **tack hammer (Part I, Chapter 1)**, is difficult but can be done by holding the tack with a hairpin instead of your fingers.

Nail-like Fasteners

Also Known As: Corrugated fastener, corrugated nail

Types:

Chevron

Corrugated fastener

Staple

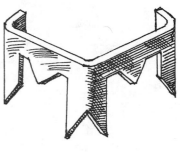

Chevron

Description:

Chevron: Small, thin metal piece bent at 90 degrees with several sharpened points on one side.

Corrugated fastener: Short, wide, wavy piece of thin metal with one sharpened side.

Staple: Small U- or J-shaped wire with sharpened ends.

Use:

Chevron: Nailed into corners of boxes and the like.

Corrugated fastener: Nailed across miter joints, such as in picture frames and boxes.

Staple: Usually driven into wood to hold wire or screening.

Masonry Nail

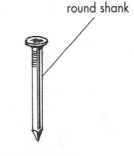

round shank

Masonry Nail

Also Known As: Concrete nail

Description: Looks like a thick common nail but is made of case-hardened and tempered steel. Its shank comes four ways: *round, fluted* (or knurled), *flat* (cut), or *square*. The cut-type masonry nail looks just like the old-fashioned normal cut nail. Another version is the *hammer drive pin,* a $1/4''$ diameter pin inside a flanged sleeve.

Use: Securing items such as electrical conduit furring strips to masonry (brick, concrete, block, etc.), where great holding power is not needed. Hammered in.

> **Use Tips:** You should use a two-pound or bricklayer's hammer to drive these nails. Definitely wear safety glasses to protect against flying masonry chips, and use as few blows as possible.

Screws, Screw Eyes, and Screw Hooks

About Wood Screws

Screws should be the choice when a woodworking job calls for strength. They can be removed—unscrewed—without damaging the item. All screws are driven with screwdrivers except a **lag screw,** or **lag bolt (below)**, which is driven with a wrench, and all are pointed and tapered (unlike *bolts,* which have blunt ends and are straight) except for the machine screw, which is actually a **bolt (Chapter 22)**. Still with us? *Lag* means threaded only on about a third of a long screw or screw eye.

When selecting a screw for a job, a number of factors come into play: finish, length, gauge (diameter), head style, and slot type, as follows:

Finish may be plain steel, blued, or dipped—partially immune to weather—galvanized, brass, brass-plated, chrome-plated, or stainless steel **(Appendix A, Metals and Metal Finishes)**. Remember that brass is softer than brass-plated steel, and thus brass screws' slots are more easily damaged than those of brass-plated screws.

Screws range in size from $1/4$" up to around 6" long; the longer the screw the more difficult it is to turn with a screwdriver. Indeed, if you need a screw more than 4" long use a *lag bolt* or *screw,* which is turned with a wrench. Length is measured in inches.

Screw "gauge," or diameter, of the unthreaded shank under the screwhead is described according to numbers commonly ranging from No. (or #) 5 to No. 14, with the higher number being the larger. The total range is No. 2 to No. 24. A No. 5 screw is about $1/8$" in diameter. Screws of the same gauge are available in different lengths. Always order a screw by length and number: $1/2$" No. 8, for example. Screwheads may be flat, round or oval. See illustration.

Slot types differ. Most common are *slotted* (one straight slot) and *Phillips* (crisscross slots). Other slot types exist, but are not widely available. However, one specialized kind is often found on computers, car headlights, and dashboards—the **Torx head**, which resembles a small star-shaped Phillips head style **(Chapter 4)**. Another type, used often in furniture assembly, is the *square drive,* or *Robertson,* and features a small square hole in the head. All are vast improvements over the slotted type. All require their own screwdriver **(Part I, Chapter 4)**.

Standard Wood Screw

Description: Threads along three-fourths of a tapered shaft, with a variety of heads. **See About section, above.** Most common material is zinc chromate-treated steel. Commonly sold 100 to a box as well as in smaller and larger containers.

Use: Securing wood items to one another. Generally, *oval-* and *flat-head* screws are used when countersinking for decorative purposes or with hardware such as hinges, but oval head is generally easier to remove and slightly better-looking. *Round-head screws* are used with thin woods and with washers.

Slotted
Screwhead

Phillips-Type
Screwhead

> **Use Tips:** Always ensure that a screw is driven deeply enough so it holds well. When using an electric drill for driving screws, use Phillips head screws—they are easier for the bit to grip snugly. The force of the drill tends to make the driver slip out of a straight slot. Screws are easier to drive if you rub a little lubricating screw compound or wax on them first. Don't use soap—it may cause rust.

> **Buying Tip:** Small packages of screws are much more expensive than boxes of 100. The traditional, plain wood screw is easily replaced by new, innovative designs with sharper, wider threads that resemble **drywall screws (below)**. Many do not need pilot holes and work in a wide variety of materials. Try them.

Torx®
Screwhead

Flat Head
Wood Screw

Dowel Screw

Description: Slightly heavier than a regular screw, and with threads from both ends. (A similar item is the **hanger bolt,** or **hanger screw, listed in Chapter 22.)**

Use: Furniture assembly of pieces end-to-end.

Oval Head
Wood Screw

Round Head
Wood Screw

Dowel Screw

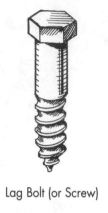

Lag Bolt (or Screw)

Lag Bolt (or Screw)

Description: Looks like a fat, oversize screw that is partly threaded (hence the name *lag*). However, it has a square or hex head for turning with a wrench (hence the name *bolt*). Always on the large side, though not in many sizes.

Use: Heavy-duty fastening when a standard wood screw is not strong enough, such as for securing framing members on a deck, for outdoor furniture, or for hanging kitchen cabinets. Think of it as the largest screw available.

> **Use Tip:** Drill pilot and shank holes so that the screw will be easier to drive. It must be turned with a wrench. Use a washer when tightening against soft wood.

> **Buying Tip:** Lag bolts are cheaper than **carriage bolts (Chapter 22)**, so if you have a choice, use a lag bolt.

Drywall Screw

Drywall Screw

Description: Thin, straight, blued (looks black) screw with deep threads, especially sharp point, and a flat Phillips head (actually a special design called a *Bugle head,* which prevents tearing the surface paper of drywall). Self-tapping—needs no predrilled hole in soft materials. Although there are two kinds—fine thread for metal studs and coarse thread for wooden studs—they are basically interchangeable. In any case the kind intended for metal works fine in wood. *Deck screws* have a coarse thread and are rust-proof galvanzied or stainless steel.

Use: Securing drywall or wood to wood or metal (stud framing, beams, furring, or joists).

> **Use Tips:** Where you are using screws just for basic construction, use drywall screws. They work quite well, due to their self-tapping design: they pull themselves right in, hold securely, and do not need a predrilled hole in soft wood. However, they are not very strong, and the heads may shear off under stress. Particularly convenient when used with a **screw gun** or an **electric drill** with a **screwdriver bit (Part VII, Chapter 50)**.

> **Buying Tip:** Drywall screws are much cheaper than other types when bought in packages of a pound or more. Avoid buying small bags or bubble packs.

Sheet Metal Screw

Description: May be flat-head, oval, or *pan* head, a buttonlike top (as shown). Unlike wood screws, they are threaded their entire length. Self-tapping (creates its own threaded hole). Heads and gauges are similar to wood screws.

Use: Fastening thin metal to thin metal. Holds extremely well in wood, too, due to its deep threads and self-tapping design.

Sheet Metal Screw

Concrete Screw

Description: Wide-threaded, incredibly hard steel screw, with either tapered flat head or hex washer head; coated against corrosion. Sold with special carbide-tipped masonry drill. Available in $1/4$" and $3/8$" diameters and a variety of lengths.

Use: Screws directly into cement and cement board **(Part VII, Chapter 50)** of all kinds. No anchor needed. Useful when attaching wood to concrete foundation, as well as for electrical installation.

 Use Tip: Carefully drill appropriately-sized hole first.

Screw Washers

Countersunk Washer

Description: Small metal circles that come in three shapes: *flat, countersunk* (slightly cone-shaped), and *flush* (slightly funnel-shaped). The latter two are known as *finishing washers*. Size matches screw being used.

Use: Washers provide a hard surface for a screw to be tightened against, thereby preventing damage to the surface and allowing a tighter fit. Countersunk (for oval-head screws) and flush (for flat-head screws) are more attractive as well. Flat washers are for use with round-head screws.

Flush Washer

About Screw Eyes and Screw Hooks

There is an entire family of devices called *screw eyes* and *screw hooks*. They are classic hardware-store items and have been around for many years. Some of these screws can be installed with hand power alone. Many are finished for outdoor use.

Both screw eyes and screw hooks are available in various wire gauges or diameters and lengths and are classified by number: As the eye gets smaller the number gets larger. For instance, a No. 000 screw eye has an inside diameter of 1" while a No. 9 would have an inside diameter only $\frac{1}{2}$". As the eye gets larger the screw eye or screw hook gets longer. Lengths generally range from $\frac{1}{2}$" to 3".

Screw Eyes

Screw Eye

Description: Metal shaft with one end formed into a ring, the other threaded and pointed like a screw. Models are available with a loose ring looped through the eye, called an *eye and ring*. Another, heavy-duty model has a round plate underneath the eye for added stability.

Screw Eye with Plate

Use: Various uses but basically for hanging objects and hooking them together. The screw eye with a plate is used for anchoring cables, such as for TV antennae.

Screw Hooks

Types:

Screw Hook

   Ceiling hook

   Cup hook

   L-hook

   Utility hook

Cup Hook

Shoulder Hook

L-Hook

Also Known As:

L-hook: Square bend screwhook, support hook, curtain rod hook

Utility hook: Bicycle hook, storage hook

Description: Same basic design as a *screw eye* but the ring part is open, forming a hook.

Ceiling hook: Very large hook for screwing directly into ceiling joists.

Cup hook: A rounded screw hook with a shoulder, or plate. Cup hooks vary from 1¼" long and, because they are decorative, are usually brass- or plastic-coated. "Safety" models have a snap across the opening.

L-hook: A screw hook in the shape of the letter L. L-hooks come up to 2" long. A *shoulder hook* is an L hook with a small shield like a cup hook.

Utility hook: Extremely large, squared-off, plastic-coated screw hook with large threads.

Use: Hanging things from wood shelves, walls, and ceilings.

Cup hook: Hanging cups in a cabinet.

L-hook: Hanging utensils, securing picture frames directly to walls (without hanging from a wire), holding curtain rods.

Utility hook: Great for hanging bicycles from a ceiling in an apartment or a garage. Screw directly into a joist. Also for rakes, shovels, lawn mowers.

> ✂ **Use Tips:** A small screw hook can be installed in soft wood by simply pushing it in place and turning it by hand.

Swag Hook

Also Known As: Ceiling hook

Description: Decorative cup hook with enlarged base and exaggerated relief. Comes in various decorator colors and with either large screw threads or a **toggle bolt (Chapter 23)**.

Use: Anchoring swag lamps and hanging plants from ceilings.

Swag Hook with Toggle Bolt

Clothesline and Hammock Hooks

Description:

Clothesline hook: Like an enlarged cup hook with a plate with holes to accept screws.

Hammock hook: Like the clothesline hook but three kinds are available. One is simply a large screw eye or hook; another has a plate with screw holes in it and a hook that hangs from it, and a third is a hook hanging from a screw eye.

Use:

Clothesline hook: For mounting clothesline, particularly where mounting material is thin.

Hammock hook: Heavy-duty anchor for hammocks.

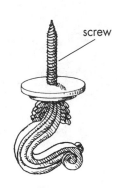

Swag Hook with Screw

> **Use Tips:** *Clothesline hook:* When mounting to thin material, such as siding, use the type with the plate on it. The plate type allows you to use small screws, which will not bite deeply into the mounting material, possibly cracking it.

Gate Hook

Gate Hook and Eye

Description: Consists of a screw eye that screws into a gate post and a corresponding screw eye and hook that is secured to the gate. Gate hooks commonly come 1" to 5" long but can be obtained up to 18" long. A "safety" version is available with a spring-loaded bolt that snaps across the hook opening to keep small children from unhooking the gate.

Use: Keeps gates and doors closed in a lightweight manner.

> **Use Tips:** Gate-hook parts must be sized to work together. This shouldn't be a problem because they come as kits.

Nuts and Bolts

About Nuts and Bolts

Bolts are generally for fastening metal to metal, not wood to wood (except for the **carriage bolt, below)**. They can be turned only with wrenches (except for **machine screws** and **stove bolts, below)**. Their threads, known as *machine threads,* cannot, unlike *wood-screw threads,* hold in anything except a nut. And they have blunt ends, not pointed ends like wood screws.

Bolt diameters are noted in inches, not in gauge numbers as with screws. Thread size is noted in a number following the diameter in terms of threads per inch, i.e., $1/4"\times 20$. Common machine bolt has 20 threads per inch. This nomenclature is often confused by various manufacturers, who may use two different systems on similar packages. Caveat emptor and good luck.

> **Note:** A **lag bolt**, also called a *lag screw,* is discussed in **Chapter 20**.

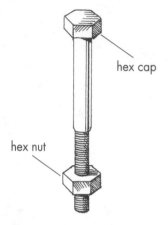

hex cap

hex nut

Machine Bolt

Machine Bolt

Description: Partially threaded with a flat end and either a square or hex head. The standard, classic bolt. Called a *tap bolt* or *hex head* capscrew when threaded its entire length; a hex head (or cap) bolt when threaded only part way up the shaft. In addition, a *capscrew* or *socketscrew* is threaded its entire length but has a round head (cap) for use with an **Allen wrench (Part I, Chapter 8)**.

Use: Assembling metal items.

> **Use Tips:** There are several ways to keep nuts from coming off of bolts because of vibration, such as on machinery: the "double-nut" technique (two nuts per bolt); using a **locknut (below)**; using a **lock washer**, either the **split-ring** type or the **internal-tooth** type **(below)**; or using **anaerobic adhesive (Part IV, Chapter 32)**, a type of adhesive that comes in small plastic tubes, one drop of which hardens inside the threads.
>
> **Carriage (below)** and machine bolts come with *rolled* or *cut* threads, but the cut thread is better. Here the thread is cut directly into the steel shaft used for the bolt, while the rolled thread is added separately after the shaft is machined. The rolled-thread type uses less metal. In smaller sizes this may not matter, but in larger sizes the shank part of the bolt may match the drilled hole perfectly but the rolled or threaded part may not. The result is a sloppy fit.

Machine Screw

Description: Threaded along its entire length, it has a flat tip, a round or flat head, and is designed primarily to be screwed into prethreaded holes in metal, though of course it works with nuts too. Actually a type of bolt, but a bolt that is driven with a screwdriver instead of a wrench.

Machine Screw

Machine screw threads are of two sizes: coarse (24 per inch) and fine (32 per inch). When a screw is specified (such as in electrical work) as a 6-32 screw, what is meant is a 6 gauge diameter, or No. 6 size, with fine threads. The length should be given in inches after the size, as in 6-32 × $^3/_4$". **See the About section, above**, for more information.

 Buying Tip: Most **electrical boxes (Part IX, Chapter 71)** need 8-32 machine screws.

Stove Bolt

Description: Usually threaded its entire length, with a round or flat head that has a straight screw slot; driven with a screwdriver. The most often used sizes (diameters) are $^1/_8$", $^5/_{32}$", and $^3/_{16}$". Exactly the same item as a **machine screw (above)**, the difference being that stove bolts are supplied to the customer with nuts and intended for use with nuts, while the machine screw is intended for use in prethreaded holes in metal (shown with a square nut).

Use: Light assembly (such as basic kitchen appliances), because a screwdriver has less tightening power than a wrench.

Round Head Stove Bolt

supplied with nut

Flat Head Stove Bolt

Carriage Bolt

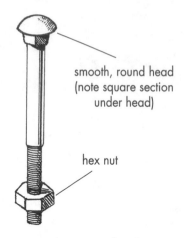

smooth, round head
(note square section
under head)

hex nut

Carriage Bolt

Also Known As: Carriage screw

Description: A large bolt, partially threaded, with a smooth, rounded head that has a square-sided portion just beneath it. That square part cuts into wood as the nut is tightened and resists the turning motion. A similar but smaller version is the *ribbed bolt*.

Use: Used in wood where particular strength is required, where you will not be able to reach the head with a wrench, or where you do not want a turnable head exposed (there is no slot in the oval head).

> **Use Tip:** Use washers under the nut on carriage bolts where the wood is very soft and you don't want the nut to dig in and cause damage, such as in outdoor redwood furniture.

Turnbuckle

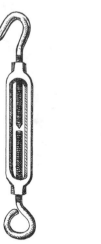

Hook-and-Eye Turnbuckle

Screen Door and
Gate Turnbuckle

Description: An open barrel-like metal device, internally threaded on both ends, with two threaded rods screwed in, one a left-handed thread, the other right-handed. The rods may have an eye at both ends, a hook on one end and an eye on the other, or hooks on each end, and are usually less than a foot long.

Use: Acts as an adjustable segment of a cable or wire. The various forms this comes in give one flexibility of use: for instance on one end a cable could be attached to a hook while on the other a snap fastener and rope. A common use for a turnbuckle is to brace a door. Another use is bracing a gate to remove a sag.

 Use Tips: The smaller sizes are zinc-plated, but the larger ones (all the way up to 2', in case you have any mountains to brace) are galvanized.

 Buying Tips: Turnbuckles can be obtained in kits, such as for straightening out a screen door.

U-bolts and J-bolts

Description: Threaded steel rod bent into either a U or J shape (rounded or squared off). Most useful U-bolt has a slotted bar across both ends that clamps down as the nuts are tightened. A very small version with a large cast-metal piece across the opening is used for clamping cable ends.

Use: Clamping odd shapes or hanging items. Often used in conjunction with *S-hooks* and *8-hooks* (figure 8-shaped steel pieces).

Buying Tip: Can be made from **threaded rod (below)** that you bend yourself.

Threaded Rod (Shown in Use)

Threaded Rod

Also Known As: All thread

Description: Metal rod threaded along its entire length. Commonly available in 2' and 3' lengths and in the following diameters: $3/16$", $1/4$", $5/16$", $3/8$", and $1/2$". Much larger sizes can also be obtained on special order. Think of it as an infinitely long bolt.

Rod may also be made of stainless steel, plain steel, electroplated, or zinc-coated; the latter is suitable for outdoor use.

Use: Used with nuts and washers for many different jobs: hanging, bracing, fastening, supporting, and mounting. Also useful where a bolt doesn't have sufficient threads to work. For example, a 6" bolt may have only $1^1/2$" of thread; a threaded rod will have sufficient threads.

> **Use Tips:** To avoid burrs when cutting rod (it may be cut with a hacksaw or bolt cutters), make the cut between two nuts, then turn the nuts off the cut ends to remove the burrs.

Eye Bolt

Hook Bolt

Square-Bend (L) Bolt

Hanger Bolt

Miscellaneous Bolts

Types:

Eye bolt

Hook bolt

Hanger bolt

Square-bend (L) bolt

Also Known As: *Hanger Bolt:* stud bolt hanger screw, handrail bolt, bolt hanger, table screw

Description:

Eye, hook, and *square-bend bolts:* These usually come galvanized or zinc-plated and resemble screw eyes or hooks, except the end is flat and it has bolt threads.

Hanger bolt: Has large screw threads on one end and bolt threads on the other, with a smooth portion between.

Use:

Eye, hook, and *square-bend bolts:* For hanging hooked items.

Hanger bolt: Commonly used to assemble commercial furniture. For do-it-yourselfers the hanger bolt is excellent for mounting in a joist or ceiling beam in order to hang fixtures.

 Buying Tips: The above bolts are available loose and are cheaper than packaged bolts.

Miscellaneous Nuts

Types:

Axle (or *axle cap) nut*

Cap nut

Fiber insert nut

Flat square nut

Cap Nut

Wing Nut

Hex nut

Locknut

Square nut

Wing nut

Also Known As: *Cap:* Acorn

Description:

Axle: Stamped, unthreaded cap.

Cap: Closed-end nut that resembles an acorn.

Fiber insert: Consists of a nut with a fiber insert.

Flat square: Thin, four-sided nut.

Hex: Standard five-sided nut.

Locknut: Thick hex nut with a plastic insert.

Square: Same thickness as a hex nut but with only four sides.

Wing: Two upward projecting wings flanking a threaded middle.

Use: All nuts screw onto bolts to tighten them against whatever is being fastened. Some have special applications though:

Axle: Caps the end of an axle to keep a wagon, baby carriage, or cart wheel on.

Cap: Decorative uses.

Fiber insert: This is self-locking and is used where much holding power is desired.

Locknut: Maintains tension even when vibrated repeatedly, such as on machinery.

Wing: Good for light use when something needs to be regularly disassembled by hand. Not intended for use with wrenches.

Nut and Bolt Washers

Split-Ring
Lock Washer

Types:

Flat washer

Split-ring lock washer

Internal tooth lock washer

External tooth lock washer

Internal Tooth
Lock Washer

Also Known As: *Split ring:* Lock washer, spring lock washer

Description: Small steel or aluminum donut-shaped pieces with holes that match the diameter of the bolt being fastened through them.

Flat: Flat circular shape. Smaller sizes provide a smooth surface for a nut or bolt head to be tightened against, while the larger ones are used with carriage bolts to prevent the nut from piercing the wood piece being attached.

Split ring: Spring action of slight spiral creates pressure that keeps a nut from loosening.

Internal tooth lock washer: Many small teeth pointing in toward hole that serve to keep nut from loosening.

External tooth lock washer: Many small teeth pointing outward that serve to keep nut from loosening. Can be used with wood screws.

Use: Provides a surface for a nut or bolt head to be tightened against, and in the case of lock washers, helps prevent the nut from loosening.

Bolt Extractor

Bolt Extractor

Also Known As: Easy Outs (brand name), screw and bolt extractor

Description: Fluted, tapered steel bar that resembles a nailset. Variety of diameters.

Use: Removing bolts or screws that cannot be turned out by normal means, such as when the threads have been completely stripped. It is driven into a hole made in the screw and then turned out; the threads, which are the reverse of the screw threads, bite into the screw and pull it out.

> **Use Tip:** As mentioned in the plumbing section **(Part VIII, Chapter 63)**, good for removing faucet seats when other means fail.

Taper Tap

Tap

Also Known As: Cut thread tap

Description: Short shaft of hardened steel with sharp, fluted threads and one squared-off end.

Types:

Taper tap

Plug tap

Bottoming tap

Tap Wrench (Stock Style)

Use: Cuts screw threads inside holes drilled in steel. The three types are sometimes numbered 1–3 and used in that order to create a properly shaped hole. Most common use would be repairing or making a new air-valve hole in a radiator.

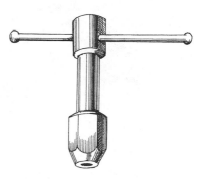

T-Handle Tap Wrench

 Use Tips: Use a T-handle tap wrench or a long tap stock handle rather than a regular wrench. Make sure everything is perfectly aligned. Back off $1/4$" turn for each full turn to break off cut material.

Die

Also Known As: Threading die

Description: Small round piece of hardened steel, resembling a cookie cutter, containing several half-holes and extremely sharp internal teeth. Held in a two-handed handle, called a *die stock,* with a circle in the center for holding dies.

Die

Use: Cutting threads on the outside of a metal rod.

Types:

Adjustable die

Solid die (most common)

Hexagonal die (can be used with a wrench instead of a handle)

Use Tip: Make sure everything is perfectly aligned.

Die Stock

Miscellaneous Fasteners, Braces, and Anchors

Cotter Pin

Description: Metal bent back upon itself, with slight open loop at the bend. Generally only about 2" long, but available in smaller and larger sizes.

Use: Generally used for holding metal rods or shafts. The cotter pin is put through a tight hole and has its tips bent to prevent it from sliding back out. The pin is removed by bending the tips straight again and pulling the ring on the other end with pliers or a hook.

Cotter Pin

> **Use Tip:** If you have to remove cotter pins repeatedly, get a small tool that looks like a hooked screwdriver, called a *cotter pin puller.*

Blind Rivet

Rivets and Other Small Fasteners

Types:

Blind rivets

Speedy rivets

Teenuts (or *T-nuts*)

Threaded inserts

Also Known As: *Blind rivets:* Pop® rivets, aluminum rivets

Description:

Blind rivet: A nail-like, two-piece item, usually made of aluminum, with a nose cap that is inserted in a drilled hole in the object to be riveted. A special **rivet gun (Part I, Chapter 14)** is then used to compress the rivet, fastening the parts together. Available in *grip range* sizes corresponding to the thickness of whatever is to be riveted.

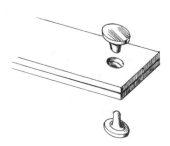

Speedy Rivet

Speedy rivet: Consists of a barbed section and threaded part. The two parts are hammered or clamped together with a special plier-like tool. Similar are *grommets,* which form a ringed hole.

Teenut fastener: Two-part fastener consisting of a threaded core and top with prongs (the "tee"). The core is inserted into a hole drilled into a piece of wood and then the top hammered in on top. A bolt screws into the core.

Threaded insert: Steel or brass cylinder with large threads on its outside and bolt threads on the inside.

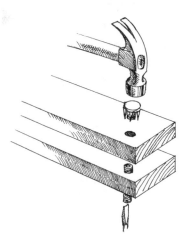

Teenut

Use:

Blind rivets: Fastening pieces of light metal, leather, or canvas on objects such as toys, bikes, and appliances as well as briefcases and suitcases when accessing from one side only.

Speedy rivets: Fastening soft materials such as canvas to canvas or canvas to leather.

Teenut fasteners: For joining wood members, such as two-by-fours.

Threaded inserts: When steel (machine) threads are required in wood, such as for furniture assembly.

Threaded Insert

Floor Squeak Eliminator

Description: Actually a system of a small metal jigs, often with three feet and a platform with a hole to guide screws in the center, and special screws. May be supplied with a special, long screwdriver bit for use with a power screwdriver. The screws are scored to break off at the surface of the floor.

Use: Eliminating floor squeaks by attaching the floor surface more securely to the subfloor, without leaving a screwhead showing.

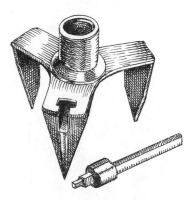

Floor Squeak Eliminator

Nylon Cable Tie

Also Known As: Nylon Tie

Description: Small piece of plastic strap 4" to 8" long, one end of which has a small fitting that the other end is pulled through. Available in self-locking and releasable versions. Disposable item. Sold by the bagful.

Nylon Tie

Use: Originally developed for binding cables together in electrical systems, can be applied to household tying tasks such as securing large plastic bags, coils of rope or hose, and so on.

Use Tips: CAUTION: Because these ties are easy to use and usually impossible to loosen, do not let unsupervised children play with them.

Inside Corner Brace

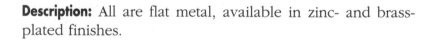

Braces and Plates

Also Known As: Door and window braces

Types:

> *Inside corner brace*
>
> *Flat corner brace* (or *iron*)
>
> *Mending plate*
>
> *T-plate*

Description: All are flat metal, available in zinc- and brass-plated finishes.

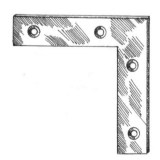

Flat Corner Brace

Inside corner brace: L-shaped piece with screw holes for mounting inside a corner. Comes in sizes 1" long and $\frac{1}{2}$" wide to 8" long and 1" wide. Screw holes are staggered rather than being in a straight line. Specialty sources sell a thicker version excellent for chairs.

Flat corner brace: L-shaped piece with screw holes for mounting on surface, at right angles to the **corner brace version (above)**. A thicker, embossed version is specially made for screens.

Mending Plate

Mending plate: Flat length of metal with screw holes.

T-plate: Flat metal piece made in the shape of the letter T; both horizontal and vertical legs of the T are the same length.

Use:

Corner brace: Strengthening and supporting box and chair corners.

Flat corner brace: Bracing corners on window frames and doors.

Mending plate: Joining two pieces of wood end-to-end. Many different applications, from reinforcing screen doors to furniture.

T-plate: Common use is for joining horizontal and vertical screen-door members.

Drop Leaf Brace

Description: Collapsible metal rod, attached to furniture parts at both ends, which snaps into place when extended.

Use: Supports table leaves or extra shelves.

 Use Tip: The shorter part is installed to go on top, or on the "leaf" side.

T-Plate

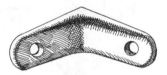

Chair Brace

Corner Brace for Screens

Drop Leaf Brace

Framing Fasteners

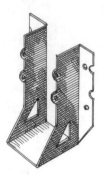

Joist Hanger

Examples:

> *Joist hangers*
>
> *Nailable truss plate*
>
> *Prong plate*
>
> *Reinforcing angles*

Also Known As: Framing, carpentry, or metal connectors, framing anchors, Tecos®, clips, structural wood fasteners, beam hangers, joist supports

Description: 16- or 18-gauge zinc-coated sheet metal in various forms with predrilled nail holes and, in some cases, metal prongs. Generally made to fit 2-by lumber, that is, 2×4's, 2×6's, etc.

Use: Conveniently connecting various framing members and assemblies, mostly at right angles. For example, there are framing fasteners to connect joists to beams, to secure roof beams, to mount posts, and much, much more. Also used as framing reinforcement in areas subject to hurricanes, tornadoes, and earthquakes. The nailable truss plate is used with special $1^1/_2$" truss nails supplied by the manufacturer.

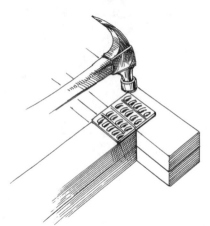

Nailing Plate

Angle Bracket

§ Buying Tips: *Hurricane anchors* are expensive and basically designed for framing that will withstand a lot of stress, such as in hurricane country. If severe weather isn't a problem in your area, then they likely aren't a good buy. However, they also enable framing to be assembled more quickly. You may count this as a plus and be willing to pay the extra money.

Framing fasteners can be bought singly, in small packages containing a few fasteners, and in bulk—25 to 50 pieces per carton. Buying in bulk can save you up to 50 percent over buying singly or in small packages.

About Wall Anchors

Wall anchors, or fasteners, are particularly useful on two kinds of wall construction—hollow wall (usually drywall), if there is no stud or solid material to simply drive a screw or nail into, and hardwall, where the wall material is too hard for screws to take hold in, such as plaster or masonry. Wall anchors come in a variety of sizes and types, and new designs and brand names appear often. Be sure to check all your sources for the best ones available in your area. Below are some of the most popular types, which fall into three categories: *light duty,* for any kind of wall; *masonry;* and *hollow-wall fasteners.*

Light-Duty Anchor

Light-Duty Anchor

Also Known As: Tubular anchor, plastic anchor, hollow anchor, plastic shield, plastic expansion anchor

Description: Plastic or jute fiber cone-shaped or cylindrical sheaths of various sizes corresponding to various-sized screws. They expand against the sides of the hole when the screw is driven into them. One version of this is made especially for use in particle board.

Use: Anchoring wood screws in plaster, drywall, or masonry. They are inserted into a predrilled hole. Not for extremely heavy objects.

> **Use Tips:** The hole must be just the right size—too big and the anchor won't hold, too small and it won't go in far enough to work.

Flat Wall Anchor

Flat Wall Anchor

Also Known As: Expanding anchor

Description: Flat, wide, nail-like item with a chisel point and a large, flat head with a hole in the middle. Made of hardened steel. Sold in various lengths (for different wall thicknesses) and styles for either hollow walls or concrete.

Use: Depending on the model, either anchoring light to medium-weight items in drywall, pegboard, wood paneling, and hollow-core doors, or concrete.

> **Use Tips:** The hollow-wall (drywall) model does not require any drilling and when removed, leaves only a small slit.

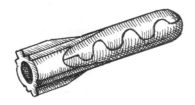

Universal Expansion Anchor

Universal Expansion Anchor

Description: Similar looking to the slightly conical plastic expansion anchor, this is made of a softer material and has two halves that mesh together with alligator-like teeth (most common brand name is Alligator® Anchor, by Toggler®). Sold in both a flange and no-flange version, in various dimensions and lengths ranging from $3/16$" to $5/16$" in diameter and about 1" to 2" in length.

Use: Heavy-duty mounting in any kind of material and with a wide range of screw sizes in the same anchor. Designed for use with a screw gun.

> **Use Tips:** Special, soft plastic conforms to the outside shape of the hole, and allows the screw to cut threads inside. Pre-installs without screw.

Buying Tip: Because of its universal applicability, a very cost-effective anchor.

Expansion Shield

Also Known As: Lead shield, shield

Description: The most common type consists of a thick, slotted metal sleeve usually made of lead. There is a one-piece design for use with wood screws and a two-piece design for use with lag bolts (most popular) and machine bolts. Another version, a *hammer drive pin,* is a nail-like device that is hammered in place. The shield expands slightly against the hole as the screw is driven into it.

Use: For anchoring items in masonry (brick, block, concrete).

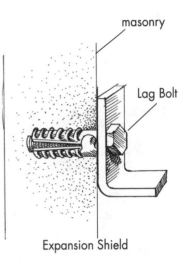

Expansion Shield

Use Tips: Bear in mind that these shields require very large holes to be drilled in masonry. You need a power drill and a **masonry (carbide-tipped) bit (Part II, Chapter 16)** to make such holes, and alignment is not always easy. An alternative may be to use simple **masonry nails (Chapter 20)** and furring strips (thin boards). If you are putting up a large job with furring strips, you may want to rent a **power hammer (Chapter 14)** powered by .22-caliber blanks for *powder-driven* or *power fasteners.*

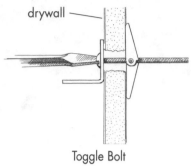

drywall

Toggle Bolt

Toggle Bolt with Decorative Head

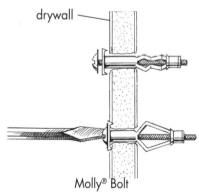

drywall

Molly® Bolt

Toggle Bolt

Also Known As: Toggles, spring-wing toggle, umbrella bolt

Description: A machine screw with collapsible "wings." One type has spring-loaded wings that squeeze together and open when released; the other type uses gravity. The wings push up against the back side of the drywall when the fastener is tightened. Available with decorative head, suitable for hanging mirrors.

Use: Hanging heavy items to hollow-wall construction (drywall), especially overhead.

 Use Tips: Note that the toggle will drop if the bolt is removed, and large holes are required.

Molly® Bolt

Also Known As: Mollies, collapsible anchors, expansion bolts, screw anchor, expansion anchor, hollow wall anchor

Description: Consists of a machine screw built into a sleeve with wings that expand out as they are tightened. A similar but smaller model is made for hollow-door anchoring, called *jack nuts.* Some brands have a plastic-tipped model that is hammered into drywall like a nail and then screwed tight.

Use: Fastening medium to heavy items to hollow-wall construction (drywall).

Use Tips: Drill a clean, solid hole so the anchor can be anchored tightly in it and not turn around as you turn the screw. The anchor will remain in place even if the screw is removed, making it slightly more convenient than a **toggle (above)**. A small wrench, a V-shaped wire device, is sometimes supplied to keep the sleeve from turning as you tighten the bolt.

Hinges, Hasps, and Latches

About Hinges

Hinges come in a tremendous array of styles and types, but there are some basics you can learn to help you make the best selection from the various models available.

Technically, hinges are "handed" —specified for use on left- or right-hand doors. But this can get complicated, and unless you're doing a special job you can forget it. Just flip the hinge over and it becomes left- or right-handed as needed.

Hinges come in different sizes to support different weights. But this, too, can get complicated. To select the proper size just determine if the hinge is in proportion, size-wise, to the door being hung and you'll be fine, even if you're undersized a bit—hinges are up to eight times stronger than they need to be.

Hinges also come in a variety of finishes, from plated brass to pure brass to paint. The variety available is virtually sure to give you the selection you require. They also are either surface-mounted or recessed ("mortised") on one or both sides. *Self-closing hinges* include spring-loaded hinges and *rising hinges* that are designed with an angular joint that uses gravity.

Because of the extreme range of models available, with minute variations in and combinations of style, prepare to ask for by

Butt Hinge

description, using a catalog or old hinge as a guide. Below is a small selection of common hinges.

Hinges

Types:

> *Butt hinge*
>
> *Loose pin hinge*
>
> *T-hinge*
>
> *Strap hinge*
>
> *Gate hinge*
>
> *Invisible hinge*
>
> *Piano hinge*
>
> *Double-acting hinge*

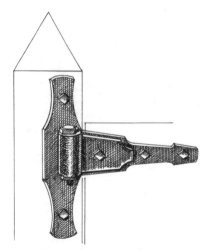

T-Hinge (Ornamental Style)

Also Known As:

> *Butt:* Utility hinge
>
> *Invisible:* Barrel hinge, Soss hinge (brand name), concealed hinge
>
> *Piano:* Continuous hinge
>
> *Double-acting:* Swing-clear hinge

Description:

Gate Hinge (Ornamental Style)

> *Butt:* Two rectangular leaves of metal with screw holes and a pin joining the leaves; to remove door, hinge must be unscrewed. Each pin hole is called a "knuckle."
>
> *Loose pin:* Similar to butt, but pin is removable for easy removal of door. Most common type.

> **Note:** Sometimes this removal distinction is not made obvious.

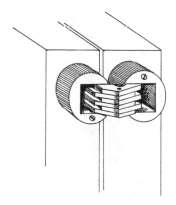

Invisible Hinge

T: Shaped like the letter T, with a vertical strap going on the doorframe and a horizontal strap in the door.

Strap: Center pin from which extend two narrow leaves.

Gate: L-shaped part that screws into a fence post and a leaf part with a knurled nut that fits over the L-shaped part and is screwed to the gate.

Invisible: Two barrel-shaped parts joined by a pin segment with both barrel-like parts recessed into the edges of the door and frame.

Piano: Two long leaves, each with many screw holes, joined by a pin.

Double-acting: Two sets of leaves and knuckles, somewhat loose-jointed, so that both leaves can be opened simultaneously.

Strap Hinge (Plain)

Strap Hinge (Ornamental Style)

Use:

Butt: Hanging regular exterior house doors. The nonremovability of the pin is a security feature.

Loose pin: The most common hinge for hanging interior doors.

T: Mostly used on gates and cabinet lids.

Strap: Gates and cabinet lids.

Gate: As the name suggests, on gates.

Invisible: Cabinet doors where you don't want the hinge to show.

Piano: Cabinet lids.

Double-acting: Folding doors that open two ways or fold flat.

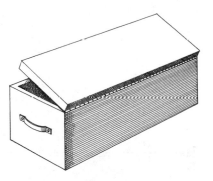

Piano Hinge

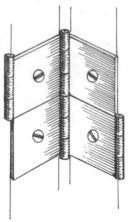

Double-Acting Hinge

Use Tips: *Butt:* These are mortised in door with a chisel; one leaf is recessed into door, one into the frame. Installation is easier using a flat template device called a *butt gauge, butt marking gage,* or *butt marker.* Also, should you want to take a door down, just remove the hinge pin, separating the leaves.

Invisible: These are very difficult to install since they must line up exactly opposite each other. There is no room for error.

Buying Tips: *T:* In addition to plain T-hinges, ornamental-looking T-hinges are available. Regular T-hinges come in plain and galvanized finishes.

Strap: Available in plain and galvanized as well as bronze finishes; the latter is ordinarily used on boats. They are available in large and small sizes. The length of the leaves makes them an unlikely selection for use on ordinary doors. They are also available in ornamental styles.

Gate: 5" and 6" sizes are commonly available, though other sizes can be obtained.

Invisible: These are very expensive.

Piano: Usually available in brass finish.

Hasps

Hasp (Safety Style)

Description: Hasps may be plain or decorative, with the length of the slotted part ranging from 2¼" to 6¼" with staples (the part with the ring for the lock) of proportionate sizes and hasp widths 1" to 2". Some models may have a key lock instead of a ring.

A *safety hasp* has a slotted part that conceals the screws securing the hasp when it is closed. Other safety hasps are heavy duty and have a square hole for insertion of a ⁵⁄₁₆" carriage bolt.

Another type of hasp is designed for use on chests and sliding doors. Here the end is upturned and also hides the mounting screws.

Decorative hasps are available with bright brass finishes.

Use: Securing doors, usually outdoor types, with a padlock that goes through the ring.

Latches

Barrel Bolt Latch

Description: Generally consists of a horizontal piece attached to the door that either slides, falls, or snaps into a catch on the door or gate post. Many different types and styles.

Basic Types:

Gate latch: Rod projects from gate and fits into catch on gate post.

Sliding, or *barrel, bolt:* Long bolt with handle projecting from middle slides in and out of curved piece on doorframe. Available in light weight for decorative purposes and in extreme heavy weight, also called a square

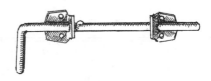

Cane Bolt

spring bolt, for security purposes, such as on the insides of exterior doors. Larger bolts come with a hole in the bolt so that it can be padlocked.

Cane bolt: L-shaped bolt that slides into two-holed mounting brackets. Installed vertically to use gravity action.

Use: Devices that keep gates and doors closed but not locked. They can also block gates open.

Cabinet and Furniture Hardware

About Cabinet Hardware

Hardware for cabinets consists of hinges, door catches, and knobs/pulls. Because so many of these items are made in decorative styles, the array of models and quality are vast.

> **Note:** See **Chapter 24** for larger items in this category.

Catches

Types:

> *Friction*
>
> *Magnetic*
>
> *Roller*

Description:

Friction: Consists of a male and female part that work by spring tension similar to roller type. Another version, used to prevent little children from opening cabinets, has a long plastic lever called a *safety catch*.

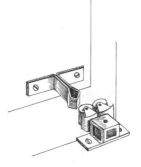

Roller Catch

Magnetic Catch

Magnetic: Part on frame is magnetic; plain metal part of this catch mounts on door.

Roller: One or two rollers set close together, mounted on the cabinet frame, that interlock with projecting part on door, similar to friction type.

Use: Keep cabinet doors shut.

> **Use Tips:** Catches are for lightweight doors only. The magnetic catch is best because it will work in situations where others won't, such as when the door warps and only part of the magnet section is contacted.

The friction catch is good when you don't want any hardware to show. This will be invisible on a **lipped door (see below)**.

About Cabinet Hinges

Cabinet hinges are made for three kinds of doors: lipped, overlay, and flush. The lipped door has a recess cut around the edge. The overlay overlaps the frame opening. The flush door's face fits flush with the face of the framework.

Hinges come in many different styles, sizes, thicknesses, and finishes. Chrome is popular, but there is also plated brass and pure brass as well as antiqued copper and black. Most hinges come carded; the card is used as a template for drilling screw holes.

On a replacement it is best to take the old hinge into the store to ensure getting the correct size. Knobs and pulls are also available in matching styles.

Cabinet Hinges

Types:

Pivot hinge

Self-closing hinge

Butterfly hinge

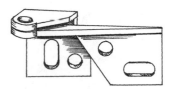

Pivot Hinge

Also Known As: *Self-closing:* S/C hinge

Description:

Pivot: One hinge is mounted on top of the door and one on the bottom, with portions of each hinge bent over and screw-mounted to frame and door. The hinge is concealed.

Self-closing: Has a spring inside and operates with just a nudge.

Butterfly: When open resembles a butterfly.

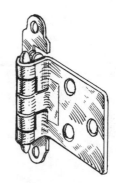

Self-Closing Hinge

Use:

Pivot hinges: Designed for use on the overlay door.

Self-closing: May be used on any door.

Butterfly: For use on flush doors only. Many people also like to use them on chest lids, where they add a decorative touch.

Butterfly Hinge

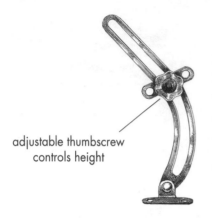

adjustable thumbscrew
controls height

Lid Support

Lid Support

Description: Long, narrow, slotted arm with small hinge on base plate and a sliding screw or thumbscrew on a flange that forms the opposing base plate. Available in a range of sizes around 5" to $6\frac{1}{2}$" long and $\frac{1}{2}$" to $\frac{3}{4}$" wide, sold in left-handed or right-handed versions. Brass or brass-plated steel.

Use: Locking cabinet or chest lids open at infinite positions. Used in conjunction with a regular hinge.

Knobs and Pulls

Description: Knobs and pulls come in a wide variety of styles and finishes. Pulls are handles mounted to doors or drawers with screws or bolts. Knobs may be mounted this way or have a screw built in, sort of like a screw with a knob for a head.

Use: Grasped to open and close cabinet doors.

Use Tips: Small knobs that have screws built in are easier to install than larger ones that require separate screws.

Chest Handles

Description: A metal plate for mounting and a handle, or "bail," for pulling. One type has no screw holes but is designed to be welded or riveted to a chest. Another type is a *trapdoor (hatch cover) ring,* in which the bail, or ring, is smaller and lies in a recess flush with the surface.

For a narrow box, chest handles may be obtained with narrow plates and larger bails. One manufacturer shows a chest handle with a plate $3^{7}/_{16}$" long but less than $1^{1}/_{2}$" wide.

Use: Handles for opening chests, cabinets, and trapdoors. Used for hatch covers on boats.

Chest Handle

> **Use Tips:** If you are installing a trapdoor type in a floor, make sure the whole thing is well recessed so no one trips over it.

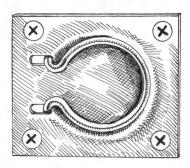
Trapdoor Ring

Flat Hook-and-Eye

Description: Similar to the hardware item of the same name mentioned above **(Chapter 21)**; a two-piece item that is flat, instead of round, and made of decorative material such as brass. The eye is the part that the hook goes into.

Use: Often used to secure cabinet and chest lids, shutters, and the like, wherever light fastening is all that's required.

Flat Hook-and-Eye

> **Use Tip:** The hook can be hooked over a plain screw or nail instead of going into an eye if precision fitting is difficult.

About Casters

Casters come in a variety of styles and for a variety of purposes. They are available to support heavy or lightweight items and the wheels may be hard plastic, rubber, or metal for particular kinds of flooring. For example, hard rubber works best on concrete floors, soft rubber on resilient flooring, and plastic best on carpet. They are available for mounting on hollow as well as solid legs and may turn 360 degrees or lock in place.

Casters come in a variety of finishes from plain to polished metal. They are characterized by wheel size: a 2" caster has wheels 2" in diameter. Other parts of the caster will be sized proportionately, and the larger the wheel, the easier it is to roll.

Stem Caster

Stem Caster

Description: Has a stem mounted above the wheel for insertion in a hollow leg.

Use: For use on any hollow-legged item.

> **Use Tips:** To remove old sockets you can drive a 10-penny nail into the socket until it catches under the top, then pull out with pliers.

Plate Caster

Plate Caster

Description: Flat plate on top with screw holes for mounting.

Use: Use on any items that have solid wood legs that can accept screws.

> ✂ **Use Tips:** First drill pilot holes for screws. Before buying a caster make sure the leg is big enough to accept it. If wood is thin, bolts work better.

Ball-Bearing Caster

Description: Plate-type caster with ball bearing instead of a wheel.

Use: Good where headroom is scarce. A ball-bearing caster only adds $1/2$" in height to the piece it's on rather than the 2" on a standard caster.

Ball-Bearing Caster

Ball-type Caster

Also Known As: Shepard (most common brand name)

Description: Ball-like metal wheels come in both plate and stem types. Usually shiny, decorative metal (chrome, brass).

Use: Usually used on furniture where there is carpeting or resilient-type flooring.

Ball-type Caster

Furniture Glides

Description: Wide range of smooth-surfaced metal and plastic designs that attach to the ends of furniture legs either by a built-in nail or screw.

Use: Allows furniture to be pushed over a floor easily.

Furniture Glide

Leg Tips and Carpet Savers

Description: Little cup-shaped plastic or rubber devices that either slide over the ends of furniture legs (leg tips) or sit on the carpet or floor underneath a caster or leg (carpet savers).

Use: Protecting wooden floors or carpets from damage by furniture legs.

Appliance Rollers

Description: Two long, flat devices with about a dozen small plastic wheels linked by an adjustable metal bar. Sold in pairs.

Use: Goes underneath a refrigerator or washing machine to make for easy removal from a recessed space and to prevent scratching floor.

 Buying Tip: Difficult to find. Used-appliance stores may help if your hardware store does not stock this item.

Drawer Hardware

Types:

Drawer track

Drawer slides

Drawer rollers

Description: Various types of guides mount either in the center or on the sides of drawers; those on the sides may be either on the bottom, middle, or top edge.

> *Track:* Metal sections mounted on the sides of drawers that interlock with sections mounted inside the drawer cabinet.

> *Slides:* Plastic sections or rollers mounted on drawers or inside cabinets.

> *Rollers:* Small rollers mounted on drawers or inside cabinets.

Use: Allows drawers to slide freely in and out.

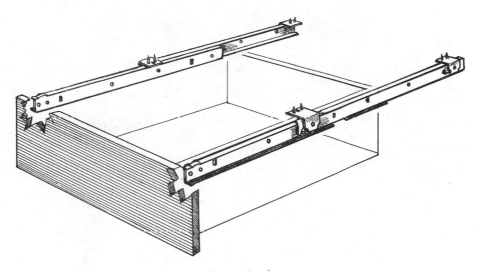

Drawer Track

Door and Window Hardware

About Door Locksets

Doorknobs and locksets, called *locks* here, are either interior or exterior. The exterior type is usually built more ruggedly for security purposes and more care is devoted to their style and finish. Following are some helpful pointers:

There is a tremendous variety of locks, which actually consist of doorknob, lock mechanism which fits into the door, escutcheon or rose (the decorative plate that fits against door), strike plate (plate that goes over the latch hole in the door jamb), and knob.

Locks are sized to fit into holes of a certain size and "backset" — a certain distance from the edge of the door, i.e., measuring from the door edge to midpoint of the knob or handle. Most locks have a $2^3/_8$" backset and are installed in a $2^1/_8$" hole; some are installed in a $1^3/_4$" hole. If the hole is backset $2^3/_8$" but is only $1^3/_4$", it can be enlarged by filling the hole and redrilling. Some locks come with a drill bit for the exact size hole needed.

Some locksets have a backset of 5". Here the bolt on the lockset wouldn't be long enough normally. A link mechanism that goes between the bolt and lock may be used to compensate.

Pin tumbler locks offer the greatest security; five tumblers are better than three.

Locksmiths can rekey your locks so one key will open all locks in a house.

Lock styles and finishes vary greatly and buying a stylish lock does not necessarily mean you'll get quality. You're more likely to get quality by buying a more costly, basic, brass-plated lock.

Heft and examine a number of different locks. Quality will soon become evident. Avoid locks made of lightweight pot metal. Following is a lineup of common interior and exterior locks.

Passage Lock
No locks on either side

Interior Doorknobs and Locksets

Also Known As: Tubular locks, tubular spring-latch locks, non-keyed locks

Types:

> *Passage lock*
>
> *Privacy lock*
>
> *Bathroom lock*

Privacy Lock
Push button lock, one side only

Description: Two doorknobs that may have lock buttons in one or both knobs, but no keys, as follows:

> *Passage:* No locking mechanism of any kind, just a latch.
>
> *Closet locks*: like passage locks but may have smaller knobs or only a turnbutton on the inside.
>
> *Privacy:* Has lock button on the inside knob only, which unlocks automatically when the knob is turned from the inside.
>
> *Bathroom:* Like a privacy lock but chrome-plated to blend with bath fittings and fixtures.

Knobs are available that are only for decoration and have no latch mechanism, called *dumb trim*. Many special use–type knobs are available, such as for hospital rooms and patios.

Use: Passage locks are used on bedroom and hall doors where privacy is not absolutely required. Privacy and bathroom locks are used on rooms where locking is required or desired.

> **Use Tips:** Privacy locks have a small slot or hole in the center of the outside doorknob that allows the door to be unlocked with a narrow screwdriver in case of an emergency.

Entry Locksets

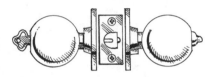

Entry Lockset
key on outside
turn button on inside

Also Known As: Entrance-door locks, exterior cylinder locks, entry locks, tubular spring-latch locks, keyed locks

Description: Two doorknobs that can be locked and unlocked from both sides. Models vary with a keyway or turn button in one or both knobs. Below are four basic types, though there are many specialized types.

1. Lock can be opened and closed from inside while outside stays locked ("all-purpose" or "communication").

2. Lock opened on the inside also unlocks the outside.

3. Unlocked on both sides by twisting a turn button inside ("dormitory" or "motel").

4. Locked with a key on both the inside and outside ("institutional").

Less common variations include models like the *vestibule lock,* which is always open from the inside and locked from the outside, and the *classroom lock,* which is always open on the inside but lockable with a key on the outside. Others include the *service station* and *storeroom* models, each with different locking combinations.

Use: As medium-security entrance-door locks.

Use Tips: Type (1) lock is usually the culprit when people lock themselves out of their homes. On the type (2) lock a drawback is that you can't try the door to see if it is unlocked without unlocking it. The type (4) lock is often used on doors with glass sections because even if a thief breaks the glass he won't be able to open the interior knob without a key. But caution: this type of lock can be hazardous in case you have to get out fast, such as in a fire, and can't find the key. It is recommended to not lock this kind when you are inside the house; the door should have a second, more easily released lock, or else the key should be kept in the lock when you are inside.

All types of locks come with different striking, or latch, mechanisms. Some allow the latch to be depressed when the door is locked, a poor security factor (a credit card can easily be used to open this lock). Better are locks that have a small rod, sometimes called a dead latch (actually a mini-deadbolt), adjacent to the latch that will prevent this.

Buying Tip: Models with just the cylinder lock itself, and no doorknobs, are also available. Keyways and cylinders are all replaceable if you have to change keys for any reason.

Deadbolt Lock

Also Known As: Deadlock

Description: A squarish lock that is mounted on the surface of the door if the lock is the older type (rim lock), or a recessed round one if of modern construction. The essence of a deadbolt lock is that the bolt, once in the strike (the part on the jamb), cannot be released without turning it with a key or turn knob—there is no spring action allowing it to be pushed or pried out of the strike. It is one solid piece of steel.

Deadbolts of both types have horizontal bolts, and the surface type can have a vertical "throw." They also come either as a single or double cylinder, meaning that they either require a key only from the outside (using a turn knob inside) or else require a key from both sides. These cylinders are easily replaceable if you need to change keys.

Use: Security locks on entrance doors. Generally backs up the cylinder lockset as an auxiliary lock. The door or the jamb would have to be pried way out in order to break through.

> **Use Tips:** Never put a lock that can only be opened from the inside by key on a sole interior exit—or else keep a key in the lock.

> **Buying Tips:** Deadbolts that are constructed of cast steel are easiest for a thief to drill through, a favorite method of entry. Deadlocks with an interior core of hardened steel are better.

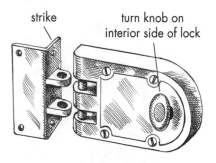

Angle Strike Surface-Mounted Vertical Deadbolt Lock

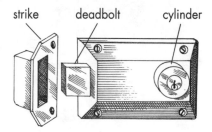

Horizontal Strike Surface-Mounted Deadbolt Lock

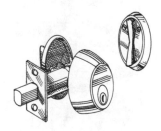

Recessed Deadbolt Lock with turnknob on inside

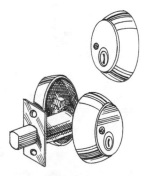

Recessed Deadbolt Lock with two keyways

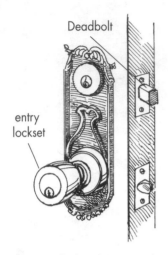

Deadbolt

entry
lockset

Deadbolt with Entry Lockset

A thief could conceivably drill out the cylinder on any deadbolt, then use a screwdriver to turn the bolt out. For this there is the *jimmy-proof deadbolt*. The cylinder may be drilled but then a spring-actuated plate will stop further penetration.

Horizontal deadlock bolts come with various "throws," the distance the bolt protrudes from the lock. Sizes are commonly 1/4", 1/2", and 1". Theoretically, the more the bolt protrudes, the greater the security, but this is questionable on a wooden door where a well-placed kick could bring the door itself down. On a steel door it would be an entirely different story. In other words, the lock is only as good as the doorframe is solid. Look for heavy steel and brass, and sturdy screws.

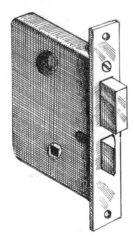

Mortise Lock

Mortise Lock

Description: Combines features of various other locks—the spring latch and the deadbolt. Consists of a flat, rectangular box, which fits into a recess in the door from the edge, and two faceplates (one for each side) containing the knobs, turn knob, and keyholes. Usually contains a deadbolt and a regular strike latch as well as two locking buttons on the side that control the locking settings. Comes left- or right-handed.

Use: Standard house entrance-door lock.

Night Latch

Also Known As: Night lock, slam lock

Description: Mounts on inside surface of door. Large, spring-loaded latch locks automatically when the door is closed.

Use: Light security, typically in addition to another lock such as a mortise or cylinder entrance lock.

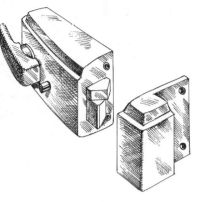

Night Latch

Storm- and Screen-Door Hardware

Main Parts:

> *Lock mechanism*
>
> *Door closer*
>
> *Retainer*

Also Known As:

> *Door closer:* Pneumatic cylinder

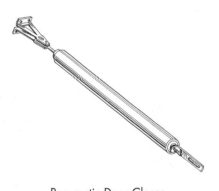

Pneumatic Door Closer

Description:

> *Lock mechanism:* Consists of small regular knob outside, mounting plates and turn handle inside. May have locking feature from outside.
>
> *Closer:* Usually a bicycle-pump type consisting of a pneumatic cylinder and plates with screw holes for mounting to door and doorframe. There is usually also an extension spring, sometimes called a *snubber,* which attaches between doorframe and door.
>
> *Retainer:* Wire chain and spring with mounting brackets.

Use:

Lock mechanism: Open, close, and lock storm door.

Door closer: Regulates speed at which door closes. The door should close quickly enough but not slam and be unable to latch. The spring keeps the door from being pulled open too far.

Retainer: Prevents damage of door closer, or, in the absence of a door closer, keeps the door from being ripped off its hinges.

> **Use Tips:** Some lock mechanisms come with a flip lever that allows you to lock the door from inside. Locks that operate with keys are also available.

> **Buying Tips:** Storm-door hardware is like window hardware—there are many variations and screw holes on replacement parts must align with the old screw holes. If you have a problem with your storm door, such as the wind always catching it, make sure that the closer used is the right size—they vary according to size and weight of door.

Sliding-Door Hardware

Description: Consists of a top metal track, wheels that attach to the door, and bottom guides (sometimes a track) that attach to the floor. Exterior, or patio, doors are similar but heavier duty. Two doors that slide past each other are *bypass doors;* doors that slide into the wall are *pocket doors.*

Use: To enable a pair of sliding doors to work.

> **Use Tips:** When part of a sliding door doesn't work properly often all that is needed is a slight hardware adjustment. Some tracks are delicate and may be bent out of shape easily.

> **Buying Tips:** Hardware for sliding doors normally comes in kits containing all parts so that when one part goes bad—say a wheel becomes misshapen—you will probably have to buy all parts. Size is by track thickness. Exterior (patio) types tend to require the original-brand replacement parts.

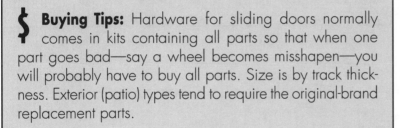

Sliding Door Hardware

Bifold-Door Hardware

Description: Six or seven different pieces of hardware, including hinges, track, top and bottom pivot, snubber, knob, and bottom jamb bracket.

Use: For mounting and using either two- or four-set bifold doors. There is a pivot on the floor that mates with a corresponding socket on the door, or the reverse—socket on the floor, pivot on the door. Four-door set also includes a bracket to align the doors at the bottom when closed.

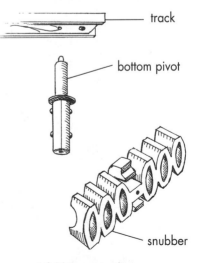

Bifold-Door Hardware

> **Use Tips:** Both top and bottom pivots can be adjusted back and forth to align the doors and there is a guide at top to make the outside door follow in the track. On a four-door set you can use two or four handles. One pair of handles should be mounted closest to the jambs. Mount the other pair of handles where the doors meet.

> **Buying Tips:** Hardware for bifold doors, like sliding doors, comes in kit form; handles are not included. Some sets include adjusting screws for raising or lowering the doors.
>
> Hinges (supplied) are usually brass-plated and may be mortised (recessed) into the door or the butt type. Get the butt type if the doors will be used frequently. Hardware for a four-panel set will be packaged as two assemblies.

Miscellaneous Door Hardware

Types:

> *Doorstop*
>
> *Peephole*

Also Known As: *Peephole:* Door viewer, viewing eye, safety door viewer

Description:

> *Doorstop:* Metal rod or spring with rubber point that mounts on the wall or floor.

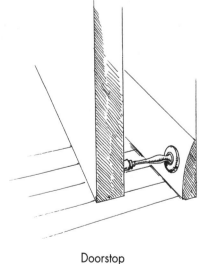

Doorstop

Peephole: Cylinder with internal viewing lens that goes in the center of the door.

Peephole

Uses:

Doorstop: Keeps doors from banging into wall when opened.

Peephole: Lets home occupants view visitors without opening the door.

Window-Opening Hardware

Typical Parts:

Casement operator for roto handle (opens window)

Casement locking handle (locks window shut)

Casement keeper (handle, above, latches onto keeper)

Double-hung tape balance (rides in track to keep window open at desired position)

Double-hung sash lock (locking mechanism)

Description: There are thousands of different window parts but they can be grouped into hardware for either wood or metal casement windows and hardware for double-hung windows.

Locking handle

Roto handle

Casement Window

 Buying Tips: Since parts vary so much, it is essential to take the old part to the store when getting a replacement.

Glazier's Point

Turn Button

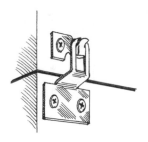

Screen- and Storm-Sash Hanger

Miscellaneous Window Hardware

Types:

Glazier's points, or *push points*

Turn button

Sash lift

Sash (window) handle

Screen- and storm-sash hangers

Storm-sash adjuster

Shutter dog

Also Known As:

Hanger: Hinge hook

Shutter dog: Shutter turnbuckle

Description:

Glazier's points: Tiny flat metal triangles or odd-shaped, pointed pieces with small flaps.

Turn button: Small galvanized or zinc-plated bow-shaped device with a raised turning edge.

Sash lift: Small metal plate with protruding lip.

Sash handle: Small pull handle.

Screen- and storm-sash hangers: Small two-part hanger consists of a hook that goes on the frame and a mating part on the storm window or screen.

Screen- and storm-sash adjuster: A folding leg, one end of which is attached to the window frame, the other to the storm sash.

Shutter dog: Bow-shaped flat metal piece on a center pivot.

Use:

Glazier's points: Pushed into wood window frame to hold glass plate in place prior to applying glazing putty.

Turn button: Retains screen or storm window.

Sash lift: Provides a small fingergrip for raising a window.

Sash handle: Provides handgrip for raising a window.

Storm-sash adjuster: For opening a storm sash to a certain point.

Screen- and storm-sash hangers: For hanging screens or storm windows.

Shutter dog: Holds exterior shutters open.

Drapery Hardware

Types:

Fixed drapery rod

Traverse drapery rod

Fixed Drapery Rod

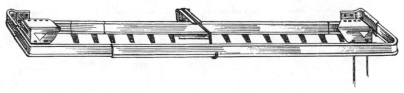

Traverse Drapery Rod

Description:

Fixed rods are hollow metal tubes that are either exposed (in full view) or concealed and come 48" and 60" long. They are also available spring-actuated to fit virtually any dimension.

Traverse rods are similar but come with an opening and closing mechanism controlled by hanging cords.

Use: Hanging drapery and enabling it to be opened and closed.

 Use Tips: Accessories for either fixed rods or traverse rods must be matched but are readily available. Fixed rods require hanging rings as they have no mechanism for moving drapes. These must be slightly bigger in diameter than the rod. For traverse rods hooks are used and the hooks must be sized to hook onto eyelets, or hangers, that move along the traverse rod. Hooks come in three basic patterns: *slip-on* (hook goes into an eyelet on the traverse rod or over a plain rod, and a double-ended long piece slides under the heading of the drape); *pin-on* (large hook goes over a rod, and a sharp pin pierces the drapery heading); and *pleater hook* (large hook goes over a rod or into an eyelet, and three or four round-tipped prongs or shanks form pleats when inserted into the drapery heading).

Buying Tip: Fixed rods and traverse rods come in kits complete with fasteners and instructions for installing them.

Curtain Hardware

Description: Commonly lightweight, C-shaped metal channels that may expand, or *telescope,* to fit a window. Not decorative per se. Another version is the *spring-tension rod,* which expands to fit within a window casing and requires no mounting—it is held in place by its own tension. And of course there are just plain metal rods, such as *cafe rods,* which are held by supports designed to go with each type of rod and are generally more decorative than the above two types. Similar to **fixed rod (above)**.

Use: Supports curtains or draperies in a fixed position or allows only limited movement.

 Buying Tip: Additional supports are needed for large expanses, such as over 48".

Spring-Tension Curtain Rod

Springs

About Springs

There are literally hundreds of kinds of springs available, but for around-home use three kinds are common: extension, compression, and torsion. Most springs are zinc-plated so they can be used outdoors. Some are painted black enamel, and these are for indoor use only. Chrome-plated springs are also available but are not common.

Springs differ in terms of gauge of wire used and number of coils. On extension springs the heavier the gauge and the more coils, the greater the springs will expand. The quickest way to get the same size replacement spring is to take the one you are replacing to the store for a match. Dealers have boards on which are mounted many different springs and you can match up what you have to what's on the board.

Springs come loose and carded; carded is more costly. Spring assortments can also be bought, but before buying determine that you'll use them—many could go unused in the average household.

Extension Spring

Extension Spring

Description: Wire in a coil shape with ends that have closed loops, hooks, or a variation.

Use: Those with long hooks are useful for getting into tight places, such as attaching a spring to an oven door—the long hook enables you to attach it more easily. Another extension spring useful on a screen door is one with a threaded eyebolt, which you can turn to make the door open and close with more or less tension. Since extension springs come with hooked and closed ends, flexibility of use is ensured—you can either hook the spring onto the item or vice versa.

Compression Spring

Compression Spring

Description: Wire in a coil but, unlike the extension spring, it does not have hooks or loops at the ends; ends are either plain or cut off.

Use: Used where you want to push parts together such as on wheels, shafts, and toys. Mostly a replacement spring. Compression springs with squared-off ends are useful where you need a spring that lies flat between two parts of a machine or toy.

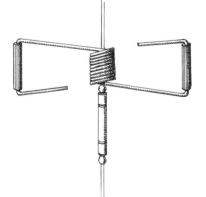

Torsion Spring

Torsion Spring

Description: Two-armed spring with the arms extended out, wing-like, several inches.

Use: Used only occasionally. It is slipped over the top of a hinge pin to give a door a spring-closing action. A similar type is a *door-closer, coil door spring,* or *gate spring,* which goes diagonally over the gap between the hinged side of a door and the wall and is attached with clamps or plates at both ends.

Chain and Cable

About Chain

Chain comes in around forty different varieties, but most of your needs will be filled by the small selection commonly available in stores, as described here. Sections are usually cut from reels to your order, though some decorative chain comes packaged. Size denominations vary from type to type, so study the label on the reel or package for important technical information.

Chain may be put into two groups: chain whose primary purpose is strength and chain whose main purpose is decoration. Whatever type you buy, however, check to make sure it's strong enough for the job at hand. All chain is classified and marked according to its *working load limit,* meaning what kind of stress may be applied before the chain snaps. Most are specifically marked "not for overhead lifting."

Load limits vary according to the thickness of the chain and the metal it's made of. So, for example, #10 (1" long links) brass jack chain, which is decorative, has a working load limit of 34 pounds. Grade 30-proof coil chain, however, in about the same size but made of steel, has a load limit of 800 pounds. And a cam-alloy version has a limit of 5,100 pounds in the same size. Check the label of the chain container or the manufacturer's catalog for the chain's working load limit.

> **General Use Tips:** Links of most lighter chain can be pried apart with fingers or pliers. Use pliers to crimp the links shut.

In addition to the specific chains detailed below, which are mainly available from reels, there are packaged chains designed for specific purposes such as dog runners, hanging porch swings, and various vehicular jobs. Chain also comes in pails, boxes, drums, and bags.

For safety, you should observe the following:

- Follow load limits on a chain—don't overload it. Dealers can supply load limits from charts they have. However, it is okay to load it right up to its limit.

- Don't use a chain for overhead lifting unless it is specified for that use.

- Don't apply tension if a chain is twisted.

- Pull a chain gradually from an at-rest position—don't jerk it.

- Don't use a chain that looks damaged.

Bead Chain

Bead Chain

Description: Hollow, round metal beads joined by dumbbell-shaped connectors. Beads may also be elliptically shaped. Comes in chrome-, brass-, and nickel-plated finishes.

Use: Used for decorative purposes around the home and as lamp pulls.

> **$ Buying Tips:** The main advantage of bead chain is that it will not kink or tangle. You can twist it every which way and it will fall out straight.

> **$ Buying Tips:** At local stores you are likely to get only a couple of sizes of bead chain, plus packaged chain for lamp pulls. Hardware stores carry catalogs that list manufacturers from whom you can get a much wider selection. You can buy connectors separately, such as when you want to lengthen a bead chain.

Decorative Chain

Also Known As: Decor chain

Description: Lightweight chain available in a variety of handsome finishes, including brass and colors—antique white, antique copper, and black. Loops are generally large ovals of wire.

Use: Hanging lamps, plants, and for hanging on draperies and other decorative effects.

Decorative Chain

Double-Loop Chain

Also Known As: Weldless, Inco (brand name), Tenso (brand name), Bowtie

Description: Lightweight steel links that are knotted into long double loops for linkage instead of being welded. Sizes run from No. 5 (smallest) though 0 to 8/0 (largest). A *single-loop,* or *lock link* version is available, primarily for use in machinery.

Use: Household jobs from decoration to shelf supports. Among the strongest of the decorative chains. Heavier sizes—over 1/0—can be used to hang hammocks and playground equipment.

Proof Coil Chain

Description: Strongest steel chain of welded, slightly oblong links. Comes in galvanized, plain steel, and zinc finishes. Comes in four grades: Grade 30 (most common), 40, 70 ("high test"), and 80 (made of alloy steel, with the highest load limits—up to 80,000 pounds). The $5/16"$ size Grade 30 has a working load limit of 1,900 pounds. The fractional sizes refer to the diameter of the steel.

Use: Very heavy pulling jobs where motorized equipment is involved, such as in agriculture or for towing cars.

Jack Chain

Jack Chain

Description: A strong decorative chain of varying load limits made of twisted figure-eight links. Comes in hot-galvanized, brass-plated, bright zinc, and solid brass, and in single and double versions.

Uses: Often used for functions where decoration and light support are needed, such as for hanging large plants, signs, and children's toys.

Welded General Use Chain

Straight-Link Machine Chain

Types:

Coil chain

Machine chain

Passing link chain

Description: Similar to but not as strong as **proof coil chain (above).** Material is less than $1/4$" thick. Sizes are measured in gauges, from No. 4 (smallest—inside of links about half an inch long) through 3, 2, 1, and on to 1/0 to 5/0 (largest—inside of links about an inch long).

Coil: Longest link of these three. Available in straight-link and twist-link styles.

Machine: Slightly shorter links. Also available in straight-link and twist-link styles.

Passing link: Slightly rounded links which prevent binding and kinking.

Use: Wherever a strong chain is needed. Commonly used on agricultural implements, tailgates, overhead doors, security purposes, general utility.

Safety Chain

Safety Chain

Also Known As: Plumber's chain

Description: Flat, stamped brass chain of oval links that resist entanglement.

Use: Used by plumbers in toilet tanks (as link between flush rod and ball valve) and as a general utility chain. It is available in bright zinc and solid brass and may also be used for decorative purposes.

Sash Chain

Sash Chain

Also Known As: Weldless flat chain

Description: Flat, teardrop-shaped stamped links that appear folded over one another.

Use: Good replacement material for sash cords on double-hung windows as it rides over window pulleys easily, and for tub and basin stoppers. Often used to hold small animals.

> **$ Buying Tips:** Sash chain comes in plain metal and bronze, but if you live in an area where sea air is present, sash chain is inadvisable—it can rust out.

Plastic Chain

Description: Available in colors, usually red and yellow, and in light as well as heavy chain shapes.

Use: Decorative jobs such as hanging light fixtures, and drape accessories.

About Chain Accessories

Generally, accessories for chain are either designed to connect chain sections permanently or temporarily. There are a couple of other useful attachment/accessory pieces that stand alone.

Temporary Chain Connectors

S-Hook

Types:

S-hook

Clevis slip hook

Clevis grab hook

Lap link

Quick link

Also Known As: *Lap Link:* Repair link

Clevis Slip Hook

Description:

S-hook: Open-ended metal link shaped like the letter S.

Clevis slip hook: Looks like a hefty fishhook.

Clevis grab hook: Shaped like a clevis slip hook but is narrower.

Clevis Grab Hook

Lap link: Partially open link that looks like it has almost been cut in half sidewise.

Quick link: Link with a gap on one side that has a nut on one end and threads on the other.

Lap Link

Use:

S-hook: Connecting chain sections; they are crimped shut with pliers after being hooked onto the sections, but they are not designed for anything that requires a high degree of safety, such as swings and other play equipment.

Clevis slip hook: Looping chain around different-sized items, such as tree stumps, and pulling them out; in effect it allows you to make a chain lasso. The clevis (pin) end of the slip hook is secured to the end of the chain while the chain is slipped through the hook to form the lasso loop.

Clevis grab hook: Works like a clevis slip hook but its narrowness allows it to lock onto one link.

Lap link: Can be used wherever life or limb does not depend on link's integrity to link two sections of any chain together.

Quick link: Similar to lap, a fast but not the strongest solution to linking.

> **Use Tips:** S-hooks come in various strengths, and for safety the hook should be the same strength as the chain links it's being used on.

Permanent Chain Connectors

Types:

Connecting link

Cold shut

Description:

Connecting link: These look like individual links cut in half sidewise, with one half of the link containing rivet projections and the other holes to accept rivets.

Cold shut: Open-ended link device designed to be hammered shut.

Connecting Link

Miscellaneous Chain Accessories

Types:

Ring

Snap

Description:

Ring: Heavy welded rings of steel.

Snap: Small metal device with spring-loaded locking device available in a variety of models, combining four features:

Swivelling or fixed *(solid)*

Eyes: round or rectangular *(strap)*

Cold Shut

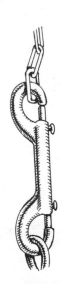

Double-Ended Bolt Snap

Snap Types: large latch *(cap);* sliding bolt; flat strap *(spring);* lever on outside of a ring *(trigger);* or solid half-circle catch *(animal tie);* and other special ones for boats, horse harnesses, and dog leashes.

Snaps on one or both ends *(double-ended)*

Uses:

Ring: A variety of chain linking jobs with other connectors or snaps.

Snap: A variety of temporary connecting jobs, such as a gate closer.

 Use Tip: Most of these accessories can be used with rope as well.

Cable

Description: Multiple small strands of wire woven together to form a strong rope. Many different types and strengths. *Aviation cable* is the smoothest and strongest.

Use: Dog runs, anchoring trees, fences, and satellite dishes, and so on. Cable does not stretch and is generally stronger than rope and easier to use than chain.

 Use Tip: Cable clamps, a type of small U-bolt with a horizontal bar, are necessary for securing cable.

Wire and Wire Products

Wire

Description: May be *single-strand drawn wire* or *twisted strand;* the first is a single piece of wire, the latter three or four strands twisted together. Both types come galvanized for outdoor use (short lengths are available in copper and aluminum too) and both may be had in various gauges, specifically 10, 12, 14, 16, and 20. Wire also comes plastic-coated. *Aviation wire* is the strongest—cut it with a **cold chisel (Part I, Chapter 2)**. Very thin wire may be called *hobby* or *flower wire. Picture wire* is woven cable of medium strength.

Use:

Twisted: Most often used, and commonly used as guy-wire support and for dog runs. In the very light gauges—18 and 20—it can be used for hanging pictures or tying Christmas wreaths.

Plastic-coated wire is used for clothesline.

Aviation wire or *cable* is for supporting the heaviest objects, such as trees or satellite dishes.

Screening

Also Known As: Bug screening, insect screening

Description: Screening is made in four different materials: aluminum, galvanized steel, bronze, and fiberglass. It is sold by the foot in a variety of widths, 24", 28", 32", and 36"—up to 4' wide—as well as in precut lengths and widths by the package. Screening is normally bright or galvanized metal, but green, gray, and gold are also available. Fiberglass may be gray, green, or charcoal. Solar screening is also available. This is made of a material and mesh that limit the amount of sun that can get through. Finally, you can buy small, prepackaged sections of screen for patching purposes.

Use: Permits open windows while providing a barrier to insects, leaves, and pets.

Use Tips: It is a simple matter to install your own screening with a pair of **C-clamps (Part I, Chapter 9)** to hold screening to the frame while you use a special **screening tool (below)** to roll it into the grooved edges of the frame.

Buying Tips: Screening bought by the foot costs a lot less than precut material.

Screening Tool

Screening Tool

Description: Cylindrical handle with blade-type wheels on each end; one wheel is convex, the other concave.

Use: Installing screening in frames with channels for this purpose.

Hardware Cloth

Also Known As: Wire mesh

Description: A kind of rugged galvanized, welded, and woven screening that is relatively flexible and comes in rolls of widths ranging from 2' to 4'. It also comes in various meshes, stated 2×2, 4×4 mesh, etc., which refers to the number of squares per inch, usually ranging from 2 to 8 mesh. As the number of squares per inch increases, the gauge of the metal gets thinner.

Use: Various: as a sifter of sand, cement, topsoil; a pet cage material; as a fence wherever you want extra security. It is frequently used to keep birds, bats, and squirrels out of houses and rabbits and deer out of gardens.

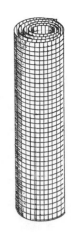

Hardware Cloth

 Use Tip: You can cut hardware cloth quite easily with **tin snips (Part I, Chapter 6).**

 Buying Tip: Hardware cloth is sold by the foot.

Wire Netting

Also Known As: (if openings are hexagonal) Chicken wire, poultry netting, hexagonal netting

Description: Galvanized wire woven—not welded—into a netting that has large squares or hexagons—1" or 2" wide— and comes in various heights up to 6' and lengths of 50' to

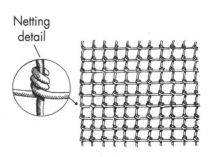

Netting detail

Wire Netting

150'. The wire is of a lighter gauge than **hardware cloth (above)**. Some brands have horizontal lines of wire through the lower hexagons to make a tighter mesh.

Use: Protection against encroachment of small animals on property; for example, installation on a split-rail fence as a way to keep a dog confined.

> **Buying Tips:** Though not as strong as hardware cloth, netting is very inexpensive and can serve well for many jobs.

Miscellaneous Hanging Hardware

Hinged Tool Holder

Also Known As: Broom hook

Description: "S"-shaped hook mounted as a hinge on a small plate. Plastic coated.

Use: Hanging light or average weight brooms, light shovels, hand tools, and the like. Items can be hung by the straight handle, as the holder design uses gravity to hold items in place.

> **$ Buying Tip:** Handy in confined areas such as closets or hallways where it is good to avoid installing hooks that stick out from the wall.

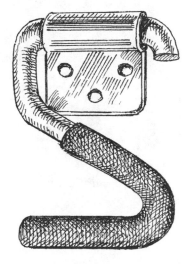

Hinged Tool Holder

Coat and Hat Hook

Description: Cast or solid metal (steel, aluminum, brass, or bronze) or wire double hook, with a short one on the bottom and a long one on top, and an integral wall plate with screw holes.

Use: Hanging coats (small hook) and hats (big hook).

> **Use Tip:** If you are prone to hanging many heavy pieces of clothing on a hook, be sure to get a solid and not cast metal hook. Otherwise it will bend.

Peg-Board® Fixtures

Description: Various shapes but designed to mount in holes in **Peg-Board (Part VI, Chapter 47).**

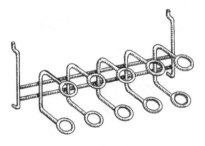

Peg-Board® Holder

Use: Hanging a wide variety of items from tools to condiment containers.

> **Use Tips:** Hooks must be sized according to the thickness of the Peg-Board—$1/4$" Peg-Board takes $1/4$" fixtures, $1/8$" Peg-Board takes $1/8$" fixtures.

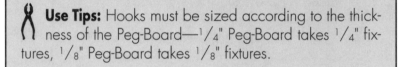

Peg-Board® Bracket   Peg-Board® Clip

Picture-Hanging Hardware

Types:

Picture hooks

Adjustable sawtooth hanger

Adhesive hanger

Hardwall hanger

Mirror hanger

Plain Picture Hook

Also Known As: *Picture hook:* Nail hanger

Description:

Picture hooks: Metal fasteners with holes for driving nails through. Come in various sizes and in plain and ornamental styles.

Adjustable sawtooth hanger: Piece of metal with serrations on one edge, nailed onto frame.

Ornamental Picture Hook

Adhesive anchor: Hook secured to adhesive strip that, in turn, is secured to wall.

Hardwall hanger: Consists of a hook with pins capable of being driven into hard material such as masonry and plaster, with the four-pin model capable of holding up to 100 pounds.

Mirror hanger: Small offset clip with screw hole in one end.

Mirror Hanger

Use: Hanging pictures, mirrors, etc. of various weights.

Hanging Plant Track

Plant-Hanging Hardware

Types:

Brackets

Chain

Macramé

Shelves

Track

Description:

Decorative Scroll-Type Bracket

Brackets: Decorative scroll hook that mounts on wall and has a small swiveling hook on the end. This allows plant to be rotated toward the sunlight.

Chain: This is decorative chain, either metal or plastic. It is secured with other hardware to the plant and ceiling. See **chain (Chapter 28)**.

Macramé: Fancy woven rope to which plant is secured at one end; the other end of the macramé is secured to a screw eye, toggle bolt, or other hanger.

Shelves: These may be as various as shelves are, but the brackets used to support them are fancier than most.

Swivel Hanger

Track: Formed metal pieces into which sliding sections are inserted and to which, in turn, hooks or swivel hangers are secured.

Use: To hang potted as well as other kinds of plants.

Shelf Supports

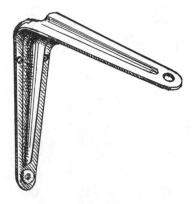

Utility Bracket

Types:

> *Utility brackets*
>
> *Standards and brackets*
>
> *Pilasters and clips*
>
> *Pin and hole*

Also Known As:

> *Utility:* Steel angle bracket.
>
> *Pilasters:* Pillars, standards.
>
> *Pin:* Plug-in clips, shelf supports, pin clips, plug-in shelf supports, clips, shelf rests, plugs.

Description:

> *Utility brackets:* L-shaped metal forms with a center ridge and screw holes for securing to walls. One leg is longer than the other. Usually gray, but also gold and black. Flat versions, called *braces,* are available. A newer version is larger and has a hooked part in front and below the shelf for a closet pole *(shelf and closet pole combination);* it has a diagonal brace that goes from the front down to the bottom of the vertical part in the rear. Fancy versions are available with some scrollwork or in solid wood.

Fancy Shelf Bracket

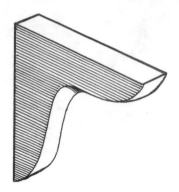

Solid Wood Shelf Bracket

Standards and brackets: C-shaped, long pieces of strong metal, with many small vertical slots, that are mounted on a wall. Brackets, which come in various lengths from 4" to 18" for corresponding shelf widths, have hook-shaped sections that slip into the slots and enable the brackets to support the shelves that are laid across them.

Pilasters: Shallow C-shaped light metal standards with horizontal slots that are placed in the sides of the cabinet or bookcase with small, V-shaped metal clips that snap into the vertical standard. Made in two versions: for surface mounting and for recessed mounting.

Pins: May be metal or plastic. Very small piece with plug on one side and flat support on the other, of various designs, including a rounded one called *spoon type.* Pins fit into predrilled $1/4$" holes in the sides of the cabinet or bookcase to support shelf ends.

Use: As the name suggests, shelf supports do just that—support shelving. All are adjustable except the utility brackets. The first two are mounted on the wall behind the shelves; the second two are mounted on the walls or sides at the ends of the shelves.

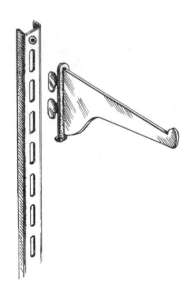

Standard and Bracket Shelf Support

Utility: Mounted on wall studs with shelves laid across them and screwed down. They are considered strictly for utility in basements and garages. Not adjustable.

Standards and brackets: Mounted directly on walls and usually considered more decorative.

Pilasters: Mounted inside cabinets and bookcases at the ends of the shelves. Clips then fit into slots at any convenient position. When recessed can be used in the finest cabinets.

Pins: Fit into holes drilled inside bookcase or cabinet sides, with shelves resting directly on them. Adjustment limited to the positions of predrilled holes, so you want a lot of holes.

Use Tips: *Standards and brackets:* For better holding mount these on studs. You can use any kind of shelving that fits across the brackets. Shelf height can be varied simply by moving brackets on the standards, enabling you to accommodate shorter or taller items. Standards may be mounted with **hollow wall fasteners (Chapter 23)** if only light items are going to be supported, but anchor in studs with screws if heavy items are going to be supported; heavy items could pull light anchors from walls.

Pilasters: These are made of both aluminum and steel; when maximum strength is needed, use steel. Shelf length should be on the short side.

Pins: Drilling a series of $1/4$" holes in a straight line is not easy. For best results, make a template for hole drilling.

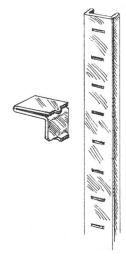

Pilaster and Clip Shelf Support

Buying Tips: *Utility:* For inexpensive shelf supports choose these.

Standards and brackets: These are more costly than utility brackets. They come in a variety of finishes. The standards and brackets of different companies are sometimes interchangeable but usually they're not.

Pins: Perhaps the simplest and least expensive adjustable shelf system.

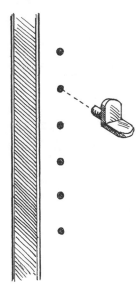

Pin-Type Shelf Support

Miscellaneous Hardware

Cleat

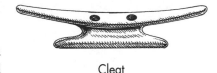

Cleat

Description: Long, narrow metal piece with screw holes on flat part in center for anchoring on wall and with ends raised slightly. Various lengths. A rope hook, which has a flat part with screw holes, is used to hold the coiled rope.

Use: Quick tying of rope to cleat from flagpoles or window blinds and the like.

 Use Tip: The larger models are easier to use.

Engine Hoist

Description: Two sets of pulleys, usually three in one and four in the other, connected by a long rope that is threaded through the pulleys; each set of pulleys has a hook or hooking device.

Use: Obviously, as its name implies, for hoisting heavy objects. However, this is not limited to engines. Smaller models are useful for raising bicycles for storage to the ceiling of a garage or hallway, for example, or when installing heavy items in holes that are filled with cement and must be supported until it sets.

Siding Wedges

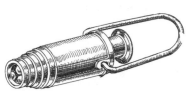

Line Tightener

Siding Wedges

Description: Small aluminum wedges.

Use: Inserted under clapboards or shingles to allow air to circulate, thereby eliminating moisture and eventually preventing peeling paint.

Line Tightener

Description: Small bullet-like cylinder with small funnel inserted in one end, ball bearings inside, and a large loop handle extending from its middle. Made of cast aluminum.

Use: Adjusting laundry lines. The line is threaded through the cylinder, which grabs onto it when the line is pulled tight and releases it when it is loose. The other end of the line is tied to the loop handle.

Padlock

Description: Small metal lock that is not mounted but attaches temporarily to hasps, lockers, or between links of chain. May be made of brass, plates of steel, or hardened or stainless steel. Opens either with a key or combination of numbers; some of the better models that require keys are called *tubular cylinder locks*.

Use: Temporary locking, both interior and exterior.

Use Tips: Lubricate often if used outside. Tubular cylinder locks offer the ability to have key changes without buying a new lock, a useful characteristic if many people have keys to the same lock.

Buying Tips: Domestic makes tend to be stronger, and hardened or stainless-steel locks are the strongest. The five-pin lock mechanism is the best.

General Materials

Adhesives, Sealers, and Caulk

About Adhesives

Adhesives and glues (the former generally refers to man-made products, the latter to natural ones) can be confusing because of their overlapping uses. They can generally be divided into products primarily used for wood and products used for other materials. Another source of confusion is that the term *glue* is used generically.

Adhesives for Wood

Types:

> *Casein glue*
>
> *Clear cement*
>
> *Hide glue*
>
> *Hot melt glue*
>
> *Plastic resin adhesive*
>
> *Waterproof adhesive*
>
> *White glue*
>
> *Woodworker's glue*

Also Known As:

Hot melt: Glue stick

Plastic resin: Urea resin, urea-formaldehyde adhesive, PRG

Waterproof: Resorcinol

White: PVA (polyvinyl acetate, polyvinyl resin)

Woodworker's: Yellow glue, carpenter's glue, aliphatic glue, aliphatic resin glue

Description:

Casein: Comes as a powder that you mix with water. Has a heavy consistency, clearish or brown.

Clear cement: Clear liquid adhesive. Sold in small tubes.

Hide: One part liquid or flake.

Hot melt: 2" to 4" long sticks sold by the box or package.

Plastic resin: Powdered material mixed with water.

Waterproof: Brown powdered material mixed with water.

White: One part white liquid glue that dries clear. Usually sold in soft plastic squeeze bottles. Very common, such as Elmer's Glue-All, a popular brand.

Woodworker's: One part yellowish liquid glue. Sold in soft plastic squeeze bottles. Relatively thick.

Use:

Casein: Good gap-filling characteristic for furniture with loose joints that must be filled. Stains wood and may attract mold. Good on high-moisture and oily woods such as teak.

Clear cement: For lighter wood and paper-porous materials. Somewhat water resistant.

Hot melt: Extruded by an **electric glue gun (Part I, Chapter 14)**. Excellent general-purpose, fast-setting adhesive particularly suited for complicated fits without clamping, such as household repairs and crafts using a variety of materials.

Hide: Traditional furniture glue, for both construction and repair, though not waterproof and with a longer "set up" time than white or yellow glue.

Plastic resin: Any kind of interior wood. Water resistant.

Waterproof: Designed for gluing wood indoors, resists chemicals and temperature changes. Good for wooden bowls and trays.

White: Excellent general-use glue, including wood, but not moisture or heat resistant and too thin for some jobs. Thinned with water can be used as an edge-sealer. Tends to run—not gap-filling. Medium strength.

Woodworker's: Strong glue, good and easy to use for general indoor woodworking jobs. Medium heat and moisture resistance. Excellent gap-filling characteristics.

Use Tips: Read adhesive labels very carefully. Be sure to use as much adhesive as needed to ensure total coverage (it should squeeze out of the joints), and try to match the adhesive closely to the usage. Clamping is necessary with most adhesives. Mix two-part glues very carefully.

Buying Tips: Glue is cheaper when bought in the larger-sized containers. For all-around use every household should have a bottle of either white or yellow glue around.

Adhesives for Other Uses

Types:

> *Acrylic resin adhesive*
>
> *Anaerobic adhesive*
>
> *Contact cement*
>
> *Cyanoacrylate adhesive*
>
> *Epoxy adhesive*
>
> *Mastic adhesive*
>
> *Urethane adhesive*

Also Known As:

> *Anaerobic:* Liquid lock washer, thread-locking compound
>
> *Cyanoacrylate:* Instant glue, super glue
>
> *Mastic:* Construction adhesive, construction mastic, Liquid Nails®, panel adhesive

Description:

> *Acrylic resin:* Two-part adhesive that sets in less than a minute without clamping. Will adhere even if surface is oily.
>
> *Anaerobic:* One-part adhesive that cures without air. Common brand is Loc-Tite®, which has almost become a generic term.
>
> *Contact cement:* Heavy, sticky adhesive that is allowed to become tacky before surfaces are bonded.
>
> *Cyanoacrylate:* One-part clear glue that bonds items instantly with just a drop or two. Made for either porous or nonporous surfaces.

Epoxy: Two-part material consisting of a catalyst and hardener. Available in clear, metallic, and white. Often sold in two-tube syringe. Not to be confused with **epoxy putty (Part VIII, Chapter 60)**, which is for filling holes and patching pipes.

Mastic: A general term applied to any thick adhesive, especially asphalt, rubber, or resin-based, thick, doughy material. Usually sold in cartridges used in **caulking guns (below)** as well as in cans or tubes for application by **notched trowel (Part VII, Chapter 51)**. Includes rubbery, all-purpose adhesive.

Urethane: One-part, multipurpose, expensive adhesive that requires at least 24 hours to set.

Use:

Acrylic resin: Waterproof; good for repairs to two dissimilar materials, exterior or interior. Excellent for filling gaps and extremely strong. Mix to preference for job. Cleans up with acetone. Sold with syringe.

Anaerobic: Good for sealing nuts and bolts that are subject to vibration and otherwise tend to loosen, such as on machinery, doorknobs, or eyeglasses.

Contact cement: Bonds on contact (after it becomes tacky) and is a favorite material for bonding plastic laminate countertops and veneers. Also used to secure hardboard to metal. Applied with a paint brush or roller.

Cyanoacrylate: One version of this glue instantly bonds all kinds of nonporous materials like metal and glass instantly and another bonds porous materials—cardboard, leather, etc. Dangerous to use due to instant bonding quality. Not gap-filling.

Epoxy: For bonding just about anything to anything—masonry, metal, plastic—inside or outside the house. Waterproof, oil-resistant, strong. Excellent for china repairs. Difficult cleanup with acetone.

Mastic: Heavy-duty. Bonding paneling, flooring, drywall, or ceiling tiles to wood, metal, or masonry. Different formulations are made for different types of materials.

Urethane: Can be used anywhere you would use an epoxy, including wood. Can be applied with electric glue gun, brush, or as a stick. Waterproof, very stainable, slightly elastic, and almost invisible.

> **Use Tips:** Make sure surfaces to be bonded are clean and dry. Most contact cements are dangerously volatile and should be used with caution. On top of that, once the two pieces being glued are put together, they cannot be repositioned.

> **Buying Tips:** When you have a job that you can't imagine a glue doing, think epoxy. Some rubbery mastics labeled for special uses are actually all-purpose adhesives handy for most household and plumbing repair or sealing jobs. Keep some on hand.

Blacktop Sealer

Also Known As: Driveway sealer

Description: Heavy black liquid with coal tar or neoprene base. Ordinarily comes in 5-gallon cans but also available in smaller containers as a *crack patcher*.

Use: To renew the appearance of asphalt driveways and to provide a waterproof coating that also protects against oil and other staining materials. Also for sealing small cracks.

> **Use Tips:** Blacktop sealer can be applied with brush, roller, or push broom. Using a roller on a stick or a push broom makes the job easier.

> **Buying Tips:** Blacktop sealer can vary in quality greatly; poor-quality material can be as thin as water. The thicker the material, the better.

Blacktop Patcher

Also Known As: Cold patcher, cold-mix asphalt

Description: Chunky black material with the consistency of very soft tar. Comes ready to use in various-sized bags; also available in standard 10.5-ounce caulk cartridges.

Use: Repair cracks and holes in asphalt driveways; used to pave small walks.

> **Use Tips:** Cold-mix patcher is poured in place and then tamped to a solid density. Driving a car back and forth over a small patch is one good way to compress it, or use a heavy lawn roller.

Caulk

Also Known As: Sealant, sealer

Caulking Cartridge

Description: Elastomeric (flexible) and adhesive goo of various materials and colors most often sold in 6-ounce squeeze tubes or 10–11 ounce, 8" long cartridges made to be used with a **caulking gun (below)**. May or may not be paintable; may or may not be mildew-resistant; more or less flexible or adhesive depending on formulation and quality. Sold either by binder material or by specialized use. The terms "caulk" and "sealant" are interchangeable and are used differently by each manufacturer. Some of the common binders and combinations are:

Silicone caulk

Siliconized acrylic latex caulk

Silicone latex caulk

Acrylic or vinyl latex caulk

Latex caulk

Butyl rubber caulk

Polyurethane (also known as *urethane*) *caulk*

Rope caulk (also known as *caulking cord*)

Neoprene (also known as *rubber adhesive*) *caulk*

Use: Filling gaps or sealing between a wide variety of materials. Each kind has a different degree of flexibility, resistance, and adhesion. General use caulk is used to seal out water and/or air or just to fill in gaps around the house. Specialized uses run from driveway repair to roof repair to duct and gutter work. *Liquid caulk* is for sealing small cracks. General purpose caulks are listed under **Buying Tips.**

All replace the old-fashioned limestone-and -linseed oil product called putty. Following are some special use caulks listed by main ingredient:

Butyl rubber caulk: For metal-to-metal or metal-to-masonry joints (gutters, window and door frames, etc.).

Neoprene caulk: For metal-to-metal, metal-to-masonry, and masonry-to-masonry joints (driveway/foundation joints, window and door frames, foundations, etc.), plumbing and miscellaneous household repairs.

Polyurethane caulk: For masonry-to-masonry joints, highly stressed joints (driveway joints, marine construction).

Rope caulk: For temporary use and for large gaps. Applied by hand. Often called by the brand name Mortite®.

Use Tips: Experiment with the kind of caulk you find easiest to use. Have plenty of water and rags or paper towels around for quick cleanup. Fill extra-large gaps part way with foam rubber, fiberglass insulation, or **oakum (Part VIII, Chapter 60)** first to keep the caulked part relatively thin. Remember to have a long, thin nail on hand to puncture a new tube top, and a thick nail or plastic cap to seal it when you are done.

Buying Tips: In general, get the good stuff and avoid the cheap stuff. There are plenty of specialized caulks that are worthwhile for their particular purposes. Read the labels carefully. Always note whether a caulk is labeled paintable.

Among the general purpose caulks, there are some basic price and quality differences as ingredients (silicone, acrylic or vinyl compounds, and latex binders) are mixed in various recipes by different manufacturers under confusing names. Ultimately, price may be the best indication of quality as it relates to flexibility, durability, and adhesion (you need to decide which qualities are most important).

As with paints, the less expensive stuff has more water and filler in it. The cheap stuff is going to peel away or crack in a couple of years while the better stuff is going to last for decades, though some "lesser" quality caulks might be more suitable for a particular job than those of "greater" quality, such as filling small holes, depending on the manufacturer.

Listed here are the most basic formulas, with the most generally durable at the top:

100% silicone caulk: The most durable, flexible, water-repellent, and adhesive of all caulk products, but it cannot be painted (it is offered clear and in a range of colors), is a little harder to work with (because it is so sticky, though it doesn't stick to some materials), is slightly toxic in its uncured state (and cleans up with mineral spirits), and is often more than twice the cost of all other caulks. It is typically guaranteed for 50 years or even life. Best all-purpose caulk, especially for bathtubs. Worth the price.

Siliconized acrylic latex caulk: A hybrid of the lesser and greater types of caulk listed here, with some of the benefits and drawbacks of both. Most likely a general-purpose caulk. 15–35 year life.

Silicone latex caulk: Good adhesion and flexibility (depending on the brand) make this a common exterior general purpose caulk. 15-year life.

Acrylic or vinyl latex caulk: Suitable as a spackling compound for small holes and cracks prior to painting. Often marketed for its adhesive qualities or as a general purpose caulk. May be marketed as *painter's caulk.* Good for 10 to 15 years exterior use, longer indoors.

Latex caulk: Easily applied, easily cleaned up, inexpensive. May not be very flexible after a short time. May be marketed as *painter's caulk.* Best for stress-free interior use. Five- to 10-year life.

Accessories include different-sized *caulk tips, cartridge nozzles,* and the money- and caulk-saving *cartridge caps,* all worthwhile. Always avoid "bargain" caulks. They aren't!

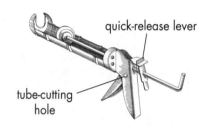

Caulking Gun

Caulking Gun

Description: Metal device about a foot long with a trigger handle and an L-shaped rod coming out the back. When the trigger is squeezed the rod is forced forward and squeezes caulk out of the cartridge in a ratchet or spring-pressure action. A cordless electric model is also available.

Use: Applying caulk and sealant from standard 10.1-ounce cartridges. This is the only way such cartridges can be used.

Cordless Caulking Gun

Use Tips: Keep the caulking gun moving evenly as caulk is forced out the tip of the cartridge to get an even "bead." Remove caulk tubes after use and clean gun.

$ Buying Tips: Get a model with a little lever that re- leases easily, with one hand. The choice between a ratchet action and spring-pressure action is one of per- sonal preference. Both have points that tend to wear out and are a little hard to use because of the constant squeez- ing. Definitely get a model with a metal spike attached for piercing the liner seals on new caulk cartridges—a tre- mendous help. Also look for models with new tube cutting holes. For smoothest and steadiest flow, use the cordless electric caulking gun.

Caulk Smoothing Tool

secondary trim tabs

handle

primary trim tabs

direction of tool

Caulk Smoothing Tool

Also Known As: Caulk finishing tool

Description: Small, open-winged, plastic trowel-like item with a slight scoop shape. Sold in a kit with two sizes ($1/4$" or $5/16$") and a specially shaped flat piece for cleaning it out. An alter- native, a *caulk and putty square,* is a flat piece of plastic with different-sized rounded corners.

Use: Perfect smoothing of freshly caulked or glazed joints without using your finger or a plastic spoon. Works by trim- ming excess.

$ Buying Tip: For the perfectionist, mostly. For everyday small jobs, fingers or plastic spoons aren't that bad, but for larger jobs or more toxic caulks, fingers and spoons do have their disadvantages.

Caulk Remover

Description: 6" long, flat, plastic tool with a slightly hooked tip.

Use: Removing old caulk/sealant from around bathtubs or other areas. The small point is pushed under the caulk to loosen it and the hooked tip is pulled under the loosened caulk to remove it.

Caulk Remover

> **$ Buying Tip:** Excellent for hard-to-remove caulk, but not necessary for most caulk, which can be pulled away by hand.

Roofing Materials

About Roofing

Roofing materials come in many more varieties and styles than can be described here. The intention is simply to give you a general orientation concerning the stuff that you may need in order to make minor repairs.

All roofing is available in a variety of colors. If you live in a very hot climate, consider the use of a light-colored roof; it absorbs less heat than a dark-colored one.

Roofing is sold by the square, meaning a 10' × 10' area or 100 square feet.

Working on a roof can be a hazardous activity, so it would be well to observe safety considerations. Professionals use safety hooks called *roof jacks* on which boards can be mounted. These are a good idea and can be rented.

Roofing Material

Types:

> *Asphalt roofing*
>
> *Built-up roofing*

Glass fiber shingles

Modified bitumen roofing

Roll roofing

Slate shingles

Tile roofing

Wood shingles

Also Known As: *Glass fiber:* Fiberglas (brand name), fiberglass

Description:

Asphalt: Usually comes in strip form with two, three, or four tabs per shingle and heavily coated with mineral granules on the weather side. Shingles range from around 11" to 22" wide and 36" to 40" long.

Built-up: Made of layers of tar-impregnated **roofing felt (below)** and base sheet with hot moppings of tar between the layers and a layer of asphalt on the very top. May also be all asphalt.

Glass fiber: These are partly asphalt and partly glass fiber, i.e., fiberglass is used as a base for asphalt and mineral granules instead of felt. (All asphalt shingles may be called *organic.)*

Modified bitumen: 36" wide, 10 square foot roll of rubbery material, similar to **roll roofing (below)**. Applied with a torch so that it melts into the surface adjoining rolls. Often called *rubber roofing;* it isn't.

Roll: 36" wide asphalt-impregnated material made in rolls containing 108 square feet. The weather side of this material is plain or covered in part with mineral granules (the uncovered part is the *selvage*). Sold in *weights;* typical is 90-pound type, and it may be sold in two *exposures*—half exposure being for use in double layers.

Slate: Available in various colors—green, gray, black, purple—depending on the quarry it's from. Slate has a nominal size $3/16$" and an overall size 10" × 6" and 24" × 16".

Tile: A burned clay or shale or concrete product. Shapes vary greatly.

Wood: Made of cypress, cedar, or redwood. Comes in lengths of 16" to 18" and in bundles containing random widths 3" to 12". Available in either *shingle form,* which is machine-made, or *shakes,* which are hand-split. Some communities require expensive fireproofing treatment.

Use: To protect a home from weather and, in some cases, provide a degree of insulation. *Modified bitumen* and *roll roofing* are for flat roofs.

Use Tips: All roof installation is really a professional task. Installing or repairing slate and tile especially are better left to professional roofers; special tools and much experience is required to do the job right. In fact, you should limit your roofing work to repairs.

Buying Tips: The cheapest roofing materials are asphalt and fiberglass shingles. They are relatively easy to install. The heavier the shingle the better. Manufacturers guarantee their products, some types for 15 years and some for 25.

Use Tips: Even though it is flat, a built-up roof is harder to install than it might seem. It is not that simple to make it leak-free. Keep some **asphalt plastic cement (below)** on hand for patching. You may want to coat it occasionally with asphalt or aluminum roof coating to extend the life of the roof.

Roofing Felts

Also Known As: Saturated felts, perforated felts, base sheet, tar paper

Description: Dry felt impregnated with an asphalt saturant and perforated to avoid trapping air. Different weights are available, the most common being No. 30, which weighs about 30 pounds per square. Comes in squares about 30" wide and in rolls.

Use: General patching of flat roofs, but mainly constructing bottom layers of a built-up roof. It is placed over the sheathing paper, which simply protects the basic roof from the asphalt in the felts.

Use Tips: Felt can be installed with a staple gun or, for patches, plenty of roofing nails.

Roofing Cements

Types:

Asphalt plastic roof cement

Damp patch roof cement

Lap/double-coverage roof cement

Quick-setting asphalt roof cement

Also Known As: Mastic

Description: All these roofing cements contain petroleum solvents. Use outdoors only.

Asphalt plastic cement: Fairly viscous black goo of asphalt and mineral fibers. Comes in two grades, regular and flashing, which is thicker. Adheres to any dry surface. Like most cements, comes in 1- and 5-gallon cans. However, some similar products are available in standard 10.5-ounce caulking cartridges for application with a **caulking gun (Part IV, Chapter 32).**

Damp patch cement (also known as *wet or dry roof cement*): Similar to the above, but specially formulated to adhere to wet surfaces.

Lap cement: Thick black adhesive, similar to the above cement but thinner.

Quick-setting asphalt cement: As the name implies, this sets very quickly. Basically an asphalt plastic cement with more solvent in it. Comes in various consistencies from fluid to thick.

Use:

Asphalt plastic cement: The standard material for sealing edges of flashing and patches in flat roofs, as well as installation of the bottom layers of roll roofing. Also for repairing leaks in gutters. Applied with a trowel over *reinforcement fabric* or *roofing tape*, a 4" to 6" wide loosely-woven glass fiber or cotton mesh membrane, sold in long rolls.

Damp patch cement: Emergency repairs under extreme dampness, such as leaks under snow buildup or during a major rainstorm. Applied with a trowel.

Lap cement: Used to seal overlapping strips of roll roofing or shingle tabs. Applied with a brush or roller.

Quick-setting asphalt cement: Adhering strip shingles in windy areas.

Use Tips: Patching over and over again may indicate a more serious problem that needs to be solved by a new roof or an overall coating with a material called *roof coating*, or *asphalt roof paint*, which is applied with a big brush. This will fill small gaps. Roof coating, also called *foundation coating*, is a masonry waterproofer. Both can extend the life of a flat roof.

Buying Tips: Always keep repair material on hand. Consult with manufacturers for best product in your situation (there are many variations on the themes noted here). Try the convenient 10.1 oz cartridges, used with a **caulking gun (Part IV, Chapter 32)**.

Reflective Roof Coating

Also Known As: Roof paint

Description: Either of two kinds, aluminum flakes suspended in an asphalt and solvent mixture, or white acrylic elastomeric suspension.

Use: Coating asphalt, modified bitumen, rubber, or metal roofs to protect them from damaging sunlight (U.V. rays) as well as to reduce thermal transmission.

> **Use Tips:** Worthwhile to apply every few years or so to extend the life of your roof. Easily applied with large brush or roller.

Flashing

Types:

Metal flashing

Metalized flashing

Mineralized roll roofing

Description:

Metal: This may be copper .01" thick or more, but aluminum is much more common. It is available in 6" and 8" squares and in rolls in 6" to 20" widths in 50' rolls. Other materials available are galvanized steel, lead, plastic, felt, and rubber.

Metalized: Very flexible paper-backed aluminum, almost like heavy aluminum foil.

Mineralized roll roofing: This is standard 36"-wide roll roofing cut to sizes desired.

> **Note:** *Flashing* is also a verb and may refer to the use of roof cement products around chimneys, skylights, and edges of roofs.

Use: Flashing is used to fill the gaps in a roofing job, such as at peaks, in valleys (where sloping roof sections abut), around chimneys and vent pipes, at roof edges, or against walls to carry off water. It is also used for repairs.

> **Use Tips:** Make sure that the flashing used is compatible with the roofing. For example, don't use copper with red cedar shakes because copper will darken the cedar. Be sure to seal it at the edges.

> **Buying Tips:** Metalized flashing is poor-quality material. The most commonly used flashing is aluminum. Roofing manufacturers also offer specialized products not listed here. Be sure to ask for them.

Soffit Vent

Soffit Vent

Also Known As: Vent louver, vent plug

Description: Small, round, metal, or plastic louvered vents ranging in size from 1" to 4" in diameter. Screen inside. Also available in rectangular lengths to run all the width of a house.

Use: Ventilation of the *soffit,* the part of the roof that over-hangs the outside wall of a house. Helps prevent paint peel-ing and blistering.

 Use Tips: Be sure to keep paint off these small vents or it may close them up.

Shanty Cap

Also Known As: Coolie hat, rain cap

Description: Cone-shaped galvanized sheet-metal construction of large pipe section with roof suspended like a gazebo on top. Comes in diameters from 3" to 12" to fit pipe as needed (adjustable models are available). Other types are *turbine* and ones with *multiple cones.*

Use: Covers top of roof vent (drain stack or other vent) or chimney to keep rain out.

Shanty Cap

Ridge Vent

Description: Two Types: The stand-alone type is 5' or 10' lengths of either plastic, aluminum, or galvanized steel formed to fit over the open ridge of a roof; internal baffles on the underside allow for air circulation. The other type is a dense, synthetic mesh material about 1" high which is secured over the ridge gap, to which shingles are nailed. Each model has a specific ventilation capacity measured in square feet.

Use: Ventilating attics and barns efficiently of both moisture and heat.

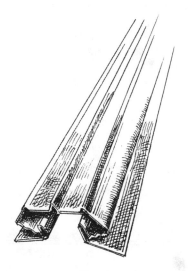

Ridge Vent

Shingle Puller

Shingle Puller

Also Known As: Slate ripper, slater's ripper, shingle remover, shingle ripper, shingle nail remover

Description: 24" long, 2" wide flat steel bar with two fishhook notches on one end and an offset, thick, in-line handle.

Use: Driven up under and down to either shear off or pull out shingle nails or hooks when removing shingles carefully for a repair or remodeling job.

Buying Tips: This is not the tool for removing an entire roof; for that use a *roofing shovel*, which generally looks like a flat garden spade with a notched edge for cutting nails and wedges for prying up shingles, or a garden hoe–like *shingle removal tool* that has a flat, angled blade instead of a shovel blade. Both can be used from a standing position. Handle asbestos shingles only after checking with authorities about their proper removal and safe disposal.

CHAPTER 33

Gutter and Fittings

Types:

Aluminum, standard cut gutter

Aluminum, custom cut gutter

Copper gutter

Galvanized gutter

Vinyl gutter

Wood gutter

Gutter accessories and fittings

Also Known As:

Aluminum, standard and *custom cut:* Reynolds wrap
(if thin gauge)

Aluminum, custom cut: Seamless

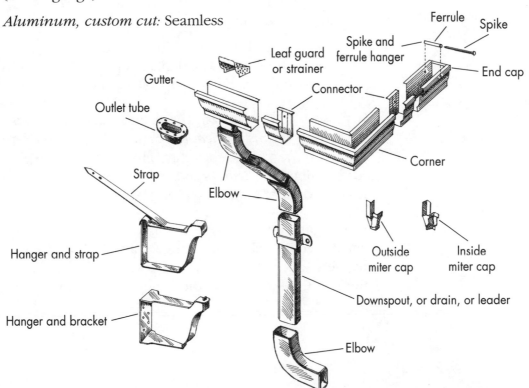

Description: Gutter is made of five different materials: copper, wood, vinyl, galvanized metal, and aluminum.

Aluminum, standard cut: Normal thickness, or gauge, is .027", but it also comes in 32' lengths of .032" at building supply houses that specialize in gutter. Standard-cut gutter is ordinarily available only in white.

Aluminum custom cut: Cut on the site by a jobber to the exact length desired; it is seamless. It is commonly available in white, brown, black, gold, and green.

Copper: This comes in standard 10' lengths; joints are soldered.

Galvanized: Comes in various baked enamel finishes and in lengths of 10' and 20'. It also comes 4" or 5" wide, rectangular or round and fluted.

Vinyl: This is PVC (polyvinyl chloride). It is available in one width, 5", and in lengths of 10', 16', 21', and 32' and in white and brown. Components snap together easily.

Wood: Usually made of fir, redwood, or red cedar, available at lumberyards in lengths up to 50'. It weighs five or six times as much as a metal gutter.

Accessories and fittings: These include *downspouts* (also known as *drains,* or *leaders*), *end tubes, leader hangers, spikes and ferrules* (tubes through which gutter spikes fit) for hanging, and *leaf guards,* which are grids that prevent leaves from entering the gutter.

Gutters are hung by one of three ways, and fittings will attach accordingly: with hangers attached to straps, with hangers attached to brackets, and with spikes that are driven through the ferrules and the gutter into the house.

Use: To carry water off the roof and away from the house.

Use Tips: The most common mistake in installing gutter is to assume that the house is level and pitch the gutter off that. Houses are rarely level. A level line must be established and the gutter pitched according to that for water to run down it properly. Clean gutters often.

Buying Tips: The best gutter buy is probably custom-cut aluminum. Besides being available in different colors, it is seamless—fewer places for leaks to occur—and .032 gauge; when you lean a ladder against it, it won't buckle, like the thinner (.027) aluminum will. But vinyl systems are easier to install and maintain by the homeowner.

Plastic, Metal, and Fiberglass

About Do-It-Yourself Materials

Plain, small sheets and lengths of aluminum and plastic can easily be used in a variety of innovative projects around the house. Many shapes are available; below are the basic ones. The first three items below are actually sold as "do-it-yourself materials" and are often found in specially designed display units.

Metal Sheets

Types:

Aluminum sheet, plain

Aluminum sheet, perforated

Galvanized steel sheet

Also Known As:

Aluminum sheet, perforated: Radiator grill, decorative aluminum panel

Galvanized steel: Sheet metal

Description: Thin metal (less than $^3/_{16}$" thick) that is easily bent and cut without special equipment other than tin snips.

Aluminum sheet, plain: Most often sold in 2' × 3' and 3' × 3' squares.

Aluminum sheet, perforated: Sold in 3' × 3' squares and 3' × 8' sheets in various perforations. Available also in anodized finishes, such as gold, and many different patterns.

Galvanized steel: Sold in rolls 2' wide, commonly 8' long.

Use:

Aluminum sheet, plain: Lining walls next to stoves, hobby projects, etc.

Aluminum sheet, perforated: Forms a grill in front of a radiator for decorative purposes.

Galvanized steel: Variety of repair and hole-patching jobs.

Angle Iron and Bar Stock

Description: L-shaped or flat aluminum or steel pieces in a variety of sizes up to about $1^1/_2$" wide, up to around $^1/_4$" thick, and sold by the foot. Generally available up to 8'. Some kinds of heavier steel angle iron or barstock come with slots and holes for bolts, allowing for easy construction of shelving or support brackets.

Use: Protecting corners, supporting shelves, and so on.

Rigid Plastic Sheet

Also Known As: Plexiglas®, Lucite®

Description: The most common rigid plastic is acrylic, and comes clear or in textures and colors. Generally cut to order from a 4' × 8' sheet, it comes covered with a protective paper coating that must be removed by the user. Most dealers stock a variety of sizes—2' × 3' is common. Lumberyards have larger pieces. Available in various thicknesses, of which $^1/_8$" and $^1/_4$" are typical.

Use: Extremely versatile product used in an infinite array of decorative and functional projects, including art, hobbies, small shelves, and repairs. Can be bent by heating slightly, drilled at slow speed, cut with fine-toothed saw blades, glued, sanded, and polished.

> **Use Tips:** Easily cut with a special knife called a **plastic cutter (Part I, Chapter 6)**. Just score it several times along a line and then break it off. When drilling holes support it directly underneath the hole with a block of wood.

Plastic Film

Also Known As: Clear poly sheeting, plastic sheeting, plastic sheet

Description: Available in roll form and in various gauges—2 mil, 4 mil, etc.—and widths.

Use: Many different uses, but chiefly as covers and drop cloths or for insulating windows.

Use Tip: Do not use thin plastic film on floors—it is extrememly slippery.

Buying Tips: Plastic film is just as effective an insulation material as glass, which is to say it stops drafts but transmits temperature. If you are using plastic as a drop cloth, make sure you get the thicker kind—the thinnest ones available tear very easily, making them worthless for that purpose (and are generally hard to use).

Fiberglass Panels

Description: Most commonly these are available in sheets 8', 10', and 12' long and 26" wide, with corrugations $2^{1}/_{2}$" apart. Fiberglass comes in a variety of colors and in various light weights—4, 5, 6, and 8 ounces per square foot. Installation is with aluminum nails. Fiberglass is also available in flat sheets and rolls up to 4' wide.

Use: As awnings over patios, carport roofs, porches, and the like. They let light in but keep out some of the sun's rays and heat.

 Use Tip: Fiberglass panels can be cut with a fine-toothed hand- or power saw.

Plastic Tubing

Description: Clear and frosted flexible vinyl in a wide variety of diameters and in lengths cut to suit. Often a large variety is for sale on a stand of reels.

Uses: Any number of uses, including making very long **liquid levels (Part I, Chapter 10)** for measuring levelness over long distances, such as in construction of a room's ceiling.

Plastic Laminate

Also Known As: Laminate, 'mica, Formica®, Micarta®

Description: Hard and brittle $1/16$" thick, sheet material sold by length and from 24" to 60" wide. One type has a hard plastic color surface and a base or core that's brown; newer material has the top color all the way through (color core). Plastic laminate has great stain resistance and easy-clean qualities and, once installed, can take a lot of punishment.

Use: Plastic laminate is considered the standard material installed on kitchen and bathroom countertops because of its easy clean feature and its imperviousness to water.

 Use Tips: Handle plastic laminate with care before installation. It's very brittle. *Contact cement* is used to install it. An easier way to apply this is with a paint roller. Laminate with color clear through makes trimming edges easier.

Buying Tip: Color core is triple the cost of regular laminate.

Roll Laminate

Description: Plastic laminate in roll form, which is thinner than the better-quality laminate.

Use: Same as **sheet laminate (above)**.

 Buying Tip: Roll laminate is not as good as sheet laminate but it does work.

Vinyl Patching Kit

Description: Kit containing patching material, graining "papers," and backing material.

Use: For repairing holes in vinyl upholstery.

 Use Tip: Don't expect color-match perfection when using one of these kits.

Synthetic Marble

Also Known As: Corian®, 2000X®

Description: This is acrylic plastic combined with minerals to form an extremely hard material. It comes 30" wide and up to 10' long and in thicknesses of $1/4$", $1/2$", and $3/4$". It is a very heavy material and comes in a limited number of colors simulating marble.

Use: To cover countertops in kitchen or bath. Can be used as a cutting surface and repaired with minor sanding, but it dulls knives quickly.

 Use Tips: Cut Corian® with carbide-tipped tools. Very easy to work with, perhaps even more so than plastic laminate.

Buying Tip: Synthetic marble is very expensive.

Insulation and Weatherizers

About Insulation

This is a highly technical field in which many specialized products are found. Below is only a basic overview of the main types commonly available. Thorough research for your specific application is necessary; many helpful publications are available at your local library, bookstore, or utility company. And of course from the manufacturer.

House Insulation

Types:

Batt and blanket (or *quilt) insulation*

Fill (or *loose fill) insulation*

Foam (or *foamed-in-place) insulation*

Rigid board insulation

Siding with insulation

Description: All insulation comes in a variety of thicknesses for different degrees of performance. All work on the same principle of tiny pockets of air trapped in something fluffy or foamy. The most common types of material are such fibers as rock or mineral wool, fiberglass, and cellulose.

Batts and blankets: Batts are precut flexible sections of insulation 4' or 8' long and 16" or 24" wide and are designed to fit between framing members. Blankets are as wide but come in lengths up to 100'. Both batts and blankets consist of mineral wool or fiberglass and have a vapor barrier, either kraft paper or aluminum. Both types also have edging strips or flanges, which are nailed or stapled to framing members (studs or joists).

Fill: A granular material, such as vermiculite, or chopped-up and chemically treated paper, which is poured or blown into place.

Foam: Applied as a liquid, it foams up instantly and becomes rigid.

Rigid: This comes in board form anywhere from 8" squares to 4' × 12' sheets (2' 8" sheets are the most popular, it seems) and may be urethane, expanded polystyrene or beadboard, fiberglass, Styrofoam®, or composition. Runs from $1/2$" to 2" thick.

Siding with insulation: Siding, wood sheating or aluminum, with insulation sheets adhered to the back side or in a sandwich form.

Use:

Batts and blankets: Normally installed between open ceiling and wall framing members (studs and joists).

Fill: May be poured in place between attic joists or blown into walls inaccessible to other kinds of insulation. Good for retrofitting.

Foam: Like fill-type installation, foam is for pumping into walls otherwise inaccessible to boards or batts and blankets. Professional installation is definitely required. Good for retrofitting. Aerosol cans of foam are excellent for filling small gaps, such as around windows, behind electrical boxes, and so on.

Rigid: Basement walls or areas with difficult access.

Siding with insulation: Exterior walls.

Use Tips: Do-it-yourselfers favor batts or blankets because they are very simple to install. Be sure to use *attic rafter vents* or *vent baffles* in attic installation to allow some movement of attic air from the *soffit,* under the sheathing. The most important area of the house to insulate is the top floor, simply because heat rises. For safety you should wear a suitable mask and gloves when handling insulation. Rigid insulation can be attached directly to walls of all kinds with **mastic adhesive (Chapter 32).**

Buying Tips: The key consideration when buying insulation is its R, or heat resistance, factor. The higher the R factor, the greater the ability of the insulation to limit heat passing through, and thus the more effective the material. Different climates require different R factors. To avoid installing too little—as well as too much—insulation, find out from your local utility what's sufficient.

Note: Foam has the highest R value per inch but gives off noxious gases in a fire.

Blanket Insulation

Pipe Insulation

Also Known As: Insulating pipe wrap, insulating pipe cover

Types:

> *Fiberglass insulation*
>
> *Foam rubber insulation*
>
> *Foam polyethylene insulation*

Description:

> *Fiberglass:* Comes in 4' and 6' lengths and in various diameters to fit all sizes of pipe, some with self-sealing tape. Paper or vinyl facing. Also in 3" wide rolls.
>
> *Foam rubber:* Sold in common pipe diameters and in 6' lengths with lengthwise seams which must be sealed with adhesive at joints, or wrapped with **cable ties (Part III, Chapter 23).** Foam rubber pipe wrap also comes in $1/4$" thick, 2" or 3" wide, 15' long rolls, with a self-adhesive foil cover. Duct wrap is similar, but 12" wide.
>
> *Foam polyethylene:* Also sold in common pipe diameters and in 6' lengths. Must be sealed lengthwise at joints with adhesive.

> **Note:** A similar but extra-large version, called an *insulation jacket* or *water heater blanket,* is available for use on hot-water heaters.

Use: Insulating hot-water pipes to conserve heat and to prevent cold water pipes from sweating.

> **Use Tip:** Self-sealing fiberglass is easiest to use.

Insulation Jacket

Outlet Seal

Description: Small pad of insulating material in the shape of a wall plate for either an outlet or a switch.

Use: Installed between the wall plate and the wall to seal out cold air.

Weatherstripping

Also Known As: Energy-saving products, weatherizers, sweeps (when installed on the bottom of a door; the vinyl or brush sweeps onto the threshold, or saddle, to make the seal).

Description: Many designs are available. Here are some basic ones:

Adhesive-backed foam: Foam rubber strip about 1" wide with peel-away paper, usually sold in rolls of 17'.

Aluminum saddle with vinyl gasket (threshold weatherstrip): Threshold with vinyl gasket in its middle.

Aluminum saddle with interlocking door bottom: See illustration.

Aluminum and vinyl strip sweep: Strips of aluminum with screw holes and a vinyl flap.

Caulking cord (Mortite®): Soft, putty-like cord supplied on a multiple-roll coil.

Felt strips: Strips of hair or cotton felt $3/4$" to 2" wide and about $1/4$" thick. Sold in 17' rolls, enough to surround an average window or door.

Foam-edged wood molding: Rigid molding with foam edging.

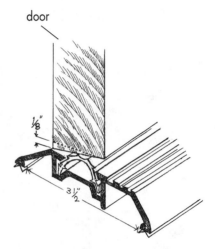

Aluminum Saddle with Vinyl Gasket Weatherstripping

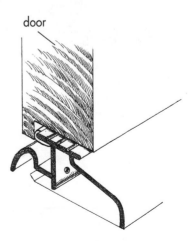

Aluminum Saddle with Interlocking Door Bottom Weatherstripping

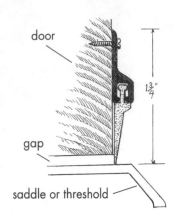

door

gap

saddle or threshold

$1\frac{3}{4}$"

Aluminum and Vinyl Stripsweep
Weatherstrip

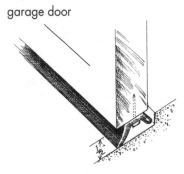

garage door

$\frac{1}{2}$"

Garage-Door-Bottom
Weatherstripping

Nylon pile: Soft, carpet-like strip with solid edge for nailing.

Polyethylene tape: Clear, wide tape.

Rubber garage-door stripping: Wide flaps of vinyl or dense foam rubber secured to bottom of garage door.

Serrated metal/felt: Felt encased in metal with holes for nailing.

Spring metal: V-shaped bronze strip with holes for nailing.

Interlocking metal: Two parts, one (male) installed on door, the other (female) on frame (see illustration).

Tubular vinyl gasket: Tube with a nailing lip; best have foam-filled tubes.

Vinyl channel: U-shaped strips.

Use: All weatherstripping prevents cold air from entering a house through gaps around doors and windows. Each of these items is more specialized, as follows:

Adhesive-backed foam: Sits on doorframe and door is closed against it.

Aluminum saddle with vinyl gasket: Sealing beneath door. Here, saddle is installed on floor, vinyl on door.

Aluminum saddle with interlocking door bottom: Interlock is installed on bottom of door.

Aluminum and vinyl strip sweep: Installed on door bottoms.

Caulking cord (Mortite®): Excellent temporary filling of large gaps. Easily applied.

Felt strips: Used to seal around windows and doors, especially over large gaps.

Foam-edged wood molding: Used around doors and windows.

Interlocking metal: Seals doors well, while also protecting against forced entry.

Nylon pile: For sealing around storm doors and windows. Nailed to bottom of door, sweeps up against the threshold.

Polyethylene tape: Seals around windows, sometimes with plastic film over the window too.

Rubber garage-door stripping: Nailed to garage door bottom, seals bottom and helps reduce shock when door hits floor.

Serrated metal/felt: Seals around windows and doors.

Spring metal: Nailed around a wooden doorframe to seal tightly when door is closed.

Tubular vinyl gasket: Nailed to door or window frame; can be used to replace factory weatherstripping on windows.

Vinyl channel: For sealing around metal casement windows.

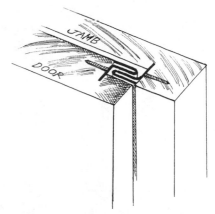

Interlocking Metal Weatherstripping

Tubular Vinyl Gasket
Weatherstripping

Use Tips: Spring metal and interlocking metal are the best permanent types; polyethylene and dense, foam rubber (EPDM) are the best nonmetal materials; nylon pile can flatten out over time; tubular vinyl is more likely to seal better. You still can't beat new, double- or triple-glazed windows (windows with several layers of glass and air spaces) for energy conservation.

Rope and Cord and Accessories

About Rope and Cord

Rope is defined as any material $1/8$" (some say $3/16$") or more in diameter while cord is anything less than $1/8$". Both rope and cord have what is known as *safe working loads*—how much pressure they can take before breaking. If you use rope or cord in any situation where safety is important, check out the safe working loads. Your choices are of material, weave, and diameter.

Rope

Types:

> *Manila rope*
>
> *Nylon rope*
>
> *Polypropylene rope*
>
> *Sisal rope*

Description:

> *Manila:* Made from hemp. Resists sunlight, doesn't melt or stretch, and ties easily. Like most rope, it is available in diameters ranging from $1/4$" to $3/4$" and is normally sold by the foot from reels.

Polypropylene Rope   Sisal Rope

Nylon: Two types: One twisted, the other solid braid. Very strong. The twist type can unravel when cut. *Polyester rope* is similar.

Polypropylene: This is rope that floats. It comes in bright yellow and sometimes red. Least expensive material.

Sisal: Another natural-fiber rope; has less strength than Manila.

Use:

Manila: Where strength is important.

Nylon: Its big advantage is that it stretches, so if you have a job where the rope may need to take a shock and stretch, by all means use nylon—but beware of jobs where stretching would be a problem.

Polypropylene: Since it floats, it is used as a marker in pools and as a tow rope for boats. Hard to tie.

Sisal: Because of its relative low strength, use it only for temporary jobs.

 Use Tip: The ends of both nylon and polypropylene ropes can be melted with a match flame to prevent unraveling.

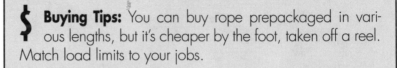 **Buying Tips:** You can buy rope prepackaged in various lengths, but it's cheaper by the foot, taken off a reel. Match load limits to your jobs.

Cord

Types:

Clothesline

Twine

Masons' line

Description: Any rope product less than $1/8$" in diameter.

Clothesline: There are various types. One is braided cotton and has a filler inside to add body and bulk. Usually sold by the hank (a convenient length, coiled and packaged). Another clothesline is plastic—a film of vinyl over a wire. Another clothesline is *poly,* which is braided.

Twine: This could be described as a lightweight version of rope and cord made of plies twisted just once. There are different kinds: *Polypropylene* is strongest and sometimes the least expensive. *Jute* and *sisal* twine have fuzzy surfaces that stick well when tied.

Masons' line: Strong thin cord that comes in balls.

Use: All twine is good for lightweight tying jobs. Masons' twine is very strong and is used to mark off masonry projects, such as rows of bricks being laid. Jute and sisal are popular in rural and gardening applications because they will rot quickly.

Twine

Swiveling Round Eye Cap Snip

Miscellaneous Rope Accessories

Types:

Pulley

Snaps

Description:

Pulley: 5" to 7" diameter grooved wheels in housings with eyes or hooks.

Snaps: Small metal device with spring-loaded locking device available in a variety of models, combining four features:

Swivelling or fixed *(solid)*

Eyes: round or rectangular *(strap)*

Snap Types: large latch *(cap);* sliding bolt; flat strap *(spring);* lever on outside of a ring *(trigger);* or solid half-circle catch *(animal tie);* and other special ones for boats, horse harnesses, and dog leashes.

Snaps on one or both ends *(double-ended)*

Uses:

Pulley: For clothesline but can also form the core of a rig winch for hauling up do-it-yourself materials.

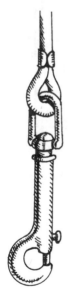

Swiveling Strap Eye Bolt Snap

Snaps: Where temporary hooking up of things is required. Swivel snaps are good for dog runs and other places where there is a lot of motion.

 Use Tip: Most of these accessories can be used with chain as well.

Lubricants

Household Oil

Also Known As: All-purpose oil, 3-in-1®

Description: Light oil in cans or sprays.

Use: Lubricating small machinery, doors, and tools around the house. Particularly good for breaking up rust. Cleans and polishes, removes tarnish.

> **Use Tip:** Although suitable for most lubrication needs, keep in mind that there are many specialized oils for sewing machines, cycles and mowers, and so on.

Dripless Oil

Also Known As: White lubricant

Description: White, high-viscosity oil—virtually a grease—that will not dry up and become ineffective (as **silicone, below,** does).

Use: For hinges and typewriters.

Graphite

Description: Comes as a powder and is applied with puffer tube.

Use: Usually used on locks but also good for squeaking floors and stairways.

Lock Fluid

Description: Graphite in fluid or spray form.

Use: Freeing up lock mechanisms.

 Use Tip: Take care when applying graphite. It can create a mess.

Penetrating Oil

Also Known As: Bolt loosener, easing oil

Description: Extremely thin petroleum/graphite mixture in liquid or aerosol spray. Liquid Wrench® is a common brand, as is WD-40®, which comes only as an aerosol spray. Both contain solvents.

Use: Loosens "frozen" nuts and bolts, "seized" machinery, or corroded galvanized-steel piping when allowed to penetrate for several minutes. WD-40® can be used as a plain solvent as well as a rust preventer on large metal items such as shovels and lawnmowers. Liquid Wrench® can also be used to remove rust.

> **Use Tip:** After applying penetrating oil, make sure you give it enough time to work. The spray type is good for spots with limited access.

> **Buying Tip:** Liquid Wrench® makes all-purpose and other specialized lubricants as well, so be sure you have the right item if you ask for it by brand.

Dry Spray Lubricant

Description: Teflon or silicone available in aerosol cans.

Use: Often used to slicken surfaces of drawers, doors, and windows for smoother operation. Works on paint, plastic, wood, glass, leather, and many other surfaces not suitable for liquids. Best lubricant for lock mechanisms.

Stick Lubricant

Also Known As: Stainless stick, stainless lubricant

Description: Comes as a grease stick and is applied like a crayon. May be made of silicone.

Use: Can be used on metal, plastic, glass, wood. Good for keeping drawers moving freely as well as enhancing the use of drills, saw blades, and other cutting tools.

Tape

About Tape

There are new kinds of tape appearing every day that combine various attributes of the ones below. This list is merely a grouping of some of the most common. All tape is known as *pressure-sensitive tape* and typically has adhesive on a backing of some sort.

Anti-Slip Tape

Description: Heavy tape with gritty surface, available in light and medium duty, and in various widths.

Use: Provides traction for bare feet around pools, on stairways, and in bathrooms.

Double-Faced Tape

Also Known As: Two-sided, cloth carpet tape

Description: Reinforced cloth with adhesive on both sides (one side protected with a removable wax-type paper).

Use: Securing carpeting and other flooring.

Duct Tape

Also Known As: Duck tape

Description: Reinforced cloth tape with a gray vinyl facing, commonly sold 2" wide (available in other widths too) and in up to 60-yard-long rolls. Most common is a rubber, waterproof adhesive, but other formulations are available that are flame-retardant or metalized.

Use: Wide variety of repairs and worksite holding jobs inside and outside the house such as gutter, leaking pipe and hose. Also seals heating and cooling ducts.

> **$ Buying Tips:** Inexpensive duct tape is not a good buy—the adhesive will be gummy and the tape may slip. Probably one of mankind's most useful inventions. Keep at least two rolls on hand.

Electrical Tape

Description: Black tape usually no more than 1" wide. Two kinds: One is a fabric that is sticky on both sides, known as *friction tape,* and adheres only to itself; the other is plastic with adhesive on one side only. The plastic tape stretches quite a bit and thus creates a tightening tension when wrapping wires.

Use: For wrapping electrical wires.

Foil Tape

Description: Thin, adhesive-backed insulation with foil face.

Use: For wrapping and insulating pipes against condensation.

 Use Tip: Does not prevent a significant energy loss as real pipe insulation would.

Masking Tape

Description: Paper-backed adhesive tape that comes in various widths up to about 3". Some have adhesive only along one half.

Use: Masking off areas to be painted, for packaging, general light use.

 Use Tips: Remove masking tape immediately after use, as otherwise it tends to leave a gummy residue that can be removed only with a strong solvent like lacquer thinner. Everyday translucent tape leaves no residue on windows. Don't use very old tape.

Buying Tip: A serious paint store is likely to have a variety of specialized tapes available.

Paints, Stains, Finishes, Wall Coverings, and Related Products and Tools

About Paints

There is no question that painting jobs are made easier and better when you use top-quality paint, brushes, and rollers. Scrimping here is not a good idea. Getting the cheapest paint will almost always yield an inferior job that takes longer, requires more paint, and needs repainting sooner. You can expect to pay more for the best-quality paint, but in the end it will cover better, be easier to apply, and last longer than lower-quality paint. Stick with the top grades of nationally advertised brands, such as Benjamin Moore, although professionals may recommend some regional brands.

To save money, comparison shop by telephone—paint prices can differ dramatically from store to store. Also, buying paint by the quart is very, very expensive—it can be over double the price per gallon, although generally it should be about a third of the gallon price. Paint does keep a long time, so buy by the gallon (or the 5-gallon container) if possible.

Check paint-can labels to get an indication of quality. Paint is made of three components: a *vehicle* (solvent or water); a *pigment* (color); and a *binder,* usually a resin, to hold it all together. Resin can be natural (old-fashioned linseed oil) or synthetic (alkyd, or acrylic polyvinyl acetate). The more pigment and resin the better; likewise, the more vehicle the cheaper it is and the less covering power it has (and what good is paint that won't cover well?). For common household paints, pigment content of about one-third and a vehicle and binder content of about two-thirds is considered good. Ask for the technical specifications sheet.

Regular decorative paints are generally divided into two types: *interior* and *exterior.* Those types are generally available in either alkyd/oil-based or latex/water-based, as explained below. Where you will be using paint defines what kind of paint you should buy. Your choice will be determined by which rooms or walls it is going on (bathroom, ceiling, shingles, etc.) and what kind of surface it is going to be used on (old glossy paint, brick, drywall, etc.).

A final note: The paint job can be torpedoed by bad surface preparation. This cannot be overemphasized. Good wall preparation will make any job that much better—and poor preparation will ruin it. When in doubt about any aspect of a job, first try a test patch of paint in an inconspicuous spot. Follow directions.

About Alkyd and Latex Paints

Almost all decorative paints are available today in either of two types—alkyd or latex, which means either oil- or water-based.

Alkyds, the modern replacement of old-fashioned linseed oil-based paint, are actually a blend of cooked vegetable oils and resins that dry faster and have less odor than the old petroleum oil paints. Alkyds are often called *oil-base* or *oil-alkyd* paints just like their old counterparts. You can use either alkyd or latex paint for most painting jobs, but not always. These differences are detailed in the items below and on the paint-can labels.

Adding to the confusion is an inconsistency on the part of manufacturers in names. Some latex paints are labeled "acrylic" or "vinyl"; these are the synthetic resins that act as binders of the paint to the water and do not define any inherent difference for the end user because each manufacturer's process and formulations are different, prohibiting direct comparison. Latex paints are also referred to as "waterborne" products.

The basic difference is that alkyd (or oil) paints are thinned and cleaned up with paint thinner, or turpentine, while latex paints are thinned and cleaned up with warm water, making them mighty popular with the average user. Latex paints dry much faster than alkyd paints, have less odor, no noxious fumes, and are slightly porous to moisture. However, alkyd paints tend to cover a bit better, are slightly more durable, and are less prone to showing brush marks. Quality and manufacturing differences make a blanket comparison impossible, though, and in the long run personal preference dictates most decisions as to which paint to use. Furthermore, paint manufacturers are putting more and more research into latex paints so that the differences are becoming less significant. One day soon latex will be the norm and alkyds the exception, especially if environmental protection laws make the manufacture of alkyd paint or high V.O.C. (volatile organic compounds) finishes impossible.

Note: Most spray paints are oil-based.

Interior Paints

Standard Interior Paint

Also Known As: Finish paint

> **Note:** This term applies to any top coat, exterior or interior.

Description: Either latex, alkyd oil, or old-fashioned linseed oil paint labeled for interior use. Interior paints are generally available in flat, semigloss, high-gloss and enamel formulations, though some manufacturers have intermediate designations of eggshell and satin between flat and semigloss, and some manufacturers consider semigloss to be satin. Actual finish depends on the manufacturer.

The term *latex enamel* is actually a misnomer, as enamels technically are oil-based varnish with pigments, but in this case latex enamel describes a hard, glossy-finish paint. In the extreme, latex paints are not as glossy as alkyd paints, and alkyd paints are not as flat as latex paints.

Most deck, floor, and other enamels are oil-base types—mostly polyurethane or varnish (oil)-based, though some are lacquer-based. (Varnish and lacquer are discussed in **Chapter 42**.) Plastic paints are good for metal and wherever extreme gloss is desired.

Use: Flat latex or alkyd is ordinarily used for walls, while semigloss, high-gloss, and enamel are for woodwork trim, bathrooms, kitchens, and furniture. (Paints for metal are covered in **Chapter 41**.)

> **Use Tips:** Flat paints dry lighter than the color on the label, while glosses tend to dry darker. Latex can be applied over old oil-base only if the surface is sanded and primed. A gallon will generally cover 400 square feet.

Interior and Exterior Primer

Types:

> *Alkali-resistant primer*
>
> *Alkyd primer*
>
> *Enamel undercoat*
>
> *Latex primer*
>
> *Stain-blocking primer*

Also Known As: Sealer, conditioner, undercoater, base coat, primer-sealer. *Stain-blocking primer:* stain killer

Description: Primers are almost always a white paint with a thin consistency. Alkyd is thinned with solvent, latex with water, and shellac-based stain-blocking primer with denatured alcohol.

Use: Providing a good, solid, even base for finish paint, because pigmented finish paints cannot sink in and bond as well as primer. Primer generally is used on previously unpainted (especially porous) surfaces, surfaces that have been heavily patched, when using high-gloss paint, and when changing from a dark to a light color. Finish print label will indicate the primer recommended. Stain-blocking primer (B-I-N, Kilz, and Enamelac are some brand names) is used when hiding stains, graffiti, soot, crayon, tape, grease, or knotholes, although some new latex and oil paints have *stain killer* in them. *Block filler* is used on masonry surfaces. *Alkali-resistant primer* is for damp masonry. (**Metal primers** are covered in **Chapter 41**.)

Use Tips: Any primer helps seal and bond. However, when a surface is water- or otherwise stained, use a shellac-based, stain-killing primer (this stuff solves more problems than any other paint).

Note: Nailheads will rust through latex primer unless they are sealed off. Alkyd is best for new drywall that is going to be wallpapered; latex primer should be used if the drywall is going to be painted. Figure coverage of about 250 square feet to the gallon. It is o.k. to paint over alkyd primer with latex.

Primers can be tinted with **colorants (below)** to give them a little more hiding power and to make the finish paint "holidays" (missed spots) less evident.

Buying Tips: Stain-blocking primer is good to have on hand for all types of problems. Always use a primer when painting or the binder in the finish coat will soak in. Spray cans designed for use on ceilings area are a big help. Shop thoroughly—many product variations now exist.

Ceiling Paint

Description: White, glare-resistant paint in both latex and alkyd formulations with more and coarser pigment than wall paint.

Use: For ceilings. Some people use ceiling paint on walls, but it is very dull and not as washable as wall paint; it gives a dead flat effect. However, wall paint is perfectly all right for use on ceilings.

 Use Tips: Painting ceilings is usually easier if you paint against the light from a window to detect wet, freshly painted areas. If white ceiling paint doesn't cover well, add a teaspoon or two of either lamp black or burnt umber **colorant (below)**.

Buying Tip: Ceiling paint costs less than wall paint.

Texture Paint

Description: Thick-bodied paint in various consistencies ranging from relatively thin liquid to material that can be worked almost like cement. Comes as a powder that is mixed with water or other base; can also be an additive, such as sand or perlite, bought separately or premixed. In any case it is tinted with colorant. Even "popcorn" texture is available, in aerosol form to boot.

Use: Excellent for covering a badly scarred and cracked ceiling or wall. Good for filling cracks in stucco. Also just for decorative purposes, such as a stipple finish.

> **Use Tips:** Many different items from crumpled paper to a trowel including **special rollers and sponges (Chapter 44)** may be used in working texture paint while wet. If you don't like one effect, you can always rework it. Cannot help badly peeling or flaking paint, as its weight will pull the rest of the old paint off; also, the cause of the damage must be cured first.

> **Buying Tip:** Because of its thick consistency, coverage per gallon of texture paint is limited, and therefore it is expensive, but it does solve minor problems.

Acoustical-Ceiling-Tile Paint

Description: Looks just like regular paint, but when it dries it is particularly porous.

Use: Painting acoustical tile. It does not interfere with the noise-absorbing qualities of the tiles.

Epoxy Paint

Description: Paint that comes in two containers, the contents of which are mixed together before use; dries to a hard, glass-like finish.

Use: Painting porcelain fixtures such as sinks and tubs, metal, concrete—just about anything.

> **Use Tips:** Epoxy is volatile and can be dangerous to use. Read cautionary material on the label and make sure area where you're working is well-ventilated. It is not cost-effective to use epoxy where other, less-expensive paints can be used.

> **Buying Tips:** A true epoxy is a two-container material. There are one-container so-called epoxy enamels but these are not true epoxies and will not perform like the two-container material.

Paint Colorant

Also Known As: Tinting colors

Description: A wide variety of colors in paste form, either oil-based or universal (oil and latex). Comes in tubes or cans.

Use: Tints primers or finish paints various colors.

> **Buying Tip:** Paint colorant is cheaper by the can than the tube.

Use Tips: Oil-based colorants can be used only with oil-based (alkyd) paint while universal colorants can be used with both latex or alkyd. Colorant cannot be used to darken a paint deeply—only to tint it. If you use too much colorant (see label for amounts suggested), the paint will become streaked with the colorant. One good use for lamp black or burnt umber colorant is to slightly darken ceiling paint so it covers better; the tinted paint may appear a bit gray in the can but will dry white.

Exterior Paints

Standard Exterior Paint

Description: Generally available in all formulations of flat and glossy. Some specialized paints are available, such as for aluminum siding or with "chalking" characteristics (a sort of weatherizing/fading process) that may or may not be desired. The final coat is called the *top* or *finish* coat.

Use: Painting siding and trim.

Use Tips: To save your energy, try to paint only in the shade. Also, many manufacturers recommend you paint only in the shade to avoid problems with the paint. In any case, do not paint late in the day, as the dew and reduced daylight will prevent the paint from drying properly.

Buying Tips: The same as for **interior paint (Chapter 39)**: buy the absolute best quality you can—and shop around for the best price. Each surface and location has particular needs, so choose paint with care.

Exterior Stains

Types:

> *Solid* (or *opaque*) *stain* (also known as *shingle paint*)
>
> *Semitransparent stain*
>
> *Preservative stain* (also known as *waterproofers*)
>
> *Specialized stains*

Description: Oil- or latex-based, with pigments and additives to resist mildew and moisture. Somewhat like a diluted paint with preservatives.

> *Solid stain:* Like flat paint, imparts an opaque finish.
>
> *Semitransparent stain:* Contains less pigment and allows the wood grain to show through.
>
> *Preservative:* Clear; merely darkens the wood slightly.
>
> *Specialized stains:* Include deck stains, weathering stains, and others.

Use: Penetrates and preserves exterior wood. Solid and semitransparent stains are designed for use on all kinds of wood siding. They color the wood to varying degrees and enable it to repel water. Preservatives enable wood to repel water and kill wood-rotting organisms, especially for wood in contact with soil or water. Among the specialized stains, deck stains are for application on decks only, while weathering stains give cedar and redwood an aged look upon application.

Use Tips: Solid and semitransparent stain is not as forgiving of incorrect techniques as paint. The chief problem is *lap marks*—stain dries so quickly that before you can apply a fresh brushful the previously applied stain is dry, causing lap marks. The key is to work in small areas quickly, always keeping a wet edge. Also, stir stain frequently to ensure that pigment is properly mixed with the vehicle. Depending on label instructions, may be applied with brushes, high-nap rollers, or spray. Wet the wood before staining on hot days or in direct sun.

Note: Observe safety precautions on can when using stains. Some are toxic, especially preservatives.

Buying Tips: Some cheaper, lower-quality stains do not contain preservatives, so all such stain does is color the wood—it offers no protection. Check label to ensure preservative is there.

Cement Paint

Also Known As: Portland cement paint, concrete paint

Description: Cement paint is available both as a powder that is mixed with water before use and premixed. Comes in various colors.

Use: Cement paints are good where a masonry surface is porous or badly damaged—the thick paint fills the cracks. Some brands are also intended to prevent damp basement walls and floors as well as for exterior use. For more serious waterproofing, see masonry sealers.

Use Tips: Read the cement paint label carefully—a special etcher, cleaner, or primer may be required and it may not work on floors or roofs. Some are made just for floors, ideal for garage floors. A specially made, pliable fiber brush is the best tool for application. The paint should be scrubbed into the surface.

Buying Tips: In many cases exterior latex paint works very well on masonry, but if the surface needs filling, use cement. Cement paint is specially formulated to not react to the powerful chemicals in cement.

Metal Paints

Metal Primers

Types:

Zinc chromate

Zinc oxide

Description: Zinc chromate is a white or yellow paint primer thinned with a chemical solvent, such as turpentine. Zinc oxide is a red primer also thinned with a chemical solvent.

Use:

Zinc chromate: For metal that is inside and not expected to be subject to moisture.

Zinc oxide: For metal that will be exposed to moisture.

> **Use Tips:** Follow primer labels for how to use the material. Once primed, you can use any finish paint—latex or alkyd—on the metal as long as it's compatible with the primer. Read the label on the paint. Alkyd primer will generally stand up better.

Rust-Inhibiting Paint

Description: Paint with a rust-inhibiting agent, or primer, that is part of the formula of the paint. In other words, the paint is primer and finish paint in one.

Use: Painting metal.

 Use Tips: Read the label carefully to ensure that the paint is a primer/finish in one. Some companies make alkyd enamels that are purportedly single-coat metal paints, but they require that a primer be used.

Aluminum Paint

Description: Aluminum-colored paint consisting of aluminum with a resin base.

Use: Painting any kind of exterior or interior metal—fences, radiators, sheds, mailboxes, flashing, etc.

 Use Tip: Aluminum paint should be allowed to dry overnight before recoating.

Buying Tips: Cheaper than other metal paints. Great results are easy in spray form.

Interior Stains and Clear Wood Finishes

About Interior Stains

Stains are an alternative to paint when you want the grain of the wood to show. As for which is best to use in which cases, it is often a matter of personal preference. Surface preparation and application are extremely important to a good job, if not more so than with paint. Some manufacturers mix stains with other products like tung oil, varnish, or polyurethane so that not only do they stain wood, but they also seal or coat it to provide protection. In most cases, however, another product is applied over the stain to protect it against moisture and wear—even when the stain totally hides the wood.

Using this kind of product correctly is almost an art. Test for results in an inconspicuous area first.

Interior Stains

Types:

> *Pigmented stain*
>
> *Dye stain*

Also Known As:

Pigmented stain: pigmented wiping stain, pigmented oil stain, wiping stain.

Dye: Aniline, spirit stain (if mixed with lacquer or other solvent), water stain, alcohol stain, NGR stain (if mixed with certain solvents), penetrating, dye-type.

Description:

Pigmented: Tiny particles of pigment suspended in either oil or latex (latex is water-based but not a water stain). Most common kind; almost like very thin paint. Designed to be brushed or wiped on with a cloth.

Dye: Aniline dye in powder form, mixed by user with water, oil or alcohol. When mixed with certain solvents becomes an NGR (non-grain-raising) stain, which dries very fast.

Use: All stains color wood and enhance its grain to varying degrees but provide no protection.

 Use Tip: Read product label closely for recommended method of application.

Pigmented: Stir constantly, as the pigment never dissolves—it is merely suspended. Wiping-type is easiest to use because you have more control over the rather slow process. Even though the colors are not as pure or transparent as dye stains, the results are quite good and colorfast.

Dye: Clearest, deepest penetrating colors—but the hardest to obtain and hardest to apply. Tends to raise grain. Surface and NGR types, or any mixed with lacquer, alcohol, or varnish, are hardest to handle and should be left to professionals. Used on the finest hardwoods; not sun-resistant.

 Buying Tip: Pigmented, or wiping, stain is the best for the typical do-it-yourselfer.

Stain Remover

Also Known As: Aniline stain remover

Use: Removes deeply imbedded stains and water marks.

Use Tips: If stains cannot be completely removed, sanding the wood will make it lighter. If it is an alcohol-based or lacquer-based stain, the wood can be lightened slightly by rubbing with denatured alcohol, lacquer thinner, or a mixture of both.

Bleach

Also Known As: Bleaching solution, wood bleach

Description: Liquid product, generally sold in two parts. Similar product but less strong (although poisonous) is *oxalic acid,* which is sold as crystals or powder.

Use: Applied to bare wood prior to final finishing to produce lighter tones, remove water marks, or to make an uneven surface color even.

 Use Tip: Use caution when working with these caustic products.

About Clear Wood Finishes

Technically, paint is just another finish for wood. But when one thinks of wood finishes one ordinarily thinks of products that allow the wood to show through to varying degrees. Here two such kinds of finishes are considered: *surface* and *penetrating*.

Clear finishes do one of two things: They protect the wood or, if they have some stain mixed in them, both color and protect it at the same time. However, even the clearest finish will darken wood somewhat. Think of varnish as oil paint without the pigment. Whatever you use, it is always a good idea to test the product on a separate piece of wood in an out-of-the-way spot to ensure that you will be getting the finish you really want.

Choosing the best finish for woodwork and furniture can be very confusing, as there are not only a number of very different products with similar end results but manufacturers blend all of them and call them by names that can be misleading. For example, someone might put a tiny amount of tung oil in a can of polyurethane and call it "tung oil varnish" or mix polyurethane with old-fashioned varnish. The end result is a blurring of some already fine distinctions. Caveat emptor: experiment.

About Surface Finishes

This group of finishes stays right on top of the wood, some-times giving a plastic-coated look, and can chip. They can be applied in successive layers to achieve a buildup.

Polyurethane

Also Known As: Urethane, poly, plastic varnish

Description: Available as both a petroleum derivative with a resin base and in a water-based formula. Very similar to tra-ditional oil-based varnish, of which it is the modern version. Dries quickly, and when thinned can act as its own primer/ sealer. Comes in satin or high-gloss, often called *gymna-sium finish*.

Use: All-around protective coating for wood furniture, trim, and floors. Resists alcohol, household chemicals, abrasion, and chipping. Most durable finish. Usually applied with a brush or lamb's-wool applicator, but also can be wiped on.

Use Tips: Can outlast traditional varnish two to one. As rugged as it is after curing, polyurethane must be carefully applied and directions for temperature, thinning, and surface preparation followed rigorously. Also, oil-based polyurethane vapors and sanding dust are potentially harm-ful, so use maximum ventilation and an appropriate respi-rator. Allow planty of time for each coat to cure—days in some cases.

> **$ Buying Tips:** Only the more expensive polyurethane is reliable. Get the very best—it is too hard to redo a floor if the finish doesn't bond correctly. Water-based finishes are generally less durable than oil-based, though some can be mixed with hardeners.

Varnish

Types:

> *Alkyd varnish*
>
> *Spar varnish*
>
> *Tung oil varnish*

Also Known As:

> *Spar:* Marine spar, outdoor, phenolic
>
> *Tung oil:* Penetrating oil varnish

> **Note:** The term *varnish* is sometimes used generically for all clear surface finishes and usually includes polyurethane, which is listed separately here because it is used so widely.

Description: Various durable formulations that dry with anywhere from a flat to a high gloss. Regular varnishes take a day or more to dry, but quick-drying, rubbing varnishes take only five hours or so to dry.

Thins with turpentine or mineral spirits (see label). New technology is being used to produce water-based varnishes.

Use: Finishing wood trim inside and outside the house.

Use Tips: Most varnishes take a long time to dry, so dust can be a problem. Varnish generally needs renewing from time to time. Spar varnish resists sunlight, water (and salt water), and alcohol more than others, but is not recommended for indoor use. Alkyd is less durable.

Buying Tips: The alkyd formulation is least expensive; tung oil the most expensive.

Shellac

Description: A mixture of a liquid traditionally made from an Indian insect, the lac bug, and alcohol. Currently artificial substitutes are used as well. Comes as a cream-colored liquid known as *white* shellac as well as an amber-colored one known as *orange*. It is available in a number of different "cuts," referring to the number of pounds of lac flakes, the basic shellac component, per gallon of denatured alcohol. For example, a 3-pound "cut" means 3 pounds of flakes mixed with one gallon of alcohol. Also available in flake form for mixing on location.

Use: Furniture finish that dries very quickly. Also used as a paint primer/sealer over hard-to-hide colors, patterns, or knotholes.

Use Tips: Shellac is not waterproof and responds badly to alcohol; it is also brittle. But as easy as it is to damage, it is easy to repair. It may be waxed for protection too.

> **$ Buying Tips:** Shellac has a short shelf life—do not buy anything over six months old. If a can is not dated, test it for clarity and drying time.

Lacquer

Description: High-gloss finish that dries almost instantly. Thins with lacquer thinner.

Use: Favored by professional furniture finishers because it dries so quickly. Somewhat similar to varnish. Goes on in thin coats.

> **Use Tips:** Apply with spray. It dries too quickly to be applied by brush unless specifically formulated. Somewhat delicate to use for amateurs, except as a touch-up using aerosol spray cans.

About Penetrating Oil Finishes

These finishes are absorbed into the fibers of the wood and actually become part of the wood. They are known for giving the more natural appearance of being "hand-rubbed" and are thus quite different from the surface finishes described above. However, the principle is similar—protecting wood.

Penetrating Oil Finishes

Types:

Linseed oil

Tung oil

Also Known As:

Blends: Danish oil, antique oil, Danish penetrating oil, drying oil finish

Tung: China wood oil, China nut oil

Description: Oil that penetrates into wood fibers and hardens (polymerizes). Typically leaves a satin finish with a hand-rubbed look. Many different types of blends are available, but most are formulations that include either tung oil and/or linseed oil and solvents and dryers. They often have stains incorporated as well. Some of the most popular brands are mostly linseed oil, which costs much less than tung oil. Some purists still use pure linseed or tung oil, but the blends solve a multitude of problems of the pure oils.

Tung oil is made from the nut of the tung tree, originally found only in China, and is a major ingredient in enamels and varnishes. Many finishes with varying amounts of tung oil in them use "tung oil" in their name, but some might only have a little in them. Check the label. Somehow it seems logical to put an oil made from a tree onto wood in your home.

Use: Protects wood trim and furniture inside the home. Easy to apply—brushes or wipes on with rag or hand. Very durable—needs little maintenance. Successive layers make for a greater sheen.

Use Tips: Some types are safe for surfaces that come into contact with food. Tung oil is highly resistant to water and mildew and dries fast. However, it is harder to get good results with pure tung oil than with the many modern penetrating oils that mix tung with various additives to give a much more predictable product. Similarly, linseed oil, squeezed from flax seeds, is the prime ingredient in some of the more popular blends but can be found pure. It should be "boiled" rather than "raw." Raw takes months to dry or may not completely dry at all.

Linseed oil tends to darken with age and need renewal. It is difficult to apply by itself. Like tung oil, it is a common ingredient in other products. Pure linseed oil is not recommended to the average do-it-yourselfer.

Sealer

Description: Clear oil that penetrates deep into wood fibers and seals surface.

Use: Protects against grain raising, moisture, and general weathering; as a conditioner and as a primer for varnish, penetrating stain, polyurethane, or high-gloss paints, preventing blotches. Can also be used as a rust inhibitor on metal.

Wood Filler

Description: Finely ground silex (rock) paste.

Use: Fills pores of open-grain wood and acts as a primer for varnish, polyurethane, and some lacquer. Can be tinted to match wood.

> **$ Buying Tips:** Some brands are available in a combination with stain and sealer for one-step usage. Others are formulated for filling small gaps.

Thinners, Cleaners, Removers, and Preparers

About Thinners

Thinners are known generally as solvents, or reducers. Most are petroleum distillates and therefore volatile and flammable. Handle with care.

Paint Thinner

Also Known As: Mineral spirits

Description: Petroleum distillate product. Lowest of a number of grades of chemicals distilled from coal, such as benzene, acetone, or naphtha. Extremely volatile and flammable. Generally has only a mild odor.

Use: Thinning and cleaning up oil-based paints; cleaning up various adhesives and other materials.

> **Use Tips:** Avoid splashing in eyes or prolonged contact with skin by wearing goggles and gloves. Avoid diluting final coats of paint; use primarily on prime coats.

> **$ Buying Tips:** Least expensive of this family of products. Can be made even cheaper by buying in bulk, using your own metal container; used thinner can also be recycled, as paint sinks to the bottom of the container. Don't buy premium-priced "odorless" thinners. It's the paint that smells, and you can't do much about that.

Turpentine

Also Known As: Pure gum spirits, turps

Description: Distilled from pine sap. Slightly lower-quality turpentine, called *steamed distilled* turpentine, is distilled from steamed pine tree bark. Has pronounced odor.

Use: Thins fine paints; particularly good for thinning exterior oil-based paints, making them easier to apply; general cleanup of all paints. Excellent for cleaning smooth surfaces.

> **Use Tip:** Better, quicker, stronger solvent than paint thinner, but has odor.

> **Buying Tip:** Much more expensive than paint thinner, which does most of the jobs that turpentine does.

Lacquer Thinner

Description: Extremely volatile petroleum-based solvent.

Use: Cleaning, removing, and thinning lacquer or other oil-based paint products. Cleaning any durable surface, especially tape or adhesive residue.

 Use Tip: Extremely flammable; use with maximum ventilation.

Denatured Alcohol

Description: Volatile solvent.

Use: Thinning and removing paints and varnishes, removing grease and other smudges, fuel for chafing dishes. Main solvent for shellac.

 Use Tip: Safer than wood or methanol alcohols, which are strong poisons.

 Buying Tip: You can buy in bulk at a very low price from a gas station that mixes its own gasohol.

Paint and Varnish Remover

Types:

> *Water wash off remover*
>
> *Solvent wash off remover*
>
> *No-wash remover*
>
> *Latex paint remover*

Also Known As: Stripper, chemical stripper, paint remover

Description: All are dangerous, strong chemicals with varying degrees of volatility.

> *Water wash off:* Liquid or paste containing detergents that allow it to be washed off with water. Very volatile, but nonflammable, unlike other removers.
>
> *Solvent wash off:* Liquid or paste that is washed away with solvent, either a petroleum distillate or denatured alcohol.
>
> *No-wash:* Remover that can be merely wiped off surface with an absorbent cloth.
>
> *Latex paint remover:* Solvent or water-based chemical that acts only on latex, not oil-based paints.

Use: Removes paint, varnishes, and other finishes from wood. Typically the remover is applied, allowed to remain a specified time, and then it—and the old finish—are scraped off. Latex paint removers also remove crayon, tape residue, gum, and grease.

Use Tips: Removers work, but most are dangerous, very strong chemicals, and are messy. You must read labels carefully for cautions. Use proper safety equipment: goggles and heavy rubber gloves, long sleeves and long pants, adequate ventilation, and keep a water source ready in case you get some caustic chemical on your skin. Do not use in direct sunlight. Note that a remover may not be necessary in the first place. Other chemicals can remove finishes. For example, denatured alcohol will remove shellac as well as some varnishes. Lacquer thinner takes off lacquer. Heat takes paint (but not varnish) off very well, through the use of **heat guns** or **plates (Part V, Chapter 45)**, and it is not toxic—though the old paint may be. Use a liquid remover only on horizontal surfaces or it will run off. A paste remover can be used on vertical and horizontal surfaces. Water-based strippers raise the wood grain. Plastic abrasive pads are excellent substitutes for steel wool when removing gooey paint residue.

Buying Tips: There are many different removers available, but only some are nontoxic. Among the toxic ones, those containing methylene chloride work best. Check labels; the more of this ingredient the better.

Roll and Brush Cleaner

Description: Caustic liquid, paint stripper with additives.

Use: Alternative to paint thinner for cleaning extremely paint-encrusted brushes and rollers.

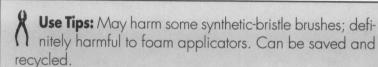

Use Tips: May harm some synthetic-bristle brushes; definitely harmful to foam applicators. Can be saved and recycled.

Sanding Liquid

Also Known As: Liquid sandpaper

Description: Liquid abrasive.

Use: Scoring glossy surfaces prior to repainting with another high-gloss or latex paint; gives the new paint a "tooth" to hold on to.

Use Tip: Dangerous, strong chemical. Use goggles and gloves.

Rubbing Agents

Types:

> *Rottenstone*
>
> *Pumice stone*
>
> *Tripoli*
>
> *Rouge*

Also Known As: Flour pumice, rubbing powder

Description: Finely ground stone powder.

Use: To rub with water or special oil (usually paraffin) to give final, delicate polish to surfaces.

Rottenstone: For high-gloss finish on varnished or lacquered wood surfaces, sometimes used after pumice.

Pumice: For soft, satin luster on varnished or lacquered surfaces.

Tripoli: Finer in texture than both the above. For polishing fine metal and jewelry.

Rouge: Finest rubbing/polishing agent for metal.

Painting Tools and Accessories

About Painting Tools

There are many kinds of painting tools, but a number of them are more gimmicky than useful. The tools presented below are all of good practical value, though in a number of cases one can be used for a variety of jobs.

Brushes

Description: Brushes come in a great variety of sizes and styles, but for the do-it-yourselfer brushes ranging from 1" to 4" wide and made of either a synthetic material or animal hair—normally Chinese hog bristle—will serve well. *Flat ends* have evenly trimmed bristles; *chisel ends* are V-shaped.

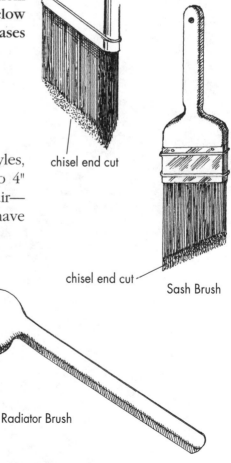

chisel end cut

chisel end cut

Sash Brush

Wall Brush

Radiator Brush

Types:

Angular or *angle sash brush* (1" to 3" wide, end cut on angle, long handle)

Calcimine brush, or *block brush* (heavy and thick, 7" wide)

Oval sash and trim, varnish and enamel brush (round, sized by number, 2-20)

Radiator brush (sash brush at 45-degree angle to long handle)

Sash and trim brush (flat end, 1" to 4" wide)

Varnish or *enamel brush* (chisel end, 2" to 3" wide)

Wall brush (chisel or flat end, 3" to 5" wide)

Use: Apply paint to any surface inside or outside the house and on a great variety of other items. Also used to apply many other finishes, such as varnish.

Use Tips: When applying paint try not to wipe the paint brush on the edge of the can. Instead, dip the brush in about one-third of the way, tap it back and forth inside the can, then apply the paint. A $2\frac{1}{2}$" brush is perfect for use with quart cans.

Brushes made of synthetic bristles serve well for both oil and latex paints, especially polyester, but do not use natural-bristle brushes with latex—they are not compatible and will soak up the water in the paint. Nylon bristles may dissolve in some solvents.

For trim a 2" brush is good. If you have large areas to paint, such as cabinets, a 3" or at most a 4" brush should be used. Brushes wider than this would be too heavy. Note special types listed above. Chisel ends and angular cuts make it possible to "cut in," or start painting from a corner, such as a window, and are generally better. Longer handles help when doing detailed trim work. *Angled radiator brushes* are helpful for painting trim in corners or at ceilings, as well as for reaching behind radiators. Large, thick block brushes are excellent for priming (indeed, sometimes they are called *priming brushes*). *Stain brushes* are thicker and bulkier than paint brushes.

> ₷ **Buying Tips:** As quality varies, compare brushes against one another. Quality brushes have a lot of bristles. The bristles are of varying lengths and the tips are *flagged*— they have split ends, just like hair—so the paint can be applied more smoothly. And they taper to a point. Good brushes cost more but stand up to repeated cleanings and do a much better job. Get good ones.

Cheap brushes lose bristles in the paint and are generally much less efficient in carrying paint, making the job take longer and you work harder. Bristles should also be relatively long. Beware of China or ox hair "blends" of bristles— they may be cheap brushes with only 1 percent of those bristles. The good ones say "100% China Bristle" or the like. The most inexpensive brushes (made for one-time use) may be called *chip brushes*.

About Paint Rollers

A paint roller actually consists of two parts, the handle and a fabric-covered cylindrical cover that slips onto it. Both parts are often called rollers whether assembled or not.

Paint Roller

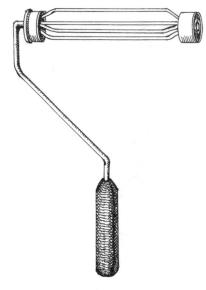

Paint Roller

Also Known As: Roller frame, roller

Description: Handle attached to metal rod that holds roller covers. Should have threads in end of handle for attachment to an extension pole for painting walls and ceilings. Handles come with either a wire cage–like section for mounting a sleeve or a wing-nut arrangement. Sold in 7" or 9" as well as 1" to 3" sizes.

Use: Painting walls and ceilings and other large, flat areas. Small rollers are for trim or radiators. Longer rollers are made for painting vast areas of flat wall.

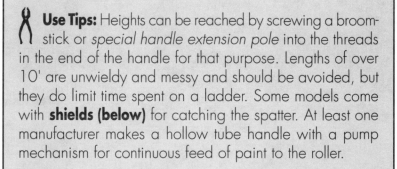

Use Tips: Heights can be reached by screwing a broomstick or *special handle extension pole* into the threads in the end of the handle for that purpose. Lengths of over 10' are unwieldy and messy and should be avoided, but they do limit time spent on a ladder. Some models come with **shields (below)** for catching the spatter. At least one manufacturer makes a hollow tube handle with a pump mechanism for continuous feed of paint to the roller.

Buying Tips: The cage-type handle works better than the kind with wing nuts. Choose a heavy-duty model where possible. More expensive but worth it.

Roller Cover

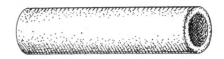

Roller Cover

Also Known As: Sleeve

Description: 9" long by about 2" thick tube made of cardboard or plastic, covered with naps or fabric coverings made of synthetic material (such as nylon or rayon) or natural lamb's wool in different thicknesses. Also available in narrower, "mini-roller" 1" to 3" long sizes. *Texture rollers*, for use with texture paint or for special effects, are also available. *End caps* fit in the end of the cover to convert roller to a full-sized corner painter.

End Cap for Roller Cover

Use: Applying paint to wide areas with a **paint roller, (above)**. Roller covers are removed after use either for cleaning or to be discarded.

> **Use Tips:** The rule is, the rougher the surface being painted, the longer the nap should be. A $3/8$" nap works well for smooth walls and ceilings, while $3/4$" is good for semirough surfaces, such as stucco. You need a short nap for satin, eggshell, and other high-gloss paints. *Texture,* or *specialty rollers*, made of plastic loops, foam, carpet, rag, leather, and other materials, are used for special effects. The whole range of naps is from $1/4$" to $1 1/4$".
>
> Nylon and some other synthetics work well, but rayon is a poor choice. Lamb's wool is fine for long-nap rollers, but never with latex paint (it will absorb all the water). Small rollers, intended for trim, work well for touch ups or when you wish to use paint directly from a can with a **bucket grid (below)**.

Leather Mottling Texture Roller

Paint Roller Spatter Shield

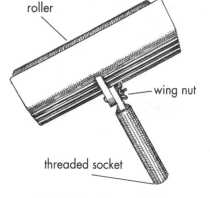

roller

wing nut

threaded socket

Paint Roller Spatter Shield

Also Known As: Spatter guard, spatter shield

Description: Plastic cover for paint rollers shaped to hide all
but the part in contact with the surface being painted. Attaches to extension poles with an adjustable wing nut and
clamp that permits use at any angle.

Use: Preventing droplets of paint from being sprayed onto
the floor and you.

Use Tips: Don't use too much paint on the roller, and
move slowly to prevent excess splatter. Empty out the
shield from time to time.

$ Buying Tip: Good insurance.

Roller Washer

Description: Plastic tube about a foot long and 2" wide with two removable cap ends, one with a drain hole and one with a garden hose attached. It is forced over a paint-laden roller.

Use: Removing leftover latex (water-based) paint from a roller by forcing it off with pressure and back into the paint can, then by washing the roller in water by attaching it directly to a faucet.

Foam Rollers

Also Known As: Trim rollers, specialty rollers

Types:

Foam corner roller

Foam paint tongs

Foam pipe roller

Foam edge roller

Foam trim roller

Description: Small foam rubber rollers of various shapes suited to specific tasks, mounted on short, special handles.

Foam corner roller: Doughnut shaped roller with pointed edge.

Foam paint tongs: Small rollers on ends of wire tongs.

Foam pipe roller: Concave roller.

Foam edge roller: 1" wide roller.

Foam trim roller: 3" wide roller, about 1" in diameter. A 3 or 4" long *tight spot roller, mini roller,* or *radiator roller* may use short foam or fabric roller covers with various naps, but on a 12" to 21" long handle.

Foam Paint Tongs

Use:

Foam corner roller: Painting corners.

Foam paint tongs: Painting fences or other thin items such as radiators two sides at a pass.

Foam pipe roller: Painting pipes, half the surface at a pass.

Foam edge roller: "Cutting in" along corners instead of using a brush.

Foam trim roller: Painting wider trim and radiators, as well as touchups. 3" and 4" rollers, with their narrow diameters, allow you to paint directly from a 1-gallon can instead of having to use a tray.

Foam Pipe Roller

Use Tip: As with full-sized rollers, don't put too much paint on at any one time or it will drip.

Buying Tips: Specialty rollers are a great time-saver and quite inexpensive to boot. Some trim rollers are sold with a small tray, excellent for small projects. Those with *covered ends* (the nap extends over one end of the roller) allow you to paint corners and walls at the same time.

Roller Tray

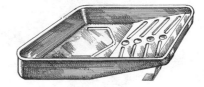
Roller Tray

Description: Shallow metal or plastic pan about 10" square, with one deep end and short legs at the upper end. May come with a grid insert. Inexpensive disposable plastic liners may be used to eliminate the need for cleaning the tray after use.

Use: Holds paint for use with rollers. Grid aids spreading paint evenly onto roller and thereby helps prevent splatter and drips.

 Buying Tip: Quality trays have deeper paint wells and hold more paint than cheaper models.

Paint Pourer

Paint Pourer

Description: Large plastic ring with spout that fits into a standard 1-gallon paint can. Some models have flip-top lid that re-seals between uses.

Use: Makes it possible to pour paint without dripping or messing up the ridge of the can. Protects label from drips, preserving it for future reference.

Buying Tips: Handy if you are pouring paint into trays. If you are anti-gadget, punch holes in the ridge to drain paint, and pour quickly, and wipe up drips immediately.

Bucket Grid

Bucket Grid

Also Known As: Paint grid, roller grid

Description: 7" square expanded steel grid with short legs, one set of which is curled (5-gallon model), or 4" × 8" plastic grid with loop handle (1-gallon model).

Use: Removing excess paint and spreading paint evenly on a roller within a can of paint, without having to use a **roller tray (above)**. The 1-gallon model can only be used with 3" or 4" long rollers.

 Use Tip: Remember to keep stirring the paint that remains in the can, and not to leave it open too long.

 Buying Tip: Great way to speed up a big job and reduce material to clean up.

Cordless Electric Paint Roller

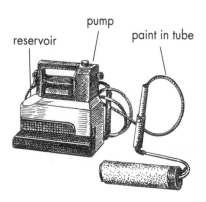

Cordless Electric Paint Roller

Description: Not just a power version of the *manual roller,* but a painting system made up of a large container for paint, an electric pump, a hose that takes paint from the pump to the roller (through the handle), and a roller with a splatter guard.

Use: Continuous painting of large surfaces, such as walls. Pump keeps roller continuously wet with new paint. Eliminates the need for a **roller tray (above)** and the related repeated pauses to use it.

Buying Tip: For big projects only.

Paint Pad

Also Known As: Painting pad, brush pad

Description: Pads of varying widths, around 1" to 8", with a rigid back with a synthetic or natural nap, like rollers, and of varying lengths. Pads slip in and are held by a handle.

Use: Painting all the surfaces that rollers can paint, but with the versatility of a brush.

Paint Pad

Use Tips: Pads are faster than a brush but not as fast as a roller. They generally do a smoother job applying paint than a roller.

Foam Brush

Also Known As: Foam paint applicator

Description: Tapered slabs of foam mounted on handles, usually wood.

Use: For testing, touch-ups, or painting trim.

Foam Brush

Use Tips: Since their cost is so low, discard foam applicators after use. People are divided as to their effectiveness, so experiment.

Lamb's-Wool Paint Applicators

Description: A short nap of natural lamb's wool mounted on wood. The two most common designs are flat sticks (often paint-mixing sticks) and a more serious model that resembles a floor sponge, about 4" by 10", attached to a broom handle.

Use: The sticks are used for painting radiators or wrought-iron fences, where you need to get into narrow spaces, and the flat floor applicator applies polyurethane to floors.

 Use Tip: Clean thoroughly and carefully.

Stippling Sponge

Stippling Sponge

Description: Foam rubber cylinder, 3" thick × 5" wide, with a textured pattern on one side and threaded extension pole socket on the back.

Use: Creating a textured effect in painted surfaces. The sponge is dabbed, swept, or rotated to create different patterns.

 Use Tips: Let yourself go! Be creative in your painting! Yields much better results than a regular sponge.

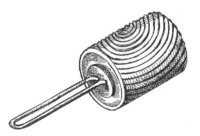

Graining Tool

Graining Tool

Also Known As: Heart grainer

Description: Quarter or half cylinder of rubber with curved, raised ribs and a handle out one side. Also available in a *graining roller* version. A similar item, a *check roller*, is made of a series of metal plates. See illustration on the facing page.

Use: Creating a heartwood grain effect with paint or stain.

> **Use Tips:** Experiment to see what grain effects you can create and how much pressure to use. Wipe off tool after each pass.

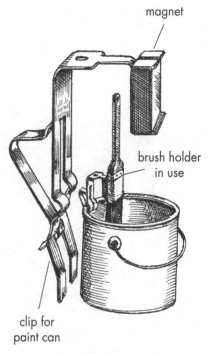

magnet

brush holder in use

clip for paint can

Magnetic Brush Holder

Magnetic Brush Holder

Description: Steel clip about 3" to 6" high that slides onto side of paint or joint compound can. Large magnet at top.

Use: Holding paint brushes or **taping knives (Chapter 50)** by their metal ferrules or blades.

Extension Brush Holder

Description: Small, hinged two-part device, one side of which clamps onto paintbrush handles, the other side of which is threaded to fit onto the end of a broomstick or *roller handle extension pole*.

Use: Painting with a paintbrush instead of a roller on the end of a long pole.

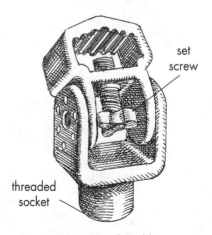

set screw

threaded socket

Extension Brush Holder

> **$ Buying Tips:** Handy for the odd touch-up or trim problem where using a ladder is too time-consuming or cumbersome, such as in a room full of furniture (or when the painter is not willing or capable of handling a large ladder).

Painter's Mitt

Description: Fabric or lamb's wool-covered mitten.

Use: The mitt is worn like a regular mitten and dipped into the paint, and then touched to whatever is being painted—your hand becomes the tool. Ideal for speedier painting of items such as pipes and wrought-iron fences, where the surface is relieved, shaped oddly, or otherwise difficult for a roller or even a brush to get into.

> **☍ Use Tip:** Dip the mitt only about one-third of the way into the paint.

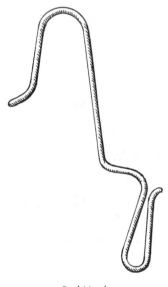

Pail Hook

Also Known As: Paint-can hook, pot hook

Description: Large, heavy wire S-hook. Also made with a swivel and snap hook.

Use: Hangs from ladder rung to hold a 1-gallon can of paint by its handle.

Pail Hook

Pail Opener

Pail Opener

Also Known As: Lid opener

Description: Plastic handle with C-shaped opening that has hooked ends.

Use: Opening plastic 5-gallon buckets of anything, such as paint or joint compound, without breaking the rim (or your tools or fingernails).

 Use Tip: Doubles as a pail hook.

 Buying Tip: A handy, inexpensive item.

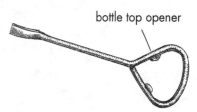

bottle top opener

Paint Can and Bottle Opener

Paint Can Openers

Description: Various types are available. The multipurpose tool model is a flat, solid bar of steel with a chisel on one end and a fishtail on the other, with a teardrop hole and a small tongue on either end. A curved and a square notch are on either side. Another version, the *paint can and bottle opener,* is made of steel wire, with a loop handle and flat, slightly bent end.

Use: Opening paint cans gently, so as to preserve the sealing ability of the lid. Also, depending on the model, for opening bottles, pulling nails, and cleaning rollers and putty knives.

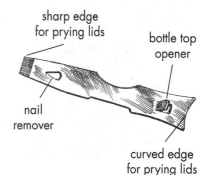

sharp edge
for prying lids

bottle top
opener

nail
remover

curved edge
for prying lids

Paint Can Opener

$ Buying Tips: Very handy and much better than screw-drivers or quarters. Some of the more successful paint stores actually give them away at times. Keep your eyes peeled for such a wondrous deal.

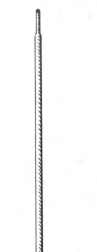

Power Paint Mixer

Also Known As: Power mixing paint mixer, mixing paddle, paint blender, power mixer, paint mixer, drill mixer

Description: Propeller, spiral, or small paddle on end of metal rod that fits into power drill. Made for 1-gallon and 5-gallon cans.

Use: Inserted into paint cans for vigorous stirring without splashing, like a kitchen blender.

Power Paint Mixer

$ Buying Tip: A must for 5-gallon cans.

Paint Shield

Also Known As: Trim guard

Description: Long, slightly curved, or flat metal or plastic with a handle.

Use: Allows the painter to "cut in" narrow areas such as trim without getting paint on adjacent surfaces. Also used as a straight edge for trimming wallpaper.

Paint Shield

Use Tips: Not particularly useful if used improperly. While the painter won't get excess paint on the window glass or whatever the shield is protecting, the shield itself must be continually wiped off or else it will smear paint in unwanted places.

Glass Masking Solution

Description: Fast-drying liquid solution applied with a wide applicator.

Use: Masking off glass without using tape, prior to painting windows. The material is scraped off with a razor knife after the paint is dry. Also used as a straight edge for trimming wallpaper.

Buying Tip: Faster and easier to use than masking tape.

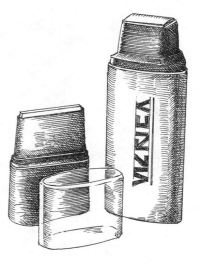

Glass Masking Solution

Drop Cloths

Also Known As: Drops

Description: Large plastic, paper and plastic, or canvas sheet, commonly 9' × 12'. Plastic comes in a variety of thicknesses as well as from 1 mil (service weight) to 4 mil (extra-heavy).

Use: Protects floors, furniture, and landscaping from paint splatter and other mess.

Use Tips: Fold up carefully after use and keep one side clean. Plastic is very slippery, so avoid using it on floors. Anything less than a 4 mil thickness is likely to tear too easily.

Buying Tips: Get a good, big canvas one—it makes work go faster. Cut into small pieces for more convenient handling on small jobs.

Brush Comb

Brush Comb/Roller cleaner

Also Known As: Comb

Description: Plastic- or wood-handled comb with long steel teeth. Also made as a *brush comb/roller cleaner,* which has jagged teeth as part of a blade and a round notch on the opposite side for cleaning rollers.

Use: For straightening and cleaning bristles of a brush or cleaning a roller at the end of a paint job.

Brush and Roller Spinner

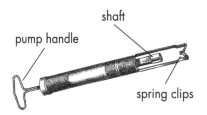

shaft

pump handle

spring clips

Brush and Roller Spinner

Also Known As: Brush cleaner, paint brush/roller cleaning tool, brush spinner, brush and roller cleaner

Description: Somewhat like a bicycle pump, with a loop handle and a metal cylinder, but with a spring-tension gripping device on one end to hold paint brushes or roller covers. Pump action spins the head very rapidly, creating strong centrifugal force on brushes and roller covers.

Use: Spinning paint brushes or roller covers at high speed to remove paint quickly and thoroughly without the use of excessive amounts of water or chemicals.

> **Use Tip:** Don't be like an unwanted wet dog. Spin inside a bag or a large bucket, as this thing makes the paint really fly. Very handy when working with a variety of colors.

> **Buying Tips:** An amazingly effective tool. Helps preserve expensive, high-quality brushes. Worth its relatively high price.

Cheesecloth

Description: Loosely woven, light cotton cloth.

Use: Originally used to strain old-fashioned paints; it's now used mainly in the kitchen (excellent for straining chicken stock). Also useful for applying stains and as a lintless cloth for wiping down surfaces with denatured alcohol before a final finish.

Tack Cloth

Description: Waxy **cheesecloth (above).**

Use: Final wiping of sawdust prior to painting or finishing. Its waxiness picks up dust.

Spray Can Handle

Spray Can Handle

Description: Pistol grip and trigger device with large ring instead of a barrel.

Use: Snaps on to almost any aerosol can to make pressing the paint can button easier, cleaner, and more controllable.

> **Buying Tip:** Makes any spray paint job easier and better.

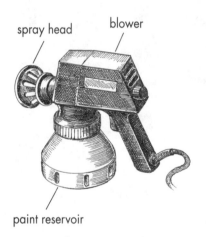

spray head   blower

paint reservoir

Airless Paint Sprayer

Airless Paint Sprayer

Description: Electronic pressurizer with trigger handle that sits atop a small paint container. Paint is atomized without mixing with additional air.

Use: Painting or staining large, irregular surfaces or items such as fences, decks, house siding, lattice, and concrete block. Also good for items such as wicker furniture, where using a brush would take too long.

Paint and Finish Removal Tools

Heat Gun

Description: Looks like a heavy-duty hair dryer—gun-shaped, electric, hot-air source (500 to 750 degrees).

Use: Softens multiple layers of paint for removal from molding or other detail.

Use Tips: Don't linger too long in one spot or a fire could start. Be especially cautious when removing lead paint.

Buying Tips: Avoid inexpensive plastic guns—they tend to drop their heat level as you work and do not have replaceable elements. The best are industrial-duty, with a cast-aluminum body and a ceramic heating element.

Heat Plate

Description: Electrified metal hot plate with handle that works up to about 1,100 degrees.

Use: Softens multiple layers of old paint for removal from large flat surfaces such as doors and clapboards.

About Scrapers

Even the semiactive handyperson frequently uses various kinds of scrapers, so it is a good idea to buy quality tools—they will last longer and be easier to use. The inexpensive ones tend to rust very easily, get dull quickly, and lose their handles.

Wall Scraper

Wall Scraper

Also Known As: Scraper, push scraper

Description: A stiff or slightly flexible, flat, triangularly shaped metal blade, commonly 3½" wide at the front, with a wooden or plastic handle. A particularly long, narrow, and stiff scraper is called a *burn-off knife*.

Use: For scraping off peeling paint (whether old or while being softened with heat or chemicals), old plaster, or wallpaper. Can also be used as a trowel for *small* patching jobs, though that is easier with **flexible knives** made for the job **(Part VII, Chapter 50)**.

> **$ Buying Tips:** Look for such signs of quality as a one-piece blade that extends through the handle, is individually ground (or shaped), mirror-finished, and is of slightly flexible high-carbon steel. Good handles have large rivets and often a reinforced end for tapping nails into place, called a *nail-setting end*.

Shave Hook

Also Known As: Molding scraper, window scraper

Description: Long handle with small triangular or variously shaped blades perpendicular to handle. Generally sold in sets of three shapes (square, circular, and triangular), although models with interchangeable heads are available and convenient when scraping different shapes of molding. A large, heavy-duty version is called a *strip,* or *glue scraper.*

Use: Scraping softened paint or other finishes from window frames, moldings, doors, and other flat and curved surfaces.

Shave Hook

> **$ Buying Tip:** Get a set of blades so that you can select a blade to match the contour of whatever you are scraping.

5-in-1 Tool

Also Known As: 6-in-1 putty knife, combination glazier's knife

Description: Stiff metal blade and handle similar to the **wall scraper (above)** that has a notched chisel end with a point on one side.

Use: Scrapes paint (with chisel end), opens cracks, cleans rollers (with large notch), removes putty (with point), and spreads adhesives.

5-in-1 Tool

> **$ Buying Tips:** Very handy to have. If it has a *nail-setting (hammer) end* (metal cap on end of handle) it can drive home small nails.

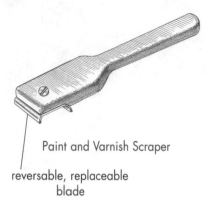

Paint and Varnish Scraper

reversable, replaceable
blade

Paint and Varnish Scraper

Also Known As: Wood scraper, hook scraper

Description: Consists of a short, hooked metal blade, 1" to 5" wide, with a long wooden, plastic, or metal handle. Blades are replaceable. Some models have four-sided blades that can be rotated around a central screw as they become dull.

Use: Removing old paint and varnish and smoothing wood.

 Use Tips: Take care not to gouge soft wood. Sharpen or replace blades often to make work easier.

Buying Tips: Blades should be of high-carbon steel; long-lasting tungsten-carbide scrapers are also available.

Razor Blade Scraper

Also Known As: Retractable blade scraper, glass scraper, window scraper

Description: Small, flat metal handle that holds a retractable single-edged razor blade.

Use: Mainly used to scrape paint off windows but can be used for other scraping jobs where you are dealing with a hard, nonporous surface.

Razor Blade Scraper

Use Tip: Blades dull quickly, so keep replacement blades handy.

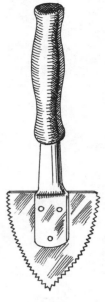

Window Opener

Also Known As: Window zipper, Windo-Zipper™

Description: Short spatula-like metal blade with toothed edges and a short handle.

Use: Cutting paint around windows that is blocking them shut.

Window Opener

Note: See **Part VII, Chapter 50** for taping and putty knives.

Wall Coverings, Materials, and Tools

About Wallcoverings

Once there was only wallpaper—a wallcovering literally made of paper—to decorate walls and ceilings. Today, wallpaper is still plentiful but a variety of other materials are used, and thus the term *wallcoverings* is more apt.

Wallcoverings

Types:

> *Wallpaper*
>
> *Vinyl wall coverings* (popular brands include Wall-Tex® and Sanitas®)
>
> *Special materials wall coverings*

Also Known As: Wallpaper (only sometimes literally accurate, but often used generically to describe material that is not paper)

Description: Wallcoverings generally come $20^{1}/_{2}$", 27", 36", and 54" wide, but almost always contain a total of 36 square feet of wallcovering per roll; more and more coverings are coming from abroad, though, and are measured in the metric system, yielding about 28 square feet per roll. Smaller widths, known as borders, are sold by the linear yard. Wallcoverings come prepasted or unpasted. Some are *dry strippable,* meaning that once installed they can be easily removed from the wall in one strip without using messy chemicals. Sold in "bolts"—one to three rolls, depending on the thickness of the material, but usually priced by the single roll. They are sold this way to cut down on waste when covering a standard 8' high wall.

Wallpaper: Simply paper on which a design has been imprinted.

Vinyl: This comes in various forms. One has a very thin clear vinyl coating over wallpaper; another has a strong fabric backing. While the vinyl may be solid, smooth, and shiny, it is also made "expanded" or textured to simulate many other materials from wood to suede. The patterns, colors, and textures are virtually endless. Vinyl may be either "washable," which can be washed mildly, or "scrubbable," which may be vigorously scrubbed.

Special materials: These are woven textile, grass cloth, and materials other than vinyl or paper, such as metal foil.

Use: Chief use is decoration of walls as an alternative to painting or paneling, but in the case of vinyl, protects from moisture as well. Borders are used along the tops of walls. Most coverings can be used on ceilings too.

Use Tips: Vinyl is highly recommended for its cleanability and variety of surface appearances. Some fabrics, and especially grass cloth, are very hard to keep clean. 54" wide rolls are extremely difficult to handle but leave fewer seams. Recommended only for nonpattern types of covering, such as canvas. Use as thick a wall covering as possible to cover walls in poor condition; a product called *lining paper*, a plain wallcovering available in many weights, is good. A new polyester fiber-fill material is heavier and more versatile. Be sure to follow the manufacturer's directions closely, especially when selecting paste and when matching covering to the surface. Avoid applying paper over latex paint less than 6 months old.

Buying Tips: The more expensive types are fabrics, grass cloth, flocked paper, embossed paper (anaglyphic), and the like. Patterns and colors that are out of style are always cheaper. How-to books have many formulas for determining how much paper to buy for a particular room. Try for a 10-percent discount when you buy wallcovering; many retailers will give it to you just for the asking. Avoid untrimmed paper that comes with *selvage*, the unprinted edge that must be trimmed off.

Wallpaper Paste

Description: Specially formulated glue for hanging wallpaper; heavy vinyl wall coverings need a specified type. Usually water soluble.

Use: Holds wall coverings to wall.

Use Tips: Follow directions carefully for wall preparation. Using **wall size (below)** is usually a good idea.

Wall Size

Also Known As: Wallpaper primer

Description: Powder sold in bags or boxes. Mixed with water for use. Some specialized mixtures contain different types of primer as well.

Use: Applied as a primer to porous, especially plaster, walls before using **wallpaper paste (above)**. Prevents the paste from soaking into a porous wall and thus not adhering to the paper, and provides a smoother surface for the paste that allows more "open time" for positioning the paper (also called *slide time*) as well as, eventually, better bonding. Generally makes for a better wallpapering job. Some primers are designated for use with "strippable" wallcoverings.

Buying Tips: *Primer/wall size* with additives to fit a variety of wall surfaces and paper is available and worthwhile. Note the details of your walls and paper and check the labels for the right one for you.

Wallpaper Remover

Description: Liquid or gel that is sprayed, rolled, sponged, or brushed onto old wallpaper. May contain wetting agents and/or enzymes.

Use: Softens old adhesive so that wallpaper may be scraped away.

 Use Tips: Gently slit or score (perforate) the paper first to foster better absorption. Wipe down the wall with remover solution after the paper is removed to eliminate any adhesive residue.

About Wallcovering Tools

One of the more common household decorating activities calls for a few specialized tools. Some typical items also often used but listed elsewhere are a **plumb bob (Part I, Chapter 10)** and a **razor knife (Part I, Chapter 6)**. Rent a *steamer* for removing stubborn old wallpaper.

Seam Roller

Seam Roller

Also Known As: Oval seam roller, hardwood roller

Description: Small wooden roller with a wooden handle.

Use: Flattens wet wallcovering seams.

 Use Tip: Wipe clean after each use.

Paste Brush

Paste Brush

Description: Typically a 6" wide, thick, long-bristle brush with a large wooden or plastic handle.

Use: Applying wallcovering paste.

Smoothing Brush

Smoothing Brush

Also Known As: Smoother, wallcovering smoother

Description: Very wide (up to 12"), very thin, flat, short-bristle brush.

Use: Smoothing wallcovering just after it is applied to the wall.

 Buying Tip: A flexible *plastic smoother*, a large flat rectangular plastic sheet with a handle, might be a good alternative.

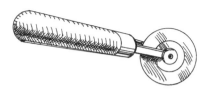

Casing Knife

Casing Knife

Also Known As: Roller knife, smooth-blade casing knife

Description: Small wheel blade with a wooden handle; resembles a pizza cutter.

Use: For safely trimming excess wallcovering from windows, doors, baseboards, and so on.

Use Tips: Even though this is the one tool specifically designed to trim wallcoverings, the **razor knife (Part I, Chapter 6)** actually works better (use a fresh blade after every cut or two; it is worth the slight expense in blades to avoid ruining a piece of wall covering with a dull blade alongside a straight edge (wallcovering tool) such as a **trim guard** or a **wide taping knife (Part VII, Chapter 50)**.

Magnetic Wrist Band

Description: Plastic wrist band, available in neon colors, with a rectangular, magnetic square instead of a watch.

Use: Holding single-edge razor blades, screws, or nails conveniently.

Magnetic Wrist Band

Use Tip: Aim carefully when putting blades back on your wrist after use.

Wallpaper Scraper

Also Known As: Wallpaper stripper, slitter

Description: Extremely sharp, flat metal blade, usually about 3" wide, housed in a long metal handle. Often has a slightly angled head.

Use: Scraping old wall coverings from wall after they have been steamed or chemically treated to release glue.

Wallpaper Scraper

Use Tips: Try to avoid gouging soft plaster wall surface. A plain **wall scraper** may be easier to use.

 Buying Tips: Keep plenty of replacement blades on hand. Angled head makes it easier to use.

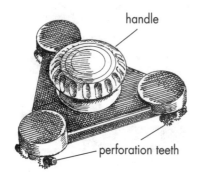

Wallpaper Scoring Tool

Wallpaper Scoring Tool

Description: Unique device made of a small, triangular, wheeled platform with a knob handle on top. The wheels are sharp-toothed blades, and there are six of them.

Use: Perforating old wallpaper so that removal chemicals or steam can penetrate more easily.

Wood and Wood Products

Manufactured Wood Products

About Manufactured Wood Products

All *manufactured wood products* are made from wood that has been cut, shaved, chipped, or ground into particles of various shapes and sizes, and then compressed under heat with synthetic resins and binders. The result is a product that is dimensionally stable and that can be designed for specific uses that go way beyond what mere boards and lumber can do.

For most people, the term *manufactured wood products* (also called *engineered wood*) does not include plywood, which is manufactured nonetheless from layers (not little pieces) of wood; indeed, some manufacturers call everything other than plywood *engineered board products*. Some of those products are smoother and flatter than plywood, or have less voids inside, or are stronger and lighter, though most are heavier because they are more dense. In most cases they are less expensive but in any case they are different from plywood.

Manufactured wood products are made with various kinds of adhesives and additives, some of which may emit slightly toxic gasses (especially when they are cut), presumably within stringent government standards. If you are particularly sensitive to formaldehyde or other gases, check with the manufacturer and note the technical specifications on the product for appropriate precautions. Often nothing more than covering the product or ventilating the room is called for.

About Plywood

Plywood is a manufactured item consisting of various thin layers of wood glued together. There are a number of characteristics to know about any plywood in order to make the proper selection. In other words, there is no such thing as "just plain plywood"—there is a specific plywood for each use.

Plywood is graded for either interior (INT) or exterior (EXT) use because of the different glues used (exterior grade is made with waterproof glue). It is also graded by the quality of its two faces, or sides, and each side may be graded differently. For grading, each plywood side, or face, has a letter designation that indicates quality. Plywood stamped Grade A should have no blemishes. Grade B will have a few blemishes and repair plugs of knotholes. Grade C will have checks (splits) as well as small knots and knotholes. In Grade D large knotholes are permitted. So, for example, if you buy Grade AC plywood, one side will be perfect while the C side will have some knotholes. This is often called *good one side* plywood. Plywood is also graded for the maximum span it can tolerate between roof rafters or floor joists.

Theoretically, you can buy any combination of sides, but in practice you will most often find: AC Exterior, AD Interior, AC Interior, and CD, or CDX (exterior), which is used for house sheathing.

Plywood

Plywood

Description: Plywood is either composed of various plies—thin panels of wood—bonded together at right angles to one another (veneer core plywood) or a single thickness of lumber sandwiched between a veneer of woods (lumber core). Some plywood is made with fine oak, birch, or lauan (Philippine mahogany) surfaces for shelving or cabinetry. Most is just plain pine, though.

Plywood is normally available in various thicknesses from $1/8$" to $3/4$" and in 4' 8' sheets and in exterior (EXT, or X) and interior (INT) use formulations. You may special-order other sizes, such as 4' × 10'. The only difference between interior and exterior plywood is that exterior plies are bonded with adhesive that can withstand harsh weather that glue for interior use cannot. *Marine plywood* is also available and has yet another specialized glue; even more specialized versions can be found, too, such as *fire-treated* or with *tongue-and-groove edges* for flooring.

A distinction between lumber and plywood is that nominal size is actual size—$3/4$" thick plywood is $3/4$" thick. In **lumber (Part VI, Chapter 48)** this is not so.

Use: A tremendous variety of building projects ranging from rough carpentry to building fine cabinets.

The following should give you an idea of how face grades are used:

A-A EXT: Outdoors, but very costly, used only when both sides show.

A-B EXT: Outside when both sides show.

A-C EXT: When only one side will show.

C-C EXT: Good for framing construction.

B-B EXT: Utility plywood for concrete forms, walks, and the like.

A-A INT: Best for cabinets and other fine furniture when both sides will show.

A-B INT: Similar to A-A, but a little less smooth-looking.

A-C INT: Paneling where one side will show.

B-D INT: Underlayment (subflooring) for flooring.

C-D: Used for sheathing, but cannot stand exposure to weather—must be kept covered.

CDX: Sheathing grade, exterior quality, for when you expect panels to be exposed awhile.

Sometimes carpenters refer to the lower grades as *construction grade* or *shop grade*.

$ Buying Tips: here are a number of ways to save money when buying plywood. One is to buy panels that are just good enough for the job at hand. If, for example, the plywood will be painted, you don't need an expensive plywood with a beautiful grain pattern. Check the so-called cut-up bin at the lumberyard where cutoffs or other scrap pieces are put. The pieces there may be big enough for the project—and the cost will be greatly reduced. Remember: If doing exterior work, make sure the pieces you buy are stamped EXT. Also, ask the dealer if he has any shop plywood available. This is material that has been chipped or otherwise damaged, but it is often possible to cut away the damaged area and use the rest of the panel. And shop plywood costs half of what nonshop plywood costs. Finally, *veneer-core* plywood is generally less expensive than *lumber-core*.

Use Tips: Plywood is a wonderful material, but the edges are unsightly. To hide them you can (1) plan the project so the plywood edges don't show in the finished item, (2) cover them with thin wood strips, or (3) cover them with **veneer tape (below)**—thin strips of wood in flexible rolls.

OSB (Oriented-Strand Board)

Also Known As: Flakeboard, waferboard, waferwood, wiggle board

Description: Usually 4' by 8' panels made by bonding layers of wood strands and flakes oriented at right angles to one another with phenolic resin. Panels range from $3/8$" to $3/4$" thick; lengths longer than 8' are also available. Panel edges are both tongue-and-groove and square. Panels are available in three different degrees of stiffness for use as roof and/or wall sheathing, subfloors and underlayment, and single-layer floors.

(OSB is actually second-generation *waferboard*, an older product that has randomly-oriented flakes and is now almost only used in industrial applications where it is prized for its uniform strength in any direction. OSB is stronger in the long dimension of a panel.)

Uses: Light framing jobs, underlayment and roof sheathing (the material that goes under roofing). Some say OSB will be the plywood of the future.

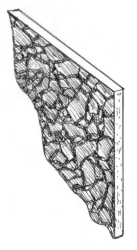

OSB

 Use Tip: Dulls saw blades quickly. Keep dry.

> **$ Buying Tip:** More environmentally friendly in fabrication and slightly more uniform than plywood. Also less expensive.

Particleboard

Also Known As: Chipboard, fiberboard (incorrect), flakeboard (incorrect)

Description: Very hard, heavy material made of small reconstituted wood particles. Available in various thicknesses—$3/8$", $1/2$", $5/8$", and $3/4$"—and 4' wide by 8', 10', and 12' long. Particleboard is also available at some lumberyards precut as shelving 8", 10", and 12" wide, sometimes with plastic laminate already on it.

Use: For a variety of interior building jobs—closets, base for kitchen countertop plastic laminate, and underlayment. It does not warp.

> **Use Tips:** Particleboard is very heavy, so its use should be carefully calculated before obtaining it. The edges do not hold screws or nails well. Particleboard is also tough on saw blades. Cutting with a carbide blade is suggested. And don't let moisture get into it—it'll swell.

This material is often made with urea formaldehyde, which emits harmful vapors (outgassing) for some time after it is cut. Let new boards sit for a few days in a well-ventilated area.

> **Buying Tips:** Particleboard costs less than half of what plywood costs and can be very good material if used for the right project. It is particularly good for kitchen countertops and underlayment. You can also build with it, but be aware of its limitations.

Hardboard

Also Known As: Masonite®

Description: Made of densely compressed, very fine wood fibers and pulp. Standard hardboard comes 4' wide and in lengths of 8', 10', and 12' and in thicknesses of $1/8$" and $1/4$". Usually comes with one side tempered, which makes a harder, more moisture-resistant surface. The tempered side is normally smooth, the untempered side crosshatched and rough (available with both sides smooth). Another, substandard version is *service grade.*

Use: Various building purposes, but particularly useful as underlayment (subflooring) prior to installing resilient flooring, although some people think it is inferior to lauan or other plywood. For this you can get 4' × 4' squares or 3' × 4' hardboard rectangles, which are easier to manage than larger sizes. Also a common material for decorative wall paneling.

> **Use Tips:** Although screws do not hold well in hardboard, you can use sheet-metal screws if there is no alternative. The $1/8$" thickness takes glue poorly; *flooring nails* are best for underlayment.

Buying Tip: Since hardboard is cheap, use it instead of plywood whenever possible.

Perforated Hardboard

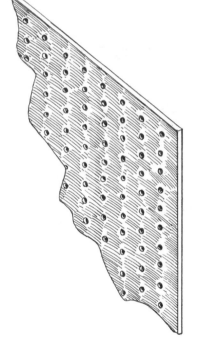

Perforated Hardboard

Also Known As: Peg-Board®

Description: Hardboard (above) with holes that can accept various hooks and hangers. Peg-Board comes either plain or prepainted and $1/8$" and $1/4$" thick.

Use: For hanging a wide variety of items, from tools in the shop to kitchen utensils. Special **Peg-Board fixtures** are used **(Part III, Chapter 30)**.

Use Tips: When mounting Peg-Board make sure there's enough clearance behind the board for the hooks. Use special rubber spacers that go over the wall mounting screws.

MDF

Also Known As: Medium density fiberboard

Description: Heavy, flat, smooth panels of various sizes, most often $1/2$" or $3/4$" thick but in fact made from $1/4$" to $1^1/2$" or more thick. All edges are smooth; may come with shaped edges intended for use as bookshelves, stair treads, or flooring. Also sold as *molding*. Made from extra-fine wood fibers

and resins or other bonding agents (glue) compressed under heat. Studier than particle board.

Use: Shelving (needs much support), cabinets, paneling, millwork, and furniture. Extra-smooth surfaces take paint and
veneers extremely well.

Use Tips: Stable, but not structural. Smooth edges are
ready to paint (doesn't take stains). Routs easily.

Buying Tip: Often half the price of birch veneer
plywood, and two-thirds the cost of pine molding.

Fiberboard

Description: Very soft, low-density, light brown material made
from wood fibers, available $1/2$" thick in panels of various
sizes. A thicker, softer version of **hardboard (above)**. May be
treated with chemicals for fire resistance. *Homosote® panels*
are a similar, lighter item.

Use: As a light building material—closets and the like—and
for sound deadening. Also as a "backer board" for nailing
shingles.

Use Tips: Fiberboard has significant limitations. It is not
very strong and is subject to swelling from moisture; it
should not be used in the bath or kitchen. Also, it should
not be nailed to studs more than 16" apart.

Wood Scratch and Hole Fillers

Types:

> *Color stick*
>
> *Lacquer stick*
>
> *Liquid colorant*
>
> *Shellac stick*
>
> *Wood putty*

Also Known As: *Wood putty:* wood dough, Plastic Wood® (premixed type), Water Putty® (powder type), wood filler

Description:

> *Color stick:* Relatively soft, crayon-like stick in various wood colors.
>
> *Lacquer and shellac sticks:* Lacquer and shellac in hard stick form. They come in a variety of wood colors and are melted for use.
>
> *Liquid colorant:* Aniline dyes in small bottles in various colors.
>
> *Water putty:* Available two ways: cellulose fiber with a putty-like consistency, in small cans and ready to apply, and in powder form, which is mixed with water to obtain the proper consistency. Comes plain and in various wood colors.

> **Note:** These items are all made from wood fibers or wood-like products; **spackling compound (Part VII, Chapter 50),** a plaster-like substance, is one of the most common and best wood gap fillers you can use prior to painting.

Use: *Shellac, lacquer stick*, and *water putty* are for holes, though they can also be used on deep scratches. *Color sticks* and *dyes* are for scratches; the former is rubbed over the scratch while the latter is applied with a tiny brush.

Use Tips: Wood putty may be colored to suit. Professionals favor lacquer and shellac sticks, but they are more difficult for the beginner to use than putty. Color sticks and dyes are simple to use.

Buying Tips: Powdered water putty is amazingly useful. Unused portions can be stored indefinitely (the premixed kind tends to dry out), and it can be used for large holes and even as a floor leveler. No worker should be without a large can.

Wood Restoration Material

Description: A variety of either polyester, polymer, or epoxy materials. Usually a two-part mix. Liquid form is considered a consolident for soft wood; putty form is a structural adhesive that fills and replaces whole sections of wood. Can be sawed, nailed, planed, and sanded like wood. Moldable.

Use: Restoring damaged architectural wood parts where replacement with new wood is not possible or desirable, and where plaster-like patchers would fail. Common items for which this is ideal include most exterior repairs, rotted or damaged windowsills, columns, frames, structural or decorative wood components in trim, and broken furniture. Liquid form is poured onto damaged wood so it penetrates and is absorbed and impregnates the wood fibers so that it hardens into a high-strength mass within minutes. It also acts as a primer for putty or paint. The putty is applied with a knife and does not shrink or crumble when dry. Both merge totally with sound wood.

Use Tips: Follow directions for safety and use scrupulously. Some of the chemicals involved are toxic. Don't expect rotted wood to support a strong piece of this material—remove all rotted wood down to a sound base for repair. No material bonds well with wet wood. Make sure it is dry, dry, dry.

Buying Tips: Especially formulated for use with wood. Do not confuse with the **epoxy repair putty** intended for **plumbing repairs (Part VIII, Chapter 60)**. Some people like to use polyester-based auto-body repair material, which is an acceptable substitute.

Wood Veneer

Description: Extremely thin strips of various types of fine woods, sold in narrow ribbons on rolls or in wider, packaged units. $1/28$" or $1/40$" thick. Available in many different beautiful wood grains.

Use: Furniture repair, hobbies. The ribbon type is used to cover edges of plywood; the sheets for furniture.

Lumber

About Lumber

There are a number of basic systems by which lumber is classified. These may seem confusing at first but are in fact very helpful.

1. **Type of Wood.** Trees can be broken down into two basic kinds: softwood and hardwood. The names are botanical distinctions and have nothing to do with the hardness of the wood: Softwoods come from trees that have cones, while hardwoods come from leaf-bearing trees.

   Theoretically, lumber is available in a vast variety of wood types. But in reality what you'll usually find in the average lumber outlet is pine, fir, and spruce. Pine alone comes in some 25 different varieties. But names don't matter. What matters is that you get the right material for the job at hand.

2. **Length.** Lumber is sold by the *board foot*, a volume measurement meaning a 1" thick, 1' square of wood. This is a common denominator used by dealers in pricing lumber. Sometimes it is sold by the *linear* (or, incorrectly, lineal) *foot*, too, but usually only with preformed, or milled, pieces such as molding.

3. **Major Groups: Lumber and Boards.** Lumber includes all sawed wood more than 2" thick, but is divided into

two broad subgroups: lumber (or *dimension lumber* or *framing lumber*), which is used for structural purposes—to make *studs* (basic vertical framing of walls) and *joists* (horizontal framing of floors and ceilings) and the like. Boards are thinner (no more than 2" thick) and are used for siding, decking, making furniture, or for decorative purposes. And there's yet another category for lumber larger than 5" × 5"—timber **(see dimension lumber and boards, below)**.

4. **Size.** Most important, boards and lumber, like many other wood products, have nominal, or named, sizes and actual sizes. This is because when it is dressed (cut, smoothed, and dried) lumber loses some wood from its original named size. Thus, when you buy a normal 2 × 4 you will actually get a piece of wood that is $1^{1}/_{2}$" × $3^{1}/_{2}$". If you buy a 1 × 4, the board will be $^{3}/_{4}$" × $3^{1}/_{2}$". Check with your dealer on the actual sizes of material before buying.

Boards and lumber come in a tremendous array of sizes, of course, but lumberyards don't carry everything, and in reality you will likely find boards ranging in size from 1" × 2" to 1" × 18" wide, with sizes increasing by 2" increments after 3". Lumber sizes start at 2" × 2" and go up in 2" increments after 3". Carpenters often call lumber by its dimensions only, such as a "2 × 4" or a "2 × 6." The "2×" dimension is so common that it is sometimes just called a "2-by," as in the most common lumber cuts, 2 × 2, 2 × 3, 2 × 4.

5. **Grading.** The most common boards are classified according to the amount of defects, such as knotholes, that they contain and are roughly divided into boards that have none or few defects, called *clear* or *select,* and boards that have varying degrees of defects are called *common.* Each of those has subcategories, too, and there are so many grades and systems (some regional, and some just

for one species!) that we've outlined them in a separate section **(below)**. However, many outlets just group their boards into these broad categories, or perhaps clear or select and two or three categories of common (No. 1 common, No. 2 common, on down in quality). For average projects that is all you need to know.

About Lumber and Boards Grading

Like plywood, lumber is graded according to quality, and prices reflect this quite strongly. *White pine,* one of the most common pines carried by lumberyards, is graded in nine categories for boards, though only about half of these grades are normally carried in your average, small lumberyard.

There are two basic divisions: *clear,* or *appearance* (almost perfect, clear of imperfections), and *common* (which has varying numbers of knotholes); these are in turn divided into four and five subdivisions. Again, most lumberyards do not carry all grades.

Here is how white pine is graded, from the top, or best, grades to the bottom:

Clear Grades:

A Select: Also known as: Clear

B Select: Also known as: A and B are sometimes lumped together and called *B or Better* or *1 and 2 Clear*—no knots or blemishes.

C Select: Perhaps only a few blemishes on one side.

D Select: Slight blemishes on both sides. Most widely obtainable of this group.

Common Grades:

> *No. 1 Common:* Also known as: 1C, Select Merchantable; overlaps with D Select.
>
> *No. 2 Common:* Also known as: 2C. Some knots and blemishes. Good for most projects.
>
> *No. 3 Common:* Also known as: 3C, Standard; knots and holes, okay for shelving; generally needs painting or staining.
>
> *No. 4 Common:* Also known as: Utility; much cheaper; okay for construction.
>
> *No. 5 Common:* Also known as: Economy; extremely unsightly; suitable for crating.

Dimension lumber (see below) is similarly graded, and ranges from select structural, the best, down to No. 1, No. 2, and No. 3, with No. 3 the lowest. However, these are commonly reduced to three names for lumber for light framing uses, or studs: *construction, standard,* and *utility.* To add to the confusion, wood intended for studs (basic vertical 2 × 3 or 2 × 4 framing) may be classified as just that: stud grade. Keep in mind that the lowest-quality grade is not as strong as the higher grades. Some low grades may be referred to by a rather descriptive term, *sound wormy.*

Here again, grade names really don't matter so much—just examine the wood and match it to the job at hand. If you want wood grain and pattern to show, buy lumber that has such qualities.

A final note: This grading system holds for white pine. Some of the more special woods have their own grading systems, so when you buy Idaho pine, redwood, and most hardwoods, ask to have that particular grading system explained to you. For example, hardwoods have a top category called *firsts and seconds,* abbreviated FaS.

Dimension Lumber and Boards

Also Known As: Lumber, construction lumber, framing lumber

Description: In brief, dimension lumber is anywhere from 2" to 5" thick, while boards are less than 2" nominal size. Remember, nominal means that a 1" board is actually $3/4$" thick. If dimension lumber has smoothed surfaces on four sides, it may be noted as "S4S," which is a type of **molding (below)**.

Some boards come precut or trimmed for particular purposes, especially stair building. There is *stringer* (or *carriage*—zigzag cut or grooved to hold treads), *stepping* (treads), and so on. Others may be trimmed for decorative use, such as *nosing,* boards with one rounded edge. 1" boards 6" to 10" wide are often referred to as *shelving board*. Because of these time-saving cuts, your local dealer will often ask what you intend to use the board for.

Use:

> *Dimension lumber:* Framing rooms, porches, and a wide variety of other basic construction (structural) tasks. These are your studs (vertical framing), joists, and beams (horizontal framing), etc.
>
> *Boards:* Siding building boxes, cabinets, shelves, and many other, more finished items.

Buying Tips: You'll likely get a better buy at lumber-yards than at other outlets simply because you'll have a larger choice of material. Also, some home centers some-times pick out the best pieces in a lot of common and sell them as select, so even if you can pick wood there you are not picking among the best material. Some lower-priced outlets sell lumber that lumberyards won't take. In fact, in smaller stores the only distinction made may be between clear and common—probably the No. 2 grades of each. And remember, grades are reflected in the prices. But don't fret—you can just ask for boards "with or without knots" if you have trouble with these terms.

When buying always check for the following, rather than just relying on complicated grading terms:

1. *Is it straight?* Tip the board up and sight down it. Is it flat or warped?

2. *Does it have knots?* If so, are they tight? If they are, they may not interfere with your project.

3. *Does the board have pitch pockets*—broken lines run-ning down the board? Sap pockets? If so, don't buy the board. It will eventually warp.

4. *Does the board have splits?* Edges of bark that are rounded? No good.

5. *Is it kiln-dried, or air- (surface, or seasoned) dried?* Or green (wet)? Dried lumber does not warp, which mat-ters a great deal if the wood is not nailed in place right away. Kiln-dried is the best, but air-dried is fine for most projects. The drying grade is often abbreviated, as in S-Dry for surface-dried and S-Green for high moisture content.

One Other Buying Tip: With boards, "common" is usually the cheapest material available. If your project requires clear wood, you may be able to buy common, cut away the knots, and still have enough usable material for your project. You can buy three times as much common as needed for the job, and if you can get the boards you need out of it, you'll still likely save money over buying clear—it's not that much more expensive. This is especially true for wood that you intend to paint, in the No. 2 and 3 categories, but you must paint the knots with **shellac (Part V, Chapter 42)** or other stain killer first, or else the knots will show through.

Furring

Description: Narrow strips of wood. Usually 1" × 2" boards, but sometimes 1" × 3" or 1" × 4" boards.

Use: Applied to walls and ceilings, provides a level nailing or adhesive surface for materials such as paneling, drywall, and ceiling tiles, a process known as *furring out*.

Use Tips: When using furring on walls, space the pieces horizontally. Proper spacing is more critical on ceilings than walls—especially when used as a base for tile.

Buying Tips: Select pieces of furring that are straight. Placing them length-to-length against one another and then turning them over will reveal any gaps between them and, therefore, any curves.

Pressure-Treated Lumber

Also Known As: Treated lumber, PTL, CCA (more common)

Description: Standard lumber that has had chemicals injected into it under pressure and is to varying degrees—depending on the treatment—decay- and rot-proof. CCA refers to one very common chemical used, copper chromate arsenate, but there are different ones and some manufacturers use their own formulations: Wolmanized® lumber is one very common example of this. These are strong and, in some cases, toxic chemicals.

Use: Used in place of naturally decay-resistant woods, such as redwood or cedar, in outdoor building projects such as decks, furniture, exterior trim, landscaping, and the like, where constant moisture is a problem.

Use Tips: Pressure-treated lumber was not intended to be painted for protection, at least when fresh (it "outgasses" chemicals for 4–6 months), but you may want to paint it to reduce the possibility of toxic splinters in bare feet. These days painting is being considered more often. Cut ends should be treated—ask at your lumberyard for assistance. Observe safety precautions when sawing, sanding, and handling treated lumber—the preservative chemicals used are toxic, and therefore so is its sawdust. Never burn pressure-treated lumber as it may give off toxic smoke. Make sure scrap is disposed of in a way that prevents it being used as fuel, especially for barbecue fires.

Buying Tips: Treatment is often done locally, and some communities are banning this work for environmental reasons. New, nontoxic treatments are being developed and some are already in use.

Milled and Preformed Wood Products

About Milled Wood Products

A stroll through the average lumberyard or home center can turn up a number of useful items, all assembled, milled into special shapes, or otherwise ready for use. Also known as *millwork.*

About Molding

Molding, or interior trim, is the material used to trim a job, and it often spells the difference between a job well or poorly done. There is a wide array of molding available, and lumberyards usually have a board on which are displayed their variety of moldings. The descriptions and illustrations here describe only a fraction of what's available.

Molding may be made of hardwood or softwood, depending on wood availability in the area you live in. Cedar, pine, fir, larch, poplar, and hemlock are common.

Molding comes unfinished in 2' increments up to 16' long, and the increments can be odd or even. 8' and 10' lengths are the most common and useful. Widths vary from a fraction of an inch up to 6", but molding, like lumber, is described in nominal and actual sizes—a 3" nominal size, for example, will only be $2^5/_8$" wide.

Although this is a section on wood products, note that a common substitute for base molding around a floor-wall joint is

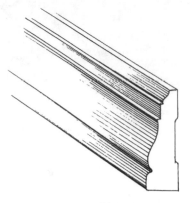

Base Molding

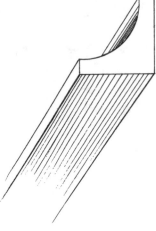

Shoe Molding

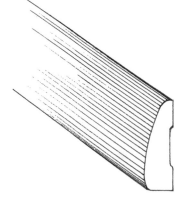

Casing Molding

vinyl strip, cove, or *straight base molding,* a 2" to 6" wide strip sold in various lengths and easily installed with its own adhesive. It is available in a range of colors.

Molding

Types:

Base molding

Base cap molding

Base shoe molding

Casing molding

Chair rail molding

Corner guard molding

Cove molding

Crown molding

Half round molding

Mullion

Quarter round molding

Stool

Stop

Threshold

Also Known As:

Base shoe: Shoe, toe

Base: Baseboard, clam, clamshell

Casing: Case

Corner guard: Corner bead (same term as metal base for joint compound)

Threshold: Saddle

Description: Sold in lengths of 3' to 20' (usually stocked in the longer lengths only) and generally not cut to order. Dozens of shapes available, with many similarities. Here are a few of the most common.

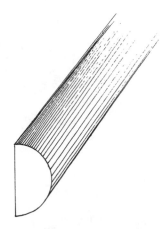

Half Round Molding

Base: Flatish with square bottom and tapered top, various surface patterns. Plain surface called *clam base.*

Base cap: Square bottom and convex or concave top, generally small.

Base shoe: In profile looks like a slightly offset quarter of a circle. Another type is concave with a square bottom. Always small.

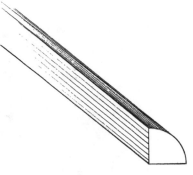

Quarter Round Molding

Casing: Flatish to slightly convex with almost square bottom and top with slight taper; fancier ones with more curves in the surface may be called *Colonial casing.*

Chair rail: Flat, grooved, or fluted; generally fairly wide.

Corner guard: V-shaped channel.

Cove: Slightly curved, a little like the letter C. Also similar to a concave base shoe.

Crown: Curved face on flat back with 45-degree beveled edges.

Half round: Half-circle profile.

Mullion: Fluted molding.

Quarter round: A quarter of a circle.

Stool: One square and one molded edge.

Stop: Thin molding with one square and one tapered edge.

Threshold: Usually oak, flat, beveled piece.

Use:

Base: Goes along bottom of walls.

Base cap: Goes over top of base for added trim.

Base shoe: Covers the gap between baseboard molding and floor.

Casing: Trim around outside of doors and windows.

Chair rail: Placed a few feet up a wall to divide the space and protect from chairs rubbing against the wall.

Corner guard: Covers corners to protect from damage.

Cove: Standard moldings usually forming an inside corner if small, such as on stairs, or if larger, trim at the wall-ceiling juncture, like crown molding.

Crown: Decorative cover of the wall-ceiling juncture; greatly enhances any room.

Half round: Variety of uses, including enhancing other moldings.

Mullion: Vertical trim between windows.

Quarter round: Fills the cap between wall and floor. Often used in small sizes on stairways.

Stool: Inside horizontal section of window molding (sill is outside section).

Stop: As trim that abuts windows and doors; actually "stops" the door at its closing point.

Threshold: Doorways, over joint between floors of two rooms.

Use Tips: When cutting molding at an angle, use a **miter box (Part I, Chapter 5)**—don't try to do it free-hand. Keep in mind when determining how much molding to get that these cuts create waste by themselves as well as in the unfortunate case of errors. You can create very distinctive and fancy-looking trim by combining some of the simplest molding shapes. Old-fashioned trim often consists of three or four moldings—some just plain, flat boards—placed together with some simple shapes. Molding may be nailed or glued, and often both are used in difficult spots.

Buying Tips: Molding described as the same size can differ fractionally if produced by different mills. This can affect the looks of a job so hold pieces against one another to make sure they match. Buy more than you think you'll need to cover cutting errors. Also, beware of buying *paint grade molding* that's not one continuous piece but, rather, joined by so-called finger joints. Molding of this quality is suitable for only one finish—paint. For staining, get *clear-grade molding* (or *select-grade* or *stain grade*). If you want molding that has fancy designs milled in it, this is also available. Every metropolitan area has at least one major lumberyard that is a major supplier of finish wood trim. They would have, or sometimes even produce, a catalog or a sheet showing all kinds of shapes. Finally, shop around for molding prices—they vary greatly. One trick of lumberyards is to offer paneling at a great discount and companion molding at a great markup.

Wood Shims

Description: 6" to 8" long wooden wedges, no more than about $1/2$" thick at the "heel" end, and about 2" wide. Generally sold in bundles of a dozen or so.

Use: Stabilizing and leveling counters, appliances, and walls under construction.

> **Buying Tips:** Although your own scrap pile can help, having many of these on hand is a good way to speed up a major job. Alternatives are wooden shingles, or *shakes.*

Dowels

Also Known As: Dowel rods

Description: Wood rods, sold usually in 3' or 4' lengths and ranging in diameter from $1/8$" to $1\frac{1}{4}$" in $1/16$" and $1/8$" increments. Larger sizes—$1\frac{3}{8}$" and $1\frac{5}{16}$" diameter—are sold as *closet rods* or *poles; socket sets* are sold for installation, and come with cup-like parts that attach to the closet walls.

Use: Various woodworking projects, including making glued joints with perfectly matched holes and short lengths of dowel rod.

> **Buying Tip:** These are often sold in a DIY materials floor display.

Dowel Pins

Dowel Pins

Description: Short, specially milled dowels with spiral grooves or channels (fluted).

Use: Gluing two pieces of wood together, especially furniture parts. They are inserted in holes drilled in the edges with glue; the spirals or flutes are paths for excess glue and air to escape. Makes a very strong joint.

 Use Tip: Drill accurately matched holes in the two pieces with the aid of a **dowel jig (Part II, Chapter 16)**.

 Buying Tip: Although they are available commercially, you can easily make your own pins from dowel rods.

Furniture Legs

Description: Legs are available in unfinished wood as well as other materials—wrought iron, tube steel, and in a variety of styles from modern to Mediterranean. Lengths range up to around 30". Sold alone or with metal mounting plates.

Use: Used in the making of new furniture as well as repairing and resuscitating older pieces. They screw right into existing mounts.

Furniture Leg

Lattice

Lattice

Description: Thin boards assembled in crisscross fashion into panels of various sizes—2' × 4', 2' × 8', and 4' × 8'—and made of interior or exterior wood. Also now available in plastic, which resists termites. Unassembled boards are sold as molding.

Use: Decorative material for inside and outside the house, such as for dividers, trellises, flanking entryways, to wall off the space between deck and ground to keep rubbish from blowing in.

Spindles

Description: Turned-wood posts of various lengths of around 6" to 72" and diameters of 1" to 4". In some cases the spindles screw together. Posts may be unfinished, raw wood, or finished. Related parts include finials, spacers, bases, and connectors.

Use: Spindles can be assembled to serve a variety of decorative and functional purposes, including dividers, shelf supports, candle and lamp holders, and stair or porch railings.

> **Use Tips:** Prefinished spindles are available in a wide variety of finishes, so if you want to avoid having to finish the wood yourself, it's likely you can find what you need in prefinished form.

Shutters

Types:

Exterior shutters

Interior shutters

Description:

Exterior shutters: Made of plastic or wood that is primed.

Interior: Almost always made of pine, these come in widths from 6" to 12" and heights from 16" to 48". They may be unfinished and without hardware or finished with hanging hardware attached. Shutters are available with *louvers* (slats) and panels into which fabric or other decorative material may be inserted.

Use: Interior shutters can be used over interior windows or as cafe doors. Exterior shutters usually aren't operative and are intended for decoration only.

 Use Tip: If shutters require painting, aerosol spray paint is usually the easiest way to a smooth finish.

VII

Wall, Floor, and Ceiling Materials and Tools; Doors and Windows

Drywall, Plaster, Materials, and Tools

Drywall

Also Known As: Sheetrock®, wallboard, gypsum wallboard, gypsum board, gypsum drywall, gypsum panel, gypboard, plasterboard, GyProc®.

> **Note:** Sheetrock®, U.S. Gypsum's trade name, is used generically.

Description: Sheet material composed of a core of gypsum or other plaster-like material, covered on both sides with heavy paper. The paper on the backing and face is different according to use: drywall is available with both sides of backing paper, for use when another piece of drywall is going to be glued right to it (*backer board*); with green paper (*greenboard*) that is moisture-resistant, and with blue paper (*blueboard*) for skim-coating. Other specialized types are available.

Drywall panels come 4' wide and in 6', 7', 8', 10', 12', and 16' lengths with 8' the most common and $1/4$", $3/8$", $1/2$", and $5/8$" thick. Edges may be tapered, straight, beveled, tongue-and-groove, rounded, or square; tapered is most often sold and allows for three layers of **joint compound (below)** to be applied to the gap between panels without bulging out. Although all gypsum is somewhat fire-resistant, *Type X fire-rated* ("Firestop") or *boiler-room*, drywall types are also available.

Use: New walls and ceilings, resurfacing damaged walls. Moisture-resistant drywall is excellent for baths. It is secured with special **drywall nails** or **screws (Part III, Chapters 20 and 21)** to wooden or metal studs (the vertical framing members of the wall) or glued to existing walls and to ceilings with special **panel adhesive (Part VII, Chapter 51)**.

Use Tips: Install panels so that the number of seams is minimized. This reduces the amount of joint taping you must do. $1/2$" thick drywall is generally used for light residential purposes and $5/8$" for everything else; $1/4$" can be used to cover an existing but damaged surface. Don't use moisture-resistant drywall on ceilings. Drywall is one of the heaviest materials around, so plan carefully how to transport it from the store to your home and within the construction site. Not a job for one person in any way. Even with two, look into renting a special hoist (called a *panel lift* or *drywall jack*) for holding panels in place on ceilings prior to screwing, or construct a "dead man," a cross of 1" × 2" or similar lumber that is jammed up against the panel while you screw it in. For best painting results, especially with glossy paint, put a "skim coat" of joint compound over all. Prime properly. Rent or buy a **screw gun (Part II, Chapter 16)**, if you are installing any large quantity.

$ Buying Tips: As building materials go, drywall is the same: one manufacturer's product will be the same as another; there are no hidden defects. This material is either smooth and solid or it isn't. If you see it on sale, buy it. Drywall is cheap, but the price can vary somewhat from lumberyard to lumberyard, so check it out.

Cement Board

Also Known As: Backer board, tile backer board, underlayment board

Description: Cement version of gypsum **drywall (above)**, consisting of an aggregated portland cement core sandwiched between two layers of glass fiber mesh. One side is smooth and one textured; the side edges are smooth and rounded to allow for joint mortar, but the ends are square cut. Resistant to water damage. Standard board is $1/2$" or $5/8$" thick and 32", 3', or 4' wide in 4', 5', 6', or 8' lengths. Underlayment board made specifically for floors and countertops is $5/16$" thick and 4' × 4'. Should be sold with joint tape and polymer-coated screws made specifically for use with cement board.

Use: Substrate or underlayment for ceramic tile in wet areas such as bathrooms or kitchens, or for floors.

> **Use Tips:** Smooth side is for adhesives, rough side for thin-set mortar. Use only alkali-resistant glass fiber tape on joints, and only latex-fortified, thin-set mortar or Type 1 organic adhesive, as well as either $1^1/_2$" hot-dipped galvanized roofing nails or polymer-coated screws made specifically for use with cement board. Otherwise the strong chemicals (alkalis) in the cement or the moisture in the environment will corrode the screws and tape. Floor underlayment must be totally secured according to directions, using $^5/_8$" plywood.

Corner Bead

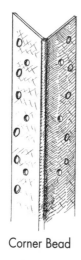

Corner Bead

Description: Long galvanized steel strip with an L-shaped profile. Sold in 8' lengths. Available also in a flexible version, *metal corner tape*, made of a steel strip sealed into paper tape. Many specialized designs available, such as J-profile, Bullnose, or offset.

Use: Finishes off corners where drywall panels abut. Provides base for **joint compound (below)**. Corner tape is for arches, cathedral ceilings, or any odd angle.

Joint Compound

Also Known As: Drywall compound, mud

Description: Comes both as a ready-mixed paste and in powder form that is mixed with water. Dries fast and is very easily sanded wet or dry, or smoothed with a wet sponge. Specially formulated for easy workability over large surfaces, made with the finest granules of the **wall patching/preparing products (below)**, including gypsum, vinyl, and other additives. Setting (*taping*) and *topping compound* are for professionals using a two-product system; *all-purpose joint compound* is the most common for the DIY market. Available also in a "light" formulation.

Use: Sealing drywall joints with joint tape as well as extremely shallow patching, such as in areas where paint has peeled. Intended for use over wide areas in thin, successive coats. A number of applications will likely be required because joint compound shrinks as it dries. Must be primed prior to painting; diluted flat latex wall paint is recommended. Only setting-type joint compound should be used with **fiberglass tape (below)**.

> **Use Tips:** Joint compound is always applied in thin, multiple, smooth layers, each layer feathered out beyond the previous one. Use lots of joint compound and a proper **taping knife (below)**—it is an easy material to work with. Don't let any dried chips fall into your fresh supply (working out of a 14" long mud pan or mud tray instead of the compound container may help). If used in a high-traffic area, remember that joint compound is much softer than its cousin, plaster, and easily damaged. Nor is it as smooth. Sanding (done with fine-grade sandpaper) produces lots of bad dust, so use a proper respirator or use wet sanding or a damp sponge to limit your dust. Try using a damp sponge or a stiff felt pad *blister brush* instead of sandpaper but avoid wetting the surface paper. If you have much sanding along the ceiling or high walls, use a **drywall sander (below)** with a broom handle–type attachment. Sanding can be limited by proper application in the first place. "Light" compound generally needs less sanding (it is also easier to sand) and doesn't shrink or crack. Supposedly only two coats are needed. Some brands may be used as texture paint when diluted with water. Can replace **spackling compound (below)**. Powdered *setting-type joint compound* is a good plaster-like patcher.

> **Buying Tips:** Premixed "all-purpose" joint compound is recommended. It is always at the proper consistency and stores well. "Light" compound is usually more expensive, but you might use less, and it is easier to sand. Fiberglass tape requires setting-type compound that you must mix, but needs only two quick-setting coats and can be finished in one day.

Joint Tape

Types:

>*Paper joint tape*
>
>*Fiberglass mesh joint tape*

Also Known As: Wallboard tape, perforated tape, drywall tape

Description: 2" wide, strong, perforated (and nonperforated) paper or fiberglass mesh in various lengths, usually 75 and 250 feet. Paper tape comes in rolls as long as 500' and with a convenient crease down the middle (*corner tape* has steel strips in the middle). The perforations are necessary for the tape to imbed itself in the joint compound. Fiberglass mesh is also available in 36" by 75' or 150' rolls.

Use: Component in sealing and reinforcing the seams between drywall panels; always used in conjunction with **joint compound (above)**. Large rolls of fiberglass mesh are used to repair entire walls or ceilings of old, cracked plaster.

Use Tips: Fiberglass mesh is applied with staples or is self-adhesive and may be easier to use, especially when patching holes (the adhesive eliminates the need for a first coat of joint compound). It also makes for a stronger joint. Fiberglass tape requires the use of the stronger *setting-type joint compound* and may be covered with two coats in only one day.

Self-Adhesive Wall Patch

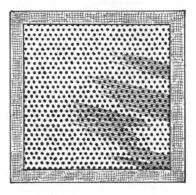

Self-Adhesive Wall Patch

Also Known As: Metal drywall repair patch

Description: 4" to 8" square piece of fiberglass mesh with adhesive backing, containing a perforated aluminum plate in its center. Peel-and-stick *patching tape* has no metal and is slightly flexible.

Use: Patching large holes in drywall, plaster, or hollow-core doors with a minimum of patching material. The aluminum eliminates the need to fill the hole and the adhesive mesh eliminates the need for preplastering. Also eliminates the need to cut drywall patches and holes to size. Smaller versions, made only of very stiff mesh, are specifically designed to bridge the gap between drywall and electrical boxes, a gap that is particularly hard to fill without cracking. They are placed over the whole hole and then the inside is cut out to leave the electrical box open while providing surface around it for patching compound. *Patching tape* is for small holes and cracks in plaster.

Buying Tip: Another good effort in the search to simplify hole patching.

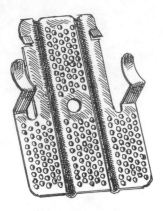

Drywall Repair Clip

Drywall Repair Clip

Description: Small, perforated, flat metal clip with openings on opposite sides.

Use: Provides instant bracing for repair of large holes in drywall. The "filler" piece of drywall is simply clipped in place and then covered with patching compound. Eliminates the need to cut back the good wall to studs or to create a home-made brace.

Wall Patchers

Types:

> *Plaster*
>
> *Patching plaster*
>
> *Spackling compound*

Also Known As:

> *Plaster:* Plaster of Paris, painter's plaster, wet-wall plaster
>
> *Patching plaster:* Wall patch
>
> *Spackling compound:* Spackle®, spackling putty, spackling paste

Description: Plaster, or plaster of Paris, is the generic name for a very common product made of ground-up and treated gypsum rock (originally mined near Paris) that comes as a white powder that is mixed with water for use. Different manufacturers use different additives and manufacturing processes, much as with paints, to produce similar products that they market under various names. The three basic groups of products noted here differ in their drying, or *set,* times, their ease of application, their plasticity or "workability," and their strength. These differences are due to chemical additives and the different grades of ground gypsum rock used.

Plaster: Mixed with lime to form the basic material in wet-wall construction, i.e., commonly known as *plaster walls.* Sets in about ten minutes and forms an extremely hard surface. May be mixed with aggregates such as sand for base coats and varying amounts of lime for different finishes and hardnesses. Must be applied over a proper surface, such as wooden or metal lath, a net-like metal sheet.

Patching plaster: Plaster that contains additives that make it dry much more slowly and has a slightly more plastic "feel" to it when being applied, making it slightly easier to work. **Setting-type joint compound (above)** is almost the same.

Spackling compound: Finest ground gypsum, with many additives. Extremely fast-setting and nonshrinking. Also available in paste form ready to apply (in tubs, tubes, and even pencil-like dispensers), as well as in versions with additives such as vinyl that make it more flexible or adhesive. The verb "to spackle" comes from the German verb *spachteln,* meaning to fill or smooth a surface; Spackle® is a popular brand name that is used—incorrectly—in a generic way for this family of products.

Use:

Plaster of Paris: Constructing walls, filling very large patches, anchoring ceramic bathroom fixtures, hobby projects. Making plaster walls is an art done only by seasoned professionals.

Patching plaster: Filling large cracks and breaks in plaster surfaces, but not holes.

Spackling compound: For small holes and cracks in drywall, plaster, or wood. If in powder form, use only inside the house; for outside use a *spackling paste,* made for both interior and exterior work. Lately manufacturers have been coming out with so-called *light* spackling mixtures that permit coverage of larger patches than before, though **joint compound (above)** suits this purpose, too. They cover well but are not as hard. Light spackling dries instantly and can be painted right after application.

Use Tips: Plaster sets so quickly that it can create problems. But you can triple the setting time by adding a dash of vinegar to every batch you mix. Use a **bonding agent (below)** to assure adhesion. Regular plaster is extremely hard to apply just right, and also hard to sand, so use spackling compound as a final leveler of uneven surfaces—spackling compound, like joint compound, is extremely easy to sand down.

Buying Tips: Plaster is available in 4- and 8-pound plastic tubs and 5-pound bags, but it is suggested you buy only what you need; it doesn't stand up to moisture well in storage. Take care when buying spackling paste—some brands are relatively gritty, while the better ones are very smooth. Stick with major brands. Specialized mixtures abound—even *popcorn ceiling patch* is available.

Bonding Agent

Description: Resinous emulsion that is brushed or rolled onto wall surface and allowed to dry until it becomes tacky.

Use: Dramatically increases bonding of new plaster or cement to any structurally sound surface. Virtually welds the patch to the old material. Useful for applying skim coats of plaster.

> **Use Tip:** While it is necessary to wait until this becomes tacky, it is o.k. to wait as much as two weeks after application to apply the plaster to it.

> **Buying Tips:** Yields excellent results. Some types are made specifically for plaster or concrete, while others work with both or are marked for interior or exterior use. Check the label carefully.

About Drywall Finishing Tools

A number of tools have been specifically developed to help in this common job of installing drywall, and you should not hesitate to buy them if you are doing a job even as small as one room.

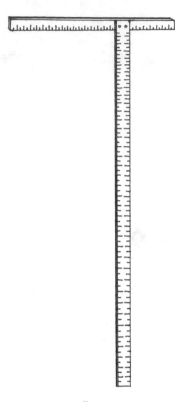

Drywall T-Square

Drywall T-Square

Also Known As: Wallboard T-square, drywall paneling T-square

Description: Flat aluminum 'T' usually 22" wide and just over 4' long with measuring markings. The crosspiece is either off-set or has a lip to catch the edge of the drywall sheet, and may be adjustable.

Use: Acts as a guide for cutting drywall with a **utility knife (Part I, Chapter 6)**; extremely useful for marking any large sheet material (plywood, sheet metal, etc.). This is for cutting square shapes; for holes use a **drywall saw (below)**.

Drywall Saw

Also Known As: Wallboard saw, jab saw, Sheetrock® saw, utility saw

Description: Big-toothed saw with narrow, pointed, stiff blade and in-line handle, like a knife with a jagged edge. Teeth are specially hardened. Same name is given to a saw with similar large teeth, which has a blade that resembles a regular crosscut saw, but this is a rarely used version. Quite similar to a **keyhole saw (Part I, Chapter 5)**.

Use: Cutting openings in drywall for pipes and electrical outlets. (Larger sections should be cut side to side with a **utility knife, Part I, Chapter 6**, not a saw.)

> **Use Tips:** You can start a cut by jabbing the point of the saw into the drywall or else punching it with a screwdriver and a hammer.

> **$ Buying Tips:** Stick with a knife for small jobs. Use a compass-like *drywall circle cutter* or **cutout tool (Part II, Chapter 18)** for big jobs.

Taping Knife

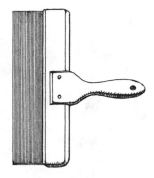

Taping Knife

Also Known As: Joint knife, tape knife, drywall knife, drywall tool, filling knife, broad knife, finishing knife, spackling knife, wallboard knife

Description: Wide, flexible metal blade with a riveted handle. Two types are made: a triangular shape about 4" to 8" wide at the tip *(broad knife)* and a rectangular shape, commonly 10" to 12" long *(finishing knife)*. The triangular type is sometimes called an *elastic knife,* referring to its flexibility; and the rectangular one, which is usually blued steel, may be called a *blue steel knife.* Some pros use a rectangular trowel with a slight curve to it, called a *drywall trowel.*

> **Note:** The triangular knife is often erroneously confused with a **wall scraper (Part V, Chapter 45),** which is narrower and stiffer but looks very similar.

Broad Taping Knife

Use: Spreading **joint compound (above)** smoothly over the **joint tape (above)** covering seams between **drywall panels (above)** or surface patches.

> **⚒ Use Tips:** Using the widest knife possible for the finish application makes the job easier, as there are fewer edge beads of compound created. Narrower knives are acceptable for the first application. Use a long, narrow *mud pan* to hold the compound for wide knives.

> **$ Buying Tips:** The key consideration in getting a quality joint knife that makes the job easier is flexibility in the middle of the blade itself—a *hollow ground blade*. Good knives have "give" while poor ones are stiff.

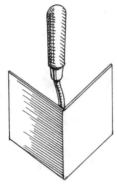

Corner Taping Tool

Corner Taping Tool

Also Known As: Corner tool, corner trowel, angle plow, inside corner wipedown tool, butterfly trowel

Description: A large, slightly flexible metal blade bent at just over 90 degrees; has a wooden handle. Outside corner versions, bent the opposite ways, are available as well.

Use: Applying joint compound or plaster to inside or outside corners.

> **Use Tip:** With this tool you can apply compound to both sides of a corner simultaneously—without it you have to wait for each side to dry before touching the other.

> **$ Buying Tip:** Hard to use well—not for everyone.

Spackling and Putty Knife

Putty Knife

Also Known As: Spackling knife

Description: Narrow blade, usually about 1" wide, with squared-off end and a simple handle.

Use: Applying *glazing compound* (putty) to windows, small scraping jobs, very small spackling jobs, such as nail holes and hairline cracks.

 Use Tip: The more flexible knives are for patching and the stiffer ones for scraping.

 Buying Tip: Like many tools, putty knives come in varying degrees of quality. Cheap ones don't work very well.

Drywall Sander

Description: Open-mesh abrasive sanding screen made of steel, about 3" × 7", with a handle with a threaded hole so it can be attached to a broomstick or roller extension pole. The *vacuum drywall sander* attaches to the hose of shop vacuum. *Drywall sanding screens*, open metal mesh pieces that fit directly onto the sander, are sold separately, and in several levels of abrasiveness, or grit (80-120-150 grit, or coarse-medium-fine).

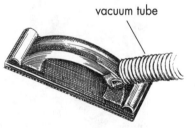

vacuum tube

Drywall Sander

Use: Sanding joint compound smooth in preparation for painting. The vacuum drywall sander sucks up all the fine dust produced by sanding.

 Use Tips: Joint compound sands so easily that it is likely you will remove too much or gouge it. Go lightly.

> **Buying Tips:** Try to avoid sanding joint compound. The dust is fine, voluminous, and potentially unhealthy. Apply the compound carefully, use wet sandpaper or a damp sponge, or use the *vacuum drywall sander.*

Panel Carrier

Description: 15" long plastic, L-shaped handle with slight bend in it.

Use: Carrying large, heavy panels of gypsum drywall.

> **Buying Tip:** Drywall is heavy and delicate. This helps overcome both attributes.

Drywall Lifter

Also Known As: Foot fulcrum, dry wall foot lift

Description: A number of small accessories are available that are generally a foot or so long, with a fulcrum. Some have small rollers for short movements.

Use: Placing and moving panels of drywall.

Panel Carrier

Crack Opener

Crack Opener

Description: 6" long tool consisting of a hooked, stiff steel rod with a point, and a simple in-line hardwood handle.

Use: Cleaning and opening small cracks in plaster sufficiently for the most efficient filling and anchoring of patching material.

 Use Tip: Try to create a wider base to better anchor the patch.

Crack Patcher

Crack Patcher

Also Known As: Utility patcher and trowel

Description: Small, lightweight plated steel trowel with one pointed end and one rectangular end. Slightly flexible.

Use: Patching small holes and cracks in drywall, masonry, and plaster with various patching materials.

Cement Board Knife

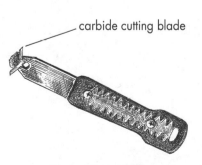
carbide cutting blade

Cement Board Knife

Description: Carbide-tipped hand knife. Tip is semicircular with sharp points on either end of oval.

Use: Cutting **cement board (above)**. Carbide tip in handle is for chiseling and shaping. Score the fiberglass mesh on BOTH sides and then snap the board.

Use Tips: Score deeply and hope for the best (it is rough material). For more, longer cuts, try a **carbide-tipped saw blade in a circular saw (Part II, Chapter 17)**.

Buying Tip: Cutting cement is not for your usual razor knife.

Paneling and Tile

Wall Paneling

Types:

Manufactured wood product paneling with paper, vinyl, or wood veneer face

Plastic laminate wall paneling

Wood planks (solid board panels)

Description:

Manufactured wood product: **Hardboard, plywood, particleboard**, or similar product **(Part VI, Chapter 47)** with a thin layer of decorative paper or vinyl attached that is generally a simulated wood-grain pattern; grooves are usually incorporated to give the impression of narrow wood panels. A fancier type is a fine hardwood veneer such as birch on plywood and may be used to cover cabinets as well as walls. Typically available in 4' × 8' panels $^1/_8$" to $^1/_4$" thick.

Plastic laminate: $^1/_{16}$" thick plastic sheet with a decorative style laminated to a backing panel generally of particle board but may be applied directly to **drywall (Part VII, Chapter 50)**. In any case a strong adhesive is required. Comes in 4' × 8' sheets.

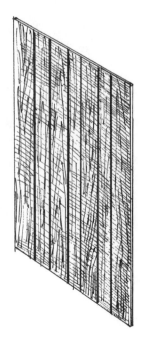

Wood Paneling

Wood planks: Solid hardwood or softwood boards 3" to 12" wide and $1/2$" to $7/8$" thick with smooth and rough as well as knotty and clear wood grades. Edges are *tongue-and-groove.* Length varies, and patterns can be custom-ordered (indeed, may have to be ordered, as this classic product is less and less commonly found).

Uses: Paneling walls in new construction and to cover badly damaged walls—or just to change the look of the room. May go directly over layer of **drywall (Part VII, Chapter 50)**.

Use Tips: Use a **router (Part II, Chapter 18)** for cutting and trimming paneling and laminate. It's faster and allows intricate cuts. If paneling is going to be applied directly to furring strips or studs, it should be at least $1/4$" thick; use **panel nails (Part III, Chapter 20)**. Thinner panels can be secured to plaster with special adhesive. Panels that are $1/4$" thick are best for installation directly on drywall.

Buying Tips: The plywood types are considered best; vinyl or paper wood-grain patterns never look as good as veneer does. There is a vast range of quality, and you should insist on fire-rated panels, because some are highly flammable and give off much smoke when burning.

Ceramic Wall Tile

Description: Extremely hard product that comes in various shapes from square to octagonal and various thicknesses and textures. Standard tile is $4^{1}/_{4}$" by $4^{1}/_{4}$" with projections, or nibs, on the edges for proper spacing.

Use: Wherever an easy-to-clean, waterproof surface is desired. Mainly in the bath, but also on kitchen countertops.

 Use Tip: Installing tile is a difficult, meticulous job.

Tile Spacers

Description: Little white plastic crosses, ranging in size from $^{1}/_{16}$" to $^{3}/_{8}$" thick; all are less than an inch across. Sold in bags of 50 to 300, and boxes of up to 1500 pieces. Different types for wall tile or floor tile. Best quality models are molded, not extruded, for consistency.

Use: Maintaining even spacing between tiles prior to applying grout. Also to speed up the layout process.

Tile Spacers

$ Buying Tip: Necessary for a professional, even installation when the grout space between tiles is bigger than the space made by the bumps on the tile sides.

Grout

Description: A cement-based material. Comes as a powder in various sizes and colors that is mixed with water for use; also in tubes.

Use: Filling gaps between ceramic tiles up to $1/8$". Sand is added when grout is intended for joints wider than $1/8$". Think of it as a thin mortar.

> **Use Tips:** Mix grout with *acrylic latex additive* for surfaces that will have water on them. Seal it later with *silicone grout sealer*. On large jobs, or when using sanded grout, use a **rubber float** or **grout float (Part X, Chapter 75)** instead of a sponge.

Grout Saw

carbide grit

Grout Saw

Also Known As: Grout rake, grout scraper

Description: Plastic palm-sized handle with a short, round blade of tungston-carbide grit or hardened steel teeth.

Use: Removing old grout prior to regrouting.

> **Use Tip:** Take it easy—you need to remove the loose grout only to a depth of an eighth of an inch for the new grout to hold. No need to remove everything.

Buying Tips: Get replacement blades if available for your model. Some people get the same result with an old beer-can opener.

Notched Trowel

Also Known As: Trowel spreader, serrated trowel

Description: Rectangular metal or plastic blade with a handle and with notches of varying shapes and dimensions along the edges.

Use: Spreading adhesive (mastic) for tiles and panels of all kinds.

Notched Trowel

 Use Tip: Use tooth size specified by adhesive manufacturer.

 Buying Tip: Dealers will often give you a free notched trowel when you buy adhesive and tiles.

Tile Pliers

Also Known As: Tile-cutting pliers, tile cutter

Description: Pliers-like device with one flat jaw and one vertical blade, and a sharp, carbide wheel cutter.

Use: Splitting ceramic tiles along straight, scored lines.

carbide wheel cutter

Tile Pliers

> **Use Tips:** For small quantities only. For large jobs rent specialized tile-cutting tools—they are great time-savers. The most common is the *tile cutter,* or *snap cutter,* with a blade that slides on two guide rods. Dealers will often lend you these tools.

Tile Nippers

Tile Nippers

Description: Blunt-headed pliers with wide pincer-like blades.

Use: Nibbling away at ceramic tiles to remove curved sections for fitting around plumbing, etc.

CHAPTER 52

Doors and Windows

Doors

Types:

Interior doors

Exterior doors

Insulated doors

Folding doors

Bifold doors

Sliding doors

Swinging doors

Garage doors

Storm doors

Also Known As:

Swinging: Cafe

Exterior: "Entrance" doors

Description: Most doors are 6' 8" high and come in various widths. They also may come prehung, complete with frames and hinges.

Interior: Either hollow-core construction—sheets of wood veneer over a ribbed core of cardboard or wood strips—or solid-core. Usually 1 ³/₈" or 1 ³/₄" thick.

Exterior: Made of solid wood or wood material, such as particleboard. Usually 1 ³/₄" thick and assembled with exterior glue (interior doors use interior glue). Available insulated. Both interior and exterior doors come in two types: *panel* or *sash* doors, meaning they are composed of separate wood sections with visible joints (stiles, rails, and as many as 15 panels), and *flush* types, meaning the exterior is one homogenous, solid piece of wood veneer. Both types come with "lights," or windows. Doors come in a variety of widths and heights.

Insulated: Core of wood or particleboard encased in galvanized steel sheets. Such doors have R values up to R-15.

Folding: May be woven or laminated. Woven have louvers and may be made of wood or PVC. Laminated doors are commonly laminated to steel.

Bifold: Two folding doors with each of the two sections hinged together. They come solid and louvered.

Sliding: Made of wood, glass, and metal as well as vinyl-covered wood and metal. Exterior, or patio, doors of glass panels are normally insulated; there is a dead air space between the sheets of glass used in their construction. *Bypass doors* slide past each other; *pocket doors* go into the wall.

Swinging: Mounted on the sides of a doorway and swing open and shut when pushed.

Garage: Consists of panels hinged together. Panels may be wood or have air spaces or polystyrene inside for insulation. Doors ride on track and may be automatic or operated by hand.

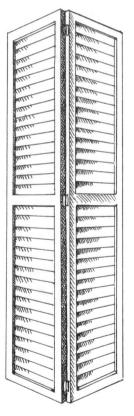

Louvered Bifold Door

Storm: Metal- or wood-framed doors with glass or plexiglas windows. Available ready-made or as a do-it-yourself package. *Cross Buck doors,* with an X-pattern on the bottom and a window on top, are a common model.

> **Use Tips:** Because of the close tolerances, hanging most doors is a very difficult job, and prehung doors, where possible, are a great advantage. Hollow-core doors make excellent office tables when placed across low file cabinets. Prehung steel doors are the best for security.

> **Buying Tips:** Doors are available in much greater variety in "panel" types. Doors covered with veneer are usually suitable only for painting rather than clear finishing. Wooden doors usually come unfinished.

About Windows

There are far too many types and details concerning windows to do justice in this book, so only a general classification will be given to guide you at the very start of your purchase. One term is helpful: *sash* refers to the wooden or metal framework that the glass panes are attached to.

Windows

Types:

Double-hung windows

Sliding windows

Casement windows

Fixed, or *picture windows*

Description:

Double-hung: Most common, with two units, or sashes, that slide up and down on separate tracks.

Sliding: Similar to double-hung, but horizontal.

Casement: Window swings outward from a side hinge. May be operated by a small crank. If they are out-swinging, hinged at the top, they are called *awning windows;* bottom-hinged, in-swinging models are called *hopper windows.*

Fixed: Generally large window, mounted permanently in a non-opening frame.

Use: Installed in walls to allow entry of light and air.

Glass

Types:

Safety glass

Standard glass

Composition glass

Description:

Safety: There are a number of types: wire-reinforced, laminated, tempered. Wire-reinforced: $1/4$" thick, has wire embedded in it that keeps the glass from shattering on impact. Laminated: $1/4$" thick and consists of two pieces of glass adhered to a middle layer of plastic to make it shatterproof. Tempered: if this breaks, it crumbles into zillions of harmless pieces rather than sharp shards.

Standard: Standard door and window glass, nonsafety, comes in three grades: B for general work, A for superior, and AA, the highest grade.

Composition: This glass has metal particles embedded in it with the result, manufacturers say, of retaining heat from the sun's rays longer, thereby keeping a house warmer in the winter and cooler in the summer.

Use: Use safety glass in storm doors, shower and bath doors, patio doors, interior and exterior doors—wherever there is a possibility the glass may accidentally be broken by a person's body.

Glazing Compound

Also Known As: glazing putty, window putty

Description: Soft, pliable material worked with fingers and/or **putty knife (Chapter 50)**. Sold in cans, tubs and cartridges. Also available in roll form, called *glazing tape*. Oil or latex (water) based.

Use: Glazing (attaching glass to window frame) and patching small exterior holes. Not a substitute for caulk.

Use Tips: When dealing with bare wood, apply a coat of paint before applying the glazing compound. This keeps the wood from absorbing oils from the compound. Check the label for both suitability to either wooden or metal frames and for painting directions—it should be sealed with either latex or oil paint. Apply with a **putty knife** designed for this purpose **(below)**. Glazing tape needs no knifing, nor does compound sold in cartridges used with **caulking guns (Part IV, Chapter 32)**.

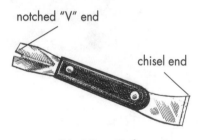

notched "V" end

chisel end

2-in-1 Putty Knife

2-in-1 Putty Knife

Also Known As: Double-ended window tool, glazing tool, glazier putty knife

Description: Small, hand-sized tool with hardened steel blades on each end, one of which is wide, and has a sharp, chisel end, and one of which is angled and folded into a V shape, with a small notch in the middle.

Use: Chisel end removes old putty from around windows, and notched V end smoothes new window putty or glazing compound.

 Buying Tips: A combination of two other tools, the bent putty knife and the putty chisel. A good buy.

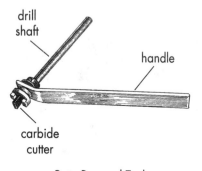

drill shaft

handle

carbide cutter

Putty Removal Tool

Putty Removal Tool

Also Known As: Putty Chaser™

Description: 6" long steel shaft with small carbide blade on one end, as well as a 6" long flat handle extending from the blade end. Fits into a power drill like a drill bit. The distance that the blade protrudes from the guide to cut over the sash is adjustable by a small collar on the shaft.

Use: Quickly removing old, hardened window putty without cracking the glass.

Use Tip: Works only with corded drills, as a minimum of 2,000 rpm is required. Wear safety glasses and a respirator. Hand removal of putty is onerous and usually involves removal of the window frame as well as breaking of the glass.

Buying Tip: Highly efficient solution to a big problem.

Floor and Ceiling Materials

About Flooring Materials

If there ever was a mantra to keep in mind while preparing a job, it is "make the floor level and solid" prior to laying floor covering. Anything else and things pop, crack, loosen, trip, wear out, and so on. Do it right the first time. Rent a variety of professional installation tools.

Resilient Flooring

Groups:

> *Tile*
>
> *Sheet goods; sheet goods types:*
>
> > *Inlaid structure*
> >
> > *Rotovinyl*

Vinyl Floor Tile

Also Known As:

> *Sheet goods:* Sheet flooring; vinyl sheet flooring; roll flooring; linoleum (no longer manufactured in the U.S.)
>
> *Rotovinyl:* Roto flooring, flexible

Description:

Tile: Vinyl and vinyl composition tile dominate tile flooring today. It commonly comes in 12" squares. It is approximately $^3/_{32}$" to $^1/_8$" thick and is available in a tremendous number of colors and styles. It is also available 3" wide by random lengths up to 36" to simulate wood planks. *Vinyl composition tile* has for the most part replaced asphalt tile, a 9" × 9" brittle material. Tile is available in self-stick form; the "dry-back" kinds must be laid in a bed of special adhesive, or **mastic**, made for this purpose **(Part IV, Chapter 32)**. Tile manufacturer should specify type of mastic required as well as other installation requirements.

Sheet goods: All sheet goods are available in a wide variety of colors and patterns and are generally cut to order off a large roll or else sold in rolls of convenient dimensions. *Inlaid structure vinyl* is a thick, durable material with color and pattern manufactured as one piece through to the backing material and a glossy, "no-wax" finish. It usually comes 6' and 12' wide and is relatively stiff; top-quality flooring. Rotovinyl consists of a core of vinyl with pattern and color printed on top and covered with a clear vinyl wear layer of varying thicknesses and perhaps a urethane coating. Rotovinyl is usually "waxless" —no waxing is required for maintenance. Rotovinyl is available 9', 12', and 15' wide. May be very thin and not long-lasting, and may have a cushion layer. Some come with kits of specialized installation tools.

Use: Tile and sheet goods can be used as flooring in any room in the house and on virtually all smooth and secure surfaces, but asphalt tile is still used for commercial installations and in below-grade basements, where it can "take" moisture.

Use Tips: Tile is easier to install than sheet goods; self-adhesive tiles are easier to put down than dry-back—those that require a separate adhesive. Among the sheet goods, inlaid is difficult to install and best left to professionals, while rotovinyl and cushioned flooring are easier because of their lighter weight and flexibility. Some manufacturers make a cushioned flooring that has to be held down only by molding or cemented at the edges rather than over the entire floor, the normal procedure. This makes for easy removal later on, which is convenient with the cheaper, thinner types that are bound to wear out quickly. Vinyl composition tile is more durable than plain vinyl.

Buying Tips: Better-quality tile is also thicker. Asphalt tile is much cheaper than vinyl composition tile, and plain vinyl is the most expensive. Inlaid, generally the best kind of sheet vinyl, comes with $1/16$" and $1/8$" wear layers; the $1/8$" thickness is best. The wear layer on rotovinyl is measured in thousandths of an inch; experts figure five thousandths of an inch equals about five years' wear. Hence, the thicker the wear layer the better the quality. In general, quality sheet goods are more expensive than tile. Get the kits with specialized installation tools.

About Carpeting

Carpeting is available in either roll form with padding—widths are usually 36", 54", 72", 108", and 144" —and tiles that are 12" × 12". Carpet materials vary, but the test of quality is the density of the pile. Bend the carpet. The less backing you can see, the better the carpet. The underlayment should be strong rubber padding for carpet used in high-traffic areas. Indoor/outdoor carpet can be used in high-moisture areas as well as outside the house. Rent a variety of specialized tools for installation.

Carpet Tiles

Description: As mentioned above, made of various materials. Some are self-adhesive, some installed with mastic, others installed with double-faced tape.

Use: Carpeting most rooms of the house and patio area, if outdoor type. Such tiles can also be used in the bath.

> **Use Tips:** Carpet tiles are easier to install than roll goods.

Roll Carpeting

Also Known As: Roll goods

Description: As mentioned in the **About section**, roll carpeting is made of various materials, such as nylon, acrylic, polyester, wool, and others. It comes in a variety of piles from velvet to plush. Paddings are made of felt, horsehair, rubber, or foam plastic. It may have to be glued down or held with a *pad and tackless strip,* which is a wooden strip with the points of tacks protruding from underneath; the carpet is laid upon it. In either case the carpet backing determines the method.

Use: Carpeting any room in the house.

> **Use Tips:** Roll carpeting is normally glued to the floor, but it can also be tacked in place, a professional job. Put metal strips called **carpet binder bars (below)** at doorway edges in high-traffic areas.

Ceramic Floor Tile

Description: Extremely hard ceramic pieces usually $4^1/_4'' \times 4^1/_4''$ (often stated "4 × 4") but also 1", 2", 6", 8", and 12" in square as well as hexagonal and octagonal shapes. Texture may be smooth or rough, shiny or dull, and colors and patterns vary greatly. Tiles are also available in a variety of other shapes. Additionally, ceramic tile is also available in *mosaic* form—a number of small tiles on a mesh backing. **Grout (Part VII, Chapter 51)** is used to fill gaps between tiles.

Use: Normally used as bath or kitchen flooring but also used outside on patios, walks, etc.

Use Tips: Ceramic floor tiles can be installed on either a thin set sand/cement mortar mixture or adhesive; each will vary according to the tile being installed. Installation on adhesive is easiest for the do-it-yourselfer. Different tiles require different adhesives, so check. Keep in mind that the additional thickness of tile may cause problems for various built-in appliances. Use a slightly rough finish for traction in bathrooms and other areas likely to be wet. Dealers will normally furnish the tools, either free or for rent, for installing tiles. Tools would include a *trowel* for the adhesive, a *cutter* for square cuts, and *nippers* for odd-shaped cuts. Remember that a good, solid underlayment is particularly important. No "give" can be allowed.

Note: Floor tile is laid on a bed of mastic and filled with grout the same as wall tile, and the tools used are the same except that a *rubber float* is used to push the grout into the tile spaces. **See Chapter 51**, for the **notched trowel** and **tile cutters** and **nippers**.

Wood Flooring

Types:

> *Parquet (wood block) flooring*
>
> *Plank flooring*
>
> *Strip (prepackaged) flooring*

Description: Usually hardwood—oak, maple, pecan, birch—but also softwoods such as redwood and southern pine—in flooring form. Flooring is available either finished or unfinished and most of it is $3/4$" thick.

> *Parquet flooring:* Comes in 9" to 36" squares but sometimes in rectangular shapes or in individual strips that are assembled to form parquet blocks. It is $13/16$" thick and usually prefinished.
>
> *Plank flooring:* Also tongue-and-groove and comes in standard widths $6^1/2$" to $7^3/4$" and random widths from 3" to 7" wide. Attachment is by installing screws in predrilled holes in the ends, which are covered with plugs; the result is a "pegged" effect.
>
> *Strip flooring:* Narrow boards $1^1/2$" to 3" wide that come in random lengths and go together tongue-and-groove fashion. Usually $3/8$" thick, though pros use $3/4$" thick wood. May be prefinished.

Use: As flooring in all rooms of the house.

Use Tips: Strip and plank flooring is normally nailed in place but there are planks with square edges that can be installed on a mastic base. Parquet is normally installed with **mastic (Part IV, Chapter 32)**. Do not install if there is excessive humidity present. If you are nailing tongue-and-groove flooring, rent a *nailing machine* especially designed for the purpose of shooting nails into wood flooring at a precise and low angle.

Floor Leveler

Also Known As: Floor and wall patch

Description: Cementitious plaster-like product that usually comes as powder that is mixed with water for use. A very common brand is Dash Patch®. Latex liquid binder may be added for more strength and adhesiveness.

Use: Leveling floors to provide a smooth base for floor coverings such as resilient tile or carpeting. Also general large area patching.

Ceiling Tiles and Panels

Also Known As: Panels, suspended ceiling, lay-in panels, pads

Description: Tiles are normally 12" square and made of either fiber or fiberglass. They are usually white but come in other colors as well. Tile faces have a striated or fissured surface for sound absorbency. Some also have a vinyl surface so they can be cleaned easily. Tiles are tongue-and-grooved, made to fit together when installed, either by bonding them directly to the ceiling or *furring* strips with adhesive or by stapling them. Ceiling panels normally are 2' × 4' and are designed to be installed in a grid system. They are made of fiber, fiberglass, or plastic.

Use: Ceiling installations for nonformal rooms. Panels installed in a grid system form a suspended, or dropped, ceiling, useful if you want to hide a ceiling with pipes running on it, such as in the basement. Translucent plastic panels are used to form a luminous ceiling in which lights are installed above the panels.

> **Use Tips:** Take care when installing mineral fiber panels on a suspended ceiling: The wires to support the grid can cut through a panel easily. Also, panels are fairly delicate and can chip. Check your building code before installing. Getting a ceiling perfectly level is very difficult. Make extensive use of a **flexible tube level (Part I, Chapter 10)**. A good time to call in the professionals.

Binder Bar

Description: Long, thin, narrow metal strip, either gold or silver colored, with a slight bend down its length and several screw holes.

Use: Protecting the edge of floor covering when it is a little higher than the floor, especially in doorways.

> **Buying Tips:** Cheap insurance for an extended life of floor covering. Don't hesitate to use it.

Floor Scraper

Also Known As: Floor stripping tool

Description: Long-handled, broom-sized steel tool with hardened steel business end and a sliding weight inside the tubular handle. The weight is slammed down to create 150 pounds per square inch of impact. Other versions, with no sliding weight, merely have a slightly angled steel head.

Use: Removing tile, linoleum, carpet, roofing, ceramic tile, and other adhesive floor coverings. Also helpful in removing old shingles from rooftops.

> **$ Buying Tips:** Certain jobs are incredibly tough without specialized tools. Removing old flooring is one of them, and this tool helps make it easier.

VIII

Plumbing Hardware, Materials, and Tools

$ General Buying Tips: Before shopping for any plumbing products, bear in mind the following, which could save you a lot of money.

- High-quality plumbing tools are worth the price difference in efficiency and safety. Cheap tools can truly interfere with a job.

- Many plumbing parts come both packaged and loose. The loose items can be as much as 30 percent less expensive than the items in "view," or plastic bubble packages.

- Some packaged products contain a number of the same item, meaning that they include many unneeded parts. For example, you'll most often need only one "O" ring to repair a faucet but a package contains at least four or five.

- In the same vein, washerless faucet-repair kits contain multiple parts but only one or two are usually needed for repair. A well-stocked hardware store or plumbing supply shop carries all kinds of individual parts for washerless faucets at much less than the kit price. To ensure getting the correct parts we heartily recommend that you make a habit of taking in the old part to identify the brand and the model of the faucet. You will always be better and more quickly served. Such a tremendous array of plumbing parts is sold that virtually any part of any plumbing device can be replaced. For example, an old toilet can be kept going virtually forever—there would likely be no need to replace it. A good hardware store stocks an amazingly wide variety of parts or will order what you need, as will a plumbing supply store.

- At this writing American-made plumbing products are generally better than ones imported from the Far East, as are most products imported from Germany. The country of origin must, by law, be on the package or product. The price difference is worth it.

- Check closely when buying a brand name to make sure that it is indeed the real brand. Some companies in the Far East make inferior products (especially tools) and package them to look just like well-known American brands.

- Look for "loss leaders" when buying at home centers. They often offer big discounts on common items such as faucets and tools. On the other hand, their prices on smaller, more unusual items tend to be higher than at hardware stores.

- You needn't buy an expensive, specialized tool that you may need only once or very rarely. You can rent virtually anything from a rental store, hardware or plumbing supply store, and such tools are generally of a heavier duty and higher quality than the average person would be inclined to buy. On the other hand, if you cannot find one to rent, and you are confident that you know what to do, then the purchase of a specialized tool to avoid the expense of a plumber's house call may be worthwhile.

- A plumbing supply store or good hardware store might be open to giving a 10 percent discount if you are planning to buy a large quantity of pipe and fittings, such as when you are renovating a house or apartment.

A Note About Plumbing Code

Any consideration of what plumbing products to purchase should take into account local building and plumbing codes, which are sets of rules and regulations set up by local governmental authorities on what products may be used and how the installations must be done. Similar codes exist for electrical and general construction work.

Plumbing codes have a simple purpose—to ensure that the installed plumbing is done safely and does not jeopardize the health of a building's occupants. However, despite this seemingly straightforward goal, plumbing codes vary greatly from community to community, sometimes in a contradictory manner. But they must be followed. If they are not, a plumbing inspector can order the removal of any installation that violates the code, even though the installation may be perfectly safe. This can also be a problem when selling a house and the prospective buyers have it inspected professionally. For example, plastic pipe may have been used where the code allows only metal.

Before embarking on a home improvement project by all means check the plans out with the local building code authority to ensure that they conform with the law. Your local plumbing supply or hardware store can usually advise.

Pipe and Accessories

About Pipe and Fittings

Three kinds of pipe are used for home plumbing, *water supply, water distribution,* and *waste.* Water supply pipe supplies clean cold water, water distribution pipe carries hot and cold water inside the house, and waste pipe transports waste, "used," or soiled water to a sewer, cesspool, or other disposal facility. Water piping in the home is rarely over 1" in diameter; waste piping is always of a larger diameter, like 2" to 4".

Water supply pipe is also known as *supply pipe* or simply *water pipe.* Waste pipe is also known as *drainage pipe*, *soil pipe*, *sewer pipe*, *drain pipe*, *DWV pipe* (for *drain-waste-vent*), and *discharge pipe*, although technically waste pipes do not carry toilet discharge, only soil pipes do, as they carry all waste. A *stack* is the general term for any vertical line of this kind of drain piping; *riser* is the general term for any vertical water supply piping. It's simple—the former goes down, the latter goes up.

Pipe sections are connected with **fittings (Chapters 55 and 56)** that allow piping to be routed around turns throughout a building and connect them to fixtures such as sinks, tubs, and toilets. Every type of pipe has its own type and kind of fittings, i.e., copper pipe/copper fittings.

Pipe size is almost always described and ordered in terms of its inside diameter—a 1" pipe has a 1" inside diameter. This is the "nominal" size; it is not meant to be exact. The outside diameter varies with the wall thickness of whatever the pipe is made of. For example, cast-iron pipe is thicker than copper pipe of the same nominal size. You do not have to specify it for retail purchases, but if the outside dimension is critical to the job, such as when fitting it through a hole in a wall, be sure to ask for specifications as sizes do vary.

Pipe is considered *male* and the fittings into which it fits *female.* Male pipe has threads on the outside; female fittings have threads on the inside. This male-female designation is used to describe all fittings.

On a large project it is advisable to buy all the fittings from the same manufacturer to ensure a better fit, as the manufacturing tolerances can vary from one brand to another.

Also, you should avoid mixing types of pipe, such as galvanized, brass, plastic, copper, and so on, as well as different thicknesses of the same type. Where different types must be connected you can use specialized fittings to avoid creating *electrolytic action,* a corroding condition that occurs when dissimilar metals are in contact with one another.

Galvanized Steel Pipe

Also Known As: Iron pipe, malleable pipe, steel pipe

Description: Gray, zinc-treated steel. The zinc, or galvanized, treatment, makes the steel rust-resistant if not scratched. Commonly comes in 21' lengths, which plumbing stores and larger hardware stores will cut to order, as well as in shorter precut lengths, usually in sections of 6" up to 6', threaded on both ends. Pipe diameters range from $1/8$" to 6". Common water sizes are $3/8$" to 1". Common waste sizes are $1^1/2$", 2", and 3". Both ends should be threaded to be screwed into correspondingly threaded fittings; lengths can be threaded on one end only (T.O.E.) if you want.

Use: Carries water or waste as needed in a building.

> **Use Tips:** Most hardware or plumbing supply stores will custom cut and thread lengths for you. Galvanized pipe cannot be used for gas or steam.

> **Buying Tips:** Check to see that the threads are not damaged before leaving the store. Because galvanized pipes can eventually rust out, copper, brass, or PVC is usually used.

Black Iron Pipe

Also Known As: B.I. pipe, black pipe

Description: Similar to galvanized steel pipe, but not treated for rust resistance. Darker and often seamless. Slightly greasy to the touch.

Use: For steam or gas.

> **Use Tips:** Only black fittings can be used with black iron pipe. Best left to a professional plumber.

Cast-Iron Pipe

Also Known As: Soil pipe, soil stack

Description: Very heavy pipe that comes in two weights—*service* and *extra-heavy*. It is commonly sold in lengths of 5' and 10' and in diameters of 2", 3", and 4". Two kinds exist. The old, classic kind has a bell hub on one end and a spigot hub (raised end) on the other, but the new kind is plain and known as No-Hub® or *hubless*. Sections of the old kind are joined with a packing of oakum and lead, while the hubless kind is joined with a special **hubless fitting (Chapter 55)** that is simply tightened down over the joint.

Use: As a waste pipe.

Use Tips: Only a professional should tackle oakum and lead joints. The new, hubless pipe can be done by the do-it-yourselfer, if allowed by local code, but the pipe is so heavy and hard to handle that is not recommended. Your supplier may cut pieces to length for you or you can rent a device called a *snap-cutter* for the purpose. It can also be cut with a cold chisel and a hammer. You can remove unneeded cast-iron pipe, such as during renovations, by shattering it with a sledgehammer.

Plastic Pipe

Types:

ABS (acrylonitrile-butadiene-styrene) pipe

CPVC (chlorinated polyvinyl chloride) pipe

PB (polybutylene) pipe

PE (polyethylene) pipe

PEX (crosslink polyethylene)

PP (polypropylene) pipe

PVC (polyvinyl chloride or *vinyl) pipe*

SR (styrene rubber) pipe

Description: Two basic kinds, *flexible* (PE, PEX, PB, PP) or *rigid* (PVC, CPVC, ABS, SR) some with ends prepared for joining in various ways, such as flared or threaded. Wall thickness for home use is generally referred to as "Schedule 40." Comes in same nominal diameters as all other water or waste pipe and in lengths of 10' and 20', as well as in 25' and 100' coils of flexible tubing. PVC, CPVC, and ABS are the most common kinds in general use.

Use: Different materials are made for use as either water supply (cold potable water), water distribution (hot and cold), or DWV (waste). PVC and ABS are commonly used for DWV. CPVC, ABS, PEX, and PB are used for water distribution; PB, PEX, and PE pipes can withstand freezing with water inside them without bursting and are often used outdoors. PB and PP are most popular for traps due to their excellent chemical resistance.

Use Tips: Plastic pipe can be cut with a special, large-bladed *plastic pipe saw*, **hacksaw (Part I, Chapter 5)**, or a special pruning shear–like *PVC cutter* or *plastic tubing cutter*, a great work-saver with pipes up to 1" diameter. PE and PEX not only can withstand freezing water but remain flexible in extreme cold. You can use **transition fittings**, or **adapters (Part VIII, Chapter 55)**, to join plastic to copper or steel plumbing systems. Be sure to get the kind of fittings specified for your pipe.

Buying Tips: Plastic is less expensive than steel or copper (by half), easier to use (it is one-twentieth the weight of steel and has a simpler method of joining), and works just fine. Use various plastic pipe accessories, such as a *deburring cone* or *edge bevel*, to speed your work and ensure tight joints. But make sure it is acceptable by your local plumbing code.

Copper Pipe and Tubing

Description: Rigid copper pipe for water comes in diameters from $1/8$" to 12" (measured on the outside diameter, or "O.D."), and of various wall thicknesses known as types K (thick), L (medium), and M (thin), as well as DWV type (thin). Available in rigid 20' or 21' lengths with unthreaded ends, 10' lengths with threaded ends capped for protection, and coils of 45', 60', 100', and 200' (types K and L). *Drawn* is hard; *annealed* is soft.

Use: Water or waste pipe.

Use Tips: Type L is most common for residential use. It can be cut with a hacksaw but a specialized tool called a **tubing cutter (Part VIII, Chapter 65)** makes it easier. Connections are usually made with **sweat-soldered fittings (Chapter 55)**, but **compression and flare fittings (Chapter 55)** can also be used to avoid using the propane torch necessary for soldered fittings. Use only the same thickness (types K, L, or M) in one line of plumbing.

Buying Tips: If copper tube is on sale for a very low cost, make sure that it is indeed type L and not the thinner-walled type M. Although type M is suitable for some uses, it has been called *see-through pipe* by some plumbers who think it is too lightweight. Copper is the highest quality pipe, but it is relatively expensive and connections must be made with care and specialized tools. This said, it can be worked by the average handyperson.

Brass Pipe

Description: Solid brass, usually sold in unthreaded 12' lengths and in all standard sizes. Comes in various weights.

Use: Water supply and distribution, where resistance to corrosion is the main concern.

 Use Tips: All threaded connections. Not commonly used in homes.

 Buying Tip: More expensive than other types of pipe.

About Tubular Goods

Tubular goods are drain pipes used underneath sinks, basins, and tubs. They have their own type of joining system, using slip nuts, and are easy to work with.

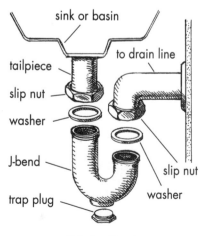

Tubular Goods

Tubular Goods

Also Known As: Drainage fittings, drain pipes, drain fittings, drainage pipes, slip-joint pipe.

Description: Large diameter, variously shaped lightweight brass or plastic pipes. Those that are exposed to view are often chrome-plated or nickel-plated brass. Others are satin-finish brass (unpolished chrome-plated) or plastic, including chrome-covered plastic. Kitchen-sink tubular goods are usually $1^1/_2$"; lavatory tubular goods are $1^1/_4$". All are usually held together and made watertight by hexagonal slip nuts and plastic or rubber washers called *slip-joints*—though some tailpieces that attach to sink strainers have threaded ends. Washers may be called *cut sj washers*.

The long piece with an L-bend at one end is often called a *waste ell* for kitchen piping ($1^1/_2$") and a *slip ell* for bathroom basin piping ($1^1/_4$"). *Corrugated flexible drain* is plastic tubular goods that can be bent with the bare hands and is an option if there is more than the usual distance to cover between the sink and the drain line, particularly if precise alignment is difficult.

Types: Typical parts are tailpiece, tail pipe, branch tailpiece, extension piece (also known as *extension tube*), trap, repair trap, offset, waste ell, waste bend, J-bend (also known as *trap bend, replacement trap bend, kitchen-sink drain bend)*, P-trap, S-trap, continuous waste line. The most common is the tailpiece (descends from the sink) and the P-trap (from the tailpiece to the drain).

Use: To route waste water from a sink, disposer, or tub to other drain pipes. *Traps* (J- and P-bends) retain water in their curved part, which acts as a seal against sewer odors and vermin.

Use Tips: A variety of configurations are possible with tubular goods; it is a simple matter of assembling the right shapes so that everything fits together. Occasional rinsing with extremely hot water helps clear debris from the trap. This pipe and especially the chrome finish is delicate, so use a **strap wrench** and special tools such as **spud wrenches** instead of regular **pipe wrenches (Part VIII, Chapter 63)** or **tongue-and-groove pliers (Part I, Chapter 7)** and extra care when handling. Forcing one of these pipes might crush it.

A reducing slip nut with an extra large rubber washer can connect $1^1/_2$" to $1^1/_4$" tubular goods if necessary. If for some reason you are using galvanized piping in the drain line, a slip joint nut and washer can be "borrowed" from tubular goods and used on galvanized. You can also use a device called a **flexible coupling (Part VIII, Chapter 55)**, which consists of soft rubber fittings in various sizes that are clamped onto the pipes.

Buying Tips: Plain plastic is the cheapest material, but not the best-looking. If the lines will be out of sight, then plastic or rough brass is suitable. If it is visible, chrome-plated brass is recommended; chrome-covered plastic is new and relatively untested. Some brands come with fittings and others do not; be sure to check before leaving the store. Because a J-bend (trap) comes off easily for cleaning, the more expensive model with a cleanout plug is unnecessary. Parts for P- and S-traps are sometimes sold in kits, though this can be more costly than buying parts individually.

Water Supply Tubes

Also Known As: Speedies, Speedees, basin tubes, sink supply tube, lavatory supply tubes or pipe, lav supply tubes, water connectors, water supply pipe, inlet pipe, flex line, toilet supply tube, tank tube (latter two for toilets)

Description: Short $3/8$" diameter tubes made of plastic, rough brass (raw copper), chrome-plated copper or brass, copper, corrugated copper, nylon weave in clear plastic, and nylon covered with stainless-steel weave. Corrugated is plain or chrome-plated copper and may be corrugated in a central section or for its entire length for bending ease.

Use: Makes the connection between the **water supply valve (Part VIII, Chapter 59)**—the water supply—and the sink faucet or toilet tank.

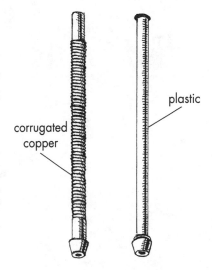

corrugated copper

plastic

Water Supply Tubes

Use Tips: Always get tube longer than needed and trim the excess. Plastic is easiest to connect, cut, and bend; the metal types, except for corrugated, may kink. Nylon can withstand any kind of bending—pretzel shape if you want—and attaches like a garden hose.

Buying Tips: Nylon is five or six times as costly as other plastics. Nylon supply tube is usually sold in kit form, i.e., with necessary connectors attached.

Pipe-Hanging Tape

Pipe-Hanging Tape

Also Known As: Hanger strap, pipe hanger, band iron, band clamp

Description: Steel or copper band with holes at regular intervals, sold in coils.

Use: Suspending pipes of all sizes from walls and ceilings. Infinitely adjustable to fit. Tightened with a **machine screw (Part III, Chapter 21).**

 Use Tip: Use copper tape on copper pipe, not steel.

Pipe Strap and Tube Strap

Description: Pipe strap is a U-shaped piece of galvanized steel with two holes in flanges; tube strap is similar but made of copper for copper tubing.

Use: Screwed or nailed to wall to hold small pipe.

 Buying Tip: Serves the same purpose as *pipe hanging tape,* but only when the pipe can be snug against the wall or ceiling.

Hose Clamp

Hose Clamp

Description: Stainless-steel band with notches and a closing gear. The gear is in the form of a $^5/_{16}$" nut.

Use: To apply even pressure around pipe or hose; in particular to clamp a hose or a gasket onto a tube or pipe. Also used with **insert fittings (Chapter 55)**.

> **Use Tips:** Don't overtighten. If you have many to do, use a $^5/_{16}$" **nut driver (Part I, Chapter 8)** or a **T-handle torque wrench (Chapter 63)**.

> **Buying Tips:** New plastic types—one brand is Speedy Clamp®—are becoming available. No tool is required. Instead of a worm gear, they have sawtooth-edged ends that lock in when you squeeze them together and come apart when you twist them. *Spring-type clamps,* used on cars and appliances such as clothes dryers, are just thick wire loops, and are harder to use.

Floor and Ceiling Plates

Description: Chrome-plated split doughnut-shaped flat metal piece. A tiny rivet acts as a hinge for the two halves, which open up for installation.

Use: Goes around radiator pipes for decorative purposes where they enter a ceiling or a floor.

Radiator Air Valve

Radiator Air Valve

Also Known As: Steam vent, air vent, vapor equalizing valve, air eliminator

Description: Small round or cylindrical metal device that screws into small hole on top or side of a steam radiator or at end of run of steam pipe. Comes in various sizes, 1–5 and C–D, for placing different distances from the boiler.

Use: Allows cold air to escape steam-system radiators as steam enters, closing automatically when steam fills the radiator or pipe.

 Use Tip: Boil valves in vinegar from time to time to remove scale.

Buying Tips: Choose category carefully in order to balance system. Be sure you get the technical brochure that is usually packaged with the valves.

3-in-One Radiator Repair Tool

3-in-One Radiator Repair Tool

Description: Metal, three-armed tool with a tap, a screw extractor, and a die.

Use: Repairing worn-out holes in radiators where an air vent has broken off or stripped the threads. Extracts broken air valves, retaps radiator, rethreads air valve.

Use Tip: Make sure radiator valve is closed when removing vent.

Radiator Air Bleeder Valve Key

Description: Tiny metal key with square opening, similar to a roller skate key.

Use: Opens air bleeder valve on hot-water-system radiators to let air out.

Radiator Air Bleeder Valve Key

$ Buying Tip: These are inexpensive and important enough to warrant buying several to ensure that you can find one when you need it.

Flexible Gas Hose

Also Known As: Gas range or dryer connector

Description: Brass (old style) or gray epoxy-coated (new style) flexible, corrugated hose with brass hex fittings on the ends. Comes in a range of sizes from 18" to 6' in $1/2$" or $3/4$" diameter. Modern appliances have $1/2$" fittings but typical supply lines are $3/4$". Adapters for reducing the connection are available with the hose.

Use: Connects gas supply line to kitchen gas stove or clothes dryer.

Use Tips: Use plenty of **pipe dope (Part VIII, Chapter 60)**—not tape—and care. Make sure no kinks are in the line. Test by brushing with soapy water and examining connection for bubbles.

Fitting Types

About Fittings

Fittings are devices that allow pipe to be connected to increase length and to change direction. For each kind of pipe there are fittings made of the same material, wall thickness, and sizes, with a few exceptions. For quality check to make sure that there are not too many rough edges.

Galvanized, plastic, and copper fittings come in two variations, for *water supply* and for *waste,* or drainage. Waste fittings have recessed threads that leave a smooth inside—when connected they do not impede the flow of waste and thereby avoid causing blockages. They are not available in all sizes. They may also be called *Durham fittings,* after an old manufacturer. Supply fittings are also known as *malleable steel fittings.* When purchasing fittings you should, of course, specify if they are for water supply or waste lines. *Black iron fittings* come either for gas or for steam. *Cast iron* is made for waste only.

Fittings are made of copper, plastic, galvanized steel, black iron, cast iron, brass, and so on to go with pipes of the same material and wall thickness. All fittings have similar functions, shapes, and names but have notable differences as to type. Entries for both types and shapes follow. An almost infinite total of combinations are manufactured, so these represent the basic ones.

Some terms are shorthand for one style in a variety of fitting shapes. For example, the term *reducer* refers to any fitting that will go on to one size of pipe at one end, and another size pipe at the other end, but may be incorrectly used to refer to such items as a *reducing bushing, reducing coupling, reducing nipple*, or *reducing wye*, etc. For example, you would use a *reducing tee* to branch off a 1½" water pipe to two 1" pipes. And an *adapter* can mean almost anything, but we make an attempt to define them in Chapter 55.

Threaded Fitting

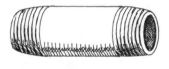

Nipple

Description: The most common type of fitting, with male (exterior) or female (interior) threads at each opening. Comes in most materials and sizes.

Use: Connecting water supply, waste, steam, and gas piping systems in all kinds of threaded pipe.

> **Use Tips:** Use plenty of *pipe dope* or **Teflon® pipe tape (Part VIII, Chapter 60)** on the threads of metal pipes to prevent leaks and reduce corrosion.

Sweat-Soldered Fitting

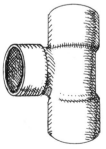

Sweat-Soldered Fitting

Also Known As: Copper fitting (incorrect), sweats

Description: Smooth-ended (no threads) copper pipe fitting with a slightly enlarged end that receives copper pipe.

Use: Connecting copper pipe or tube.

Use Tips: Ensure that fittings are clean before soldering and that plenty of **flux (Part VIII, Chapter 60)** is used. Soldering *copper pipe joints* is not all that difficult. Do not use lead solder on water supply lines.

Buying Tip: Now available with solder pre-applied.

Compression Fitting

Description: Two-piece copper or plastic device that uses a nut and a metal or plastic ring on the end of a pipe that is inserted into a fitting. As the nut is tightened the ring presses into the fitting and the pipe, making a watertight seal.

Use: Connecting water supply tubes under faucets, or wherever one wants to avoid using a torch and sweat fittings. *Plastic grip fittings* are for use with **flexible plastic (PB) pipe (above)**.

 Buying Tip: The small rings and nuts can be bought individually in case one is lost.

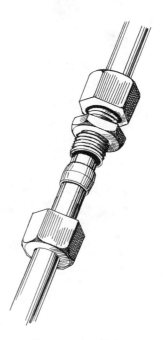

Compression Fitting

Flare Fitting

Also Known As: S.A.E. flare

Description: Similar to a **compression fitting (above)** but with an end that is expanded, or flared, and that fits against the beveled end of the fitting.

Use: Mostly for refrigeration and oil heating systems and small appliance lines. Similar to *sweat-soldered fittings* but installed without using a torch, which can be important in areas where fire would be a risk. Prohibited by some codes.

Solvent-Welded Fittings

Also Known As: Glued fittings, cemented fittings

Description: Plastic fittings with slightly enlarged, threadless openings designed for use with special solvent, sometimes called *glue*. They look similar to **copper sweat-soldered fittings (above)**. Considered the best joining method for plastic pipe and fittings.

Use: Rigid plastic plumbing connections.

Insert Fitting

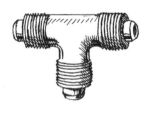

Insert Fitting

Also Known As: Insert

Description: Ridged plastic or metal piece that is inserted into the end of flexible plastic pipe and clamped in place with a stainless-steel **hose-type clamp (Chapter 54)**. Made of nylon, polypropylene, or polystyrene.

Use: To connect flexible plastic pipe to other pieces or fittings, including to standard female threads. Common on lawn sprinkler systems.

Hubless Fitting

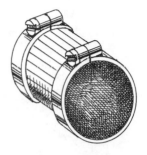

Also Known As: No-Hub®, no-hub clamp, no-hub band, clamp, banded coupling

Description: A neoprene (black rubber) sleeve, or gasket, covered by a corrugated metal sleeve, or *clamp band,* with hose-type clamps on each end.

Hubless Fitting

Use: Connecting hubless or No-Hub® cast-iron pipe sections and fittings. Also cast iron-to-plastic.

> **Use Tips:** Clamp nuts can be tightened down with a small wrench, screwdriver, a $5/16$" **nut driver (Part I, Chapter 8)**, or a special tool called a **T-handle**, or **No-Hub® torque wrench (Part VIII, Chapter 63)**. The latter tool contains an internal mechanism that prevents overtightening and speeds the job.

Adapter

Also Known As: Transition fitting

Description: Common term for virtually anything that helps connect two normally incompatible things—hoses to pipes, or whatever. As for fittings, though, it is a type of coupling or union with a different type of joining method on each end, i.e., thread/sweat, thread/solvent weld, etc.

Adapter

Types:

Transition union adapter: Special fitting designed to compensate for thermal differences in expansion and contraction between metal and plastic pipe.

Dielectric adapter: For connecting galvanized to copper.

Use:

Transition union: Allows connecting different kinds of pipe, such as plastic to galvanized, or copper to plastic, etc.

Dielectric fitting: Allows connecting dissimilar metals and prevents destructive *galvanic* or *electrolytic* action, a major cause of rust and corrosion. Typically used under faucets where copper pipe connects with galvanized. Suitable for water and waste.

Flexible Coupling

Also Known As: Fernco Coupling (brand name)

Description: Length of soft plastic (elastomeric PVC or polyurethane) that slips over the outside ends of waste pipe and is secured by hose clamps. Heavier yet more flexible than **hubless fittings (above)**. Comes in a variety of dimensions and shapes as a **reducer coupling (Chapter 56)**.

Use: Waste lines only, but fits over any kind of pipe. Especially useful where precise alignment is not possible or where some flexibility is needed and where connecting two pipes of different diameters. A "forgiving" fitting.

Tap-On Fitting

Also Known As: Saddle valve

Description: Short nipple with heavy saddle end and a U-bolt. Comes with a **sillcock (Chapter 57)** or similar valve.

Use: Clamps onto a copper, brass, or galvanized supply line with the U-bolt and, after a hole is drilled and the valve installed, provides a new source of water. Typically used in small sizes to install an ice-maker.

Fitting Shapes and Forms

About Fitting Shapes and Forms

These shapes, or forms, are made in all the various pipe materials, but regardless of the material, they resemble each other (the illustrations show galvanized fittings). The nomenclature is the same.

Cap

Also Known As: End, end cap

Description: A short piece with female threads on one end and the other closed.

Use: Seals male end of pipe at the end of a run or when a fitting or valve has been removed.

Cap

Coupling, Reducing Coupling

Also Known As: Straight coupling, reducing bell (reducing coupling), reducer (reducing coupling)

Coupling

Reducing Coupling

Description: Short length of pipe with female threads, generally no longer than the threaded area itself. Reducing couplings have two different-sized openings.

Use: Connects lengths of pipe that are not intended to be disconnected. Reducing coupling connects pipes of different sizes up to 3". Can also be used in combination with **bushings (below)** when there are large differences in pipe diameters.

Buying Tip: When buying a reducing coupling state the larger dimension first—2 × 1$\frac{1}{2}$" etc.

Cross

Cross

Also Known As: 4-way tee, straight cross

Description: Four female threaded openings of the same size set at 90-degree angles (straight cross); a side-outlet cross has a fifth opening on the side, in the center, and is extremely rare.

Use: Joining four (or, with a side outlet, five) pipes.

Use Tip: Using a fitting with five openings is extremely difficult and unusual.

Dresser Coupling

Also Known As: Mender coupler, slip fitting, "no-thread" fitting, mender dresser

Description: Similar to a *nipple* with hex or ribbed nuts on each end, inside of which is a compression fitting containing rubber and metal washers. Available in copper, steel, and plastic.

Use: Slips onto unthreaded pipe ends to make a convenient connection, often used to cover a leaking section (after the pipe has been cut through) or where a very slight flexibility is needed.

> **Use Tips:** May be used on supply or waste lines. Helpful where threading is impossible, such as when replacing a damaged section.

Dresser Coupling

Elbow

Types:

90-degree elbow

45-degree elbow

Drop-ear elbow

Side-outlet elbow

Also Known As: Ell, L, S.O. ell (side-outlet ell)

90-Degree Ell

45-Degree Ell

> **Note:** Similar to and easily confused with cast-iron fittings $1/4$ bend (90-degree) and $1/8$ bend (45-degree).

Description: Female threads at both ends, or in the case of side-outlet ells, all three, with openings at angles corresponding to the type of elbow. *Drop-ear* (also known as *drop ells*) have a *flange* for attaching to a wall. The ell that brings water from a toilet tank to flush a toilet bowl is known as a *closet bend*.

Use: Joins pipes for corners at 90- and 45-degree angles.

> **Use Tips:** Side-outlet ells are useful in corners of construction or for making railings or fences. If placed outdoors, protect exposed threads to keep from rusting.

Flange

Also Known As: Floor flange

Description: Round, female-threaded fitting that can take pipe up to 2", surrounded by flat flange with holes that permit attaching to a floor or a wall with screws or bolts.

Use: Often a nonplumbing use, such as making a railing or a table. Pipe just screws into the flange and is relatively solid.

Hex Bushing, Flush Bushing

Also Known As: Bushing

Description: Short plug (threaded, with hexagonal top) or nipple (flush)-type piece with female threads inside.

Use: Joining pipe of dissimilar size. Bushings fit inside other fittings, especially couplings, and can be combined to reduce pipe as required.

Hex Brushing

Nipple

Also Known As: Close (if threads from each end of a straight nipple meet or almost meet in the middle), straight nipple

Description: Any piece of pipe that is less than 12" and male threaded on both ends. Generally stocked in lengths from *close* (minimum) to 12"; lengths beyond this are usually considered *cut pipe* and are available in 6" intervals. Diameters are standard nominal pipe sizes, from $1/8$" to 4". *Reducing nipple* has different diameter ends. Reducing nipples are particularly short, available only up to 2" maximum diameter, and are very rare.

Use: Links longer pipe sections where the final "fit" is being made, such as the span between two fittings in a run of pipe. Reducing nipple connects different sizes of pipe in place of a **bushing** and **coupling (above)** combination. Provides a smoother, neater connection.

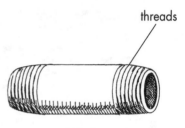

threads

Nipple

Pipe Clamp, Repair Plate

Also Known As: Often the two items above are confused and considered the same thing.

Description: A *hinged pipe clamp* consists of two concave stainless-steel pieces a few inches long with a hinge on one side and flanges with two carriage bolts on the other. It comes with a rubber gasket that fits over the pipe when the clamp is bolted down. A *repair plate* is one concave steel piece a few inches long with two flanges and two U-bolts, also supplied with a rubber gasket.

Use: Covering small holes and cracks in drain pipes.

> **Use Tips:** Not for use on supply lines. Pipe usually has to be replaced where leaks occur on any line with pressure.

Plug

Plug

Also Known As: Hex head plug, square head plug, round head plug

Description: A short, solid piece with male threads and a hexagonal, square, or round head. A large cleanout plug has a square protrusion in the middle for a wrench to grab.

Use: Seals female ends of fittings or valves and the like.

Street Ell

Also Known As: Street elbow

Description: 90- or 45-degree elbow with male threads on one end and female threads on the other.

Use: Joins pipes at corners with the male end going into a fitting or valve.

Street Ell

Sweep

Description: Similar to an elbow in that it consists of two openings at 90 degrees or 45 degrees to each other. Comes in "long" version as well as normal to create a longer curve to fit different situations.

Use: Same as elbows, but with longer dimensions and more gradual configurations.

> **Use Tips:** If replacing an existing piece of plumbing, be sure to measure the sweep to see if it is "long" or normal.

Tee

Also Known As: T, straight tee, reducing tee, sanitary tee

Description: Three openings, two in a line and one on the side, in a T shape. *Straight tees* have the same size openings; *reducing tees* have one opening of a different size. *Sanitary tees,* used in waste lines, have a curved branch that is slightly offset for a cleanout plug and a smooth inside.

Tee

Use: Connecting three pipes. Sanitary tees are for waste lines where lack of obstruction is important.

$ **Buying Tips:** When ordering a reducing tee specify the lateral, or horizontal, dimensions first, followed by the vertical branch. Keep the letter T in mind. For example, $1" \times 1" \times 1\frac{1}{2}"$. Be sure to mention the use you have in mind, as there is some variety in sanitary tees.

Union

Also Known As: Ground joint union

Union

Description: An assembly of one (sweat) or three (threaded) hex nuts. Its two halves are separated and screwed onto the ends of the pipes to be joined, then the larger, central hex nut is tightened down to join them.

Use: Connecting pipe sections of similar size that are expected to be disassembled or that are being fit into a position between two fixed pipes.

 Use Tip: Because this is a sort of compression fitting the surfaces must be clean to avoid leaks.

Y Branch, Reducing Y

Also Known As: Y bend, wye

Description: Three openings, with two in a line and one at an angle, that can be the same or a different size in the case of a reducing Y.

Use: Bringing together two pipes from similar directions.

Wye (Y)

Faucets and Faucet Parts

About Faucets

Kitchen sink, laundry, and lavatory faucets come in a tremendous array of styles and colors. Some have separate handles for hot and cold water, while others—mixing, or combination, faucets—have a single lever. Materials include chrome-plated brass, chrome-plated plastic, plain plastic, and pot metal.

When buying a faucet the key dimension to specify is center-to-center, or "centers"—the distance between the center of one handle and the center of the other. Kitchen sinks usually have 8" centers but may be 6". Lavatory faucets mounted on the basin are called *deck-mounted* and are usually 4" apart but 8" is not uncommon. Wall-mounted lavatory faucets are usually on $4^1/_2$" centers but may be 6".

Selecting a faucet can be a complicated exercise, dependent on a variety of factors, but one thing that experts suggest is buying a good-quality, name-brand model. It will be more expensive, but it will work better, and replacement parts, which are generally unique to each brand, will be available when needed.

Faucet types include ledge- or deck-mounted (exposed, on the countertop; concealed (plumbing is below countertop), shelf-back (on vertical splash back of counter). And all can be dual or single knob-controlled, with or without spray.

There can be no doubt about sizes or types when repairing or replacing faucet parts. Always take the old parts into the store, or at least the brand and model names.

 General Buying Tips:

- Avoid pure plastic or chrome-covered plastic faucets, often known as "builder's specials." They can deteriorate rapidly. Also avoid pot-metal faucets.

- Cast brass is much better than tubular brass; chrome-plated pot metal is inferior. Both metals look similar, but brass is much heavier.

- Avoid faucets manufactured in the Far East. They are generally of inferior quality. Again, some German-made faucets are very good.

- If you are a reasonably handy do-it-yourselfer, you can install any kind of standard faucet. Some come with installation kits and don't even require tools.

- Major, advertised name brands of kitchen and bathroom faucets such as Moen, Delta, and Kohler can be much more expensive than their average counterparts but worth it.

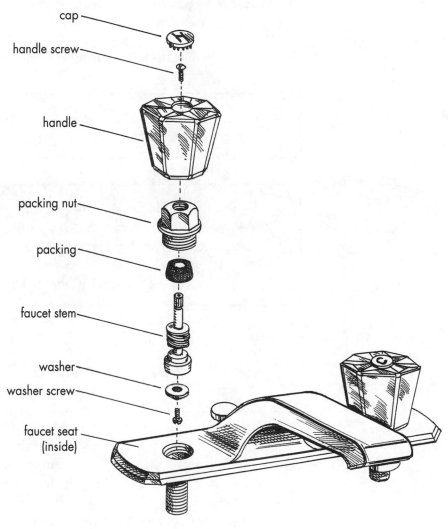

cap

handle screw

handle

packing nut

packing

faucet stem

washer

washer screw

faucet seat
(inside)

Compression Faucet

Compression Faucet

Also Known As: Basin faucet (in lavatory)

Description: Common faucet that has a threaded *spindle* or *stem,* with a washer on the end that presses against a hole, the *faucet seat,* where the water emerges from the supply pipe.

Use: Controls water flow into basins or sinks.

 Use Tips: Leaks are usually due to a worn-out washer or a pitted, corroded seat.

Buying Tips: Get faucets with a replaceable or renewable "seat"—the part that the washer presses against. If a nonreplaceable seat goes bad, the entire faucet may have to be replaced or perhaps saved by regrinding the seat with a **faucet seat reamer (Chapter 65)**.

Washerless Faucet

Description: Regular faucet operated by an internal mechanism, either a cartridge or a ball, controlling the water flow. Strictly speaking, a washerless faucet is not without a washer—there has to be some soft substance between the cartridge or ball and the faucet seat. In a washerless faucet this may be a gasket, O-ring, or a rubber diaphragm. Manipulating the faucet handle moves the cartridge or ball over the hole where the water emerges. Single-handled mixing faucets, such as those invented by Moen, are always washerless; those with two handles may be washerless or compression type.

Use: Controls water flow into sinks and basins, especially in single-handled, or mixing, faucets.

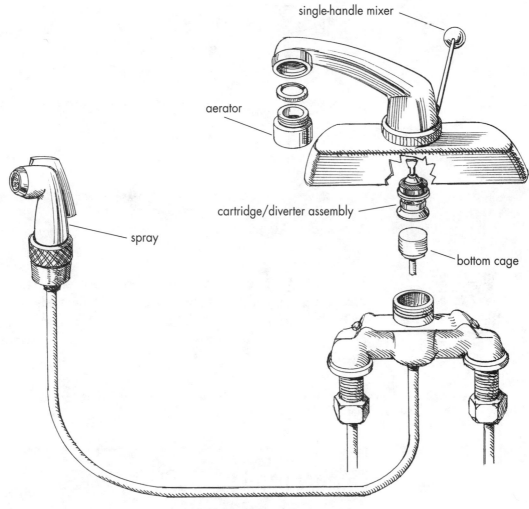

single-handle mixer

aerator

cartridge/diverter assembly

bottom cage

spray

Washerless Faucet

Use Tips: Parts vary quite a bit from brand to brand, but repair of parts or replacement of the whole internal mechanism is possible. Leaks are usually due to worn gaskets or springs in the ball type or the O-ring in a cartridge type.

> **$ Buying Tips:** Washerless faucets tend to have fewer leaks than compression faucets and are easier to repair when they do have problems. Some models require a special device to remove the cartridge. It is included in the package and should be saved for the next repair.

Faucet Stem

Faucet Stem

Also Known As: Stem (not to be confused with cartridge), spindle

Description: Metal or plastic bar fluted at one end. The **faucet handle (below)** is attached to one end and the **faucet seat washer (below)** to the other end. Sold as "hot" or "cold" with threads corresponding to the way a handle is turned to open or close the faucet.

Use: The internal mechanism of a compression faucet and a common replacement part.

> **Use Tips:** On some models the screw that holds the handle to the stem (always smack in the center) is concealed by a small decorative cap that must be pried up to gain access to the screw.

> **$ Buying Tips:** Stems vary greatly from brand to brand and model to model, so you must take the old one in to get a duplicate. Don't hesitate to replace old, corroded, leaky stems if replacing washers and cleaning and greasing the threads doesn't work. They are inexpensive, especially third-party (non-name) brands. Be sure to specify hot or cold.

Faucet Washer

Also Known As: Gasket (incorrect)

Description: Doughnut-shaped part usually made of neoprene plastic or rubber, flat or beveled, black or red. Fits into a cup on the end of the stem and is held with a brass screw.

Use: Seals off the supply of water by pressing against the faucet seat when a **compression faucet (above)** is closed.

> **Use Tips:** Keep a supply of various sizes of washers and stainless-steel or brass screws on hand because washers are the most common part of a faucet to wear out.

> **Buying Tips:** Beveled washers are usually better for repair than flat ones as they seal better if the seat is worn and pitted. Neoprene is better than rubber. Even nominal sizes vary by manufacturer; a quarter-inch washer of one make may actually not fit where another manufacturer's "quarter-inch" washer did. The only way to ensure that a washer fits is to try it. Keep an assortment on hand so you'll have one that fits an old faucet just right. Washers are commonly sold in boxes of 12 and 20 assorted sizes, with brass screws included, as well as singly.
>
> If the cup or rim on the end of the stem where the washer goes is worn or missing, the washer will not seat properly. You can try a new rim that attaches with a screw or a *no-rotate washer* or *5-year faucet washer*, which snaps into place and, in effect, has its own rim built on. However, these are not long-lasting. You may end up having to replace the whole stem.

Flat Faucet Washer

Beveled Faucet Washer

No-Rotate Washer

Faucet Seat, Removable

Faucet Seat, Removable

Description: Small, doughnut-shaped brass device that screws into the top of the water supply pipe; water flows through its center hole, which is either hex-shaped or square (in the case of removable seats).

Use: The part against which the *faucet stem washer* presses in order to seal off the flow of water.

Use Tips: If the seat is worn, the faucet will leak. To remove a worn seat use a **faucet seat wrench (Part VIII, Chapter 63)**, or if not replaceable, grind it down so the washer will fit snugly against it with an inexpensive **faucet seat reamer (Chapter 65)**. You can use a **screw extractor (Part III, Chapter 22)** if it is difficult to use a wrench.

Buying Tips: Seats rival stems in the number of different sizes available. While packages of assorted sizes are available, buying this way is poor economy as the ones that don't fit will never be used. Take the old one into the store to get the exact size and make needed.

O-Rings

O-Ring

Also Known As: Gasket (incorrect)

Description: Rubber ring that comes in various diameters.

Use: Fits over spindle of some faucets to make a seal.

Buying Tips: If difficult to remove, use a dental tool or other small, pointed tool for getting underneath the O-ring.

Aerator

Aerator

Also Known As: Spray diffuser

Description: Small barrel-like metal or plastic part that screws onto the end of a spout with either inside or outside threads and a screen inside. Made in a variety of sizes and types.

Use: Makes the stream of water coming from a faucet spout smooth and prevents splashing.

 Use Tips: Unscrew occasionally and clean debris from screen. If it doesn't unscrew by hand, use **tongue-and-groove pliers (Part I, Chapter 7)** with a rag to protect the chrome finish of the aerator.

Buying Tip: Universal aerators are available that fit most faucets.

Lavatory Faucet Handle

Lavatory Faucet Handle

Also Known As: Faucet handle

Description: Plastic or metal piece that attaches to faucet stem. Available in an almost infinite number of shapes and styles.

Use: To open and close faucet.

hex wrench for
tightening setscrew

Universal Faucet Handle

Use Tips: On some handles the screws that hold the handle on the stem are concealed under a decorative cap, often marked "Hot" or "Cold." These must be pried up to gain access to the screws.

Buying Tips: For the best fit buy a duplicate replacement handle. Failing this, buy a *universal handle*. Types with two setscrews are more secure but may still slip and damage the stem.

Bathtub and Shower Faucets

Also Known As: Valves, diverters

Description: A variety of types: three-valve faucets have hot- and cold-water faucets with another faucet in the middle for diverting water to the shower. Two-valve faucets have hot- and cold-water faucets with a lift-up device on the tub spout for diverting the water to the shower. Two-valve shower fittings have hot- and cold-water faucets only. Two-valve tub fillers have faucets that fill the tub only. Single-control faucets have one lever that controls the flow and mix of hot and cold water.

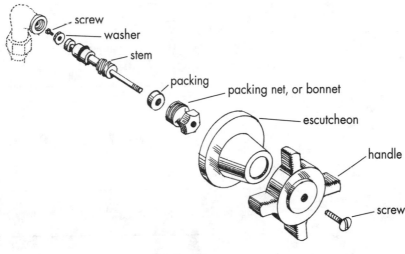

Tub Faucet

The standard center-to-center measurement on tub faucets is 8", though 6" and 11" centers are also used. The center measurement on old-style free-standing tubs with exposed plumbing is 3½". Tub faucets are available in chrome-plated brass or plastic, pot metal, and plain plastic.

Use: Controlling water flow and temperature in a shower or bathtub.

Use Tips: To remove the stem after the handle is removed, a bonnet nut must be removed. This is usually best done with a **deep-throat socket wrench (Part VIII, Chapter 63)**.

Buying Tips: Same as for sink and lavatory faucets except that kits are usually not available. Five brands stand out: Delta, Kohler, Moen, Powers, and Symmons.

Tub Faucet Parts

Note: Same as sink and lavatory faucets.

Tub and Kitchen Spouts

Also Known As: Tub-filler spout, over-the-rim spout

Description: Chrome-plated brass piece that screws onto the water pipe in the tub or is part of faucet assembly in the kitchen.

Use: Routes water from faucets into tub or sink.

 Use Tip: Before unscrewing tub spout (easily done by hand) remove the faucet handles if they interfere.

Buying Tips: Finding a duplicate kitchen spout is difficult and expensive. It's better to replace the whole faucet.

Shower Arm and Head

Description: A shower arm is a chrome-plated pipe threaded on both ends if new type or threaded on one end if old type. The newer one has a removable shower head, while the arm and head are permanently attached with a ball joint in the old style. Shower heads are made of chrome-plated brass or plastic.

Shower Arm

Use: The shower arm carries water from supply pipe to shower stall, and the head directs and sprays it.

Use Tips: Shower arms are removable, but care must be exercised when removing. You don't want to lose anything inside the wall.

Shower Head

Buying Tips: Plastic shower heads are less expensive than metal ones and may be of lesser quality. Many water-saving characteristics have been developed and incorporated into the better models. Massaging shower heads provide a pulsating stream; continental shower heads are attached by flexible hose and hand-held, as in Europe.

Sillcock

Also Known As: Outside faucet, hose bib, male hose faucet

Description: Bronze faucet with valve handle and a flange to go against a wall and a male-threaded spout for connecting to hoses ("plain" faucet has no threads). Frostproof version

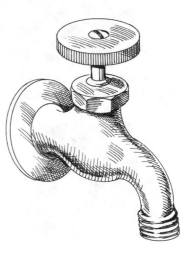

Sillcock

has a pipe connected to valve to keep water inside the house and unfrozen.

Use: Exterior water supply, especially to hoses.

> **Use Tips:** Old-style can be unscrewed; new-style sillcocks are usually soldered in place and are therefore unremovable. Leaks can be repaired the same ways as other faucets. If you are concerned about unauthorized people turning on the sillcock, such as on the exterior of public buildings, remove the handle and open or close the faucet with a **sillcock key (below)** that you carry with you.

> **$ Buying Tips:** If a difficult-to-repair leak occurs, a small **Y connector (below)**, can be screwed on to act like a new valve. This is handy anyway, as it creates two faucets in the place of one. Cast-brass decorative handles are also available.

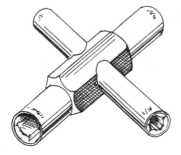

4-Way Sillcock Key

4-Way Sillcock Key

Description: Crisscross metal bar with hex-shaped openings at each end.

Use: For opening sillcocks without handles.

> **Use Tip:** Helpful when it is inconvenient to leave handles on faucets, such as in public buildings.

Y Connector

Also Known As: Siamese connection

Y Connector

Description: Female threads at base with two male-threaded legs that have small shut-off valves built in. Bronze or plastic.

Use: Screws onto **sillcock (above)** or other hose connection and provides two hose connections in the place of one, with individual valves. Useful when supplying cold water to a washing machine and a garden hose from the same pipe, for example, or when a sillcock valve is broken.

 Use Tip: Make sure only the side you want open is open when turning on the main valve.

 Buying Tip: Avoid plastic—it is not strong enough.

Drains and Accessories

Tub Drain Mechanisms

Types:

Spring drain

Weight drain

Also Known As:

Spring type: Pop-up drain, rocker arm

Weight type: Trip lever

Description:

Spring type: Consists of a chrome-plated escutcheon, or decorative faceplate, through which a trip lever sticks. Connected to the lever, inside the overflow pipe behind the tub wall, is a linkage that presses against a rocker arm assembly that controls a chrome pop-up stopper with an O-ring.

Weight type: Similar to the spring type but the linkage terminates in a weight that lifts up or down out of a drain hole, depending on whether the lever is flipped up or down.

Use: Controls tub draining.

> **Use Tips:** Most of the problems associated with tubs concern clogging, usually caused by hair. It is simple to unscrew the escutcheon, lift out the linkage, and clear away the debris. The mechanism itself rarely fails, but the spring behind the lever and escutcheon often loses its tension due to corrosion. This is easily replaced. The O-ring on a spring type must also be replaced from time to time.

> **$ Buying Tip:** If repairing the weight type seems too difficult, just use an inexpensive rubber drain plug instead.

Pop-Up Drain Assembly

Also Known As: P.O. drain

Description: Metal stopper and linkage found on the interior walls of a sink.

Use: Controls the pop-up drain in a lavatory basin or bathroom sink to plug or unplug the drain.

> **Use Tips:** When removing the drain itself or the piping, use a **P.O. plug wrench (Part VIII, Chapter 63)** or a pair of pliers inserted into the drain to hold it stationary while the nut is turned with pliers or a wrench underneath.

Buying Tips: The top part, or insert, on a basin pop-up assembly comes in a large variety of styles and sizes. Only the manufacturer's replacement insert will do, so buying a complete linkage is recommended if replacement is required. Or use a simple rubber drain plug.

Basin and Tub Drain Strainer

Description: Cylindrical chrome metal basket, either 1 $5/16$" in diameter for bathtubs or 1" in diameter for wash basins.

Use: Catches hair, toothpaste-tube caps, and other things that you don't want down the drain, like the occasional errant earring.

Basin and Tub Drain Strainer

Use Tips: Easily kept on hand even if drain plugs are in use—simple to toss into place when desired.

Kitchen Sink Strainer

Also Known As: Strainer cup, strainer, duo strainer, duo cup strainer, basket strainer

Description: A perforated, cup-shaped metal device that fits into the drain opening of a kitchen sink. The strainer insert usually has a rubber washer on the bottom.

Use: Catches debris from water. The insert acts as a stopper when its rubber washer is snug against the bottom.

Kitchen Sink Strainer

Use Tips: When installing or removing a strainer an **internal spud wrench**, or **basket strainer wrench**, may be used from above to resist the turning of a **spud wrench (Chapter 63)** below. A hammer and chisel or screwdriver may also be used to turn the spud nut that holds the strainer. The rubber washer on the bottom of the strainer insert may need replacement regularly.

Valves

About Valves

Valves, like faucets, control the flow of water or steam, but they are stronger and have more specialized characteristics than faucets. Valves and sillcocks are found on plumbing; faucets are simply valves that are used on fixtures such as sinks. Valves are made in all the sizes and types that pipe is made and in most of those materials as well, although cast brass is most common. The type of fitting must be specified, such as "threaded" or "sweat."

Ball Valve

Description: Large lever controls an interior plastic ball that covers or uncovers an opening for water.

Use: Controls water flow where quick action is a premium—one quick, easy twist of the lever and the valve is opened or closed.

> **$ Buying Tips:** Best valve available—shuts water off quickly and it's easy to see if valve is open or closed, unlike other valves.

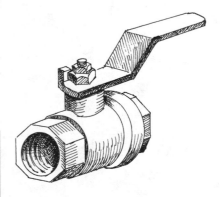

Ball Valve

Check Valve

Description: Regular and swing type, some for installation on vertical lines. Handle-less valve with loose flap inside that closes when water flows the "wrong" way and swings open when it flows properly, allowing water to flow in one way only.

Use: To prevent backflow.

> **Use Tips:** Models designed for use on vertical lines will not work if installed upside down; arrow on body denotes basic "open" direction.

Drainable Valve

Also Known As: Stop and waste valve, bleeder valve

Description: Essentially a globe or gate valve with a drain opening.

Use: Draining pipe (on the nonpressure side) to prevent it from freezing in cold weather.

Gate Valve

Description: Faucet-like handle controlling a metal wedge that slides up and down into a seat. A *connector gate valve* has a union fitting on one side, handy when connecting to a radiator.

Use: Controls water flow where total, unimpeded opening is required, such as on a water main, and is recommended wherever a constant flow is expected.

> **Use Tips:** Usually best to keep completely, rather than partially, open or closed. Leaks from the stem sometimes can be fixed by tightening the outside hex nut or else removing it and adding **stem packing (Part VIII, Chapter 60)**. Repair is not usually possible, though, so replacement is your only course if there are problems.

> **Buying Tips:** Buy only the very best quality, especially for a water main. No other valve in a residence is so important.

Gate Valve

Globe Valve

Also Known As: Compression valve

Description: Rounded body with a seat on its bottom that a stem with a replaceable washer presses against. Rounded body is what gives this valve its name. Comes in most pipe sizes. Also available with openings at right angles to change the direction of the flow 90 degrees, known as an *angle*

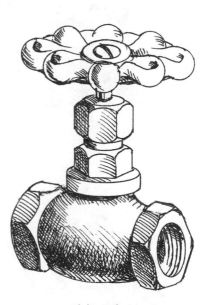

Globe Valve

valve (regular is called *straight*). A *connector globe valve* has a union fitting on one side, which, like the **gate valve (above)**, is handy for connecting to radiators.

Use: Controls water or steam flow, especially suitable for high pressure and frequent use.

> ✂ **Use Tips:** Washers and seats can be replaced, as is necessary on radiators. Leaks from the stem can usually be fixed by tightening the hex nut or else removing it and adding **stem packing (Chapter 60)**.

> 💲 **Buying Tip:** Search out the better quality brands.

Water Supply Valve

Also Known As: Speedy valve, angle stop, shutoff valve, lavatory straight valve, cutoff valve, stops

Description: A small globe-type valve, usually chrome-plated, made of plastic or metal. Can be 90-degree (angle) or straight.

Use: Controls water flow of the **water supply tubes (Part VIII, Chapter 54)** to toilets and sinks. The tubes are often called *speedies* (they have built-in fittings and are quickly installed).

> ✂ **Use Tips:** The handle has great leverage, making it all too easy to strip the plastic kind. Take care.

Angle Speedy Valve

Speedy Valve

Buying Tip: Using metal-stemmed valves limits the risk of stripping.

Gasket

Description: A generic term for soft material that fits between two hard items in order to make a seal. It may be made of rubber, plastic, or strong paper and is shaped for each particular use.

Use: Seals joints in fittings, between parts of valves, and so on.

Buying Tips: Formed gaskets as well as sheets for making your own are available. In some low-pressure cases you can form your own small gasket in between parts of leaking radiator valves and the like by using a liquid (sold in tubes) made for that purpose.

Joint and Fitting Materials

Pipe Joint Compound

Also Known As: Pipe dope, thread sealant

> **Note:** Do not confuse with **drywall joint compound (Part VII, Chapter 50)**, which is a totally different material.

Description: Thick, oily paste applied to pipe threads before assembly. Sold in containers as small as 1-ounce tubes.

> **Note:** Different types of compound are available for pipes carrying oils and gases.

Use: Helps prevent leaks and makes for easier disassembly; also helps prevent corrosion of exposed threads where the zinc coating has been removed during the threading process.

> **Use Tips:** Use gloves—some kinds of pipe dopes are extremely difficult to clean off of hands. Apply liberally.

Buying Tip: Works well, but **Teflon® pipe tape (below)** is neater and faster for the same job.

Teflon® Pipe Tape

Also Known As: Pipe tape, Teflon® tape

Description: Extremely thin, white tape sold in rolls from $1/4$" to $3/4$" wide and in various lengths.

Use: Applied to pipe threads before assembly, same as **pipe joint compound (above)**. Not for use on gas pipes.

 Use Tip: Do not overwrap; once around is sufficient.

Epoxy Repair Material

Also Known As: Epoxy putty, epoxy

Description: Two-part putty material mixed together just before use. May be a long package resembling a candy bar, or a tube, or a small package resembling a packet of chewing gum. You break off as much as you need of this clay-like substance and massage it a bit, mixing the two parts together.

Use: Repairs small leaks in pipes.

Use Tips: While epoxy cannot be depended on 100 percent to stop a leak, it may work for years. Some kinds work even when applied to a wet pipe.

Solder

Description: Soft, silver-colored wire sold on a small reel; 95-5 solder is the most common type, made of 95 percent tin and no lead.

Use: Used in sweat-soldering of copper pipe joints.

 Use Tip: Parts to be soldered must be very clean.

Buying Tips: The old-fashioned kind with lead was outlawed nationally in 1986; use 95-5. If you can't find 95-5 at your hardware store, try a plumbing supply store.

Flux

Description: Jelly-like paste.

Use: To ensure proper fusion of solder to copper sweat-solder joints.

Use Tip: Use liberally.

Buying Tip: Use the *noncorrosive* type, sometimes called *self-cleaning* or *nonacid* type.

Flux Brush

Also Known As: Acid brush, utility brush

Description: Light $^1/_4$" wide metal-handled brush with short bristles, about 6" long.

Use: Applying solder to copper fittings or for cleaning threads.

Buying Tips: Very cheap. Buy a large number and use for touch-up or anything else around the shop and dispose of after use.

Copper Fitting Cleaning Brush

Also Known As: Sweat fitting wire cleaning brush

Description: Wire handle with cylindrical black bristle brush on the end. A *combination brush* has $^1/_2$" and $^3/_4$" brushes on either end.

Use: For scrubbing copper fittings clean prior to soldering.

Plumber's Putty

Description: Soft putty.

Use: Applied to sink rims, drain plugs, and faucets before installation to ensure seal.

 Use Tip: Remove all old putty before applying fresh material.

Buying Tip: Buy only what you can use right away as it tends to dry out. Use **caulk (Part IV, Chapter 32)** to seal sinks and countertops.

Stem Packing

Also Known As: Faucet packing, packing, gasket rope, plumber's twine

Description: Graphite or Teflon®-impregnated string.

Use: Wrapped around valve stems to prevent leaks.

Stem Packing

 Use Tips: If a slow leak at a handle stem cannot be stopped by tightening the nut, just back it off and add more packing—but first make sure the water is off!

Oakum

Description: Short lengths of shredded rope or hemp fiber, sold dry or tarred (oiled). White oakum has a thin woven coating and is impregnated with a type of cement powder.

Use: Originally used mostly for sealing old-fashioned hub-and-spigot cast-iron waste pipe along with molten lead, but useful for packing any kind of large gap. For example, it could be stuffed into a crack and used as a base for caulking. White oakum, which has dry cement in it, swells when brought into contact with water. Interestingly, oakum and tar were the traditional materials used to caulk the planks of ancient ships' hulls.

 Use Tip: Wear gloves to avoid a nasty clean-up job.

Toilet Parts

About Toilets

The mechanism for operating a toilet hasn't changed much since it was invented in the nineteenth century. It is a marvel of ingenious operation. Improvements have been made only on some parts, but not on the concept.

Many toilet part names still reflect the first name for a toilet—water closet. Hence, a *closet bend* is the pipe that brings the water from the tank to the bowl, a closet, or closet floor, flange sits over the drain opening, etc. Additionally, probably because the openings between the tank and bowl are very big, they are often called *spuds,* so related tools and parts have spud in their names—spud pipe, spud wrench, etc. Confusing and inconsistent but not impossible.

A toilet works simply. When you push the handle a trip lever it is attached to inside the tank lifts the tank ball or the flapper off the flush valve seat by means of two linked rods or a chain. Clean water in the tank then rushes out the hole and into the bowl, flushing out its contents.

The float ball, which floats on the tank water (that's the big thing you see first when you take the top off the tank), goes down as the water level goes down. The end of the rod is screwed to the ballcock mechanism and its movement opens a valve in the ballcock that lets new water into the tank. Think of the ballcock as the faucet that fills the tank. At the same time some water is routed down a *refill tube* into the bowl.

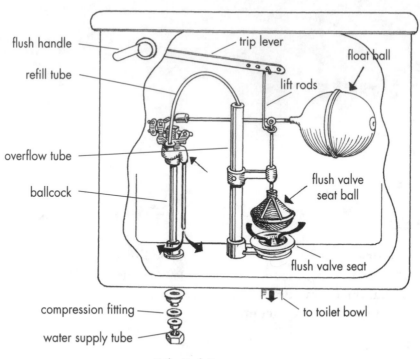

flush handle

refill tube

overflow tube

ballcock

trip lever

float ball

lift rods

flush valve
seat ball

flush valve seat

compression fitting

water supply tube

to toilet bowl

Toilet Tank Parts

As the water level rises the end of the float-ball rod gradually closes the ballcock valve and when the tank is full—and the float is again at the top of the tank—it shuts down completely, ready for the next flush. In fact, if you have a tank leak or a flood while you are working on the tank, just lift the float ball and arm up to the top position, which will shut off the water that is flowing into the tank (you can hold it up with **duct tape [Part IV, Chapter 38]** in an emergency). Best is to shut off the water supply, of course, at the water supply valve or main line.

Toilet Flush Handle

Description: Chrome-plated lever on side or front of tank. Usually supplied with the lever or arm attached.

Use: Raises *flush valve ball* to start flushing process.

> **Use Tips:** Unlike most things, to remove the handle unscrew in a clockwise direction. It is held on by a *left-hand threaded nut*.

Float Ball

Also Known As: Float

Description: Plastic or copper ball $2^{1}/_{2}$" to 3" in diameter, sometimes ribbed, attached to the end of the float arm.

> **Use Tips:** Ball sometimes develops small holes (caused by corrosion) and water enters. It should be replaced if you can hear water inside.

> **Buying Tip:** Plastic is recommended but copper works well too.

Lift Rod, Upper and Lower

Also Known As: Upper or lower lift chain or wire

Description: Metal rod with eye in the end.

Use: Connects tank ball to trip lever; this is the part that lifts the tank ball out of its seat and starts the water flushing.

§ **Buying Tips:** Available individually or as part of pre-packaged assemblies. Often replaced by the new flapper-type mechanism.

Flush Valve Ball

Also Known As: Tank ball, flush ball, valve seat ball

Description: Rubber ball-like device, suspended by lift rods or wire, which fits into flush valve seat. The older models are called *Douglas flush valve balls*.

Use: Controls water flow from bottom of tank. When it is lifted the tank water rushes out and flushing is started.

Flapper

§ **Buying Tips:** The traditional flush valve ball design is frequently the culprit when a tank leaks. It is easily replaced by a new design called a *flapper* or *flapper ball*. The flapper is connected to the float arm by a chain, and one size fits all toilets—$2^1/_2$". Very easy to install; just be sure to adjust the height until it seals properly. It eliminates the easily jammed wires or rods, guide or guide arm, and the cursed tank ball.

Flush Valve Seat

Also Known As: Valve seat, flush ball seat, tank outlet, seat

Description: Round rubber seat at bottom of tank that "lines" tank outlet to bowl. Two types exist: one for toilets connected to but separated from the tank by a short elbow, called a *closet bend*, and one for tanks that sit directly on the bowl.

> **$ Buying Tips:** Replacing a seat is difficult. Better to leave it in place and use a modern replacement, such as the Fluidmaster Fixer Kit. This consists of a stainless-steel cup, which is epoxied to the old seat, and a flapper ball.

Ballcock

Also Known As: Ballcock assembly, inlet valve

Description: Tubular valve device that has a main pipe that screws onto the water supply piping and has a smaller, parallel tube called a *filler tube* attached. Newer *float-cup ballcocks* have just one big shaft.

Use: Controls water supply to the tank and bowl. Activated by the float ball arm or float cup.

> **Buying Tips:** Although replacement ballcock parts can be bought, this may be a problem for older toilets. The solution is to install a complete new ballcock. Standard ballcocks are easy to install. Newer ones that operate by water pressure and have no float ball are best, such as the one made by Fluidmaster. Both regular and "antisiphon" types are made, but the antisiphon is better because it protects against toilet water backing up into the water supply lines.

Refill Tube

Also Known As: Bowl refill tube

Description: Small tube that screws into the ballcock mechanism and empties into the overflow tube. Made of plastic, brass, or aluminum.

Use: Fills bowl with water after flushing to keep sewer odors out.

> **Buying Tip:** Plastic is normally better than metal as the metal tubes tend to break off at the threads.

Overflow Tube

Also Known As: Douglas valve, Douglas flush valve

Description: Copper, brass, or aluminum tube 1" or $1\frac{1}{8}$" in diameter that screws into flush valve seat.

> **Buying Tips:** Sold with *flush valve seats* or individually. Get the largest thickness, or gauge, available and avoid aluminum, which corrodes quickly.

Tank-to-Bowl Attachment Hardware

Description: Long brass bolts with large rubber washers and a very large foam-rubber washer. These items are usually available in small packages. Standard size for all brands.

Use: The two items necessary to secure a close coupled standard tank to the toilet bowl. The two brass bolts and nuts go in small holes for that purpose in the bottom of the tank, and the large (bagel-sized) washer fits around the open drain hole that the water goes through on its way into the toilet bowl.

> **Buying Tips:** Make sure the connections are clean and don't hesitate to add **caulk (Part IV, Chapter 32)** or **plumber's putty (Part VIII, Chapter 60)** to ensure a seal. Stand ready with sponge and bucket when testing as you can't tell if the seal is good until you actually flush the toilet.

Closet Flange Bolt

Also Known As: Closet bolt, toilet bolt, hold-down bolt

Description: Bolt with flanges at middle and one end; a *closet screw* screws into a wooden floor and thus has screw threads on one end.

Use: Secures toilet to floor and flange to toilet base.

Wax Ring and Closet Flange

Description: Literally a wax ring and a metal ring with inside diameters the size of the drain pipe and toilet bowl bottom opening.

Use: Sealing toilet bowl to drain piping.

 Buying Tip: Buy and use a double wax ring for the best seal.

Special Products for Boilers and Furnaces

Boiler Cleaner

Also Known As: Boiler liquid

Description: Liquid or powder chemical sold in convenient containers for steam, hot water, or both kinds of heating systems.

Use: Cleans out and prevents rust and sludge deposits in boilers of heating systems; may help prevent additional wear and tear on the system. Poured directly into the boiler.

> **Use Tips:** The liquid form is easier to use if you must pour it through a small opening, such as a *pressure relief valve.*

Boiler Solder

Description: Liquid chemical sold in convenient containers for either steam or hot-water heating systems.

Use: Settles into and plugs hairline cracks or pinholes in boilers of heating systems. Poured directly into the boiler.

Oil Tank Treatment

Also Known As: Sludge treatment

Description: Powder or liquid chemical.

Use: Dissolves dirt and sludge and absorbs water found in the bottom of oil tanks. Apply just prior to being refilled with oil.

Soot Destroyer Stick

Description: About 1"× 8" cylinder of chemical that is merely tossed into the active hot chamber or firebox of oil, gas, coal, or wood heating units. Similar material available in aerosol spray can as well.

Use: Removes soot and creosote from flues.

Furnace Cement

Description: Heat-resistant premixed patching cement.

Use: Cementing furnace or boiler flues into masonry.

> **Use Tips:** Amazingly gooey and sticky. Very hard to use neatly but good to use for simple and important repairs. Helps prevent exhaust gas leaks.

Plumbing Wrenches

About Plumbing Tools

Following are some commonly needed tools for plumbing. You needn't buy many of them—perhaps only the plunger and a snake or other drain-cleaning tool. But you should be aware of them so you can purchase or rent them on the occasion when you decide to do without a professional plumber. Sometimes even the purchase of a fairly specialized tool for a one-time use can be worthwhile, considering the price of a plumber's visit.

About Plumbing Wrenches

A wrench is not always a wrench, because sometimes a wrench is a *plumbing wrench*, as described here, and other times it is a *combination wrench*, or an *adjustable wrench*, or one of many other specialized machinist's or carpenter's wrenches, as described up front in **Part I, Chapter 8.** Also, some folks in the British Isles tend to refer to all wrenches as *spanners.* When you are ordering a wrench, be specific.

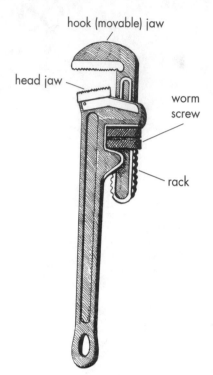

hook (movable) jaw

head jaw

worm screw

rack

Pipe Wrench

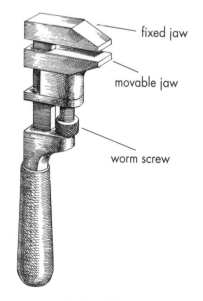

fixed jaw

movable jaw

worm screw

Monkey Wrench

Pipe Wrench

Also Known As: Stillson (or Stilson) wrench

Description: Heavy metal tool with serrated jaws—one fixed and one adjustable and slightly offset. Comes in *straight pattern* (standard), *end-pattern* (slightly offset), and *offset* (jaws at 90 degrees to the handle). The teeth of the jaws dig into steel pipes. Another type, a *compound pipe wrench*, has a head that is a combination of **end-pattern and chain wrench (below)**.

Uses: Turning steel pipe and fittings, or, in a pinch, anything round.

Use Tips: Pipe wrench jaws can leave marks on metal so use only where this is not a concern, or use tape or cloth to protect the finish. Two pipe wrenches are needed when working with pipe, one for holding the fitting and the other for turning the pipe, so keep two on hand. Turn toward the lower jaw to "set" the teeth firmly.

Buying Tips: Wrenches come in various lengths, with the jaw capacity increasing as the wrench gets longer. Two wrenches, one 8" and one 10", should serve well.

Monkey Wrench

Also Known As: Ford wrench, automotive wrench, auto wrench

Description: Large wrench with parallel smooth jaws, one fixed and one adjustable, that are always parallel. Unlike a pipe wrench, jaws are smooth. Some manufacturers call a thin, large-opening, smooth-jawed pipe wrench a **spud wrench (below)** for large spud nuts—but it looks like the classic monkey wrench.

Use: Turning nuts or fittings wherever there are flat sides for the wrench to grip. Good on chrome because the jaws won't mark it.

 Use Tips: Stronger than a pipe wrench. Always pull the wrench toward you rather than pushing it.

Buying Tips: These days large, **smooth-jawed, tongue-and-groove pliers, adjustable wrenches (Part I, Chapters 7 and 8)**, or **pipe wrenches (above)** are generally used in place of monkey wrenches. No longer commonly available.

Spud Wrench

Types:

Fixed spud wrench

Adjustable spud wrench

4-in-1 combination spud wrench

Closet spud wrench

Internal spud wrench

Radiator valve spud wrench

Also Known As: *Adjustable:* sink wrench

Adjustable Spud Wrench

4-In-1 Spud Wrench

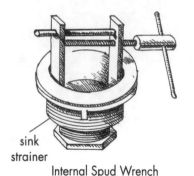

sink
strainer

Internal Spud Wrench

Radiator Valve Spud Wrench

Description: Metal tool, various models of which have large, flat-sided jaws, except for the *radiator valve spud wrench,* which is a long, solid metal tapered rod with angular sides for turning with a pipe wrench.

Use:

Fixed: To turn large spud nuts, i.e., the nuts that hold the toilet tank to the toilet, or the locknut under a kitchen sink strainer, or really any large nut.

Adjustable: Jaws are especially notched for use on various sizes of strainer nuts or any large nut. All-purpose adjustable locknut wrench. Available in a combination model.

4-in-1: For turning large locknuts on closet, or toilet tank, spuds and basket strainers, similar to the fixed model.

Closet: Especially for spuds on toilet tanks and bowls.

Internal: Removing and installing closet spuds, large and small sink strainers, pop-up plugs, bath strainers. Holds strainer in place while you are turning locknuts below with a wrench.

Radiator valve: For removing or tightening radiator spud nut.

 Buying Tips: The adjustable spud, or sink, wrench is the handiest for general purpose use.

Spanner Wrench

Also Known As: Duo strainer wrench, hook spanner, strainer nut wrench

> **Note:** Many Britishers call all wrenches *spanners*, and indeed any flat, open-end wrench that fits only particular devices can be referred to as a spanner by U.S. manufacturers.

Description: Flat metal handle with a half-circle jaw with one or two hooks at either end. A *face spanner* (also known as a *pin spanner*) has two pins perpendicular to a full C-shaped arc.

Use: Tightening or loosening large nuts especially designed for this wrench, usually found under a kitchen sink drain or strainer.

Duo Strainer Wrench

Strap Wrench

Description: Wrench-like handle on one end of which is an adjustable fabric strap.

Use: For turning chrome-plated or polished pipe while avoiding scratches.

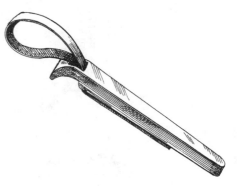

Strap Wrench

> **Use Tips:** Never force tubular goods—they are thin-walled and might crush.

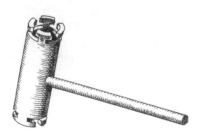

Basket Strainer Wrench

 Buying Tip: A small strap wrench is usually adequate for most jobs.

Chain Wrench

Description: Wrench-like handle with a chain on one end.

Use: Turning pipe, tubing, or fittings, particularly where there is limited space for a conventional wrench and great turning power is required.

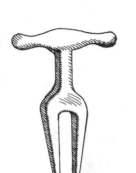

P.O. Plug Wrench

Basket Strainer Wrench

Description: Hammer-shaped steel tool with notched cylinder for a head and short rod for a handle.

Use: Keeping kitchen sink or tub strainer in place during installation.

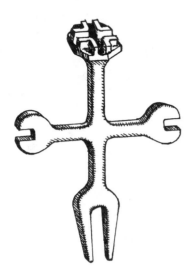

P.O. Plug Wrench

Description: Small cast-metal wrench with a fork-like end and a T-handle. A 4-way model has two arms.

Use: Removing P.O. ("Pop Up" or "Pop Out") plug from basin drain opening. Holds plug stationary in basin while nut is turned underneath.

4-Way P.O. Plug Wrench

Use Tip: 4-way model is for use with a variety of strainer types, including basket strainers.

T-Handle Torque Wrench

Also Known As: No-Hub® torque wrench

Description: Ratchet tool consisting of T-handle, bar coming off to side, and a hex opening at the bottom.

Use: For tightening fittings on hose clamps, such as on No-Hub® fittings.

 Use Tips: Easier to use than a nut driver or screwdriver as it has an internal mechanism that prevents overtightening. The T-handle provides more torque, or force.

Deep-Throat Socket Wrench

Also Known As: Plumber's wrench, wall socket set, tub/shower valve nut socket wrench, tub-and-shower valve wrench

Description: Short, hex-shaped hollow steel tube. Usually sold in sets of five graduated sizes.

Use: Removing and driving nuts and valves, especially on bathroom faucets, such as are found in showers.

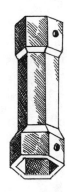

Deep-Throat Socket Wrench

Eccentric Nipple Extractor

Eccentric Nipple Extractor

Also Known As: Internal pipe wrench, tube extractor, nipple puller, nipple extractor

Description: Hexagonal cylinder with a serrated floating (loose), offset (eccentric) part on one end.

Use: Removing pieces of pipe or tube that have broken off or corroded inside fittings. It is inserted inside the pipe and turned with a wrench.

Basin Wrench

Also Known As: Faucet wrench, faucet nut wrench, crowfoot faucet wrench

Description: Bar with a rod through one end and knurled hook on the other.

Use: Essential, unique tool for loosening and tightening the nuts that hold a faucet in place.

Faucet Seat Wrench

Also Known As: Faucet seal tool, seat wrench

Description: L-shaped or straight bar of metal with one end machined to four flat sides and the other to five.

Use: Removing **faucet seats (Part VIII, Chapter 57)**.

Basin Wrench

Use Tips: Check with flashlight to see if hole (faucet seat) has four or five sides. Press firmly into place before unscrewing seat. If it has a round hole, it is not replaceable, and either the entire faucet must be replaced or the seat reamed out instead with a **faucet seat reamer (Part VIII, Chapter 65)**. If it is difficult to use this wrench because it can't "grab," try a **screw extractor (Part III, Chapter 22)**.

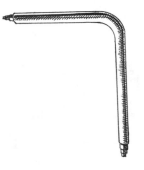

Faucet Seat Wrench

Handle Puller

Also Known As: Faucet handle puller, faucet valve handle remover

Description: Two hook-like parts with a rod down the center and a turning handle.

Use: For freeing frozen faucet handles.

Use Tip: Applying a little **penetrating oil (Part IV, Chapter 37)** to the parts first helps loosen them.

Faucet Spanner

Description: Flat metal bar with various-sized wrench openings at each end and along its length. Actually a simple wrench.

Handle Puller

Use: Tightening or loosening faucet parts during installation or removal.

 Buying Tip: These are supplied along with some brands of new faucets.

Drain-Clearing Tools

About Drain-Clearing Tools

Tools are better for clearing drains than chemicals. Try the plunger first, then a small snake, then renting a *power snake* if these other options have failed. Among other reasons, the power snake might work just because it is longer and can go around corners more easily.

Drain Opener

Also Known As: Drain line opener

Description: Chemical product in powder or liquid form. Often strong acid or caustic, though some natural products that dissolve hair are available. Lye is a common component of this product.

Use: Poured into slow drains to dissolve whatever might be blocking the line.

 Use Tip: Follow directions carefully if using any of the acids or caustics.

Note: Exercise caution when you deal with chemical drain openers. While chemicals can be useful, they can be problematic if they don't work—they may solidify and leave you with a caustic, clogged line. If you do call a plumber after having poured caustic chemicals into the drain, you must tell him so—he might be putting his hands in the water or splash his face by accident and get serious chemical burns. Also, certain chemicals may damage plastic piping and solvents.

Plunger

Also Known As: Plumber's friend, force cup, force pump, handyman's helper

Description: Short, broomstick-like handle on the end of which is a cup-shaped piece of rubber. Some models, called *combination plungers,* have two cups, one inside the other. Typical diameter is 2½" to 5½". Another type has an accordion-like bellows for pushing massive amounts of air.

Use: For clearing blockages in sinks, tubs, and toilets.

Plunger

Use Tips: Make sure that the edges of the plunger are immersed in water for a good seal. Rubbing the edge with petroleum jelly helps. The models with a smaller cup inside a larger one are for toilets; the extended smaller cup fits snugly in the bowl hole. It can be retracted for use on sinks.

Bellows Type Plunger

§ Buying Tips: Combination plungers made of black rubber are of better quality than the red ones, which are for sinks only. Quality plungers are thick and rigid.

Snake

Also Known As: Auger, drain auger, trap auger, drain-clearing or -cleaning tool, plumber's snake, drain snake

Description: Coiled spiral cable, about $\frac{1}{4}$" thick, in various lengths up to 25', with a removable or fixed handle on one end and a slightly open coil at the business end. Another type, which is much more efficient, has a crank mechanism in a wide funnel-shaped container. Professionals use power versions with power supplied by an electric drill-like tool. The best DIY model has no handle but instead an end that goes into a portable electric drill.

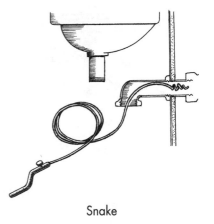

Snake

Use: Clearing sink and basin drain lines. (For toilets, see next item, **closet auger**.)

✂ Use Tips: Feed snake in gradually. Don't push too hard or you might kink it. If you have no success, try renting a heavy-duty power snake. Not only can they clear tough obstructions, but it is easier for them to turn corners in pipes, and they are longer.

§ Buying Tips: Get a top-quality snake as a low-quality one can kink at turns in the pipes.

hose
connection

Drain Unclogger

Drain Unclogger

Description: Oblong rubber bulb a few inches long, with openings on either end. One end is threaded to receive a garden hose, and the other is an open nozzle.

Use: Forcing obstructions from pipes by using water pressure from the garden hose. The bulb expands with the hose water to prevent backflow.

 Use Tips: Beware of creating problems with delicate plumbing when using high pressure.

Closet Auger

Also Known As: Auger, toilet auger, closet snake

Description: Short, thick, spiral cable with a hooked end in a rigid tube; has a crank handle.

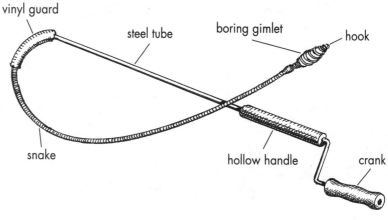

Closet Auger

Use: Clearing clogged toilets. Better than a regular snake because of its rigidity.

Sewer Tape

Also Known As: Drain-clearing tool, sewer rod

Description: Flat metal band 40 or 50 feet long, sold in a coil, with a coiled hook or point on one end.

Use: Clearing blockages located between the main house trap and the sewer or other disposal area.

> **Use Tips:** If the tape doesn't work, a rented *heavy-duty auger* or *power rooter* is recommended. These are sharper and stronger and longer. If this fails, call a plumber.

Special Plumbing Tools

Faucet Seat Reamer

Also Known As: Valve seat grinding tool, faucet seat dressing tool, cone bibb reamer, faucet reseater, seat dresser, T-handle reamer, taper reamer (one version), seat-dressing tool

Description: Comes in various versions but essentially consists of a turning handle and metal shaft on the bottom of which is a cutter, either replaceable or fixed.

Use: Smoothing a faucet seat that has become rough with wear, corrosion, or calcium deposits.

Faucet Seat Reamer

Use Tips: Work slowly and carefully. Be sure to cut perfectly horizontally or else the washer may not seat well.

Flaring Tool

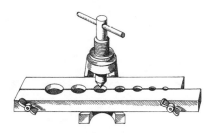

Description: Two bars that clamp closed and form openings for various sizes of copper tube, and a vise-like part called a *yoke* with a drive screw and cone that slides along the bars and locks in place.

Flaring Tool

Use: Flaring the ends of copper tubing prior to joining with flare fittings.

> **Use Tip:** Proceed slowly and carefully when flaring pipe.

Lever-type Tube Bender

Also Known As: Hickey, pipe bender

Description: A clamp-type device with two legs and a gauge showing angle of bend.

Uses: Bending rigid copper, brass, aluminum, steel, and stainless-steel tube up to $5/8$" outside diameter ("O.D.").

> **Buying Tips:** Tubing heads can be purchased separately. Hickeys can be rented.

Reamer

Also Known As: Pipe reamer

Description: Metal fluted cone with sharpened edges and a handle or chuck for turning.

Use: Removing burrs from the ends of various kinds of metal pipe after cutting.

Pipe Reamer

Tube Bender

Also Known As: Spring bender, tubing bender, copper bending spring

Description: Tightly coiled length of spring in various diameters.

Use: Bending copper tube without kinks.

 Use Tips: Bend very slowly; don't force it, or you risk getting kinks.

Tube Bender

Tubing Cutter

Also Known As: Tube cutter

Description: Metal device with a cutting wheel and a knurled knob for bringing the cutting wheel into snug contact with the tube. Comes in midget size for tubing up to $1/2$" outside diameter and another size for larger pipe.

Use: Cutting copper tubing.

Tubing Cutter

 **Use Tips:** Just as easy to cut small pipes with a hacksaw or *PVC saw* and file off ends, but the cutter does it at perfect right angles and leaves a cleaner cut than a saw.

Buying Tips: Cutters also available for cutting steel and plastic pipe. Some models have reamers attached for taking burrs off pipe after cutting. Larger size can cut tubular goods.

Electrical Products and Tools

Note: The type of electrical product used and the way it is installed are governed by local building codes throughout the country. These are enforceable laws that must be checked out before you make any major installations. Many codes prohibit the use of some of the items listed here, even though they are mostly standard items.

About Polarized Plugs and Receptacles

Electrical devices manufactured nowadays are polarized to minimize the chances of electric shock. This means that the "hot" wires (carrying the current) and "ground" wires must remain consistent through the entire electrical circuit—hot wires must be linked only to hot wires and ground wires only to ground. In practice today's appliances are polarized to keep them consistent with receptacles. To do this one prong of a plug is made larger than the other; one slot of each receptacle is made larger than the other. The result is that the device can't be plugged in any way but correctly.

About Grounding

The third prong on plugs is the *grounding plug,* which is a safety feature that routes errant electrical current to the ground instead of letting it go through your body when an electrical malfunction occurs. It is therefore recommended that grounding plugs be used wherever possible, and that **adapters (see 3-to-2 adapter, below)** are used properly in two-slot receptacles.

Taps, Adapters, and Plugs

About Taps and Adapters

Receptacles and light sockets are not always where we need them, nor are there even enough, it seems. Happily, a whole array of household devices exists that convert and multiply receptacles and sockets to bring power—whether an outlet or a socket—to where we want it by tapping into the current.

Each manufacturer calls their items by different names, and the terms they choose are not always very descriptive. Following, then, are our terms, which we think will help your understanding. There are two groups of devices—those that plug directly into a receptacle, or outlet (*extension cords*, *outlet strips*, and *outlet adapters*), and those that screw into lightbulb sockets (*socket* or *lamp-holder adapters*).

Thoughout this section the terms *male* and *female* are used to denote whether a device has prongs or threads that protrude on the outside (male) or slots or openings with springs and threads on the inside for receiving male prongs and threads (female).

About Extension Cords and Outlet Adapters

The following six items can be extremely convenient, but one cardinal rule must be followed: do not ever overload the circuit by plugging in many different adapters on top of one another. You might find yourself blowing fuses and circuit breakers unnecessarily and dangerously.

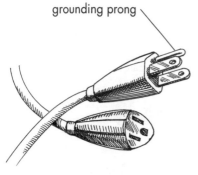

grounding prong

Extension Cord Ends

Extension Cords

Description: Available in various lengths from 3' to 100' and in various colors; wire may be two- or the heavier three-wire (grounded) type (recommended). Extension cords are typically supplied with a female plug on one end and a male plug on the other. Latest innovations are a cord with three female receptacles and another with a receptacle box with six female receptacles and a built-in *circuit breaker* or **GFI (Chapter 69),** sometimes called a *portable outlet center.*

Use: Provides power at a remote location.

> **Use Tips:** Extension cords are sized to handle a certain amount of current and should be matched to the device at hand. Most cords will be marked for the kinds of items they should be used with, such as air conditioners and hedge trimmers. For safety use only highly visible yellow or orange cords for gardening devices and in the workshop. A triple female plug is convenient when you are switching between several power tools on a job—but not for using them all at once.

Multiple Outlet Strip

Description: Rectangular plastic strip containing multiple receptacles and a long cord to plug into a nearby outlet. Available in different sizes from a few inches long with two outlets to 18" long with a dozen outlets and in two- and three-wire types. Some surface-mounted types are specially adapted for mounting on walls. Newer models may have **built-in circuit breakers (Chapter 68)**.

Surface-Mounted Multiple Outlet Strip

Another version is the *power strip,* which is a 6" to 12" long plastic device that has two slots along its length instead of individual receptacles and can take as many as 15 plugs. In any case, this is still a sort of multiple-outlet extension cord.

Still other models of this and other taps may have a *surge protector* built in, a device that protects your electronic equipment from sudden surges in electricity due to lightning or power supply malfunctions. These are generally not sophisticated enough to protect computer equipment from minor fluctuations, though.

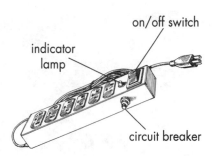

Power Strip with Circuit Breaker and On/Off Switch

Use: Provides power for a variety of items at a distance from one receptacle.

Table Tap

Also Known As: Plug-in strip, plug-in outlet adapter, outlet tap

Description: One-piece plastic unit containing two to six pairs of slots for plugs. Comes either with third grounding prong or not.

Table Tap

Use: Plugs into any outlet to provide multiple receptacle capacity.

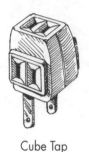

Cube Tap

Cube Tap

Also Known As: Cube adapter, plug-in outlet adapter

Description: Small plastic or rubber device with one set of prongs (either two or three if grounding type) and two or three female receptacles for other plugs. Smaller version of **table tap (above)**.

Use: Provides extra capacity at a receptacle.

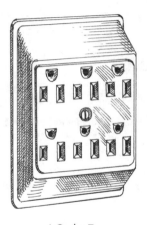

6-Outlet Tap

6-Outlet Tap

Also Known As: Multioutlet, multiple tap

Description: Plastic receptacle shaped roughly like a truncated pyramid that plugs into an existing duplex outlet and can accommodate four or six plugs, depending on the model. Comes polarized and/or grounded; some models contain circuit breakers or surge protectors.

Use: Converts a two-plug receptacle to six.

 Buying Tip: Small surge protectors are not necessarily sufficient for delicate computer equipment.

Outlet-to-Lamp-Holder Adapter

Outlet-to-Lamp-Holder Adapter

Also Known As: Outlet adapter, socket adapter (manufacturer's terminology is unclear)

Description: Lightbulb socket with prongs on end for plugging into standard receptacle or extension cord.

Use: Creates an extra light source, generally for temporary use only.

About Socket Adapters

Socket adapters, sometimes called *current taps,* differ from the taps described above in that they screw into sockets rather than plug into outlets. They also should be used sparingly and are generally intended for temporary use, although if used appropriately, they work as well as permanent products.

The term *lamp-holder* is the manufacturers' term for a socket, the device that holds a lightbulb ("lamp"), as well as for the larger porcelain or metal device that serves as a base to attach a socket to an electrical box. This latter item is described in **Chapter 67.**

Socket-to-Lamp-Holder/Outlet Adapter

Also Known As: Current tap, socket adapter (often confused with other outlet-to-lamp-holder adapter, above), socket switch

Description: Round, ivory or brown plastic device with lightbulb-like threads on each end (male on one, female on the other) and receptacle slots on each side. Some models have a *pull chain* or *toggle switch* that turns off the bulb but not the outlets. If it has no pull chain, it is called a *keyless adapter.*

Socket-to-Lamp-Holder/Outlet Adapter

Use: Provides two outlets wherever there's a light socket without sacrificing the bulb.

Use Tip: Plugging in numerous extension cords risks overloading the socket.

Lamp-Holder-to-Outlet Adapter

Lamp-Holder-to-Outlet Adapter

Also Known As: Plug body

Description: Single receptacle with lightbulb-type threads on one end.

Use: Creates a single receptacle wherever there's a light socket.

Single-to-Twin Lamp-Holder Adapter

Single-to-Twin Lamp-Holder Adapter

Also Known As: Twin light adapter

Description: Siamese (V-shaped) device that holds two lightbulbs at an angle to one another, with one threaded end that screws into a regular socket.

Use: Provides a double socket in the place of a single one.

About Plugs

Electrical plugs come in two basic forms, male or female. Male plugs have prongs while female plugs have slots. Male plugs may also have either two or three prongs (one U-shaped prong for grounding and two flat ones).

Male plugs are either *open construction* or *dead-front* type. The former, popular for years, has an insulating disk covering the screw terminals inside the plug; the disk can be pried up to access the wires' ends. It is no longer being manufactured and should be replaced as necessary. Dead-front plugs are safer. To get at wires in the dead-front type a thick cap must be unscrewed; wires are looped around terminal screws on the cap or mounted in pressure slots.

Like other electrical devices, plugs are rated in terms of amperage to handle particular currents.

 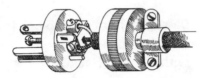

Open Construction-Type Plug   Dead Front-Type Plug

Standard Plug

Also Known As: Plug

Description: Male plug with two or three prongs as described in **About Plugs (above)**. Plugs may be of light or heavy construction, such as black rubber (for appliances) or light plastic in brown, black, and/or ivory. Side-outlet plugs have the wire coming out the side. A plug is technically a **male receptacle (Part IX, Chapter 69)**. Nonstandard currents, such as for major appliances, may require different shapes and types of prongs.

Use: Terminal device on wire that plugs into **receptacles (outlets) (Chapter 69)** to provide power for whatever device it is connected to. Black rubber plugs are used on appliances while plastic plugs are used on lamps and other devices with minimal electrical consumption. Side-outlet plugs can be used effectively where there is little clearance, such as behind furniture.

Buying Tip: Plugs are available in ivory, brown, black, and white for decoration purposes.

3-to-2 Adapter Plug

Also Known As: Grounding adapter

3-to-2 Adapter Plug

Description: Small, cube-shaped plastic or rubber plug with two prongs on one end and three openings in the other, with a small, U-shaped metal piece (lug) attached directly to the plug. Older models have a 3" grounding wire (lead)— usually green in color—coming directly out of the middle with the U-shaped lug on its end.

Use: Allows use of three-pronged (grounded) plug in a two-slot receptacle.

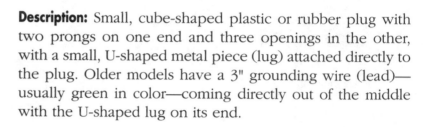 **Use Tips:** Be sure to attach the grounding metal (U-shaped piece) to the screw in the middle of the receptacle. Failure to do so exposes you to a potentially severe electric shock. You will have defeated the purpose of the safety grounding system. Best to avoid using this kind of plug except for temporary situations; better to install three-hole grounded receptacles.

Clamp-On Plug

Also Known As: Snap-on

Description: Comes in various forms. A common one is a plug with a hole in the back for wire; there are prongs that have small teeth for making electrical contact that can be removed and spread apart. Other types are *cam* and *squeeze.*

Use: Clamp-on plugs are used to replace damaged plugs on lamps or similarly small electrical devices.

Clamp-On Plug

> **Use Tips:** Clamp-on plugs are quick and easy to use but some electricians question their safeness. If you have any doubts, you can use a standard type as described above.

Female Appliance Plug

Description: Black or ivory plastic plug that can be separated in half by unscrewing the screws that hold the halves together.

Use: Plugs into small appliances to make electrical connection at one end of electrical wire; the male end plugs into the wall outlet.

Female Appliance Plug (shown open)

Lighting Fixtures and Bulbs

Fluorescent Fixtures

Types:

Rapid start: Goes on the instant the fixture is turned on.

Starter: Flickers a bit before going on.

Instant: Goes on after a momentary pause.

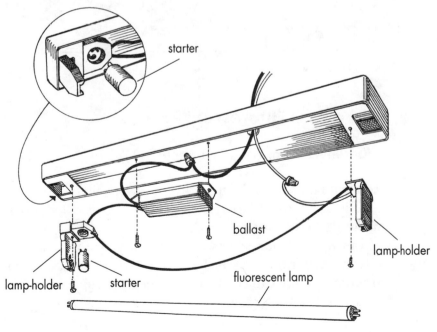

starter

ballast

lamp-holder

lamp-holder   starter   fluorescent lamp

Fluorescent Light Fixture

Description: Fluorescent fixtures are rectangular or circular and contain *sockets,* or lamp holders, which house the ends of the bulbs used, and a *ballast,* a heavy black metal box that is a kind of transformer that reduces the regular high voltage so it can be used by the fixture, which operates on a lower than normal voltage. Rapid start types have a starter and ballast in one piece. Starter types contain a smaller ballast and a small aluminum barrel, the starter, a special type of automatic switch.

Use: Holding fluorescent tubes or bulbs.

 Use Tips: Almost all the parts of a fluorescent fixture are replaceable, including the ballast, starter, and lamp holders. Of course new parts must match those being replaced.

 **Buying Tip:** Fluorescent fixtures are much cheaper to operate than incandescent ones.

Fluorescent Lamps

Also Known As: Fluorescent lightbulbs

Description: Fluorescent lamps or tubes are available in a variety of lengths from 6" to 96". They are mercury-filled tubes of white glass with capped ends that have two pins extending from them. Fluorescents come in varying light intensities, from giving off a rather harsh light to one that's much warmer. A mixture can create a daylight effect; special intensities are available for uses including examination of color

Compact Fluorescent Electric Bulb

printing and growing plants indoors. 9,000-hour bulbs, or *compact fluorescent bulbs* have a screw-in base and screw into regular sockets like incandescents—a unique design. They are squat cylinders.

Use: All bulbs supply light. Tubes are for use only in fluorescent fixtures, except as noted above.

Use Tips: Fluorescents are designed to be left on—they last much longer if you don't keep turning them off and on.

Buying Tips: Fluorescent lamps supply the same light at much less cost than incandescent bulbs. They are simply rated at less wattage for the same luminosity.

About Incandescent Light Fixtures

There are a large variety of light fixtures available. Styles vary tremendously—there are entire stores devoted to nothing but light fixtures of different design—but all have essentially the same internal mechanism and one simple purpose—to hold lightbulbs.

When hanging any fixture make sure the hardware used is strong enough to support it.

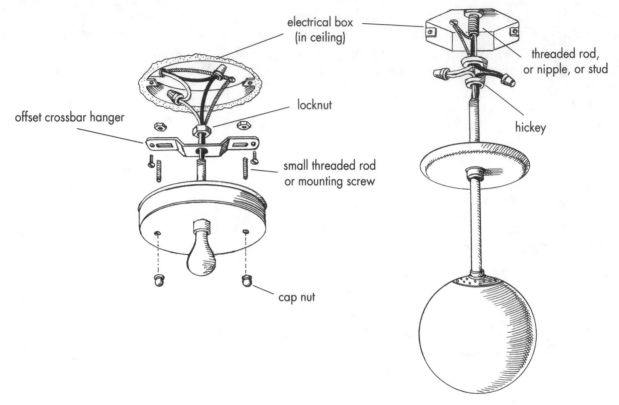

electrical box
(in ceiling)

threaded rod,
or nipple, or stud

offset crossbar hanger

locknut

hickey

small threaded rod
or mounting screw

cap nut

Incandescent Light Fixtures

Incandescent Ceiling and Wall Fixtures

Description: There exist an almost infinite variety of styles and shapes of lighting fixtures, but they usually have three wires and are mounted on an **electrical box (Part IX, Chapter 71)** that accepts the shape and size of the fixture. Mounting is either to an existing threaded *stud* (threaded rod) with a device called a *hickey* or, if there is no stud, a *crossbar hanger,* or *strap,* may be used. These are available flat, offset, and adjustable. Or a Rube Goldberg arrangement of various mounting parts—mixing *nipples* (short lengths of threaded rod) straps, hickeys, and *locknuts*—may be required to hang the fixture. Hickeys and nipples come with ends of different sizes. There is even a part called a *crow's foot*, which provides a stud where there is no electrical box. *Track lighting* is a series of fixtures mounted on a metal track that contains wiring. Fixtures can be moved along the track to any position without rewiring.

Use: Holds lightbulbs.

$ **Buying Tips:** Don't be afraid to look for miscellaneous individual items for mounting a fixture to an electrical box. In old houses, especially, each location may be different. All parts are available loose. There are various sizes of nipples and studs, so bring in the old piece or buy several to be sure of getting the right fit.

Indoor Incandescent Light Bulbs

Also Known As: Lamps, bulbs

Description: Glass spheres with necks and screw-in metal bases, containing a delicate wire element that glows when electricity flows through it. Various-sized bases are available; *Edison-base* is standard. Socket reducers are available for fitting small bases into large sockets. 130 volt bulbs and other *energy-saving bulbs* look just like regular incandescent bulbs but have a heavier, stronger filament. *Appliance bulbs* are similar, designed for use in ovens and refrigerators. *Construction grade bulbs* (also called *coated lamp* and *rough service* or *extended service*) are more resistant to breakage. They are made with a slight "skin" for protection and have stronger filaments than normal bulbs.

Use: To supply light. Construction grade bulbs are suitable for portable work lights that must "take" some vibration. For more intense light, use interior high-intensity lamps known as **halogen lamps (Part I, Chapter 15),** which require their own special fixtures and transformers.

> **$ Buying Tips:** The energy-saving bulbs will not save money at time of purchase but will, because they use less energy, save money over a long period of time. Some will last 5 years at 8 hours per day.

Outdoor Fixture

Outdoor Light Fixture

Also Known As: Weatherproof fixture, weatherproof lamp holder

Description: A variety is available, some round and others square. They are made of cast aluminum or galvanized steel. Many weatherproof fixtures have ¹/₂" pipe threads for screwing into covers or boxes; others, the *canopy* type, screw onto the box and cover it at the same time.

Use: Provides light outside the home.

Outdoor Bulbs

Types:

> *Incandescent*
>
> *High-intensity—mercury, sodium vapor, metal halide*

Also Known As:

> *Sodium vapor:* Sodium
>
> *High-intensity:* HID (high-intensity discharge)

Description:

Incandescent: These are regular bulbs designed for outdoor use. Types include yellow-colored, spotlights, floodlights, etc., that are flat or teardrop shaped. Spotlights and floodlights, often called just *spots* or *floods*, have a reflective coating on the back of the inside. They may be referred to as *reflector* spotlights or floodlights.

High-intensity: Vapor-filled bulbs of various shapes that give off strong, intense light.

Various types of high-intensity bulbs include

Mercury: Yields twice the light of an incandescent of the same wattage. Oval shape.

Sodium: High-wattage bulbs—250 to 1,000 watts—many times more efficient than incandescents. Light cast has a yellowish hue.

Metal halide: Emits a greenish light; available in various wattages from 50 to 1,000 watts.

Use:

Incandescent: Yellow bulbs are used because they don't attract insects. Spots are chiefly for decorative purposes to highlight detail. Floods are for security and to illuminate entrances.

High-intensity: Security.

Use Tips: Handle broken high-intensity bulbs with extreme care because they contain toxic materials. High-intensity bulbs take about 15 minutes to reach full brightness when turned on and are often used with timers.

$ Buying Tip: High-intensity bulbs last much longer than incandescents.

outdoor floodlight

Bulb Changer

Bulb Changer

Description: Suction cup or basket made of springs mounted on a handle with a release mechanism.

Use: Holding bulbs in order to change them without having to use a ladder.

$ Buying Tip: Note that some brands have different models for different styles of bulbs, i.e. regular incandescent lamp bulbs or outdoor floodlights.

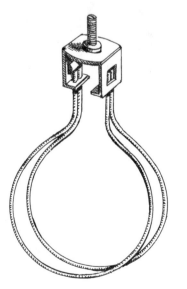

Clip Adapter

Lamp Parts

Part:

Clip adapter

Coupling

Finial

Harp

Locknut

Reducing bushing

Socket

Threaded rod (also known as *all-thread*)

Wire (also known as *lamp cord* and *flexible cord*)

Coupling

Description:

Clip adapter: Two oblong wire forms with stems in a metal piece that has a short threaded rod.

Coupling: Small, tube-like fitting threaded on the inside.

Finial: Small, decorative cap with female threads in one end.

Finial

Harp: Oblong-shaped wire form around six inches high and several inches wide, with a connecting fitting at the narrow end.

Locknut: Small, flat metal ring, sometimes with an opening and a slight spiral shape, sometimes hexagonal.

Reducing bushing: Small, round fitting threaded on the inside and outside.

Socket: Cylindrical metal part with electrical switch, two screws for securing wires, and inside threads for screwing in the bulb.

Threaded rod: Hollow metal tube threaded along its entire length. It is available with $1/8$" internal diameter and an outside diameter of $3/8$".

Wire: Lamp wire is 18-2 SPT-1 **(see wire, Chapter 70)** and may be bought with or without a plug.

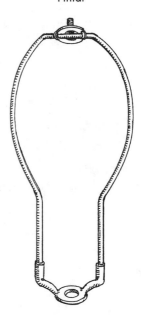

Harp

Use:

Clip adapter: Clips onto bulb and is used when a lamp has no harp to hold the lampshade.

Coupling: For joining two lengths of rod.

Locknuts

Reducing Bushings

Threaded Rod

Socket Reducer

Clamp-on Lamp

Finial: Screws on to secure lampshade to top of harp.

Harp: Holds lampshade.

Reducing bushing: Reduces the inside diameter of rod from $1/4$" to $1/8$"; to change from one rod size to another.

Socket: Electrical heart of lamp, containing switch mechanism, where the bulb is screwed in.

Threaded rod: The spine of the lamp. The lamp wire runs through it and all the lamp parts—the "head" of the lamp—are supported by it.

Wire: Provides electrical power.

> **$ Buying Tips:** Lamp parts are sold in kit form but it is more economical to buy individual parts. Socket parts may also be bought individually and can result in slight savings for repair **(see socket, below)**. *Socket reducers* are available that screw into a larger socket and permit use of bulbs with small *candelabra bases*.

Clamp-On Lamp

Also Known As: Utility lamp

Description: Normal socket, but with a large metal reflector and a spring clamp about 8" long. Reflectors come in a small variety of styles.

Use: Clamp allows temporary placement anywhere, especially at a worksite.

Use Tips: Deep, large, bell-shape reflector is most efficient. Cord set and clamp can be purchased separately from the reflector.

Lamp Holder

Incandescent Lamp-Holder
(Rear View)

Also Known As: Porcelain fixture, outlet-box lamp holder

Description: Round porcelain or Bakelite® fixture with socket, either with screw terminals or prewired with leads—white and black wires—ready for connecting. Porcelain fixtures come 3", 4", and 5¼" in diameter. Available in three styles—with pull chain, with pull chain and receptacle for plugging into, and without a pull chain, or *keyless.*

Use: Lamp holders are mounted on electrical boxes so they are exposed. They are normally used in garages, shops, and other areas where just lighting function rather than fixture good looks is the key.

 Use Tip: The two-separate-lead-type fixture is easiest to install.

Buying Tip: *Pigtails,* sockets with two wire leads, are used for temporary installations, as well as for testing.

Socket

Socket
Mechanism

Standard Socket

Also Known As: Incandescent lamp holder

Description: Metal cylinder with a threaded portion (female threads), which lightbulbs (male threads) are screwed into, and a switch mechanism—toggle or chain. Despite their various on-off actions, the wiring is the same—there are two screws, one copper and the other nickel, for each electrical supply wire.

Use: To control on-off action of incandescent lightbulbs. Some sockets have simple on-off actions while others provide three levels of light—30, 70, and 100 watt.

 Use Tip: When securing two wires to a socket it does not matter which wire goes to which screw.

$ Buying Tips: All parts of a standard socket—shell and switch mechanism—are replaceable. To save money you can buy either part, though some users say that fitting a new part to an old socket can be difficult because machining is not precise.

Dimmer Socket

Description: Looks like a **standard socket (above)**.

Use: Used to change a standard socket to a dimmer, which can be adjusted to provide graduated levels of light.

Fuses and Circuit Breakers

About Fuses

A fuse can be considered the weak link in an electrical circuit. When an electrical malfunction occurs and passes too much current through the wires, the linkage inside the fuse heats up and melts—"blows"—and the flow of electricity is stopped—it has no more wire to "ride" on. It's like part of a road, a bridge, dropping away—vehicles can't continue.

There are a variety of fuses available. You must make sure that before installing a new fuse the reason for blowing has been corrected. Usually, if the fuse window is blackened, it indicates a short circuit; if the metal linkage just melted, then it indicates an overload.

The most common fuses screw into sockets in fuse boxes. Such fuse boxes are usually found in the basement of a home. Each fuse protects one circuit; circuits have different switches and outlets on them and are distributed in different rooms. Circuits may go through several rooms and floors, particularly in older homes.

Fuses are rated according to amperage, or "amps," and are designed to protect electrical devices whose total amperage is equal to the fuse's amperage rating. Hence, when selecting a fuse never select one bigger than specified—too big and the wire will heat up and possibly start a fire before the fuse blows.

Fuses are simple to replace: just unscrew or remove the bad one and screw or push in the good one. For convenience, it's good to have some spares on hand, plus a flashlight in case the lights are out or if the lighting in the area of the fuse box is very dim.

Many fuses have been replaced by **circuit-breakers (below)**. These have a metallic strip inside that heats up in case of a problem and trips a switch from on to off. As mentioned earlier, it's a simple matter, after correcting the electrical malfunction, to flip it back on. If need be, circuit breakers can also be replaced.

Plug Fuse

Plug Fuse

Also Known As: Edison base fuse, plug-in fuse, glass fuse

Description: This used to be the most commonly used fuse. It is a round device about 1" long with a small window on one end for viewing a tiny metal linkage and a threaded base like a light bulb's.

Use: Safety device in electrical circuits **(see About Fuses, above)**. Screws into panel in fuse box.

> **Use Tips:** If the window of the blown fuse is blackened, it likely means that a short circuit is the problem; a broken linkage (no blackness) usually means a circuit overload.

$ Buying Tips: Electricians favor plug-in fuses over circuit breakers, whose internal mechanism can malfunction. Plug-in fuses are available in 5-, 10-, 20-, 25-, and 30-amp sizes; the amperage is stamped on the top of the fuse. In a pinch, plug-in fuses can usually be bought at supermarkets and drugstores.

Type "S" Fuse

Type "S" Fuse

Also Known As: Nontamperable, nontamp, Fustats®

Description: Consists of two parts—a narrow, threaded adapter, which screws into the fuse box, and the fuse proper, which screws into the adapter. Adapter and fuse are color-coded and should be the same color. Has become one of the most common types of fuses.

Use: Used where there is fear of someone accidentally using the wrong fuse, such as in rental property, because these fuses are tamperproof. For example, only a 15-amp type S fuse can screw into a 15-amp adapter, whereas different *plug-type fuses* can be screwed into the same opening because all are the same physical size.

Use Tips: Good for replacing all your existing plug-type fuses. Type S fuses are available in the same amp ratings as plug-in fuses and are interchangeable with them. Be sure to tighten them down as far as possible when inserting them. May be required in new construction.

Knife-Blade Contact Cartridge Fuse

Ferrule Contact Cartride Fuse

Cartridge Fuse

Also Known As: If for a circuit above 60 amps, known as *knife-blade cartridge* or *knife-blade contact fuse;* for 60 amps and below, known as a *ferrule contact* type.

Description: Looks like a rifle cartridge casing with metal caps, or *ferrules,* at the ends, or else blades that stick out. Cartridge fuses for 60 amps and below have the plain capped ends; those for above 60 amps have blades and are, as noted above, known as **knife-blade cartridge fuses**.

Use: Works like any fuse but for larger devices such as air conditioners and appliances. Unlike plug-type fuses, you cannot tell if it is "blown" by looking at it.

> **Use Tips:** Be sure to observe safety precautions when removing and installing fuses. If installing them in an appliance, make sure the device is turned off. There is a special pliers, a **fuse puller (Chapter 73)**, available for installing and removing cartridge fuses.

> **Buying Tips:** Both *one-time* and *renewable* cartridge fuses are available. One-time fuses melt and must be replaced; renewable fuses have a linkage that can be replaced. The ends of the fuse are unscrewed to get at it.

Time Delay Fuse

Time Delay Fuse

Description: Similar to a **plug-in fuse, above**, but contains a different element.

Use: Protects circuits for motor-operated devices that cause momentary high surges of electricity when turned on. A regular fuse would blow needlessly.

Circuit Breaker

Also Known As: Breaker

Types:

> *Push button circuit breaker*
>
> *Toggle circuit breaker*

Description: Typically a small, narrow, black plastic box that resembles a switch and is activated by either a *push button* or a *toggle* switch. Circuit breakers are plugged, snapped, or clipped into place on the house electrical panel—the metal cabinet found near where the power supply enters the house. An average house might have as many as a dozen circuit breakers on a panel.

Other than the typical models described here, circuit-breaker mechanisms are found in small **multiple outlets (Chapter 66)** and also in fuses with **plug-type bases (above)**.

Use: Circuit breakers serve the same function as **fuses (above)**. They cut the circuit off—"break" it—if there is a "short" or other hazardous malfunction that would possibly cause a fire. Like fuses, they are sized in terms of amperage to handle from 15- to 100-amp circuits. 15 to 20 amps are commonly used—20 in modern construction. Unlike fuses, they do not need to be replaced after functioning. The switches merely "trip," or "flip," and you just push or flip them back to reset once the offending problem has been eliminated.

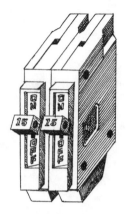

Circuit Breaker

Plug-Type (Screw-In) Circuit Breaker

Use Tips: When replacing a circuit breaker make sure the main power supply is off. Also, take the old breaker to the store to ensure getting the correct replacement—one manufacturer's breaker will not necessarily fit where another's did.

Buying Tip: Much easier to use than fuses.

Switches and Receptacles

About Switches

Switches function by interrupting electrical flow. There are many types of switches but they can be divided between those linked to the main house wiring and those that are used elsewhere, such as on wires of electrical devices. Within the category of house-wiring switches there are some that are commonly used and some that are uncommonly used; this distinction is observed when describing them below.

Regarding house-wiring switches, terminal screws—the screws that wires are connected to—may come on one side or both sides of the switch and this can make installation more or less difficult depending on the situation. The screws are color-coded for correct wiring—check your manuals.

All house-wiring switches have some sort of mounting attachments for installation in **electrical boxes (Chapter 71)**. Mounting is usually done with No. 6-32 machine screws but sometimes No. 8-32. If unsure, buy both—they cost only a few cents each.

Common House Switches

Single-Pole, Duplex Switch

Types:

> *Single-pole switch*
>
> *Double-pole switch*
>
> *Three-way switch*
>
> *Four-way switch*
>
> *Dimmer switch*
>
> *Fluorescent dimmer switch*

Also Known As:

> *Single-pole:* S.P.
>
> *Dimmer:* Rheostat

Description: All come in a variety of voltage and amperage ratings, which must be specified.

> *Single-pole:* Identified by the presence of two brass terminal screws.
>
> *Double-pole:* Has four terminal screws.

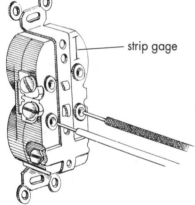

strip gage

Clamp-Type Switch (Rear View)

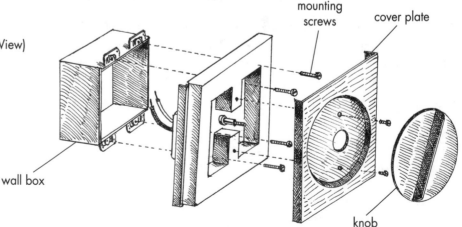

mounting screws

cover plate

wall box

knob

Fluorescent Dimmer Switch

Three-way: Has three terminal screws—there may also be a green grounding screw.

Four-way: Has four terminal screws—and possibly a green grounding screw.

Dimmer: Looks like a regular switch but may have a turning or sliding knob instead of a toggle, and wire leads instead of terminals.

Fluorescent dimmer: Three times the size of a standard dimmer switch but with a knob instead of a toggle.

Single-pole, three-way, and four-way switches come with three types of on-off action:

Snap: Flip a switch and there is an audible click.

Quiet: A slight click is heard when the switch is flipped.

Mercury: This toggle is controlled by a tilting tube of mercury and no sound at all is heard when the switch is flipped.

Switches may also be obtained with illuminated toggles.

Use: Controlling light or, in the case of dimmers, the level of light.

Use Tips: Most models are available in a *push-in* or *clamp-type* style, which means you can just slide the end of a wire into them without having to wrap the wire end around the terminal screws, making for a much simpler job.

§ **Buying Tips:** Like other electrical devices, switches come in *standard* or *spec* (specification) grade. For normal house use standard grade is fine. The least expensive switches are those with the loudest action—mercury, the quietest, is the costliest. Switches, like receptacles, can be bought in bulk by the box for less money than if bought individually.

Switch with Pilot Light

Specialized House Switches

Types:

Combination switch

Pilot light switch

Nontamperable switch

Timer switch

Outdoor switch

Safety switch

Miniaturized switch

Photoelectric switch

Also Known As: *Miniaturized:* Despard®

Description:

Combination: Regular switch that also contains a receptacle.

Pilot light: Regular switch but with a light to indicate if the switch is on.

Nontamperable: Regular switch that must be turned on and off with a key.

Timer: Like an oven timer with a spring-loaded rotary knob.

Outdoor: Consists of a turning lever built onto a weatherproof box cover and a regular toggle switch. The regular switch is mounted inside the box and the box cover over it.

Safety: Also built like a regular switch but may or may not have a fuse; remove the fuse and the switch will not work.

Miniaturized: Small self-contained toggle switch.

Photoelectric: Contains a light-sensing "eye" that operates the switch according to whether there is daylight present.

Use:

Combination: Use wherever a switch and receptacle are required at one location.

Pilot light: Alerts you to when an electrical device is on. Particularly good when the device it controls is in a remote location, such as an attic fan or light.

Nontamperable: Good on machines, particularly where children are around, such as near swimming pools, or in offices.

Timer: For turning lights on automatically, for security or for safety's sake, or for preventing an iron or other appliance from being left on.

Outdoor: Where convenient power is needed outside the house.

Miniaturized: Allows installation of as many as three separate switches in a normal wall box, often in combination with a pilot light and a single receptacle.

Photoelectric: Turns lights on at sundown and off at dawn, for security, especially outdoors.

About Line Switches

Line switches are those that are installed in the electrical cord. They interrupt the flow of electricity in the same way as regular and specialized switches.

In-Line Cord Switch

Canopy Switch

Line Switches

Types:

> *Cord switch*
>
> *Canopy switch*
>
> *Rotary switch*
>
> *Toggle switch*
>
> *Push-button fluorescent starter switch*
>
> *Push-button momentary on-off switch*

Also Known As:

> *Cord:* In-line, feed through
>
> *Toggle:* Tumbler

Description:

> *Cord:* A typical cord switch is made of two small, separable plastic halves that have prongs inside that push through the wire's insulation when the halves are screwed back together, making electrical contact.
>
> *Canopy:* Small switch with knurled metal pushbutton and wires stripped ready for attaching to the existing wires.
>
> *Rotary:* Similar to canopy, but with turnbutton.
>
> *Toggle:* Similar to canopy, but with toggle lever.

Push-button fluorescent starter: Small, round switch with a push button and four wire leads.

Push-button momentary on-off: Small switch with leads for wiring into power-tool circuits. Inch-long switch that looks like a bell.

Use:

Cord: For installation on a lamp cord for convenience, such as for bedside lamps or radios.

Canopy: Also for use on floor and lamp cord.

Rotary: A variety of uses including controlling table and floor lamps and small appliances; for controlling two individual or built-in units in an appliance or for controlling two circuits.

Toggle: For use on table and floor lamps and small appliances. Toggles are also available for heavy-duty appliances such as vacuum cleaners, portable tools, and motors.

Push-button fluorescent starter: This switch has a starter built in and its small size makes it good for use where space is cramped. Typical use is to operate fluorescents under hanging kitchen cabinets.

Push-button momentary on-off: Operates only when it is pressed—spring action closes it—so it can be used anywhere intermittent power is required.

Timers

Description: Timers vary in shape and function. They can be simple box-like affairs that plug into a wall outlet, or designed to be linked to house wiring, or they can be tabletop models. They can be bought with capacities up to 1,000 watts. In all cases they contain clock mechanisms.

Uses: Various. One is for turning on lights at certain times for security. Another is for turning on appliances such as televisions or air conditioners.

 Use Tip: Like other electrical devices, the wiring of the timer must be heavy enough to do the job required.

 Buying Tips: Basic kind tends to wear out and make noise. Electronic types are superior but much more costly.

Thermostats

Description: A form of electronic or electromechanical switch sensitive to temperature and time settings, depending on the model. Generally powered by a low-voltage circuit (24 volts). Many different types: the more advanced models have some computerization and can be programmed for different temperatures at different times in different rooms on different days; the most basic ones are set manually for minimum temperature.

Use: Turns a heating or cooling system on and off in response to a chosen temperature and time setting.

> **Use Tips:** Remember that the temperature of the room containing the thermostat determines the temperature of the rest of the house. Therefore you should place a thermostat in an average room, away from any drafts or heat sources. Wiring is usually done with a special lightweight wire called a *thermo*, or *thermostat wire*, and uses a transformer to reduce the house electricity to 24 volts. Each model comes with specific wiring diagrams.

> **Buying Tips:** Recent advances in computers have spawned a whole range of elaborate thermostats; some are too sensitive to be useful, though, and we highly recommend a thorough study of magazine articles and the like prior to purchasing one of the newest electronic models.

About Receptacles

Receptacles, commonly called *outlets,* come in a variety of styles. Like other electrical devices, they are rated to handle a specific amount of current. Capacity is stamped on the receptacle. For lights, receptacles rated at 15 amps and 125 volts are used. Receptacles that are designed for different devices may have different shapes but they are all geared to do one job—provide a link between the plug of a particular device and the house power supply.

Although some may be linked to room switches, most receptacles are always on, so exercise caution when plugging something in. Above all, be sure to turn off the power to a particular receptacle before working on it. Check to see if it is off with a **test lamp (Chapter 73).**

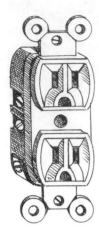

Duplex Receptacle

Standard Receptacle

Also Known As: Outlet (technically incorrect)

Description: Plastic device with two pairs of vertical slots for plugs or two vertical slots and a third hole, in the standard "duplex" model, for a grounding prong of a plug. Available in a single model too. Comes with metal attachments for mounting in an electrical box. Standard receptacles are usually ivory or brown plastic. (An outlet is technically just the point at which current is supplied—i.e., where the receptacle is installed.)

Use: Provides connection with current when a plug is inserted.

Use Tips: Like switches, terminal screws are mounted in different side positions. You may want to try using a new, more convenient clamp type with no terminal screws for wires to be wrapped around—just push wire in holes in back and it is clamped in.

Buying Tips: If you want top-quality receptacles, get *spec* (for specification) *grade receptacles;* the term *spec* will be stamped on the receptacle. Spec grade receptacles are costly, however, and for around-home use would not seem to be warranted; use *standard* grade. If you are going to need a number of receptacles, buy them in bulk to save money.

Appliance Receptacle

Description: Contains one pair of vertical or slanted slots and one vertical or U-shaped slot. Designed to be surface-mounted.

Use: For heavier-duty plugs and appliances, such as dryers and air conditioners.

Appliance Receptacle

Ground Fault Circuit Interrupter

Also Known As: GFI, GFCI, ground fault interrupter

Description: Comes in three different kinds but basically resembles a standard grounded receptacle, usually with a small reset button in the middle.

Use: The GFCI's job is to sense hazardous leakage of electricity instantaneously and shut off the circuit. It works far faster than a standard circuit breaker or fuse. One type of GFCI is designed to be installed in the circuit breaker box, another kind is installed in a standard electrical box in place of a standard receptacle, and the third kind is portable—it plugs into a grounded outlet.

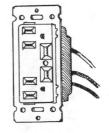

Ground Fault Circuit Interrupter

Use Tips: GFCIs are useful (and, in many cases of new construction, required) in kitchens, bathrooms, and around pools or wherever electrical hazards are magnified.

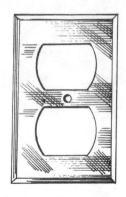

Duplex Outlet Wall Plate

Wall Plates

Also Known As: Faceplates, covers

Description: Flat metal, wood, or plastic piece with openings for receptacles or switches; generally a couple of inches across and four or five inches long. Available in a wide range of colors and shapes. Supplied with screws for attaching to an electrical box. Available to go over "ganged" boxes for groups of switches—up to a dozen.

Use: Covers switches and receptacles in electrical boxes. Mounts with a No. 6-32 machine screw.

> **Use Tips:** Some wall plates are available in oversized dimensions, especially in wood, and are handy for covering a too-large opening that a receptacle or switch is housed in or to cover a gap in wallpaper around the box.

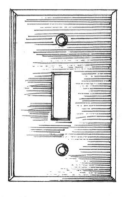

Toggle Switch Wall Plate

> **Buying Tips:** Fancily packaged wall plates can be very expensive. It's cheaper to buy them loose or in plain cellophane wrappers. They can easily be painted or covered with wallpaper.

Electrical Wire and Connectors

About Electrical Wire

The term *wire* is a misnomer because wire actually means metal conductors—lengths of metal—encased in some sort of insulation—perhaps plastic, rubber, or cloth composition.

Conductors are made of copper and will either be solid or stranded. Strands are easier to bend than the solid material.

Wire is characterized according to gauge number and runs from 0000 to No. 40, with the numbers getting smaller as the wire gets thicker—a No. 38 wire would be about the diameter of a human hair while a No. 2 wire would be the diameter of a pencil. The most common gauges used in the home range from 10 to 20.

Wire is also described by letters according to the kind of insulation (covering) and electrical capacity; for example, lamp wire is SPT-1, as in strippable, pendant thermoplastic. But technical nomenclature is not required—you should simply specify your intended use for the wire. The descriptions below are a guide to what is commonly available.

When wire is temporarily run around walls it should be protected from possible damage. It may be held in place by insulated staples, which are driven in with a small hammer. Regular house wiring requires conduit or other special material, discussed in **Chapters 71 and 72**.

Heat-Resistant appliance Cord Set

Lighting and Small-Appliance Wire

Types:

> *Bell, or hookup wire*
>
> *Conductor, or Thermo (for thermostat) wire*
>
> *SJ wire*
>
> *SPT-1 wire*

Also Known As: SPT-1

Description: Insulated copper wire in a range of gauges.

Use:

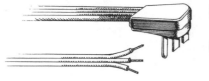

Large Appliance Cord Set

> *Bell:* For doorbells, thermostats, and low-voltage hobby work.
>
> *Conductor:* For thermostats.
>
> *SJ:* For appliances and power tools.
>
> *SPT-1:* For lamps, chandeliers, and commonly used hanging lighting fixtures.

> **$ Buying Tips:** There are a variety of wires available for many uses, such as making your own extension cords, heat-resistant cord, and more. Such cord can be identified by letter according to the insulation used, but this can get complicated—just ask the dealer for it by use. For example, ask for a cord for a toaster. If you wish, you can also buy cord sets in which the cord comes with a plug on one end and bare wires or leads on the other for attaching to a large electrical device, such as an air conditioner.

House Wire

Types:

BX

Romex®

THHN, THWN, and *MTWN*

Also Known As:

BX: Armored metallic cable, armored electrical cable, armored electrical cable, bushed armored cable, spiral armored cable

Romex®: Nonmetallic sheathed cable, NM cable, loom wire

Description:

BX: Two or three individually insulated wires, each wrapped with spiral layers of tough paper (bushing), running inside a galvanized-steel spiral casing. Two-wire BX has one black and one white wire. All BX has a bonding wire that runs along its length. The casing acts as the ground wire; the bond wire serves as a backup in case the casing breaks.

Romex®: Consists of a flat, beige thermoplastic jacket with two or three wires, each covered with insulation and wrapped with spiral paper tape and a paper-covered copper wire. Type NM is for indoor use; NMC for damp indoor or outdoor use; and UF for underground outdoor use.

THHN, THWN, and *MTWN* are heavy-duty insulated copper wires.

BX (Armored Cable)

Romex (Nonmetallic Cable)

Use: All are used for standard interior house wiring. BX is one of the most enduring and common items found in house construction. THHN, THWN, and MTWN are used inside **conduit** and **greenfield (Chapter 72)**. *Service cable,* which is not included here, is used outside the house to bring power from the municipal supply to your house.

Use Tips: BX is cut either with a hacksaw (works best in a vise) or a special cutting tool that clamps onto the cable and has a cranked circular blade. Cutting Romex® is simpler using a special tool called a **splitter (Chapter 73)**. It is held to walls and joists by nonmetallic cable straps, similar to **conduit straps (Chapter 72)**. Romex® and BX connect to electrical boxes with their own individual type of connector fittings, called *connectors,* or *cable clamps.*

Buying Tips: Romex® and BX are sold in precut lengths of 25' and 50' per box and in bulk, cut to the length you require. Buying by bulk is usually less expensive because you buy only exactly what you need.

About BX, Greenfield, and Romex® and Where Their Names Came From

As I researched this book I encountered terms that intrigued me as to what their origins were—how various items got their names. I figured out most, but the names for three very common items kept defying explanation—Romex®, which is plastic-covered cable; greenfield, which describes a hollow steel cable through which electric wires are pulled; and BX (armored cable), which is really greenfield with the wires already in place. Romex is just one of the most popular brands—that was easy. But for the others, I asked at many, many hardware stores, I asked at electrical supply stores, I asked electricians, I even asked executives at wire companies... No one knew. A real mystery.

But I finally found the answer from James C. Dollins, a vice president of AFC (American Flexible Conduit), in New Bedford, Massachusetts, which makes armored cable. Dollins brought the terms to ground, as it were, a few years ago. He explained that he learned from an old-timer that around the turn of the century there was a company run by two men, Harry Greenfield and Gus Johnson. They made this hollow metal product called—what else—*greenfield*. End of mystery one.

One day, while manufacturing greenfield, there was a problem with a cord used to bind the material and the cord accidentally was run all the way through it. An idea was born. What if they could do that with wire—sell the greenfield with the wires already in place? They worked up an experimental batch of the stuff and gave it to an electrician they knew to try it out.

His response was a rave—it saved him many hours of pulling the wire through the usual hollow cable. He wanted more of it—all they could get to him. But he had one question: What do you call it?

Up to that point they had made only one product, so they hadn't given a name any thought. "BX," said one of the quick-thinking partners. "B because it's our 'B' product line, and 'X' because it's experimental."

And that's how greenfield—and BX—got their names.

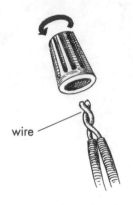

wire

Wire Nut

Wire Nuts

Also Known As: Scotchloks®, solderless connectors, twist connectors, wire connectors, connectors, spring wire locks, screw-on wire connectors

Description: Plastic caps with threaded insides; come in various colors according to size.

Use: Connects and insulates the ends of wires that have been twisted together, generally inside an electrical box or lighting fixture.

 Use Tip: Specific size nuts must be used with specific size wires.

Crimp Connectors

Description: Small metal wire connectors that are crimped (squeezed) onto the ends of small-gauge wires. Color-coded for wire gauge—red is for 22 to 18; blue is for 16 to 14 gauge.

Use: Connecting small-gauge wires.

 Use Tip: Easily used with a special **crimping,** or **combination, tool (Chapter 73).**

Electrical Boxes

About Electrical Boxes

No bare wires secured to receptacles or in other junctions can be left exposed—the wires must be enclosed for safety, and this is the job of the electrical box.

Boxes come in dozens of different shapes and sizes but can generally be broken down into boxes for walls, boxes for ceilings, and outdoor boxes. Most boxes are made of galvanized metal, but plastic wall boxes, for interior use only, are coming on strong because they cost a lot less than metal. Before using plastic make sure your local electrical code allows them. Using something that isn't allowed and then having it cause a fire could result in your fire insurance being invalidated.

Boxes are made with open holes or holes plugged with easily-removed *knockouts* that can be either pried out (if they have little slots for screwdrivers in them) or (guess what) knocked out with a hammer. For whatever kind of cable or conduit you are passing through (**BX, conduit, or plastic sheathed, Chapter 70)**, there are specialized connectors and cable clamps either built in or sold separately under the catchy name of *connectors*, complete with setscrews or locknuts and various bushings (sleeves). Similarly, there is a whole set of elbows, couplings, and other fittings for the various types of conduit available. Make sure you get everything you need the first time you go to the hardware store.

Some wall boxes have plaster *ears,* which are metal brackets or tabs for mounting the box in existing construction. The ears grip the wall and keep the box close to the surface. If the box does not have ears, it will have holes for nailing to studs. Most components are attached to boxes with 8-32 **machine screws (Part III, Chapter 22)**.

Boxes must be installed with holes in gypsum wallboard that match their size exactly. Take care to mark holes for accurate cutting.

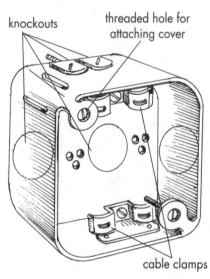

4-Inch Square Electrical Box

Wall Boxes

Types:

> *Four-inch square box*
>
> *Gem box*
>
> *Handy box*
>
> *Plastic box*
>
> *Sheetrock® box*
>
> *Stud box*

Also Known As:

> *Four-inch:* "1900" box
>
> *Handy:* Utility, surface-mounted
>
> *Sheetrock®:* Drywall
>
> *Stud:* nail-on
>
> *Wall box (general):* Outlet box, junction box, switch box

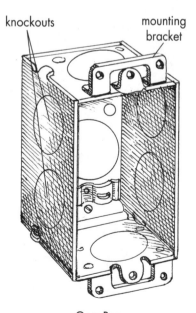

Gem Box

Description: Most are made of either galvanized steel or aluminum. Some are made of plastic.

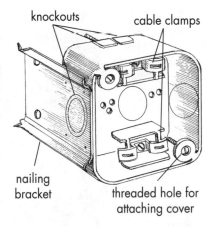

Four-inch square: Four-inch square box but only $1^{1}/_{2}$" or $2^{1}/_{8}$" deep.

Gem box: Gem is a term used to describe a commonly used box made by various manufacturers. It is metal and commonly 2" wide, 3" high, and $2^{1}/_{2}$" deep, but it does come deeper.

Handy: Small rectangular box with rounded corners.

Plastic: Various sizes, made of plastic.

Sheetrock®: Various-shaped metal box with expandable arms.

Stud: Various-sized box with a nailing bracket for attachment to studs.

Stud Box

Use: All wall boxes are for housing switches and receptacles, sometimes referred to as *outlets*. However, please note the following differences:

Four-inch square: In some cases the wall will be too shallow to mount a gem box. Here the shallower four-inch box can be used because it still has the cubic-inch capacity to accommodate the wires. May also be used on the ceiling.

Gem: Standard box for mounting switches or receptacles.

Handy: Surface-mounted. Its rounded corners make it a safer box.

Plastic: This comes in various sizes but is basically for use on new work because it must be nailed to studs, an impossibility if wall material is present.

Sheetrock®: Designed to be mounted on gypsum wallboard.

Stud: Metal boxes designed to be nailed to framing members in new construction.

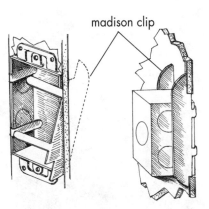

Gem Box with Madison Clips

Use Tips: Many boxes can be *ganged*—sides taken apart and the boxes linked together—if you have many outlets or switches to accommodate. If you use plastic boxes, make sure the wires are properly grounded. A simple way to mount gem boxes in walls is with *Madison clips*, also known as *battleships, bracket set*, or *switch box supports* because of their shape; they bend around the box's side and pull it up against the wall. Sheetrock® boxes are easier to mount.

Buying Tips: Plastic boxes cost far less than galvanized, but as mentioned in the **About section** are not permitted by some local building codes.

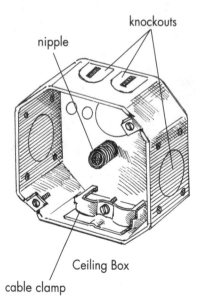

knockouts

nipple

Ceiling Box

cable clamp

Ceiling Box

Also Known As: Junction box, splice box

Description: Comes in two different forms—4" octagonal or round—and in two depths—$1^1/_2$" and $2^1/_8$". It may have *extendable* or *adjustable* mounting hangers (also called *bars, box hangers, barhangers,* or *brackets*). Hangers, which can be purchased separately, provide the short threaded rod (the *stud* or *nipple*) that fixtures attach to. Flat, shallow boxes may be called *pancake boxes*.

Use: Anchors ceiling fixtures or serves as a junction box where any wires meet, are connected, and then run to some other area of the home.

Weatherproof Box

Also Known As: Outside box, outdoor box

Description: Usually round or square box in double ("duplex") or single form with threaded holes in sides to accept correspondingly threaded light fixtures. Rubber gasket between box and cover keeps moisture out; receptacles have either screw- or snap-type covers. Slightly thicker than interior boxes.

Use: Housing exterior switches, receptacles, and mounting fixtures.

Use Tips: Covers that screw in place on weatherproof boxes should be used only where you do not need ready access to the receptacle or outlet; use the snap-type cover instead.

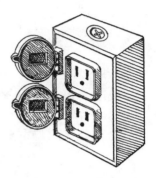

Weatherproof Receptacle
with Snap Covers

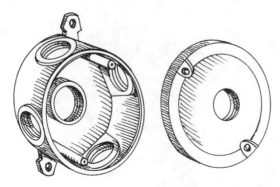

Weatherproof Box

Box Covers

Switch Box Cover

Blank Box Cover

Duplex Receptacle Box Cover

Collar-Type Box Cover

Description: Covers of boxes for inside use are metal or plastic in a variety of shapes—round, square, octagonal—to fit over boxes. Covers may be solid or have cutouts to accommodate switch toggles or receptacles. Covers are secured to the box by **machine screws,** usually No. 8-32 **(Part III, Chapter 22)**. Weatherproof (exterior use) box covers also vary in shape but many have threaded holes to accommodate light fixtures, or snap covers to protect receptacle slots when not in use, or a lever switch that operates an inside toggle switch. A lidded type houses GFCI receptacles. Partial covers, called *collars* or *plaster rings,* have a shoulder design and provide additional depth to the box.

Use: Both inside and outside covers protect wiring and devices; outside covers have a gasket that makes the box weatherproof too. Collar-type covers serve as a base for **wall plates (Chapter 69)** and also provide a border for applying plaster.

Conduit

About Conduit

Conduit comes in a variety of types but you will be required to use whatever your local electrical code specifies.

Thin-Wall Conduit

Also Known As: EMT (electric metallic tubing)

Description: Light steel thin-wall pipe that comes in inside diameters of ½" to 4", and even larger, and in 10' lengths; the ½" size is most common.

Use: For carrying house wiring in areas where it must be left exposed, such as along unfinished garage or basement walls or for outdoor lighting.

> **Use Tips:** Thin-wall pipe should not be used underground, nor is it practical to use in an existing house because walls and the like would have to be removed to accommodate it. It is used for new construction but even here much sawing of framing members has to be done. Once installed, however, new wires can easily be pulled through it.

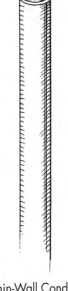

Thin-Wall Conduit

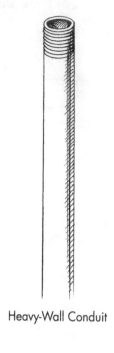

Heavy-Wall Conduit

Heavy-Wall Conduit

Also Known As: Rigid conduit

Description: Comes in the same length and diameters as **thin-wall (above)** but is galvanized and has thicker walls and is threaded for connections. Also available in plastic.

Use: For carrying wire outdoors, underground, where it is exposed to elements or perhaps subject to physical abuse, such as in a lawn where it might be run over by a mower. Typical use is to extend wiring between a house and room addition.

 Use Tip: Like thin-wall, not for use in existing construction, but may be used for new construction.

Electrical Cable and Conduit Connectors

Description: They come in a wide variety of shapes, some resembling plumbing fittings (elbows, couplings, and the like), some galvanized for exterior use, called *condulets*. Exterior fittings have covers and gaskets. Made in three versions—for **BX**, **EMT**, and **Romex® (Chapter 70)**.

Use: Connecting conduit of various kinds so that longer runs can be made and to enable it to turn or do whatever else is required for a particular installation.

 Use Tip: Be sure to use antishort collars on BX wherever you cut it to protect it from damage through vibration.

Conduit Fasteners

Types:

Cable Staples

Conduit Straps

Also Known As:

Straps: One-hole: Conduit half strap; Two-hole: Conduit full strap

Description:

Staples: U-shaped metal piece with sharp points, either plain or covered with plastic insulation.

Straps: Formed metal pieces with either one (for one-hole strap) or two holes (for two-hole strap).

Use: Plain metal staples and straps secure *conduit* and *greenfield* to walls, ceilings, or framing members. *Plastic-covered,* or *insulated,* staples are used to secure extension-cord wire and the like to walls inside the house.

Cable Staple

One-Hole Conduit Strap

Two-Hole Conduit Strap

> **Use Tips:** Straps (one- or two-hole) work best for securing thin-wall, heavy-wall, and plastic conduit. The general rule electricians have is that they use straps outside the house and staples inside. The two-hole strap makes the most secure job.

Plastic Conduit

Description: Rigid plastic pipe.

Use: Housing wire inside and outside the home.

> **Buying Tip:** Simple and easy to use where permitted by code.

Greenfield

Also Known As: Flex, flexible metal conduit

Description: Consists of a fairly flexible hollow spiral metal jacket and resembles **BX (see Part IX, Chapter 70)** but is available in larger diameters to allow wires to be pulled through it. Specialized fittings and connectors are available.

Use: Housing wire running inside the home.

Greenfield

> **Use Tip:** Greenfield may be installed the same way as BX, requiring small holes to be drilled in the wall.

Wire Channels

Also Known As: Raceway, wire mold

Description: Metal or plastic channels about $1/2$" square designed to contain house wiring; switch and receptacle boxes are designed to work with each specific brand or type of channel.

Use: Housing wiring on the surface of masonry or other walls in the place of conduit. Enables house wiring, both permanent and temporary, to be installed without piercing walls.

Use Tip: Metal channels have an advantage over plastic in that they ensure a grounded circuit if installed correctly.

Electrical Tools

About Electrical Tools

Only a few tools are needed for everyday electrical jobs, but if you get into large home improvements or repair jobs there are others that can serve one well. Following is a roundup that should handle all but the basic needs.

Test Lamp

Also Known As: Circuit tester, neon lamp tester, neon tester, testlight, voltage tester, line tester, neon circuit tester

Description: Basically a plastic housing with a small neon bulb with two 6" insulated wire probes. Large variations in design.

Use: To see whether there is electricity in an electrical circuit (if it is "live") or whether a circuit is properly grounded.

> **Use Tips:** A test lamp is a very important safety device and no one working on electrical projects, no matter how small, should be without one.

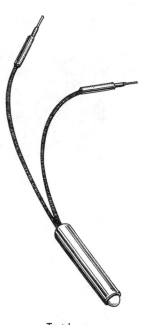

Test Lamp

Continuity Tester

Description: Usually a slender plastic housing about half a foot long containing batteries, two probes (one may be an alligator clip), and a small indicator light; works off battery power. Comes in various forms.

Use: To check if wires, such as appliance cords, or any circuit can carry a flow of electricity from one end to the other. Also used to check fuses.

 Buying Tip: Better to get a combination tool called a *multitester* then such a specialized item.

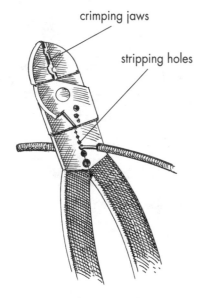

crimping jaws

stripping holes

Combination Tool

Combination Tool

Also Known As: Wire crimper and cutter, wiring tool, crimper, wire crimper-stripper, multipurpose tool, combination stripper-crimper, combination stripper-pliers, sheath stripper

Description: Similar to flat pliers, jaws have different-sized holes and notches for insertion of corresponding sizes of wire, allowing the insulation to be stripped off without touching the wire when the jaws are closed. Other parts of jaws have flat lips for crimping and pulling wire.

Use: For cutting and stripping wires of various diameters, or gauges, but also for crimping solderless wire connectors. Can cut screws without damaging threads too.

 Buying Tips: Combination tools that have multiple holes are of better quality than tools with only hole.

Fish Tape

Also Known As: Fish wire, snake, electrician's or electrical snake

Description: Stiff, flat wire, $1/2"$ to $3/4"$ wide, with a hook on one end, which is coiled in a case and comes in 25' and 50' lengths.

Use: For pulling the wire through conduit or greenfield tubing as well as for probing wall cavities to determine the best paths for wire.

> **Use Tip:** Before using a fish tape to probe walls, try to calculate as much as possible where framing members are so that you avoid hitting them.

Wire Cutter/Stripper

Description: Two flat metal bars that crisscross and have sharpened ends, with a small notch for stripping wire.

Use: Cuts and strips small-gauge wire.

> **Use Tips:** If you need to cut something thicker than wire, such as a bolt, a lock hasp, chain, or cable, use a **bolt cutter (Part II, Chapter 6),** a huge version of a wire cutter—$1^1/2"$ to over 3' long—with great mechanical advantage.

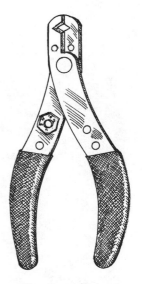

Wire Cutter/Stripper

Buying Tips: Much the same work can be done with various pliers designed to serve this purpose, such as **diagonal side cutters, etc. (Part I, Chapter 7)**.

Splitter

Also Known As: Cable ripper

Description: T-shaped galvanized piece about 6" long with triangular cutter notches and holes in the handle to measure wire gauges. A similar item with a hand crank and a small blade, is a *cablesplitter*.

Use: Strips outside insulation from Romex® cable. The bladed model splits BX.

 Use Tips: This tool saves much time. Stripping Romex® or splitting BX without it is difficult.

Electrical Tape

Types:

> *Friction tape*
>
> *Plastic tape*

Also Known As: Electrician's tape

Description: Both types sold by the roll.

Friction: Cloth-like material impregnated with chemicals, usually ¹/₂" to ³/₄" wide.

Plastic: Thin black plastic usually ³/₄" wide.

Use: Various uses, but in electrical work tape is mainly used to cover bare wire after it has been stripped of insulation.

> **Buying Tips:** Friction tape has largely been outmoded by plastic tape, which is actually much less costly, works better, and lasts longer, but some people find it is harder to tear.

Fuse Puller

Also Known As: Cartridge fuse puller

Description: Plastic pliers-like tool with hinge in the middle and with rounded jaws.

Use: Removing cartridge-type fuses.

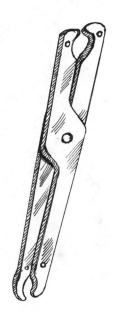

Cartridge Fuse Puller

Masonry Materials, Products, and Tools

Masonry Materials

About Masonry

The term *masonry* is generally understood to mean any of a variety of products made with cement or cement-like substances. Most masonry jobs are best left to professional masons, but for small repair jobs the following items will help orient you to the basics.

Brick

Types:

> *Face brick*
>
> *Fire brick*
>
> *Used brick*

Also Known As:

> *Face:* Common, facing, paint-grade common
>
> *Used:* Reclaimed

Description: Standard building brick comes about 8" long, 3³/₄" wide, and 2¹/₄" high, but it is made in a wide variety of dimensions both wide and thin—8" × 8", 4" × 8" pavers, for terrace patterns, and so on. It may be *cored* (have holes) or *frogged* (have a shallow depression) and comes in a variety of colors—red, cream, brown, yellow, white, pink—and with the surface glazed, smooth, enameled, or rough. In short, brick types exist to fit different jobs. Dimensions may include the intended thickness of the mortar joint, or the "nominal" versus the "actual" dimensions, incorporating the $1/2$" mortar joint.

Face: Standard, finished brick used in exterior walls. ("Construction" brick is a slightly lower grade used for basic construction of walls.)

Fire: A light yellow brick that has been fired to stand high heat.

Used: Literally used brick—recovered from demolished old buildings. Varies as much as brick itself varies and has absolutely no manufacturing standard.

Use: Brick may be used for a variety of building projects inside and outside the home. A typical exterior wall is known as a *masonry* or *brick* veneer wall.

Fire: Lining fireplaces. Fire clay is used instead of regular mortar. Dimensions are different from common brick, such as $4 1/2$" × 9" and so on.

Used: Any of a variety of building projects where the aesthetic appeal of oldness is desired; also may be cheaper to buy.

Use Tips: Any brick used outside the house may be designated SW, for *severe weathering* capability, or MW, *medium weathering,* for more moderate climates. NW, for *no weathering,* is used indoors only. You'll often find these marks, which refer to how the brick reacts to the seasonal freeze-thaw cycles, on the brick. Brick dimensions are proportional so that they may be used conveniently in patterns—a brick is approximately a third as high as it is long and half as wide. Experienced masons will remeasure bricks on site and refigure the quantity needed for a particular job no matter how many calculations have been made beforehand.

Brick—SW grade only—is often laid on a bed of gravel and sand to make walks and terraces. Gravel is graded according to the maximum size of each stone, though it is mixed with smaller stones and some sand. Item 4 gravel is best for this kind of use (6" to 8") and on top of that a 1" to 2" layer of sand; bluestone chips are highly recommended instead of sand, though. 4" × 8" pavers, solid bricks available in both regular and half, or "thin," thickness, are recommended, especially if you want to make the traditional basket-weave pattern, which requires that bricks be twice as long as they are wide.

> **$ Buying Tips:** As the many brick types exist to match type to job, ask questions of your supplier about as many characteristics of the brick as possible before delivery. The more new bricks you buy, the cheaper they are—the smallest unit being a *strap,* or 100 bricks bound with a metal strap. A *cube* is 500 bricks. Dimensions and terms vary by region of this country.
>
> Before buying used brick make sure that it is not heavily coated with mortar, as removing it could add hours to the job. To test used bricks for quality, tap them together—they should ring. Also, rap each brick with a hammer—it should not crumble or crack. You can sometimes buy brick from nonuniform runs at a discount price if dimensions are not important to you.

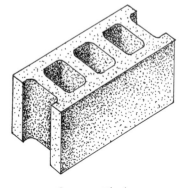

Concrete Block

Concrete Block

Also Known As: Block, cinder block

Description: Concrete block comes in a variety of styles, sizes, materials, and colors. The standard concrete block is made with cement, sand, and small stones as aggregate, while others use light aggregates such as volcanic cinders or pumice. Some are made of slag clay or shale. All are graded as to water resistance and therefore as to use above or below ground, interior or exterior, load- or nonload-bearing.

The standard, common, hollow-core block, called a *stretcher,* is just under 8" × 8" × 16" and weighs around 40 pounds. Other kinds (slag, clay, shale) can weigh as little as 25 pounds.

Most blocks have voids but some are solid, and all come in various shapes, such as bullnose, corner (or pier), or half units to facilitate building. Depth ranges from 2" to 12", and

height either 4" or 8". Other block is strictly decorative—
split, *slump*, and *screen* block are examples. And some block
comes with special finishes—marbelized, glazed, and so on.

Use: Depending on the type, could be used for building privacy walls, foundations, or as a decorative element outside
the house.

> **Use Tips:** Do not use concrete blocks outdoors—they
> don't stand up to moisture well. They are also so heavy
> to work with that we recommend avoiding their use alto-
> gether. Use a pro.

Stone

Terms:

> *Dressed stone*
>
> *Semidressed stone*
>
> *Undressed stone*
>
> *Rounded stone*
>
> *Veneer stone*
>
> *Mortar stone*
>
> *Brick or stone veneer panels*

Types: Limestone, bluestone, granite, marble, and other materials, depending on the local quarries.

Description:

> *Dressed:* Stones cut and trimmed to set sizes.

Semidressed: Rough-cut stones that need to be trimmed before use.

Undressed: Rough, just the way they are cut from the quarry.

Rounded: Local fieldstone, just the way it is found, rounded by glacial or river action.

Veneer: Various types of stone that are cut 2" to 3" thick, leaving front as is and back flat.

Mortar: Veneer stones composed of grindings of some sort of rock chips.

Brick or stone veneer panels: Made of plastic and stone or brick dust embedded in the surface. There is one grade for outdoor use and one for indoor use.

Use: All stone is used for walks, walls, retaining walls, barbecues, and a wide variety of other projects, with some specialties:

Veneer: Installed outside a home on steel studs and lath.

Mortar: Also used as siding.

Brick or stone veneer panels: Used outside or inside, as the grade permits.

> **Use Tips:** Larger stones are more difficult to handle than small- or medium-sized ones but quicker to install. Stones can be laid without mortar, but usually only for landscaping projects and walks. If you feel you need a **mortar (below)**, use regular sand **mix (below)**, as mortar will tend to dry out and crumble.

Premixed Cement Products

Types:

Concrete mix

Mortar mix

Sand mix

Description: Premixed cements are available in 10- to 80-pound bags and are mixed only with water. Cement refers to Portland cement, a mixture of different types of crushed and treated rock. Cement is mixed with gravel to form concrete and with lime to form mortar, and with sand for general use. *Portland cement* is readily available in 94-pound bags (1 cubic foot), which you can mix yourself with clean, moist sand, generally in a 1 to 3 ratio, but for most small projects it makes sense to buy it premixed. There are five types, but type 1 is general purpose, the others being for winter work or for bridge pilings.

Concrete: Comes as a powder containing cement and gravel, or aggregate, which is available in various sizes that must be specified.

Mortar: A special cement powder containing lime and sand. Various types available for special purposes. Strength rated according to type M (strongest), S, N, O (weakest).

Sand: Comes as a powder containing cement and sand.

Use:

Concrete: Used for projects calling for concrete as well as for repairing large holes in concrete.

Mortar: Used for repairing (tuck-pointing) or making mortar joints in brick and block. Use type S for brick walls and type N for concrete block.

Sand: Used for repairing cracks, holes, and other small masonry patching jobs.

Use Tips: When mixed with water a seemingly large bag of material can be reduced to a surprisingly small amount. Before buying calculate your needs carefully so you don't over- or underbuy. Cement and concrete "cure" very slowly, and should even be kept moist at first. *Latex masonry adhesive* or *emulsion* can be added to sand mixes to increase bonding ability and curing quality. Avoid inhaling the dry dust when mixing and moving cement products. Clean excess mortar off bricks with *muriatic acid* diluted 1 to 5. And watch your back—a solid model, two-wheel luggage carrier does nicely for transporting those bags. A large plastic or metal *mortar tub* is best for mixing.

Buying Tips: In comparison to buying separate components and mixing material from scratch, premixed cement is expensive. On the other hand, it is very convenient—just mix with water. Most do-it-yourselfers are willing to pay the extra cost for this convenience.

Cement and Concrete Patchers

Types:

Anchoring cement

Epoxy cement

Hydraulic cement

Latex cement

Standard cement

Vinyl patching cement

Also Known As:

Anchoring: Expansion cement

Hydraulic: Water-stopping cement

Description: Cement mixed with a bonding agent and other additives that increase adhesion strength, and allow for thin-setting ability. Some are ready-to-use, others need water.

Anchoring: Slightly expanding, fast-setting cement, ready to use, although some brands need water added. Slower setting than hydraulic cement.

Epoxy: Comes as a bag of dry cement, hardener, and emulsion that is mixed together before use.

Hydraulic: Comes as a powder. Similar to anchoring, but faster-setting. Expands as it cures to fill cracks tightly.

Latex: Powder is mixed with a latex liquid before use. Can be troweled to $1/16$" thickness. Excellent adhering power.

Standard: Blend of cement and sand that is mixed with water for use.

Vinyl: Comes as a powder that is mixed with water for use. Can be troweled to $1/8$" thickness. Excellent adhering power, more than regular cement and sand mixtures.

Uses:

Anchoring: Anchoring wrought-iron rail and gate posts, fences, and bolts.

Epoxy: May be used to patch any kind of material, including glass and steel, particularly where strength is important, and may be used to set flagstone and other patio-paving materials.

Hydraulic: Applied directly to a water leak in masonry and quickly hardens in place.

Latex: Smoothing rough surfaces as well as repairing hairline cracks.

Standard: Repairing small holes and cracks; cracks need to be undercut first.

Vinyl: Used to repair small cracks in concrete, glass, marble, tile, and brick. Vinyl bonding is strong.

> **Use Tips:** Generally, for patchers, surface should be well cleaned before application with a *concrete cleaner,* *etching material,* or *de-greaser.* Latex sets very quickly, so no more than can be easily applied at one time should be mixed.

> **Buying Tips:** Epoxy is the most expensive patcher. Acrylic, resinous, or latex bonding agents or adhesives are also sold separately as additives or primers.

Masonry Sealers

Types:

Acrylic resin sealer

Bituminous sealer

Cement latex sealer

Cement mortar

Epoxy resins

Silicone

Also Known As: Masonry waterproofers, waterproofers, waterproof cement paint

Description: Many proprietary formulations. Most common are:

Acrylic resin: Rubber and Portland cement mixture applied by brush.

Bituminous: Thick black tar-like material that can be applied hot or cold.

Cement latex: Cement-based with latex additives.

Cement mortar: Composed of one part water and one part cement.

Epoxy: Synthetic material that sets very quickly.

Silicone: Highly viscous material that goes on like paint.

Uses: To seal masonry walls against moisture penetration, dusting, staining, spalling, and the effects of weather. Decorative as well. Bitumonious may be used as a *roof coating*.

> **Use Tips:** Before using a waterproofer make sure that the problem is moisture intruding through the walls and not condensation. Always try to cure the source of the moisture. Follow surface preparation directions exactly. Note if product requires use of *etching* and *cleaning compound*. Most won't work over old paint. Take precautions to avoid eye and skin irritations as specified on the label.

$ Buying Tips: Quality sealers penetrate and swell to become an integral part of the masonry, not just a surface coating. Some products contain a mildewcide too. Some are better whites than others; check regarding colors. May require special additives.

Masonry Tools

About Masonry Tools

It pays to buy quality tools here unless you will only be doing a very simple or small patching job. Using a cheap, low-quality bricklaying tool for an extensive job is the sure route to frustration. After all, masonry is rough, heavy work to start with. Poor-quality tools have lightweight handle connectors and thin, low-quality steel. Good-quality tools are not that much more expensive, nor do they cost much to begin with. Handles have brass ferrules, and will often be attached by parts that are integral to the tool—forged in one piece—rather than spot-welded. Materials are magnesium, bronze, stainless steel, and the like. All specialized large tools are available to rent.

Despite their differences as described below, tradesmen call many of these tools merely by their basic types, such as *trowel* or *float,* without more precision. Be sure to know the specific uses intended when purchasing these items. And it is highly recommended that the first-time user practice on small brick or concrete jobs prior to tackling anything large.

Bricklayer's Hammer

Description: Narrow head with slightly curved, long claw.

Use: To break brick to size.

Masonry Trowel

Pointing Trowel

Types:

Bucket trowel: 6", blunt, stiff blade for scooping mortar out of buckets or mortar boxes and onto hawks, etc.

Buttering trowel: Triangular, wide, and slightly curved sides, about 7" long, for "buttering" the mortar directly onto individual bricks and general use by nonprofessionals. About the right size for digging anything out of 5-gallon buckets.

Duckbill trowel: Rectangular, about 2" × 10", rounded tip, for special shaping. Similar to margin trowel.

Margin trowel: Rectangular, about 2" × 5" or 8", for small patching, cleaning other tools, very useful.

Pointing trowel: Triangular, typically about 5" long, for small patching jobs.

Also Known As: Brick trowel

Description: Triangular-shaped flat metal blade with a wooden or metal handle. 5 or 5½" wide by 11" long, the most popular length; minimum length should be 8".

Use: Handling wet mortar.

> **Use Tips:** Clean thoroughly after use; if dried mortar accumulates on bottom it causes problems when you use the trowel for smoothing.

Buying Tips: For the average amateur the buttering trowel is the best all-round choice, though the margin trowel is useful. A pointing trowel tends to be too small and cheaply made—a bad choice for your one trowel. For regular trowels the *Philadelphia pattern,* with a square heel, is handier and more popular than the *London* type, with a rounded heel. Buy only the very best—this item gets rougher use than most tools.

Tuck-Pointing Trowel

Also Known As: Joint filler, tuck-pointer, pointing trowel, caulking trowel

Description: Long, narrow flat blade secured by a dogleg to a handle, like other trowels, usually $1/4$" to 1" wide and $6^3/4$" long.

Use: For repointing—applying fresh mortar to existing brick joints.

Buying Tips: Quality models are stiff and of one-piece construction. Flexible ones tend to cause the mortar to drop off as you apply it.

Hawk

Description: A flat, thin metal platform with a perpendicular handle in the middle of the bottom. Usually square, about 14" on a side.

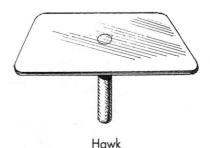

Hawk

Use: Holding "working" amounts of plaster, drywall compound, or mortar in one hand while applying it with a trowel with the other hand.

Brick Jointer

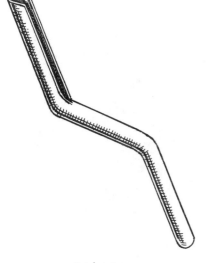

Brick Jointer

Also Known As: Jointer, jointing tool, striker, slicker, square brick jointer

Description: Narrow, S-shaped piece of metal about a foot long with differently curved, half-round ends. The ends are different widths, such as $1/2$" and $5/8$". Typical style is concave, but convex, V, and colonial (grapevine) styles are available too. May also be straight, with a wooden handle, called a *sled runner,* which is often used for long concrete-block joints.

Use: Smoothing fresh mortar in brick joints.

> **$ Buying Tips:** A jointer receives a lot of abrasive wear, so get one that's heat-treated and will therefore take the abuse. Any bent metal rod may be used on smaller jobs.

Joint Raker

Also Known As: Joint rake, skate, scratch jointer

Description: Of the two types the most convenient is a long-handled, metal device with two 1" to 2" diameter wheels and a specially hardened nail between them. A simpler model is a bent, narrow piece of metal with an offset tooth.

Use: Scraping old mortar out of a brick wall prior to tuck-pointing and recessing fresh mortar joints before the mortar sets up.

Tuck-Pointer Tool

Description: 14" to 16" long metal bar with a point on one end and a wedge on the other, both turned 90 degrees. A similar tool is the *plugging chisel,* or **flat joint chisel (below).**

Use: Scraping old, loose mortar out of brick walls prior to tuck-pointing (filling in with new mortar).

 Buying Tip: Some people prefer to use an old screw driver and a hammer for this job.

Line Blocks

Also Known As: Corner blocks, line dogs, dogs, chicken legs, line stretchers

Description: Line blocks are small wooden or plastic devices that fit on brick corners; all the other names are for variations on blocks that may be used in the middle of a wall without touching the corners.

Use: Anchoring a line stretched across a new row of bricks that is used as a guide for bricklayers.

Star Drill

Bricklayer's Chisel

Masonry Chisels

Description: Short, hexagonal tempered-steel bars with chisel points shaped according to type and use. One solid piece of steel.

Types:

General use:

> *Cape chisel:* Flat, small wedge-shaped tip for making grooves and cleaning out mortar joints.

> *Star drill:* Long, narrow, fluted; driven with a hammer to make a small hole in masonry for anchoring a fastener.

Brick:

> *Bricklayer's, also known as wide, brick, brick set, plumber's, mason's, nail, long brick chisel:* Very wide blade, about 4", for cutting bricks to size and cleaning mortar off used brick.

> *Plugging chisel:* Narrow, flat pointed blade for cleaning out mortar prior to tuck-pointing.

Stone mason's:

> *Plain chisel:* Wide blade, plain edge for cutting stone; concrete chisel is similar but with longer handle.

> *Point (also known as bull point chisel):* Hex bar beveled to a point for cutting and shaping stone, or just breaking up masonry.

> *Tooth chisel:* Wide blade, approximately 2", with toothed edge for cutting stone.

Use Tips: Always wear safety goggles when using masonry chisels. Heavy gloves are recommended too. Star drills tend to shatter bricks; **electric drills with masonry (carbide) bits (Part II, Chapter 16)** are much, much better. Many masons prefer narrower chisels than the 4" wide bricklayer's model, especially if they come with longer handles, which afford more control. Hold chisels with your thumb and first two fingers instead of your whole hand—the pain and damage will be much less if you miss the chisel with your heavy hammer. And strike these chisels only with a heavy hammer made for this purpose: a **hand drilling hammer (Part II, Chapter 16)**. Don't use a regular *claw hammer*.

About Cement Tools

Large-scale cement and concrete work is beyond the domain of the usual do-it-yourselfer, but we know some of you will attempt a small job now and then. We therefore include here some of the basic tools used, but this is by no means exhaustive. There are entire catalogs of nothing but tools for cement work. These are presented in approximate order of use.

Screed

Also Known As: Strike-off board

Description: Wood or metal plank, often just a 2 × 4, 3' to 5' long.

Use: Scrapes off the top of freshly poured concrete.

Darby

Description: Several-foot-long wood or metal plank with two handles on top.

Use: Smoothing concrete after first smoothing with a screed, prior to floats. Used with a *puddling* or spading tool sometimes to consolidate the concrete.

Float

Float

Description: Flat, rectangular piece of wood, metal (magnesium is common), cork, or wood with rubber bottom, often 5" × 12" or 3¹/₂" × 16". A *bull float* is an extremely long float—4' and even 5' long by 8" wide—with a long handle secured to it. Handle may be composed of linked sections in order to get an extreme length, up to 20'.

Use: For the first smoothing of wet concrete or plaster. If a rough surface is desired, this may be the last smoothing as well. Bull floats are used for finishing very large areas. Plaster is often smoothed with a wood float with a sponge-rubber surface. Smaller floats with rubber bottoms (*rubber floats*) are for pushing grout into ceramic tile.

Finishing Trowel

Finishing Trowel

Also Known As: Cement finishing trowel, cement trowel, plasterer's trowel

Description: Rectangular, flat metal piece with a hardwood handle attached to a rib down its middle. Typically 10" to 20" long and 3" to 4" wide.

Use: Finishing, or final, smoothing of wet cement or plaster surface. Plasterers tend to use a shorter model when building walls.

> **Use Tip:** When smoothing a patch draw the trowel across it so that the trowel edges overlap the patch edges.

Edger

Description: Metal blade, usually 3" × 6", with one end curved downward and ends flat or slightly curved up, with a handle.

Use: Rounds off edges of wet concrete slabs.

Edger

Groover

Also Known As: Cement jointer, hand jointer

Description: Flat, rectangular metal tool with curved ends usually about 6" long, with a raised projection along the bottom up to 1" deep and a handle.

Use: Cutting grooves in wet concrete slabs.

Groover

P A R T

XI

Safety Equipment

About Safety Gear

Accidents for the do-it-yourselfer can be as serious as those for professional construction workers. Risks of losing an eye or inhaling highly toxic material are present with many of the most common tasks. Top pros won't work without their safety gear, which they consider as important as quality tools, and neither should you. The key to safety is to identify potential hazards so you will know what safety gear to use and be sure to get the right equipment for the job.

Pay special attention to the chemicals you use. Certain chemical products can cause extreme allergic reactions, affect long-term health, or cause reproductive problems. Most toxic products should be avoided during pregnancy. Always refer to the label because it should tell you the hazards of use and how to protect yourself. If a product label is not specific, call the manufacturer.

Safety gear is easily obtained. Check under Industrial Safety Equipment in your commercial Yellow Pages for suppliers in your area. If you have questions about how to protect yourself, consult your federal or state OSHA (Occupational Safety and Health Administration) office or check with an industrial hygienist, found in the commercial Yellow Pages. In the cases involving the removal or disturbing of asbestos, consult a professional since it might be illegal for a nonprofessional to do the job.

Safety Clothing and Other Gear

Earplugs, Ear Protectors

Also Known As: Hearing protectors

Description: Wide range of types, from soft wax to small round rubber plugs, to ear protectors that resemble earmuffs or old-fashioned headphones.

Use: Limiting noise of power tools reaching eardrums.

Ear Protectors

Use Tips: With good earplugs you may not be able to hear someone calling to you. Keep your eyes open for possible warnings from others.

Buying Tips: Get earplugs that provide maximum amount of noise reduction (described in decibels). If ear protection is used frequently, get reusable rather than disposable protectors.

Hard Hat

Description: Hat made of metal or impact-resistant or reinforced plastic with a web lining. Some are *dielectric* (insulated against electric shock).

Use: Protects head from falling objects or from hitting against hard surfaces.

> **Use Tips:** Extremely helpful not only during any demolition but when working near an uneven ceiling, such as an attic or basement, with low beams that may have nails protruding dangerously.

> **Buying Tip:** Large variety of hardness and internal webbing available.

Protective Gloves

Also Known As: Work gloves

Description: Gloves made out of heavy material such as vinyl, leather, or canvas.

Use: Rubber gloves prevent chemicals like paint thinner or remover from entering your bloodstream through your skin. Heavy canvas and leather gloves are for handling rough or heavy objects like stone or brick or scrap lumber with random nails exposed. Heavy work gloves also prevent splinters when handling clean lumber and provide a better grip when handling materials in general.

Use cheap, lightweight cotton or plastic gloves only for painting to avoid having to clean your hands with strong chemicals.

Use Tips: Treat yourself to some peace of mind with a good, big pair of the thickest, toughest gloves you can find. For chemicals be sure to get the kind that will stand up to what you are using; black neoprene with a fabric lining is a good general choice.

Buying Tips: Invest in a variety so you can use what's appropriate. Disposable plastic gloves are a great time-saver and keep chemicals off your skin.

Protective Goggles

Also Known As: Safety goggles

Description: Plastic glasses with large front and covered sides large enough to fit over regular eyeglasses.

Use: Protects eyes from splashes of dangerous chemicals such as paint thinner or stripper. Also helpful when painting ceilings or doing demolition. Some makes are suitable for protection from impact but most aren't.

Protective Goggles

Use Tips: Don't forget to clean dust off goggles often. Obscured vision can cause accidents too—it's easy to get used to a diminished view.

§ **Buying Tips:** Get goggles with replaceable lenses and that meet ANSI (American National Standards Institute) or OSHA standards.

Protective Glasses

Also Known As: Safety glasses

Description: Regular-looking glasses frames with shatterproof lenses. Available in plain or prescription. Many have additional shields on the sides, which are recommended. Polycarbonate lenses are strong.

Use: Protects eyes from projectiles when hammering or using tools of all sorts—not from splashes.

About Respirators

Unfortunately most small respirators commonly found at hardware stores do not provide the maximum protection required. Many are unreliable at best. We recommend, as part of your tool box, a reusable (or dual) cartridge-type half-face respirator as described below.

In choosing a respirator you should keep four things in mind:

1. Get the appropriate filter for the job.

2. Be sure the respirator fits you properly.

3. Use only a government-approved respirator.

4. Regularly clean and maintain your respirator and change filters.

Respirator

Also Known As: Breathing mask, dust mask, gas mask, painter's mask

Description:

Respirator

Reusable (or dual) cartridge-type respirator: Large rubberized piece that holds two filter cartridges over mouth and nose; half-face model covers most of face; full-face model has face shield that covers entire face—necessary for anyone who must wear glasses. Special frames are required, available from the respirator manufacturer. Both are held on the head by double-wide rubber straps. Each filter cartridge should be government-approved for specific uses as marked on the package: dusts (toxic and nontoxic), mists, vapors, fumes, pesticides, radon, gases, etc.

Plastic dust (or filter) mask with replaceable filter: Small triangular plastic cup that holds a paper-like triangular filter. Fits over mouth and nose, held on the head by rubber band. Usually not government-approved.

Disposable Paper Dust Mask

Disposable paper dust mask: Small pyramid-shaped white paper cone that fits over mouth and nose, held on the head by rubber band. Also known as a painter's mask (incorrect—most do not stop paint vapors) or pinch mask. Only a few makes are government-approved.

Use:

Reusable cartridge type: Special cartridges are available to filter out a large array of dusts and toxins, ranging from serious dirt dust to chemical odors to asbestos. Must be chosen for the specific use intended, such as paint and organic vapor, pesticides, etc.

Replaceable filter type: Similar to above, and also for sanding operations. Minimum protection. Not for anything toxic or for painting.

Disposable paper type: Most brands provide below-minimum protection; possibly okay for light amounts of dust such as during housecleaning, although some newer models exist for more efficient filtration of a variety of toxins or home insulation particles.

Use Tips: In all cases, masks that fit improperly are not only useless but dangerous, especially if you get closer to poisons than normal, thinking you are protected. Respirators must be carefully, snugly fit to your face. *Disposable masks should be discarded after each use.*

Buying Tips: To emphasize: get the type of mask you need for the job being done. It is a dangerous waste to use anything too lightweight. Check packaging to see if cartridges are for the categories of dusts, mists, vapors, or fumes. And always check for the government approval from NIOSH or MSHA. If not available through your local hardware store, try the Yellow Pages for Safety Equipment or Industrial Supplies.

Fire Extinguishers

About Fire Extinguishers

Fires are characterized according to type: *Type A fires* are those involving wood, trash, cloth, and similar materials. *Type B fires* are those involving oil, gas, paint thinners, and other flammable materials. *Type C fires* are those involving electrical equipment.

Fire extinguishers are labeled with the letter or letters of the type or types of fires they can extinguish. *It is crucial that you use a fire extinguisher only on the fire types it is designed to handle.*

Extinguishers are also rated according to the size of the fire they'll put out. For example, an extinguisher rated *1A* could extinguish a burning stack of twenty-five 40" long sticks. One rated *2A* could put out a fire twice that size.

Fire extinguishers contain either pressurized water, a dry chemical propelled by nitrogen, or a gas.

General Buying Tips:

- Buy a good-quality fire extinguisher, and if you can't find one in your local hardware store, try a fire equipment dealer in the Yellow Pages—they generally carry quality equipment.

- Only buy an extinguisher approved by a testing agency, either Factory Mutual (FM) or Underwriters Laboratories (UL).

- Buy an extinguisher that is rechargeable.

- Some extinguishers don't have pressure gauges and are not as good as those that do.

- Water remains one of the best fire-fighting "chemicals" around. Small dry-chemical extinguishers only work for a matter of seconds anyway.

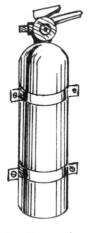

Fire Extinguisher

Multipurpose Dry Chemical Fire Extinguisher

Description: Steel, aluminum, or plastic canister, red or white, with a hand-operated valve and a gauge for reading pressure. Supplied with a strap and bracket for wall mounting. Comes rated according to types and sizes of fire it can handle, either types A, B, or C, and 1 to 10 indicating proportion of ingredients. (*A* is ordinary combustibles, *B* flammable liquids, and *C* is electrical equipment.)

Use: Extinguishing fires around the house.

Use Tips: Hang extinguishers away from stoves and near escape routes—stairwells, doorways, hallways, and the like. Also—very important—read the instructions that come with the extinguisher and make sure all family members understand them. Note that dry chemicals leave a sticky residue after use. And they spray for only a matter of seconds.

Buying Tips: While different extinguishers can be bought for different types of fires, a fire is an emotionally convulsing event that leaves little time for thought. Get a universal type that will put out anything. For the kitchen a 1A 10BC type would be good. That rating means that it handles all three types of fires, being especially strong against flammable materials. Something twice that strength against Type A fires—2A 10BC—would be good where water is not accessible and where there is lots of fire fuel, such as a basement workshop. Put several 10-pounders around your house.

Halon or CO_2 Fire Extinguisher

Description: Similar to dry chemical, above, although can be just as effective in smaller-sized canisters. Colorless, odorless, and evaporates after use. Leaves no residue.

Use: An extinguisher containing halon or CO_2 won't damage delicate electronic equipment like a **dry chemical extinguisher (above)** will.

Use Tips: Normally, halon can extinguish Type B and C fires and in the larger sizes is effective against Type A fires too. Sucks up oxygen.

Buying Tip: More expensive than the dry chemical type but generally more compact.

Metals and Metal Finishes

About Metals and Metal Finishes

It's not hard to get confused about all the finishes and metals used for hardware, tools, and materials. Following is some information that should clarify the picture and help you make more informed buying decisions.

Blued: Not really a treatment but a light coating given to items like nails to keep them from rusting in the box while waiting to be sold.

Brass: Many hardware items are made of pure brass. It is a soft metal (mostly copper and zinc) but weatherproof, though salt water or salt air will turn it green, a form of corrosion. (This condition is not serious and will not affect the integrity of the metal.) Brass screw slots are easily stripped because the metal is so soft.

Brass-Plated: Steel coated with brass. It is used when good looks count and strength is needed too. It provides a measure of protection against corrosion but is not really weatherproof.

Bright: A term meaning that hardware is not coated with anything.

Bronze: An alloy mostly made of copper and tin. Pure bronze is very strong, does not corrode, and can be used inside and outside the house. It is a favorite in marine applications. Bronze is harder than brass.

Bronze-Plated: Steel plated with bronze. Unlike pure bronze, it is not considered weatherproof, though good-quality plating can last for a number of years before corroding. Generally, though, bronze plating is just designed to add good looks and a small measure of protection against moisture.

Cast Iron: Iron made in such a way that it is more brittle than malleable iron.

Chromed: When an item is described like this it means that chrome has been added to the steel—it is an integral part of it.

Chrome-Plated: A material, say steel or even plastic, coated with chrome. It serves a decorative as well as an anticorrosive protective function. Bath items are typically chrome-plated. Items with chrome plating are not as durable as those where chrome has actually been added to the steel.

Chrome Vanadium: Steel that has had vanadium and chrome added to it. Makes a tool or other item stronger without becoming brittle.

Forged: Refers to items that have been heated and shaped to give great strength. Drop-forged items are made by pouring molten metal in a form and then dropping a great weight on it to distribute the metal in the form.

Galvanized: Most outdoor items are galvanized, which means the item has been given a zinc coating to make it weatherproof. There are two kinds of galvanizing—coated and hot-dipped. Items that are hot-dipped have a characteristically rough finish. It is by far the superior of the two finishes.

High-Carbon Steel: Also known as *tool steel*—hardened in a hot-and-cold manufacturing process. Very common, nothing special.

Hollow-Ground and Tapered: Usually refers to the way saw blades have been shaped to reduce binding—they are thinner in the middle. Hollow-ground circular saw blades are dish-shaped—the outer cutting edge is thicker than the middle to reduce binding. Hollow-ground handsaws are thicker at the cutting edge but taper to the spine, or back. Hollow-ground taping knives flex in the middle rather than at the handle, giving greater smoothing ability.

Machined: Refers to items that have been cut and shaped by grinding and polishing; simply describes the way steel is worked.

Malleable Iron: Iron that has been made so that it still has some bendability—or some capacity to be hit without cracking—without loss of strength.

Oiled: Many items such as bolts are oiled, but this in no way affords them any permanent protection, but rather, like blued items, helps them resist rust while stored.

Stainless Steel: Totally corrosion-resistant steel that contains nickel and chrome. Generally very strong and hard steel too.

Tempered: Steel that has been heated and cooled in a certain way for strength.

Zinc- or Cadmium-Plated: These two terms mean the same thing and refer to a plating given to hardware items that makes them rust-resistant rather than rust-proof. Though also treated with zinc, **galvanized items (see above)** get a much thicker shield of zinc, which makes them more weatherproof.

Basic Tools and Materials Every Homeowner Should Have

Here are some suggestions for essentials for common repairs and maintenance tasks, plus a number of things that just make it all easier, in alphabetical order. Those few with an asterisk are so basic that even an apartment dweller would do well to have them.

While it is always nice to have a fully-equipped workshop with an in-depth supply of tools and materials, it seems that most of us need to rely on a semiportable collection of things for minor and typical repairs around the house. Keep the small stuff in an open plastic tool box or canvas bag that won't scratch floors, and the larger stuff in something like a 5-gallon plastic bucket. If weight is still a problem, get a second plastic tool box that is stored empty and fill it only with the tools needed for each job. In a big house, it is also a good idea to store a few pliers, hammers, and screwdrivers (and a small container of various fasteners) in places like a kitchen drawer and an upstairs bedroom. Combination tools are no substitute for the real things, but good-quality ones can be convenient for small repairs.

Better, more pleasurable results will be yours if you keep a couple of things in mind: Always use the right tool for the job, and always try to get good-quality tools. I might add to that, *always* have some duct tape handy and *always* wear a painter's hat (request a free one along with some paint mixing sticks when you buy paint. Besides protecting your hair from paint splatter, it could just possibly make you look semiprofessional as you wander around a worksite). But that's just my thing.

Hand Tools

- 5-in-1 tool (page 393)
- adjustable wrenches* (page 56)
- allen wrenches (set) (page 63)
- awl (page 90)
- C-clamps (2 small or 2 quick-action clamps) (page 65 or 69)
- carpenter's level (24") (page 78)
- caulking gun (page 289)
- claw hammer* (page 3)
- cold chisel (page 13)
- combination wrenches (set) (page 58) or socket wrench set (page 61)
- curved jaw locking pliers (10") (page 51)
- fasteners*: various finishing nails and drywall screws (pages 174 and 184)
- four-in-hand rasp/file (page 96)
- grip light (page 112)
- hacksaw (page 34)
- Japanese saw* (ryoba) (page 30)
- latex gloves (page 678)
- long-nose pliers* (page 51)
- nail claw (page 18)
- nailsets (page 11)
- nut driver ($^5/_{16}$") (page 60)
- offset screwdriver, ratchet combination style* (page 25)
- paint and varnish scraper (page 394)
- painter's hat (above)

Absolute basics.

- Phillips head screwdrivers*: 3 sizes (Nos. 1 to 3 or at least 1 and 2), all normal length, plus one stubby (page 22)

- pipe wrenches (page 564) (if you don't have copper or plastic piping)

- pry bar (6 to 10") (page 17)

- putty knife* (flexible) (page 454)

- razor blade scraper (page 394)

- shave hook (page 393)

- slip-joint pliers* (page 47)

- slotted screwdrivers*: 3 sizes (extra-narrow, $^3/_{16}$" and $^1/_4$", plus one stubby and wide) (page 21)

- square: try or combination (page 74 or 75)

- tape measure* (page 71)

- taping knife (6" or so wide, flexible, hollow ground) (page 453)

- test lamp (page 645)

- tongue-and-groove pliers* (page 48)

- torpedo level (page 79)

- utility knife* (page 37)

- wood chisels* (set of 3 or 4 bevel-edged, $^1/_4$" to 1" wide) (page 14)

- worklights* (page 111)

Power Tools

- belt sander (page 153)

- circular saw (page 143)

- cordless drill/driver and full set of bits (page 126)

- extension cord (page 586)

Absolute basics.

Materials

- caulk*: neoprene, rubber adhesive (small tube) (page 286); general-purpose latex caulk with silicone; and 100% silicone caulk (page 286)

- damp patch roof cement or other roofing repair material (page 295)

- duct tape* (page 330) — an absolute necessity

- electrical tape (page 330)

- epoxy repair material (page 548)

- glues*: cyanoacrylate glue (page 282) and wood glue (page 279)

- joint compound* (page 442)

- penetrating oil* (aerosol form) (page 326)

- sandpaper (variety of grits) (page 99)

- spackling compound* (page 448)

- synthetic steel wool (page 101)

- teflon tape and/or pipe dope (page 547) (if you don't have copper or plastic piping)

- water putty* (page 416)

*Absolute basics.

Index

rotary tool, 140
router, 128
spade, 135–36
step, 136
tapered shank, 134
taper point, 134
twist, 133–34
Drill bit holder, 130
Drill-driver, 124. *See also* Power drill
Drill guide, 126
Drilling hammer, 8
Drill level, 126
Drill mixer. *See* Power paint mixer
Drill point, 88. *See also* Twist drill bit
Drill press, 125, 138, 139, 140, 164
Drill press stand, 126
Drill saw, 128
Drill stand, 129
Drill stop. *See* Drill stop collar
Drill stop collar, 138
Dripless oil, 325
Driver, adjustable nut, 60
Driver, brad, 7
Driver, nut, 60–61, 497, 505
Driver, right angle, 128
Driveway sealer. *See* Blacktop sealer
Drop cloths, 387–88
Drop-ear elbow, 511–12
Drop ells. *See* Drop-ear elbow
Drop leaf brace, 205
Drop light, 109
Drops. *See* Drop cloths
Drum sander, 129
Drying oil finish, 359
Dry spray lubricant, 327
Dry strippable wallcoverings, 398
Drywall, 439–41; 457–58
Drywall adapter bit, 132
Drywall bit. *See* Drywall adapter bit
Drywall box. *See* Sheetrock
Drywall circle cutter, 451

Drywall compound. *See* Joint compound
Drywall driver, 131
Drywall finishing tools, 449–56
Drywall foot lift. *See* Drywall lifter
Drywall hammer, 5, 44
Drywall hatchet. *See* Drywall hammer
Drywall jack, 440
Drywall joint compound, 545
Drywall knife. *See* Taping knife; Utility knife
Drywall lifter, 454
Drywall nails, 173–74, 440
Drywall paneling T-square. *See* Drywall T-square
Drywall panels, 451
Drywall repair clip, 446
Drywall sander, 443, 453–54
vacuum, 453–44
Drywall sanding screens, 453
Drywall saw, 29, 450–51
Drywall screw(s), 181, 182–83, 440
Drywall screw adapter bit. *See* Drywall adapter bit
Drywall screwdriver, 131
Drywall screw gun, 131
Drywall T-square, 450
Drywall tape. *See* Joint tape
Drywall tool. *See* Taping knife
Drywall trowel, 451
D system, and nail length and quantity, 170–71
Dual cartridge-type respirator, 677–78
Duckbill snips, 41, 42
Duckbill trowel, 662
Duck tape. *See* Duct tape
Duct tape, 330, 552, 689
Dumb trim, 231
Duo cup strainer. *See* Kitchen sink strainer
Duo strainer. *See* Kitchen sink strainer
Duo strainer wrench. *See* Spanner wrench

Duplex head nail, 175
Duplex nail. *See* Duplex head nail
Duplex receptable box cover, 634
Durham fittings, 501
Dust mask. *See* Respirator
DWV pipe, 485, 489. *See also* Waste pipe
Dye stain, 351–53
Dye-type stain. *See* Dye stain

Earplugs, 673
Ear protectors, 673
Easing oil. *See* Penetrating oil
Easy Outs. *See* Bolt extractor
Eccentric nipple extractor, 568
Edge bevel, 490
Edge-rounding tool. *See* Cornering tool
Edger, 669
Edison-base, 597
Edison base fuse. *See* Plug fuse
Eggbeater drill. *See* Hand drill
8-hooks, 193
Elastic knife, 451
Elbow, 511–12
Electrical boxes, 191, 596, 611, 629–34
Electrical cable and conduit connectors, 636
Electrical tape, 330, 644–45
Electrical tools, 641–45
Electrical wire, 623–
Electric boxes, 191. *See* Electrical boxes
Electric drills, 125, 181, 183
Electric glue gun, 105, 279
Electrician's (electrical) snake. *See* Fish tape
Electrician's chisel, 14
Electrician's pliers. *See* Lineman's side-cutting pliers
Electrician's screwdriver, 21, 22
Electrician's tape. *See* Electrical tape